# The *MAKING* of the
# AMERICAN
# LANDSCAPE

- FIRST NATIONAL BANK -
CUSTOMER PARKING ONLY
DURING BANKING HOURS

# The MAKING of the AMERICAN LANDSCAPE

### Edited by

## MICHAEL P. CONZEN
*University of Chicago*

**Routledge**

New York   London

First published in 1990 by HarperCollins*Academic*

Reprinted in 1994 by

Routledge
29 West 35 Street
New York, NY 10001

Published in Great Britain by

Routledge
11 New Fetter Lane
London EC4P 4EE

Printed in the United States of America on acid free paper

**Library of Congress Cataloging-in-Publication Data**

The Making of the American Landscape / edited by
Michael P. Conzen.
  p. cm.
  Includes bibliographical references.
  ISBN 0–04–917009–0. –ISBN 0–415–91178–8 (pbk.)
  1. Anthropo-geography–North America. 2. Man–Influence on
nature–North America. 3. Landscape changes–North America.
I. Conzen, Michael P.
GF501.M35 1989
304.2′097–dc20

                             89–20047
                                 CIP

**British Library Cataloguing in Publication Data**

  The making of the American landscape.
1. United States. Landscape
I. Conzen, Michael P.
719′.0973
ISBN 0-04-917009-0
ISBN 0-415-91178-8

# *Preface*

THIS BOOK HAS its roots in the fertile bicontinental traditions of landscape study nurtured by William G. Hoskins and John Brinckerhoff Jackson, and it was written in the belief that nothing quite like it yet exists in the American literature, and that there is a place for it. But its intellectual genealogy is as gnarled and sinewy as the weatherbeaten oaks that cling to the windy Cheviot foothills of England's Northumbria where the editor grew up. When he began serious exploration of the countryside and small market towns of his native region, first with his father and then on his own, Hoskins' *The making of the English landscape* was a brand new book. As time passed that volume became, for the editor, a classic statement of the humane interest all civilized souls should have in their surroundings, reaching within an historical framework for a judicious blend of understanding and appreciation of the varied ways people have marked and shaped the lands they have called home.

Discovery of and eventual commitment to life in America involved the editor in a strenuous encounter with the American landscape, not immediately through formal study but through a geographer's awareness of and interest in its significance. With Hoskins in the blood, as it were, the socioeconomic emphasis of graduate work seemed ultimately a trifle anemic, and J. B. Jackson's pungent writings on the visible American scene came as a wholly welcome native infusion, reflecting as they did the pulse and robustness of this continent and its people. However, during the 1970s no one seemed ready to write the kind of overview of the historical forces that had shaped the cultural landscape of the United States in the disciplined sort of way Hoskins had done for England. Transatlantic ties tugged further. An invitation from the editor of the *Geographical Magazine* of London to conceive and guest edit a twelve-part series of short articles on the American landscape provided the editor with the necessary impetus, and the "Fashioning of the American landscape" series, featuring contributions from a dozen American geographers, duly appeared in that journal each month between October 1979 and October 1980.

Despite the subsequent appearance of interesting interpretations by John Stilgoe, Walter Sullivan, and the contributors to an anthology on vernacular architecture edited by Dell Upton and John Vlach, there remained, it seemed, a need for a concise but systematic treatment of the major historical themes in the making of the American landscape. And so, at the—again transatlantic—behest of a British publisher who sensed the rising interest in landscape in the United States, this wholly new, more ambitious, and more integrated collection is our attempt to fill the gap. The focus is on the 48 contiguous states of the union: Hawaii and Alaska in comparative landscape terms are worlds unto themselves and require individual treatment. We harbor no illusion that the volume treats the topic comprehensively or in the only plausible way. The authors, including some veterans from the magazine series, have been given wide latitude to contribute original chapters that strongly reflect their own individual perspectives shaped by years of field and archival work. The editor makes no apology for limiting the authorship in this particular book to historical geographers because that has resulted in a certain valuable consistency of outlook and premise, notwithstanding the diversity of formal training and employment, and the irrepressible individualism apparent in the writing. The cardinal concern in involving them has been their ability not only to look, but to see.

In a critical appraisal of the style and influence of Hoskins and Jackson in English-language landscape study that appeared in *The interpretation of ordinary landscapes* (1979), Donald Meinig drew attention to the contrast and complementarity between the two writers: Hoskins's emphasis on history, documentation, and the longevity of many landscape features; Jackson's preoccupation with landscape in terms of the way we live in it, and with change and the modern scene, approached through the power of intuitive thinking. It is hoped that this book's authors represent collectively at least some fusion of these virtues. The book aims at an unabashedly evolutionary interpretation of the American landscape. It draws attention to remnants from the past embedded in today's scene (to counter the cliché that obsolescence leads quickly to replacement and effacement). And it carries themes roundly to the present, where appropriate. To these goals the editor has added further purpose: a bias in the illustrations towards modern views that remind the reader how detectable historical forms can be in today's landscapes, and an insistence on documentation that carries arguments beyond mere assertion and opens them to measurement and further reformulation. The editor is pleased to acknowledge the inspiration of W. G. Hoskins through the title of this book and in this otherwise truly American initiative to count J. B. Jackson appropriately among the authors.

Debts intellectual and practical are owed in this effort as in all others. Acknowledgement of scholarly stimulus we confine to the Notes for individual chapters. It is impractical in a multi-authored work such as this to record all debts of a practical nature, but those to a crucial few must be mentioned. The editor is grateful for the unstinting help given by research assistants Linda T. Pote and Melissa J. Morales with library checking and word-processing during editorial work on the manuscript. Maureen A. Harp

rendered singular research assistance in helping bring Chapter 6 to fruition.

*Preface*  Kathleen Neils Conzen witnessed the long maturation of this endeavor and offered countless suggestions along the way; to her the editor's deep appreciation for her interest and knowledge. Roger Jones, Academic Publishing Director at Unwin Hyman, for his part has demonstrated the confidence of a cheerleader, the toughness of a taskmaster, and the patience of Job in seeing this book into print, for which the editor will be long grateful.

Michael P. Conzen
*Chicago, Illinois, 1989*

# *Acknowledgments*

## *Photo credits*

United States Soil Conservation Service: Figs. 1.5, 1.6, 1.7, 1.8, 1.9, and 1.10. Stephen A. Hall: Figs. 2.5 and 2.6. Karl W. Butzer: Figs. 2.9 and 2.10. Michael P. Conzen: Figs. 3.2, 3.3, 3.7, 4.3, 4.5, 4.8, 6.6, 7.4, 11.4, 11.5, 12.3, 12.7, 12.8, 12.9, 12.10, 12.15, 13.1, 13.2, 13.3, 13.6, 13.7, 14.1, 14.2, 14.4, 14.5, 14.8, 14.11, 14.12 and 18.7. California State Library: Fig. 3.4. David Hornbeck: Figs. 3.8 and 3.9. State Historical Society of Wisconsin: Figs. 4.4 and 7.7. Peirce F. Lewis: Figs. 5.2, 5.3, 5.4, 5.5, 5.6, 5.7, 5.8, 5.9, 5.10, 5.13, 16.2, 16.4, 16.5, 16.7, 16.8, and 16.10. Library of Congress Geography and Map Division: Figs. 5.11, 5.12, and 5.14. Sam B. Hilliard: Figs. 6.3, 6.4, 6.7, 6.8, and 6.10. Hildegard B. Johnson: Figs. 7.6 and 7.8. Forest History Society Photographic Collection: Fig. 8.5. John C. Hudson: Figs. 9.2, 9.3, 9.4, 9.6, 9.7, 9.8, 9.9, 9.10, 9.11, 9.12, 9.13, and 9.14. State Historical Society of North Dakota, William H. Brown Collection: Fig. 9.5. United States Bureau of Reclamation: Figs. 10.3 (E. E. Herzog), 10.6, and 10.7. United States Farm Security Administration (Russell Lee): Fig. 10.5. Schwenkfelder Library: Fig. 12.1. Martin C. Perkins: Fig. 12.2. Maureen A. Harp: Fig. 12.11. David R. Meyer: Fig. 13.4. Bethlehem Steel Corporation: Fig. 13.5. Bowater Southern Paper Company (Lavoy Studio): Fig. 13.8. AMAX, Inc. (Mickey Primm, Manley Commercial Photography): Fig. 13.9. Burlington Industries: Fig. 13.10. San Jose (Calif.) Redevelopment Agency: Fig. 13.11. Edward K. Muller: Figs. 14.3 and 14.13. Carnegie Library of Pittsburgh: Figs. 14.6, 14.9, and 14.15. Johns Hopkins University Press: Fig. 14.7. Temple University Urban Archives Center: Fig. 14.10. P. Blake: Fig. 14.14. John A. Jakle: Figs. 15.1, 15.2, 15.3, 15.4, 15.5, and 15.6. Wilbur Zelinksy: Figs. 16.1, 16.3, 16.6, and 16.9. William K. Wyckoff: Figs. 17.1, 17.5, 17.6, 17.9, 17.10, and 17.11. Lawrenceville School Archives: Fig. 17.2. Fisher Island Realty Sales, Inc.: Fig. 17.4. Cartier Jewelers: Fig. 17.8. John Brinckerhoff Jackson: Figs. 18.1, 18.2, 18.4, 18.5, 18.6, and 18.8. Alex Harris: Fig. 18.3. This photograph, a color original, is reproduced with the permission of the author and of the Museum of Fine Arts, Santa Fe, New Mexico.

*Acknowledgments*

## Sources for other illustrations

Fig. 1.1. After Glenn T. Trewartha, Arthur H. Robinson, and Edwin H. Hammond, *Elements of Geography*, 5th ed. New York: McGraw-Hill Book Company, 1967. Fig. 1.2. After *U.S. Geological Survey Circular 44*. Fig. 1.3. Adapted from the *National Atlas of the United States of America*. Fig. 1.4. From Erwin Raisz, 1939. Fig. 2.1. Simplified vegetation patterns of grassy woodland—parkland—versus closed forest are based on evaluation of all published end-glacial pollen profiles, after Porter 1983, Bryant and Holloway 1985. The steppe zone of the High Plains is inferred from open vegetation and late glacial eolian activity. Fig. 2.2. Based on Driver 1961, Jennings 1978, Kehoe 1981, and Sturtevant 1978. Fig. 2.3. Urban features based in part on Fowler 1978, and Gregg 1975, abandoned channel chronology after Yerkes 1987. Fig. 2.4. Modified after Finlayson and Pihl 1980. Fig. 2.7. Modified after Midvale 1968, Masse 1981, and Nicholas and Neitzel 1984. Fig. 2.8. After Wood and McAllister 1984: Fig. 6, with permission. Fig. 2.11. Based on Driver 1961, Kehoe 1981, and Sturtevant 1978–. Fig. 7.2. U.S. Geological Survey 1:62,500 Ironton Quadrangle. Fig. 7.3. From *American State Papers, Public Lands*, Vol. 3, p. 22. Fig. 7.5. Everts and Stewart, *Illustrated Historical Atlas of Jackson County, Michigan*, 1874. Fig. 8.1. Orsamus Turner, 1851. Fig. 8.3. After Stokes 1957. Fig. 8.4. From W. B. Greeley, "The Relation of Geography to Timber Supply," *Economic Geography* 1 (1925): 1–11. Fig. 11.1. S. C. Powell 1963. Fig. 11.2. Clayton W. Woodford, *History of Cumberland County, Maine*, Philadelphia: Everts and Peck, 1880, opp. p. 220. Fig. 12.4. After Mather and Kaups 1963. Fig. 12.5 Thompson Brothers and Burr, *Historical Atlas of Kane County*, Illinois, 1874. Fig. 12.12. After William C. Sherman, *Prairie Mosaic: An Atlas of Rural North Dakota*, Fargo, ND: North Dakota Institute for Regional Studies, 1983, p. 135, with permission. Fig. 12.13. After Vogeler 1976 and Dockendorff 1986. Fig. 17.3. Data from the U.S. Polo Association.


The following figures are the work of the authors of the respective chapters: Figs. 3.5, 3.6, 5.1, 6.5, 8.2, 9.1, 10.2, 10.4, 12.6, 12.14, 17.7, 17.12, 17.13, and A.1.

The following figures are the work of the editor in collaboration with the respective chapter authors: Figs. 3.1, 4.1, 4.2, 4.6, 4.7, 6.1, 6.2, 6.9, 7.1, 7.9, 10.1, and 11.3.

# Contents

*xiii*

# Foreword

THIS IS AN important book about ourselves. It is a searching look at the home we have made, and are continually refurbishing, on this continent. It is focused on our visible surroundings, on that which we live amidst—on the landscapes we have created.

For most Americans such a book may require some adjustment of vision, some change in common ways of looking and thinking about their immediate world. It may require a considerable stretching of their usual sense of the key term: *landscape*. Americans need help with that word because it still most likely brings first to mind one of its more limited uses: the decorative design of formal parks or gardens, or the plot of ground in front of the house; or vaguely appreciative views of attractive countrysides; or a popular form of artistic rendition of such scenes. To ask us to accept, as this book does, that *landscape is comprehensive and cultural*; that it encompasses everything to be seen in our ordinary surroundings, and that virtually all that can be seen has been created or altered by human intervention, is to open up a challenging and rewarding way of thinking about our everyday world. To ask us, moreover, to see *landscape as history* adds a further dimension and enrichment, for it asks us to see that every landscape—not just those with "historic sites"—is part of a vast, cluttered, complex repository of society, an archive of tangible evidence about our character and experience as a people through all our history—if only we can learn how to read it.

One of the great virtues of landscape study is that it lies open to us all, it is accessible, every where, every day. Anyone can look, and of course we all need help to understand what we are looking at, but we can readily learn more and more and make ever better sense of what we see. Landscape study can be a lifelong education and pleasure. William G. Hoskins, one of the godfathers of this work, was wont to liken the English landscape to a symphony and to urge the importance of moving beyond a general esthetic response to a beautiful mass of sound to the point where one could clearly recognize the various themes, how they become woven together, the new harmonies that emerge, and all the subtle variations that enrich the work. It is an attractive metaphor in that it suggests an immense range of works extant, the unlimited possibilities for appreciation, the intricate relationships to be understood—and, we should also acknowledge, the fact that we may not always like what we encounter.

*The making of the American landscape* provides an unprecedented introduction to an immense composition. It sketches the general structure, describes the main themes, and offers commentary upon a great many details, dynamics, and variations. It has much to offer those already attuned to the topic, for we have never had such a comprehensive treatment, and we must hope that it will be an attractive guide to those who have never given much attention to such matters. For surely it is desirable for Americans to learn about and reflect upon this continuous shaping of their surroundings. As the metaphor of *home* suggests, it must bear, directly and subtly, in ways beyond measure if not beyond dispute, upon the quality of American life. So far we seem only dully or incoherently aware of such things. We may cry out in protest of direct threats to our own surroundings, but in general so much of our response to landscape and history seems almost pathologically crippled: a people unable to discern, or care about, the difference between a theme park and the real thing—and ready to turn the real thing into a theme park at the slightest prospect of profit. No book can cure such severe cases, but one would like to think that this one especially, and others in the burgeoning literature on landscape, might begin to provide some antidote to our long-apparent tendency to live "a life of locational and visual indifference." But I hasten to add that this book is not primarily a prescription. It is neither a critique nor a celebration of what Americans have done to their surroundings; it is, rather, a fascinating story of the building and rebuilding, the continuous tinkering and refurnishing, of their home in North America. Once one begins to look at landscapes through the help of these historical geographers any idea that even the most ordinary and familiar parts of the American scene are too simple, shallow, and monotonous to be given serious attention should be banished forever.

Michael Conzen tells something of the lineage of the book in his Preface. I would like to add just this. Half a century ago his father, M. R. G. Conzen crossed the narrow seas and brought a Germanic thoroughness to the detailed analysis of English town morphology, with enduring effect upon a whole field. A generation later the son, steeped in the tradition of English landscape studies, crossed the broader seas to continue his academic training at the premier center for historical geographic study in North America. Given that lineage, that particular combination of heredity and environment, it is perhaps no surprise that Michael Conzen soon emerged as one of our most original and penetrating geographical interpreters. It is altogether appropriate that this fine book should bear his name, but I am not sure that "editor" gives the right impression; we might better think of Michael Conzen as the commissioner, inspirer, part composer, arranger, and conductor of a grand "symphony" on the American landscape.

D. W. Meinig
*Syracuse University*

# Introduction

Life must be lived amidst that which was made before. Every landscape
is an accumulation. The past endures.

D. W. Meinig 1979, p. 44.

Landscape is not merely the world we see, it is a construction, a
composition of that world. Landscape is a way of seeing the world.

D. E. Cosgrove 1984, p. 13.

LANDSCAPES FASCINATE us because they speak through the language of
visual observation of the age-old relationship between human beings
and their environment. Our sensibility toward landscape, however, appears
to be a relatively modern development in history, emerging among the
European élite during the Renaissance. The idea of landscape took a long
time to crystallize, during which it represented a wide range of political,
social, and moral tenets expressed through painting and literature,
becoming accepted by the 18th century as a notable aspect of taste.
Although it declined in the late 19th century, when the divergence between
science and art and the advent of photography removed it as a central
cultural concept, it has continued to be important as an avenue of scientific
inquiry—especially in geography—as an approach to physical planning,
and, across a broader social spectrum, as a source of personal enjoyment.[1]

Landscapes interest people in various ways. Most would acknowledge an
elementary regard for "reading" the landscape in order to navigate through
it. We live in physical space and our need to traverse it requires at least a
fleeting attention to avenues and structures, their arrangement, and their
interrelations in terms, as it were, of a road map. For many that is also the
limit of their interest. For others there is curiosity about the landscape as an
embodiment of the cumulative evidence of human adjustment to life on
Earth. In this sense landscape holds an intellectual interest in offering a
palimpsest of signs for "decoding" and analyzing our human use of the
globe. And third, landscape can be a powerful force in shaping the
individual's emotional world of sensations and moods, thus contributing an
affective dimension to those of function and intellect.[2]

What exactly do we mean by landscape? The ambiguity of the word is
both its strength and weakness. Historically, the term dates from the Middle
Ages when it denoted "a district owned by a particular lord or inhabited by
a particular group of people."[3] The modern word stems from the 16th
century when Dutch and Italian painters used it to mean a representation of
scenery, either in general or with respect to a particular view.[4] In common
parlance, landscape as a generic term can be understood to encompass all

the visible world. A particular landscape is that characteristic portion of the world visible by an observer from a specific position. Implicit in these notions is the dual nature of landscape: as object and subject. This has caused no end of difficulty for both scientific and everyday use, since objective and subjective study employ methods usually distinct and largely incompatible. Another source of ambiguity lies in the need to distinguish between the area covered in the "scene" and its actual contents—the landscape's spatial extent and configuration, and the material features contained therein. Yet another ambiguity lies in the possibly different meanings given to landscape by those who live in it and those who see it with detachment—the dichotomy between insider and outsider.[5] A final ambiguity is introduced when we try to reconcile individual responses to landscape with collective ones. Although unable to resolve or examine at any length these intriguing issues, a few points deserve mention.

Landscape is grasped initially through its visible elements, a composition of material features in space, but its study is by no means limited to them; interpretation draws immediately on cultural expressions and related factors that may not be at all visible.[6] Whether a landscape is studied for its own sake—as a thing "out there" to be explained—or as a means to understanding the society or societies that have produced it, relevant nonmaterial phenomena such as language, moral values, and social power come readily to mind.

Landscapes are commonly distinguished as natural or cultural. This is a useful distinction for historical purposes, but in practice few landscapes in economically advanced regions have escaped some degree of human modification.[7] This is not to say that nature has lost power in shaping the visible pattern of the landscape, even in the modern age; rather, that the human imprint is by this stage so deep that even natural elements, such as forests and rivers, have not remained untouched in their extent and composition by human occupance. So in many areas, even in the United States, there are few localities that can legitimately be considered still natural or wild, and this elevates the emphasis on human factors in their transformation. The cultural landscape is, in truth, then, a composite of the historical interaction between nature and human action. Nevertheless, there is a tendency in much writing on cultural landscapes to denigrate or ignore the rôle of physical forces;[8] the scope for interpretation, it is argued, is compelling enough even when limited to the form and arrangement of settlements, the pattern of fields, roads, and other transport routes, crops, other extracted resources, and so forth.

These formal elements—the raw material of landscape study—need, certainly, to be regarded as appropriate in themselves for morphological study, but not without recognizing a more holistic, symbolic significance. The cultural meanings attached to these forms by those who created and maintained them need drawing out, for in practice they are seldom self-evident.[9]

2

There are several different approaches to landscape study current in writing on the American scene and they are worth distinguishing, for they will make the choice of content and arrangement of the chapters in this book more apparent. Donald Meinig, in a delightful essay entitled "The beholding eye," has offered a shortlist of perspectives by which people may view a landscape.[10] He distinguishes "ten versions of the same scene" in which different observers of the same prospect might see the landscape before them, depending on their proclivities, as representing *nature* (stressing the insignificance of man), *habitat* (as man's adjustment to nature), *artifact* (reflecting man's impact on nature), *system* (a scientific view of interacting processes contributing to a dynamic equilibrium), *problem* (for solving through social action), *wealth* (in terms of property), *ideology* (revealing cultural values and social philosophy), *history* (as a record of the concrete and the chronological), *place* (through the identity that locations have), and *esthetic* (according to some artistic quality possessed). Such a compendium is a valuable reminder that the eye sees what it wants to see, and this leads, even in terms of these succinct categories, to a veritable ocean of literature. How to navigate a brisk course through it that does not become distended by every local current and breeze? If we can fill our sails with writings in which landscape appears as an explicit concept and a central concern, we may group the resulting interest under four general mastheads.

There is, first, a long and honorable tradition of American landscape study that reflects what might be considered as environmental awareness. This encompasses the whole field of what we still know as natural history, in which the identification of rocks, plants, and animals, as individual elements and as associations, lies at the core of the subject. Even though the modern disciplines of geology and biology and their subfields have produced extensive documentation and theory to explain the conditions of nature, a lively industry in general interpretation feeds the lay interest in the nature around us.[11] The unification of many such themes under the rubric of ecology has excited similarly widespread interest, including even syntheses that link ecology and regional political history.[12] Ecology brings in the human element, for environmental awareness includes peoples' regard for their own relations with nature, and as such has attracted interest from anthropologists and environmental psychologists as well as geologists, biologists, and geographers.[13] In Meinig's terms, nature, habitat, artifact, and system are all represented in landscape studied as a dimension of environmental awareness.

Rudimentary and scientific awareness of the landscape is quickly matched by a subjective, judgemental dimension based on image, symbol, and representation. From early times painters and writers have captured the essence of particular American landscapes in picture and word, invariably colored by their vision of what they were seeing. Paintings and writings in the American pantheon were shaped not just by personal technique but through selection and interpretation of evidence, reflecting assumptions

about the purpose of humans in the landscape and their relations, ideal and actual, with nature. Every picture and book served as implicit recorder not merely of the visual facts of the landscape but of what they symbolized for the artist or writer. Here esthetics mingle with ideology, whether in celebration or criticism of what is contained in the scene.[14] From the Hudson School to the archetypes of Western art, from the New England transcendentalists to the regional novelists of the Middle West, representations of landscape reflect changing descriptive skills and taste, and especially changing attitudes towards the works of human kind in nature.[15] This tradition of landscape study is upheld primarily by art historians and literary analysts, but contributions have come also from cultural historians and geographers.[16]

The physiognomy of landscape can be explored not only through symbolic representation, however; it can also be considered from the practical perspective of design. Equivalent to Meinig's category of "problem," this defines landscape as something that needs managing, since in every age people who add features to the landscape face choices over which design to favor. Furthermore, past choices become subject to social criticism on both esthetic and pragmatic grounds. Hence, there is a large literature on the American landscape as a focus for normative thought—that is, about what it ought to be. Strong critiques have been mounted from the ranks of architects, landscape architects, and planners, usually decrying the depredations of the modern period.[17] Much of this writing is deeply subjective and anecdotal, but in recent years there has been a movement to codify esthetics, spurred by increasing government involvement in landscape management, producing a substantial literature on landscape assessment.[18] Not surprisingly, a consensus has yet to emerge regarding the methods for measuring human reactions to the physical and cultural landscape, let alone to the policy initiatives which they produce.

If the present condition and future direction of the cultural landscape in America stimulates lively debate, so does its history. In some ways, this is the least developed of the four principal approaches to landscape study in America.[19] To be aware of the landscape as an external context, to endow it with symbolism, and to evaluate it against some system of ideals—these are all approaches essentially independent of time. But since we exist in time we must also incorporate it in our view of landscape. Therefore to view the landscape historically is to acknowledge its cumulative character; to acknowledge that nature, symbolism, and design are not static elements of the human record but change with historical experience; and to acknowledge too that the geographically distinct quality of places is a product of the selective addition and survival over time of each new set of forms peculiar to that region or locality. This broad approach considers landscape both as history and as place (referring to Meinig's last remaining categories), and has been nourished by scholarship in geography and history, particularly the subfield of historical geography.[20] The approach has been more cultivated in Britain than America, although interest in American landscape

*4* history seems to be on the rise.[21]

Landscape history gives precedence to time as the key element in landscape formation. Each generation has inherited a landscape shaped in certain ways, and has added its own distinguishing traits while modifying or removing others as it is succeeded by the next generation. The aim of the landscape historian, then, is to distinguish the threads woven into this complex, changing fabric and account for their respective appearance, arrangement, and disappearance. Landscape elements vary widely in the speed of their formation and change, and time plays an important rôle in how historically composite a landscape may become. This idea underlies the contributions to this book.

Much has been written in one way or another about the history of the American cultural landscape, but no one has attempted to cover the ground, however cursorily, in a single volume. The most ambitious interpretation to appear in print so far is John Stilgoe's *Common landscape of America, 1580 to 1845*, but no matter how wide ranging it is the book considers developments only through the early national period and applies to less than half the country. J. B. Jackson's *American space: the centennial years, 1865–1876* covers a single, albeit significant, decade. John Fraser Hart's slim volume, *The look of the land*, looks at some rural, but not urban, landscape features in America (and elsewhere) in varying degrees of historical depth.[22] Allen Noble's *Wood, brick, and stone: the North American settlement landscape* focuses on houses and farm buildings alone, although his extensive treatment is set within a suggestive evolutionary regional framework. Anthologies abound, but even those of national scope are collections of disparate topics.[23] Books about regional cultural landscapes are beginning to give their historical evolution some attention, such as Richard Francaviglia's *The Mormon landscape*, but the majority remain in this respect cursory and anecdotal.[24]

Most other treatments are conceived along different lines. In principle the subject can be considered topically, regionally, or thematically, or through some combination of these modes. Stilgoe favors the "object" approach, devoting chapters to such elements as roads, canals, crops, cowpens, sawmills, camp meetings, fences, and furnaces, reminding us in David Lowenthal's words of the long-standing American interest in "individual features emphasized at the expense of aggregates."[25] The whole period under review is treated syncretically, with topical categories such as agriculture, community, and national design shaping the architecture of argument. Historical periods and regional variations peep through as inflection, not structure. Jackson, on the other hand, views the landscape changes that occurred immediately after the Civil War in strongly regional terms, stressing partly processes such as pioneering, reconstruction, and reform, and partly changes evident in particular settings—either general types such as woods, towns, or the countryside, or specific localities such as Boston, Chicago, Buffalo, and Kansas. Noble offers a third recipe: a richly genetic view of cultural expression and its diffusion over space through examining a highly restricted set of artifacts in the landscape, namely, houses and farmyard buildings.[26] In theory one could incorporate all these approaches in a unified study. That would present a severe challenge for the whole country in a single volume, as indeed it would even for an individual region.[27]

This book aims to draw on some of the strengths of these earlier works, and to combine ideas and evidence according to yet another principle: themes about clusters of related landscape processes set in a broadly historical and regional framework. Such a notion proceeds from the premise that the continent's landscapes were shaped most profoundly by the early colonizing peoples who affected, on the whole, different regions. That some groups prevailed in the course of time over broader territory sets the scene for a shifting of geographical focus, as major new landscape-molding forces came to prominence and modified regions in varying ways. While no sequence of chapters can maintain a perfect logical progression when trying to deal simultaneously with topics, regions, and periods, there is a perceptible if uneven movement within the book from early forces to late, from eastern regions to western, and from rural–agrarian themes to urban–industrial ones.

In the beginning there was the land. No exploration of American cultural landscapes, however oriented to the question of human impact, can ignore the majestic force of the natural environment in presenting human colonizers with certain givens. The presence of mountains, coastal configurations, long rivers, climatic regimes, and major soil and vegetation associations, and their complex interaction in a geographical matrix of relative location, define inescapable factors bound up in the evolution of basic routes of human migration and networks of economic activity. The opening chapter lays out the very minimum we should know about these things in order to make any sense of the cultural shaping that came with human occupance.

Amerindian populations have occupied North America for 15,000 years. No logic of latterday spatial dominance by Euro-Americans can alter the impact that these "first families" had over the millennia in occupying the territory of what became the United States and altering in numerous ways—some fundamental—the environment which white people would eventually penetrate and come to terms with in their own way. The second chapter paints with broad brushstrokes a picture of the aggregate effect that Amerindian settlement had at its zenith and what consequences this had for Euro-American succession.

The next four chapters turn attention to the major colonizing cultures from the European Old World that laid claim to large portions of American territory. The Spanish and French occupied at first discrete segments of the continent, so their direct legacy in today's regional landscapes is fairly apparent, if greatly diminished in modern times (Ch. 3 & 4). The British quickly secured the Atlantic seaboard of what is today the United States, and proceeded to establish a series of landscape traditions that reflected demographic variety and regional ecology. It is suggested that the traditions that carried the most influence nationwide in later landscape-forming trends emerged in the Northeast—more particularly New England and south-eastern Pennsylvania (Ch. 5), while the different agricultural and social systems that produced the plantation necessarily expanded throughout the South (Ch. 6). Both these broad, adaptive Anglo-American landscape traditions crystallized first along the eastern seaboard and spread westward in their respective latitudinal zones.

After political independence, however, a growing economy pushed the settlement frontier west far beyond the Appalachian barrier and required a colonization policy that, because of its geographical scale and rigid geometry had profound impact on the ordering of the American landscape. The land survey system served as the tangible, visible symbol of a national settlement strategy that had no counterpart anywhere in the world (Ch. 7). Extension of this landscape system, however, meant traversing three different ecological realms: the eastern forests, the interior grasslands, and the western arid lands. While the survey grid and its associated laws supplied the landholding framework for an agricultural attack on these environments, the ways in which human modification took hold in each case receive individual consideration (Ch. 8, 9, & 10).

At this point, with the continent essentially spanned as the result of a long-running and powerful agrarian initiative, it is appropriate to take stock of the symbolic and ideological foundations of this historic achievement as expressed in the resulting landscapes. Accordingly, the next two chapters consider what might be termed dominant and recessive paradigms in cultural landscape preferences. America as a would-be utopia was experimented with in several ways. Two involved leaving European precedents behind; a third, arriving with "cultural baggage." Of the first two, the dominant mode, the Anglo-American national strategy, succeeded in creating a "democratic" landscape that settled people generously across the land on single-family farms and in single-family suburbs. This soon emerged as the prevailing American ideal. In contrast, there was a recessive mode followed by those who disdained an individualistic utopia: small bands of settlers who from time to time set up tiny communitarian colonies sprinkled all over the northern half of the country, in sharp contrast to the individualistic majority around them. Their settlements nearly all proved ephemeral, but the ideological polarity represented by these two modes reveals the freedom settlers enjoyed in shaping the American landscape to their wishes (Ch. 11). A third way in which utopia was approached, also recessive, was based on retention rather than rejection of cultural roots. The ethnic background and cultural values of numerous immigrant groups have colored the American landscape in many ways, and while much muted have proven without doubt more potent and enduring than millennialism (Ch. 12).

With these issues exposed, the following three chapters take up various facets of what might be termed the advent of modernism in America, as expressed in the processes of industrialization and urbanization. The rise of large-scale manufacturing, aided by several transport revolutions that redefined distance in America, created brash new industrial landscapes (Ch. 13) and fed an unprecedented growth of towns and cities. Cities were not new to America, but cities in 19th-century America quickly gained a character quite distinct from those in other world regions (Ch. 14). While canal and railroad innovations underwrote much national economic expansion and urban layout during the 19th century, the development of the automobile has perhaps even more profoundly reshaped the lineaments of the American landscape in this century (Ch. 15).

Coursing through the veins of American history for the last two hundred years, and intimately related to questions of modernism, has been the constant tension between public and private interests. Naturally, such struggle is faithfully reflected in the landscape. This theme underlies the last three chapters which explore landscapes created through the visible hand of government (Ch. 16), and those created by private effort. The spectrum of wealth in America since at least the middle of the 19th century has been as wide as anywhere, and the landscapes of the rich, distinctive in their individual scale and opulence, sit like islands amid an ocean of more ordinary residential and recreational landscapes (Ch. 17). Many characteristics of the vernacular, or ordinary landscapes of humbler segments of society have been considered from one perspective or another in prior chapters. J. B. Jackson, with characteristic punch and perception, brings a degree of closure to the topic by reflecting on the fundamental aspects of the vernacular dwelling, contrasting its multifunctional spaces and dependence on outside public locales for family activity with the monofunctionalism and territoriality of establishment homes (Ch. 18). In comparing and contrasting the traditional house form with the non-traditional (the trailer home), this closing chapter also reminds us of the salience, indeed the sanctity, of mobility in American consciousness, as one of the cardinal freedoms Americans go far to protect. Mobility could serve, perhaps, as a metaphor to sustain much of the story of American landscape making.

# Chapter one
## Nature's continent

STANLEY W. TRIMBLE

NORTH AMERICA IS a large continent, spanning fully 115 degrees of longitude and about 75 degrees of latitude. That size is sometimes quite difficult for Europeans to comprehend. The story is told, no doubt apocryphally, that the outcome of World War II was manifest to German prisoners of war only after five days of continuous rail travel had failed to deliver them from east coast to west coast.

The continent is not only vast, it is also one of sharp contrasts. It spans tropics to tundra, searing heat to bitter cold, mild marine conditions to severe continental effects, continual wetness to permanent desiccation, mountains to almost featureless plains, absence of plant life to vegetative abundance. Perhaps, also, North America has had its physical environment transformed more rapidly at the hands of people than any other large area of the world. Generally, within less than 200 years, near-primeval land has sprouted farms and cities, forests have been removed or changed, and severe hydrologic and geomorphic disruptions have sometimes ensued.

No understanding of these profound transformations can be gained without first considering the nature of the stage upon which the human drama has unfolded. This opening chapter sketches an outline portrait of the physical environment of mid-latitude North America. The continent's size, internal contrasts and complexity can only be hinted at, and the reader is encouraged to read further, particularly with the aid of a good atlas that will complement the few illustrations that can be offered here.[1] This portrait lays out the composition of the continent's natural regions through the broad brushstrokes of climate, landform, vegetation, and soil.

### Climates

Since the dawn of time on this planet life at the surface has been conditioned by the continuous interaction of the Earth's internal forces with the enveloping atmosphere. Dynamic and historically volatile, this interaction has produced periods of apparent equilibrium in which, from the perspective of human experience, characteristic patterns of climate seem to emerge.

Many things conspire to give North America the climate it has, as one should expect for a continent so large and diverse. The first of these is the continent's very mid-latitude location. This means that the noon sun angle is low in winter, ensuring receipt of limited solar energy at that time. Also, the latitude places much of the continent in the path of the Westerlies wind belt and thus in the paths of mid-latitude cyclones or "storm-tracks." These cyclones, together with air masses, control the genesis of much of the weather over the continent.

A second climatic circumstance is the presence of source regions for varied air masses which converge upon and interact in the traveling cyclones. Because these air masses tend not to mix, their common boundaries mark the cold and warm fronts of the mid-latitude cyclones. Four air masses affect America. There is maritime tropical air which is warm and moist and originates in the South Atlantic and Gulf of Mexico, but also comes from the Pacific Ocean off the coast of California and Mexico. Maritime polar air, cool and moist, comes primarily from the North Pacific, and also from the North Atlantic. Continental polar air masses, which are cool to cold and dry, form in central to northern Canada and move south to southeasterly across the continent. Continental tropical air masses round out the symmetrical quartet, and these are warm and dry, forming over the desert of north Mexico.

The very size of the continent also conditions climate by creating a "continental" effect. Temperatures over central Canada can range from over 100°(F) in summer to perhaps −50° or below in winter. At the same time, the atmosphere over the oceans on either side has a much smaller range. The continental effect also creates a monsoon, or seasonal wind, although this is not nearly as strong as that found in southeast Asia. The cold winter air of the continental interior, being denser, produces a thermally induced high pressure zone so that the general flow of air, in conjunction with the upper Westerlies, is to the south and east. No topographic barriers exist in the mid-continent so the polar continental air can often move to the Gulf of Mexico. Texans often joke that the only barrier between them and the Arctic Ocean is a barbed-wire fence. Summer finds a reversal of flow with tropical maritime air drawn from the Gulf of Mexico and South Atlantic into the continental interior.

Ocean currents provide another control. The cold California current flows southward along the west coast and can have an effect some distance inland. The warm Gulf Stream flows northward along the southeast coast as far north as North Carolina. Meanwhile the cold Labrador current flows southward along the northeast coast, sometimes slipping in between the coast and the Gulf Stream as far south as Virginia and chilling local weather.

Another climatic influence is the wind and pressure system. The
*10* Westerlies carry with them the endless stream of mid-latitude cyclones

which attract the air masses and create much of the weather for the continent. At the surface, these Westerlies bring the marine atmospheric conditions of the Pacific Ocean onto the coast from Alaska to Oregon and, seasonally (in winter), to California. Meanwhile, there is a large subtropical high pressure cell which has a semi-permanent position over the Pacific Ocean off the coast of Mexico which keeps much of northwestern Mexico dry and seasonally (in summer) keeps California dry. Because there are no prevailing winds blowing on to the east coast, maritime influences are usually restricted to the coastline. Severe continental conditions of heat and cold thus prevail across the interior almost to the east coast. The inland suburbs of Boston, for example, record extreme winter temperatures almost as cold as those at Milwaukee, Wisconsin, which lies at the same latitude but far inland.

Some low pressure systems affecting the continent are destructive. Tropical cyclones, or hurricanes, form over the South Atlantic or Gulf of Mexico in late summer and autumn and move most often into the Gulf or northward along the east coast. The destruction along the coast from their wind, tides, and rain is well known but, once they move inland, they are less destructive and bring heavy rains, often breaking the late-summer droughts which sometimes grip the Southeast. Thus, their constructive effects offset the destructive ones to some degree. Such hurricanes also form in the Pacific and affect the Southwest, but are less common. Tornadoes are destructive cyclones caused by severe atmospheric instability (high moisture and decline in temperature with altitude) and occur in the eastern half of the continent during the warm season. Oklahoma and Kansas are the tornado kingdoms of America, as one will recall from *The Wizard of Oz*.

Mountains strongly affect climate. The chain of high mountains extending the entire length of the west coast effectively blocks most moisture from penetrating into the continental interior. Thus, the windward (western) sides of these mountains are wet while the leeward (eastern) sides are dry. Coastal mountains in Oregon get as much as 100 inches of rain annually while eastern Oregon gets as little as one-tenth of that. This process leaves the central part of the continent with little moisture: the only other source of moisture is occasional maritime tropical air from the Gulf of Mexico. Because the distances are so great and the prevailing winds blow eastward, not much of this air reaches the mid-continent, so it is relatively dry. Further east there is greater probability of such air penetrating so there is higher annual rainfall. With these genetic processes in mind, it is now possible to understand the characteristics and distribution of climates (Fig. 1.1).

The humid subtropical climate affecting the Southeast is controlled by maritime tropical air during the summer and an alternation of that with polar continental air in winter when mid-latitude cyclones are common. Summers are hot and humid, much like the wet tropics, while the winter weather alternates between cool and warm spells with frequent cyclonic rain. Very cold temperatures are then possible. Americans from the North 11 tend to perceive Alabama, for example, as "tropical," but Alabama has

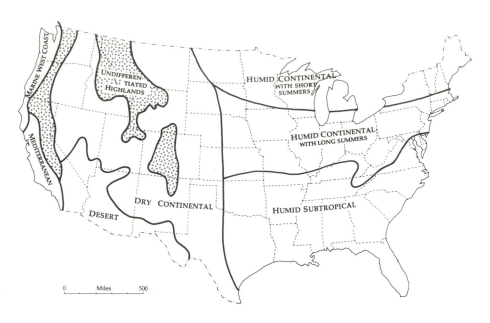

**Figure 1.1**
Major climatic regions in the
United States.

experienced temperatures as low as −18°. Precipitation may be heavy in individual storms and the area averages 40 to 80 inches per year.

Humid continental climate with a long summer found in the center and East is a cooler version of the first climate. The winter is longer, the coldest month will average below 32° and more snow and colder extremes are possible. Snowfall usually totals on the order of 20 to 40 inches. St. Louis, for example, has a January average temperature of 20° but extremes of −22° are possible. The summers have more cyclonic (frontal) activity and have slightly cooler average temperatures, but the temperature and humid extremes will be as high as in the humid subtropical further south. At least one geographer has called this zone "the misery belt," and notes that this is the perfect climate for growing corn—long summer days at mid-high latitudes, plenty of rain, warm temperatures—"but for anyone whose esthetic requirements transcend those of a cornstalk, the climate is pretty darned miserable, winter or summer."[2]

The humid continental climate with a short summer that affects a central region along the Canadian border has cyclonic rainfall all year, but summer brings some great convectional thunderstorms. Although the summer temperature may be cool, that is the result of averaging some very cool days when polar continental air dominates, with some very hot and humid days (perhaps over 100°) when tropical maritime air dominates. Mercifully, this is not too common. Winter, on the other hand, is brutal and *long*. Temperatures may go below −50°, snow may be on the ground for several months, and spring may not arrive until May with hot temperatures often coming in June. Rain may average 20 to 40 inches and there is a decided maximum during the long days of summer.

*12*     In the dry continental climatic areas of the West, mountains curtail moisture from the West while the prevailing upper Westerlies and the great distances from the Gulf limit the supply of tropical maritime air. Annual average rainfall ranges from about 10 inches in the west to about 20 inches in the east. There are great seasonal temperature contrasts. Winter temperatures to the north are more severe where there are frequent incursions of polar continental air while the summers there are shorter and milder. Snow is possible over much of the region and may remain on the ground a month or more.

The desert, located in the Southwest, is cut off from moisture on all sides. It is also influenced by the Pacific subtropical high pressure cell. The net result is a large region receiving on average less than 10 inches annual precipitation. Although summer temperatures may reach 115° or more, the winters can be quite cool and snow is possible.

The so-called Mediterranean climate prevailing along part of the West coast is also known as dry-summer subtropical. The summer dry season is controlled by the northward shift of the Pacific high pressure cell whereas the winters see a southward shifting of the Westerlies with their mid-latitude cyclones and fronts, all producing winter rainfall. Cold temperatures and frost are uncommon in winter while the summers are hot inland but greatly moderated nearer the coast. Normal rainfall is about 12 to 20 inches. An unpleasant weather feature here is the Santa Ana wind, a distant cousin of the *Mistral* and *Sirocco*. It occurs when a large high pressure air mass stalls over Utah, or nearby areas; the clockwise circulation blasts hot tropical continental air into southern California, creating discomfort and tension.

The marine west coast climate is controlled by the Westerlies importing the marine conditions of the north Pacific on to land. Winters and summers are mild and there is a small range in annual temperature averages, extremes being rare. Average annual precipitation is moderate (20 inches) with no relief, but more than 100 inches may be experienced on windward mountain slopes. Thunderstorms and downpours are uncommon.

Various remaining highland areas have such a diversity of climates depending on elevation, exposure, and other factors that it is impossible to differentiate them in this overview. Small areas within these regions may vary from subtropical to arctic and humid to desert.

Patterns of annual precipitation, then, are reasonably simple. The wettest areas are the northwest coast and the East, especially the Southeast. The dry area is the western half of the continent and the dryest is the extreme Southwest. More important than the amount of rainfall, however, is the availability of water. This balances the receipt of rainfall against the losses from direct evaporation and transpiration of plants. Potential losses to evapotranspiration are a function of temperature, relative humidity, and wind, and so are greatest in the Southwest where the rate may be over 80 inches per year. Thus, the highest natural demand for water is just where nature has been her most stingy. The Southeast has a fairly high potential rate but nature usually provides ample moisture and, usually, an excess.

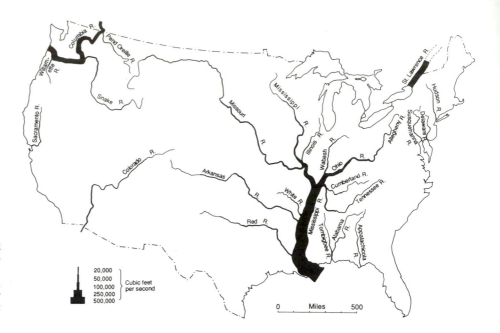

**Figure 1.2**
Average discharge of large
rivers in the United States.
Rivers shown are those with
an average flow at their
mouths of 19,000 cubic feet
(538 m$^3$) per second or more.

Minimum potential rates are found to the northwest and northeast, both humid areas, so there is surplus water found there. One sign of surplus is the amount of streamflow for the major rivers of the U.S. and southeast Canada (Fig. 1.2). The southeast coast also has much runoff, but the individual rivers there do not compare in this respect with the nation's largest.

Neither today's climates nor their causes have always been the same. During the Pleistocene epoch, approximately 1 million to 10,000 years ago, there were at least four distinct cold periods when there was a surplus of freezing water over melting water, producing continental glaciers. These glaciers advanced as far as a line from New York City southwestward down the Ohio River, thence up the Missouri River and over to Seattle. At the same time, alpine glaciers extended southward from the mountains of the West to at least the southern end of the California Sierra Nevada. The last advance of the glaciers was called the Wisconsin Stage (known as *Würm* in Europe) which ended abruptly about 10,000–15,000 years ago.[3] It is this most recent stage which left behind many of the landform features of North America. The last 10,000 years or so, the Holocene epoch, has been a period of relatively warmer and stabler temperatures. Throughout this period, and especially over the past 1,000 years, there have been cycles of warmer and colder temperatures lasting 20 to 100 years. The early 19th century was a period of cold while the first half of the 20th century was abnormally warm. Coinciding with the warmer weather, at least in some parts of the continent, there was also wetter weather. The discharge of the Colorado River was measured during this wet cycle and, based on this record, specific rights to the use of the annual flow were allocated to the states along its banks. Now that the flow has returned to what is thought to be "normal," there is insufficient water to satisfy current human expectations.

## The physiographic layout

All of North America lies on what in geotectonics is called the American Plate, except for a strip of the Southwest which sits on the Pacific Plate. The two plates join at the San Andreas Fault, a transform fault which runs from north of San Francisco to the Gulf of California. It has been the scene of many severe earthquakes, and stresses appear to be building up again. Further north, from Oregon to Alaska, the Canada Plate is subducting, or slipping, under the American Plate and a major result is the range of volcanic Cascade Mountains, part of the Pacific "Rim of Fire."

Generally, the continent may be generally described as having mountain chains roughly parallel to each coast (Fig. 1.3). In the West, the singular mass in Canada bifurcates southward, one branch remaining within 250 miles of the west coast, while the other branch, the American Rockies, extends through the west-central part of the U.S. to Mexico. In the East, the Appalachian Highlands extend from the Gaspé Peninsula to central Alabama. A low, mountainous outlier in the south center are the Ozark-Ouachita Highlands.

The physiography of mid-latitude North America is complex, but it may be simplified by grouping physical traits into regions representing composite associations between topography, soils, and vegetation (Fig. 1.3).[4] What follows can only serve as a brief introduction.

**Figure 1.3**
Landform regions of the United States, as conceived by N. M. Fenneman in 1928.

# Natural regions

### The far West

The Pacific Ranges are in the shape of a long, narrow "H" (Fig. 1.4). Running south from British Columbia are the coastal ranges, clothed in the luxuriant rain forest of that mild, moist climate. Further south, they yield to the increasingly longer dry season and are more likely to be covered with chaparral or grass. In southern California, these coast ranges veer inland in stepwise fashion and actually trend almost east–west north of Los Angeles. The lowlands of that area are increasingly covered with exotic vegetation grown under irrigation, while the rapidly expanding cities are often islands of lush tropical plants. To the northeast, the volcanic Cascades, covered with a rich growth of Douglas fir, extend from Canada almost to California. Mount St. Helens is now the most famous active member of this group, but Mounts Lassen, Baker, Hood and Ranier are also restless. Many others are dormant—or presumably so. The Columbia River has cut an impressive gorge through the Cascades (Fig. 1.5). Joining the Cascades to the coastal ranges are the Klamath Mountains: from there the magnificent Sierra Nevada trends southeastward. This mass is a huge block of granite tilted west so that the east face is extremely steep. Here is found Mt. Whitney

**Figure 1.4**
Physiographic diagram of the
United States.

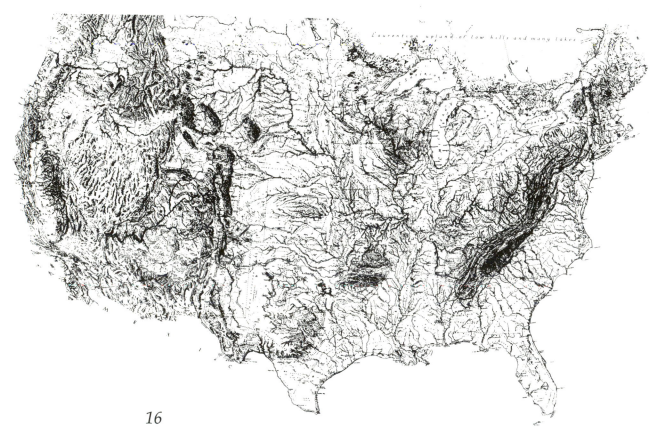

**Figure 1.5**
The gorge of the Columbia River through the Cascade Mountains at Bingen, Washington.

(14,500 feet), the highest peak in the contiguous United States. This ridge is the High Sierra, a spectacular area of peaks, glaciers, and lakes. On the gentle west slope are great forests of redwood, but to the north, parts of the deeply entrenched river valleys have been filled with gravel, the result of hydraulic mining for gold during the last century.[5] The Pacific Ranges have extensive forests of Douglas fir, spruce, and redwood. This is the most prolific supply of lumber for the continent, but the rate of cutting often exceeds regrowth.

Between the coast ranges and the Cascades is the Puget Sound Lowland-Willamette Valley, an area of good harbors, agriculture, and increasing population density. The Great Valley of California is composed of sediments of the coastal ranges and the Sierra Nevada, between which it lies. With its even surface, sunshine, and available irrigation waters, it is one of the great agricultural regions of the world, growing almost every imaginable commercial crop.

The intermontane plateaus extend from Canada south into Mexico. In the north, the Columbia Plateau is a hardened sea of lava through which the Blue Mountains and other elevated points emerge as islands. The Columbia

**Figure 1.6**
The Colorado Plateau, near
Grand Junction, Colorado.

and Snake Rivers have cut gorges through this plateau, the Snake River
Gorge being especially deep (4,000 to 6,000 feet) and spectacular. In central
Washington, the climate and excellent basaltic soils have given rise to wheat
growing and orchard planting. The Colorado Plateau is actually several
plateaus separated by escarpments or canyons (Fig. 1.6). The most
spectacular of these is the Grand Canyon, over 5,000 feet deep, which gives
a good cross-section of the geologic sequence. The main industry of this arid
region is tourism, since here are located such famous national parks as Bryce
Canyon, Cedar Breaks, Zion Canyon, Monument Valley, Dinosaur Park, the
Petrified Forest, Mesa Verde, and, of course, the Grand Canyon. The latter
inspired the composer Ferde Grofé to write his *Grand Canyon*, one of several

suites inspired by the American landscape. In the plateau area as well as elsewhere in the Southwest, there has been a severe problem with stream channel erosion or arroyos which began in the 19th century. Both climatic changes (dryer or wetter) and increased grazing (compaction of soil, replacement of perennial plants with annual plants) have been blamed, but whatever the cause, many of these arroyos have begun to fill and stabilize since about 1940.[6] The Basin and Range province extends from Oregon to Texas. It is composed of block mountains, lifted or tilted chunks of the Earth's crust, surrounded by erosional debris. To the north, drainage is to the interior with lakes often covering large areas appearing after sufficient rainfall. There, runoff has never been adequate to overflow the region and cut channels through to the outside. To the south, drainage is primarily via the Colorado River and Rio Grande.[7] Vegetation ranges from short grass in the north to desert shrubs in the south. However, where water and talent are available the area can bloom as shown by the "Mormon Garden" around Salt Lake City.

The Rocky Mountains comprise two zones, the northern and southern Rockies. The northern branch extends from Canada to the Wasatch and Uinta Mountains of Utah. It contains several ranges, often divided by deep and long valleys useful for transportation and communication. Most of these mountains were heavily glaciated and the grandeur can be seen in Glacier Park, Montana. The southern Rockies extend from Wyoming to Santa Fe, New Mexico. On the east flank, the Laramie-Park Range presents a formidable barrier and the peaks are impressive even when seen from the 5,000-foot elevation of the Great Plains. To the west, and parallel to these two ranges lie the Medicine Bow, Park, and Wasatch Ranges. Within the area bordered by these five ranges are large, basin-like areas called parks which are used for ranching (Fig. 1.7). Pioneers studiously circumnavigated the massive southern Rockies: the Oregon Trail went around the north end while the Santa Fe Trail passed around the south.

### The central interior

The Interior Plains make up the largest of the physiographic divisions and include the Great Plains, the central lowlands, and the interior low plateaus. The Great Plains extend from Canada to Mexico. They slope from elevations of 3,000 to 5,000 feet along the edge of the Rockies to about 1,500 to 2,000 feet at the edge of the central lowlands, a border often marked by a rugged escarpment called the "break of the plains." The eastern border also approximates the 20-inch annual rainfall boundary and the region generally has less than this amount. The plains are crossed west to east by the Missouri River and its tributaries, the Yellowstone, Cheyenne, Platte, and Republican. Further south are the Arkansas, Cimarron, Canadian, and Pecos Rivers. The Black Hills create a conspicuous relief feature in South Dakota. Short grass is the dominant natural vegetation of the Great Plains and many pioneer houses were built of the sod. The expansiveness of this region was eloquently recorded by one such pioneer:

**Figure 1.7**
A "park" in the southern Rocky Mountains, near Montrose, Colorado.

The long-expected valley of the Platte lay before us . . . it had not one picturesque or beautiful feature; nor had it any of the features of grandeur, other than its vast extent, its solitude, and its wildness. For league after league, a plain as level as a lake was outspread beneath us: here and there the Platte divided into a dozen threadlike sluices, was traversing it, an occasional clump of wood, rising in the midst like a shadowy island.[8]

Most agriculture other than grazing requires irrigation and this has greatly depleted the regional water source, the Ogallala Aquifer. Expansion of nonirrigated agriculture into the southern Great Plains during the humid weather of 1917–20 ended in the disaster of the Dust Bowl of the 1930s when a dry cycle again occurred (Fig. 1.8). Dust clouds covered up to 1½ square miles and were carried by the Westerlies well out into the Atlantic.

The Central Lowland is big, extending from the Great Plains to the Appalachians and from Canada to central Texas. The region was glaciated as far south as the Ohio and Missouri Rivers and, in fact, melting glaciers helped determine their present courses. Glacial features include troughs (Lake Michigan, Green Bay, and Lake Superior), various types of moraines (ground, end, recessional, and interlobate), as well as old lake floors, eskers, drumlins and outwash plains. Perhaps the greatest heritage of the glaciers is that the regional limestones were ground up and left in the glacial till as "time-release pills" of soil ameliorants, gradually feeding into and nourishing the soil. Moreover, an excellent prairie soil (a type of mollisol) fortuitously developed over much of this area. In order to improve the habitat for buffalo, it appears that the Indians kept the area burned during the centuries preceeding European settlement. This was done both to drive buffalo for the hunt and also to improve the grazing habitat. Fire not only encouraged new growth from the tall grasses (prairie), but also suppressed the forests because young undergrowth plants and seedlings were particularly vulnerable to fire. Even in the area peripheral to the prairie, most trees were more fire-resistant ones such as oak and hickory. Buffalo thriving in this habitat further suppressed trees by browsing the leaves from young forests. The prairie, allowed to remain in this state for many centuries, eventually influenced the soil by concentrating in it basic nutrients and organic materials. Thus Corn Belt farmers can thank the Indians for helping to create an enriched soil. These circumstances, together with the climate and with an unusually intelligent and industrious rural populace, have combined to create the landscape synergism known as the Corn Belt, a wonderland for corn, soybeans, hay, and other crops. It would be hard to imagine a more fortunate combination.

To the south and east, forest was the dominant presettlement vegetation, but most has been cleared for agriculture. To the northeast, near the border of the Great Plains, both wheat and corn are grown on large farms scattered across the rectilinear landscape (Fig. 1.9). In southwestern Wisconsin and extending into adjoining states is the "Driftless Area," which, for some as yet unknown reason, escaped at least the last glacial advance. Here, one may see a remnant of the pre-glacial landscape, a partially dissected plateau

**Figure 1.8**
The Dust Bowl. An abandoned farmstead near Channing, Texas, in the 1930s.

**Figure 1.9**
The western interior lowlands. A glaciated plain of rich soil in Clay County, Minnesota, used for growing corn and spring wheat. Note the rectilinear field and property pattern and the farmsteads nestled into windbreaks, scattered at regular intervals across the landscape.

with level uplands and steep slopes. Although now checked, agricultural erosion was rampant here and valleys have been buried under as much as 15 feet of sediment.[9] The unglaciated salient of the Central Lowland extending from the Missouri River to central Texas is generally less productive land than the glaciated area.

The Great Lakes are among the largest fresh water lakes in the world, but they are mere remnants of much larger lakes formed during the Pleistocene epoch. Besides their importance for navigation, their chief influence is on climate. Areas east of the lakes have their temperatures moderated, but the price they pay is more cloud cover and much more snow.

The interior low plateaus extend from north Alabama to southern Indiana. The two garden spots of this region are the "Blue Grass" basins around Lexington, Kentucky, and Nashville, Tennessee. Both basins have rich soils from the same Ordovician limestone and both are known for being the centers of prosperity, power, and talent within these states.[10] The small area of the Nashville Basin, for example, has furnished the United States with two presidents (Jackson and Polk), and many other talented individuals including Matthew Fontaine Maury, the famous maritime geographer. This Tennessee basin, known locally as the "Dimple of the Universe" is one of the few American landscape features to have inspired poetry. One poem begins:

> O, the glorious Middle Basin
> The rose in nature's wreath;
>   with her purpling sky and her hills on high
> And her blue grass underneath[11]

Interestingly, both basins are rimmed by lands that, in some areas, are among the poorest in these states. A case in point is the western highland rim of Tennessee. There, elegant ante-bellum mansions and tumble-down hillbilly cabins are literally within sight of one another. Between the two basins is the sinkhole-pocked Pennyroyal Plateau, beneath which is the Mammoth Cave System, one of the world's great networks of limestone caverns.[12]

The Ozark-Ouachita Highlands is a region composed of two divisions, the Ozark Plateaus and the Ouachita Mountains (Fig. 1.3). The former is a partially dissected plateau with poor, thin soils quite analogous to the Appalachian plateaus to the east. To the south across the valley of the Arkansas River are the Ouachita Mountains. These are folded sedimentary mountains with local relief of 2,000 to 3,000 feet and are similar to the folded Appalachians.

### The East

The Appalachian Highlands extend from the Gaspé Peninsula to mid-Alabama, comprising subareas known as the Appalachian plateaus, Ridge and Valley, Blue Ridge, Piedmont, and New England (Fig. 1.3). The Appalachian plateaus contain poor, thin soils and hardwood forests extending from central New York to central Alabama. Lying at about 2,000 to 2,500 feet elevation, the plateaus have a recognizable escarpment on all sides, but the east scarp facing the Ridge and Valley zone is the boldest. In its northern reaches, the region is heavily dissected so that it is often called the Allegheny Mountains. The north end was glaciated, producing the "Finger Lakes," among many other glacial features in New York. The southern portion is less dissected and is termed the Cumberland Plateau. Upper strata of the plateaus contain abundant coal, and mining has heavily defaced the slopes and streams of the region.

The Ridge and Valley, or Folded Appalachians, is a mostly lowland zone. The eastern part, the Great Valley, runs almost continuously from Quebec, Canada to Birmingham, Alabama and is known, depending on local drainage, as the (Lake) Champlain Valley, Hudson Valley, Kittaninny Valley, Shenandoah Valley (Fig. 1.10), and Coosa Valley. It has always been

**Figure 1.10**
A Great Valley landscape near Luray, Virginia, looking west toward the ridges of the Ridge and Valley.

an important north–south transportation corridor. Several rivers such as the Delaware, Susquehanna, Potomac and James, have cut gaps through the region which allow easy east–west movement. From Pennsylvania to Alabama, the region broadens and the western area contains many more ridges. Generally, the valleys are fertile, agriculture is productive, especially in the middle states, and many towns and cities line this region.

The Blue Ridge and Piedmont are known as the Older Appalachians. Similar to those of the Canadian Shield and the New England province, these older crystalline rocks (granites, gneisses, schists) constitute the core or basement of the North American Plate. The Blue Ridge, with its northern hardwood forests, extends from northern Georgia to southern Pennsylvania. The northern part is ridge-like, but broadens in the south to about 60 miles where the old, well-rounded mountains are the highest in the East (5,000 to 6,000 feet). The Piedmont is a semi-dissected plateau which extends from New Jersey to Alabama. It slopes from elevations of about 1,500 feet along the Blue Ridge to about 500 feet at its eastern terminus, the Fall Line. The latter is head of navigation on the many rivers flowing across the Piedmont and is thus the location of many cities including Philadelphia, Baltimore, Washington, and Richmond. From Virginia southward, the Piedmont was long used for growing tobacco and cotton. The bare fields, steep slopes, and intense rains led to disastrous erosion of the deeply weathered soil and entire stream valleys have been buried. Hence, because of the poor and eroded soils, most cultivated fields have reverted to pasture or forest. The original forest, mostly hardwood, is now largely pine regrowth.

The New England province is similar to the Older Appalachians. The major difference is that New England was glaciated so that features have been muted and many natural lakes were created, including Thoreau's famous Walden Pond. The stony, infertile hillsides offer so little opportunity for agriculture that Carl Sauer once remarked that had America been settled from the west, instead of the east, New England would never have been occupied. Nevertheless, these intelligent and hard working people *did* wrestle a living from the soil during the 18th and 19th centuries and the relics of that time—the graceful buildings, the literature, the music, and the forms of government—all attest to it as a period of high civilization. The erstwhile cropland has now reverted to forest, the farmers having gone west, but endless fences of stone, painfully hauled to the margins of those former fields, still remain beneath the forest canopies.

The Laurentian Upland, also known as the Canadian Shield, is covered by northern coniferous or hardwood forest, and extends from northern Minnesota, Wisconsin and Michigan across Canada north of the Great Lakes where it meets the St. Lawrence Valley. Although many consider the Shield and New England to be similar geologically, the Shield generally has less relief and even poorer and thinner soil. The Adirondack Mountains in upstate New York are sometimes considered part of New England, but in terms of rock formation belong to the Shield. Unfortunately, both the Shield and New England have a severe problem—acid rain. The acidic lithology, vegetation, and soil offer no innate protection, and, tragically, many of the beautiful lakes are biologically dead or dying.

The coastal plain extends from Cape Cod, Massachusetts to southern Texas. Here the natural vegetation is southern pine to the southeast, but oak-pine and even oak-hickory are dominant in the Gulf and midland areas. Cape Cod, Martha's Vineyard and Long Island, New York, are primarily terminal moraines resulting from continental glaciation. Southward the remainder is recently emerged oceanic sediments, often with the edges of strata facing landward, creating rows of low ridges parallel to the coast. At the inner edge of the coastal plain next to the higher interior regions is a discontinuous lowland, often formed on soft limestone. Examples are the "Black Belt" of Alabama and the Black Prairies of Texas. The former is the richest agricultural land in Alabama and has historically been a center of power and wealth in the state. From Virginia northward, the coastal plain is partially submerged, creating estuaries of river valleys. The chief example is Chesapeake Bay and its tributaries, but soil erosion from tobacco farming in the 18th and 19th centuries has partially filled many such estuaries, leaving some early ports as inland ghost towns. Southward and around the Gulf of Mexico, the coast is often buffered by barrier islands in the shallow offshore waters. The peninsula of Florida is created by an elongated arch. Underlain by limestone, the central part of Florida is marked by lakes and huge springs, whose waters may come all the way from Georgia. The Mississippi River valley is a wide alluvial plain created by the meandering river which is about twice as long as the 600 miles from southern Illinois to the Gulf of Mexico. By cutting channels through the necks of meander loops men shortened the river considerably in the last century. Indeed, the rate of shortening was so great that it prompted Mark Twain to speculate that in 742 years, the river would be only 1¾ miles long, so that New Orleans and Cairo, Illinois could join their streets!

This, then, is the grand stage upon which the drama of human settlement and resettlement has been enacted on the North American continent over the last millennium or so. Awesome and visually spectacular though the continent as shaped by nature is, its endless reshaping by human agency—often pleasing, often problematic—is no less intricate and absorbing a subject. That theme shapes the remainder of this book.

# Chapter two
# The Indian legacy in the American landscape

## KARL W. BUTZER

NORTH AMERICA WAS not a sparsely populated "virgin land" when the French and English first settled Québec, Plymouth Rock, and the James River estuary in the early 1600s. As generations of colonists slashed their way through the eastern forests and pushed back the "savages," their introspective and ethnocentric view excluded native Americans from the cherished image of a new European landscape. Frontiersmen and later frontier historians saw Indians as outsiders, people without legitimate claim to the land they lived on and, not surprisingly, Indians were excluded from the new society that emerged. The Spanish, who came earlier, had a very different vision. The De Soto expedition, pillaging through the Southeast in 1539–42, noted mortuary temples as a potential source of loot, and Coronado, who explored the Southwest in the same years, described pueblos such as Cibola. Whatever their motives, Spaniards "saw" the indigenous cultural landscape, and they ultimately sought to assimilate its people into their own world.

These very different visions of North America are also reflected in two traditions of cultural and historical geography, one emphasizing the indigenous roots, the other the European contributions. But America did not begin on the banks of the James River, rather, when Asian peoples crossed the Bering Straits about 15,000 years ago. Their descendants settled the continent and, over many millennia, adapted their hunting and foraging ways of life to different combinations of resources, reflecting North American environmental diversity. They created farming towns, following an independent trajectory of agricultural origins during what in Europe were the so-called Dark Ages. The farming frontier in most areas was pushed to its ecological limits, while on the west coast, alternative ways of life were developed that could support surprisingly large populations by fishing and intensified plant collecting. In the period when Gothic cathedrals were erected in medieval Europe, many thousands of native Americans built impressive towns in the Southwest and Mississippi Basin, sites now visited by tourists from both continents.

There is, then, a pre-European cultural landscape, one that represented the trial and error as well as the achievement of countless human generations. It is upon this imprint that the more familiar Euro-American landscape was grafted, rather than created anew.

## Adapting to new environments

The first peopling of the New World remains the subject of controversy. The earliest immigrants arrived from Asia via the Bering Straits, to confront the problems of an inhospitable environment, a cold water body, bleak mountain ranges, and oscillating glaciers. The persistently sparse archeological record of Siberia, Alaska, and northwestern Canada, however, hinders our interpretation of this movement.

By contrast, the environmental context of this early migration is reasonably well understood. During the last Ice Age, withdrawal of oceanic waters to feed the great continental glaciers left most of the Beringian continental shelf exposed as dry land, connecting Europe and Asia about 65,000 to 13,500 years before the present (BP).[1] However, the modern straits are ice covered in winter, and the actual crossing from Siberia to Alaska never posed a fundamental problem. Recent work on fossil animal remains and pollen indicates that a tundra vegetation dominated the vast, unglaciated tracts of Ice Age Alaska and the emergent continental shelf, while large concentrations of herbivores provided potential subsistence for hunting peoples with the necessary technology to cope with the cold and to take advantage of big game.[2] A final issue is physical access to the temperate and tropical parts of the New World via the eastern flanks of the western Cordillera, where the Laurentide ice sheet periodically approached coalescing tongues of mountain ice. Views about the exact route vary, but at the very least it would have been difficult to find and negotiate a passable and attractive way through the MacKenzie Valley and along the eastern front of the Rocky Mountains during the apogee of the last Ice Age, about 30,000 to 13,500 BP.[3]

It was technically possible for prehistoric hunters to pass from Asia into more productive regions of the New World for tens of millennia prior to 30,000 BP. But the coeval record of prehistoric settlement in eastern and northern Asia is poor, and there still is no convincing record of such antiquity in Canada or the United States. The earliest documented site in Alaska is from about 14,000 BP, and in the United States the oldest is Meadowcroft Rockshelter near Pittsburgh, of about the same age.[4] Findings at these sites include small, narrow stone "blades," an early form of hunting technology similar to that used in East Asia since about 20,000 BP. Dating from shortly after 12,000 BP, there is a veritable explosion of archeological sites in the continental United States (Fig. 2.1) and to a lesser degree in Alaska and South America. This dramatic influx of Paleoindians represents a *28* highly successful human adaptation to big-game hunting.[5] The Paleoindian

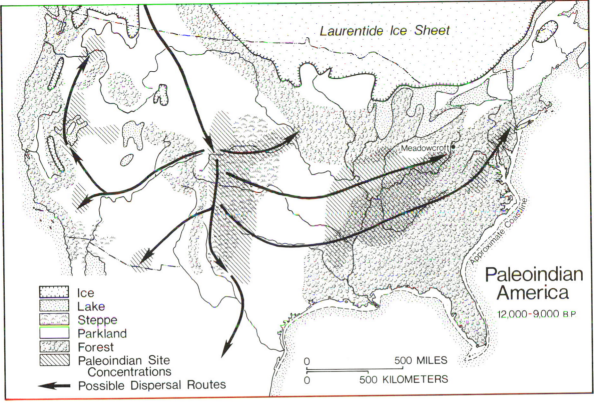

**Figure 2.1**

The Paleoindian entry into North America after about 12,000 BP. Ice margins and proglacial or pluvial lakes represent their maximum extent about 12,000–11,000 BP.

hallmark is a large, "fluted" or pressure-flaked stone projectile point, hafted to the end of a thrusting spear. This innovation is first documented in archeological writings on Japan and northeastern Siberia as dating from a little before 14,000 BP. Within 2,500 years, the Paleoindian people had settled much of the United States, and not long thereafter they appeared at the other end of South America, near Tierra del Fuego.

The Paleoindians evidently were highly mobile, efficient, and adaptable. But within the United States their site concentrations suggest a preference for relatively open environments with a high animal population: the pine-grass parklands of the High Plains and incipient Prairie Peninsula, the pine-sagebrush parkland of the western Great Basin, and the then assembling deciduous woodlands of the east-central and mid-Atlantic United States (Fig. 2.1).[6] The classic Paleoindian sites on the High Plains represent the ephemeral encampments of bison hunters. Although there also are a few associations with bones of now-extinct mammoth, mastodon, and camel, the case for a human rôle in the late glacial extinction of a large array of large mammals remains equivocal.[7] In the eastern woodlands archeological bone is poorly preserved, but white-tailed deer may have been the major game species. As the Paleoindians fanned out and penetrated further north and east, towards the margins of the retreating ice sheet, they hunted caribou.

29

Most Paleoindian sites are small, with comparatively few artifacts, even where large numbers of animals had been killed, but the fine projectile points were carefully husbanded in the course of a mobile, seasonal schedule. A millennium or two after Paleoindian dispersal into most American environments, changes in shape and size of projectile points become apparent in different areas, reflecting an adaptation to specific prey as well as the emergence of regional stylistic differences.

This transition is first apparent in the Mountain West, where once-deep lakes disappeared or were reduced to their modern shorelines no later than 10,000 BP.[8] As aridity became the rule, big-game hunting gave way to a less spectacular but more frugal foraging for nuts, seeds, berries, starchy roots, small mammals, and invertebrates. A similar, semi-nomadic way of life persisted in the marginal subdeserts of Nevada, Utah and the Snake River plains into historical times. This is but one example of the many Archaic adaptations that replaced Paleoindian traditions about 10,000 to 8000 BP. In the forest–prairie transition zone emerging on the eastern margin of the Great Plains and the Prairie Peninsula, a similar change was completed by 9000 BP and marked by a shift to hunting for deer and smaller forest game with increasing consumption of wild plant foods. Only on the High Plains did the big-game tradition persist until 8000 BP, but settlement shifted to the moister parts, where hunting remained a mainstay, despite greater attention to wild plants.[9] In the more bountiful Mississippi and Ohio Valleys, emphasis was increasingly directed to intensive gathering of wild plants and exploiting of aquatic resources such as fish, shellfish, and water fowl. Walnuts, pecan, hickory nuts, and acorns were systematically collected and seeds gleaned from wild grasses, complementing the food needs of people living in larger encampments along the river valleys.

After 5000 BP, finding food in the Late Archaic period focused more specifically on exploiting a limited range of resources, a trend apparent in different environments of North America. In the Pacific Northwest, finds of barbed antler harpoons point to the increasingly effective use of marine and river derived food such as salmon, while the existence of larger and more numerous documented sites may imply seasonal settlement. In the Mississippi, Ohio, and Tennessee drainage, manipulation of weedy seeds gradually led to domestication of marsh elder (sumpweed, *Iva*) and maygrass (*Phelaris*) by 4000 BP.[10] The native squash (*Cucurbita*) was domesticated and generally available about 3000 to 2000 BP, while the bottle gourd (*Lagenaria*), a tropical cultigen of Mexican origin, was introduced before 4300 BP and was widely cultivated by 2500 BP. In the Southwest, domesticated maize (*Zea*) of Mesoamerican origin indicates the presence of supplementary agriculture about 3000 to 2500 BP, but sites are limited to some caves near the Mexican border.

All in all, there are parallels between American Archaic and European Mesolithic developments. They were periods of environment-specific specialization and diversification, in which increased labor was devoted to raising the calorific or protein yield of food.

The potential rôle of environmental change at the end of the Ice Age and during post-glacial times has not been widely appreciated. The shift from a glacial to a non glacial environment on the Great Plains greatly reduced the complexity of the open vegetation, in favor of a more monotonous grassland with fewer plant species and specialized environments, while the faunas indicate that post-glacial climate was, contrary to expectations, more continental, despite higher temperatures.[11] Accelerated eolian sedimentation has been verified on the High Plains about 8000 to 4500 BP, contributing perhaps to the demise of the Paleoindian way of life and probably explaining the limited archeological record for the Early and Middle Archaic in this area.[12] In the Southwest and Great Basin, the disappearance of the great pluvial lakes coincided with a drastic change in potential resources. Although some modest playa lakes and many marshy floodplains persisted, with the exception of an arid period from 6500 to 2500 BP, which eased after 5500 BP,[13] the separation of plant and animal resources possibly contributed to the small-scale and peripatetic settlement patterns of Archaic peoples in the area. Demographic growth was very slow until the appearance of irrigation at a much later date.

In the Mississippi Basin, the Early and Middle Archaic period coincided with a notably drier climate. After 10,000 BP, episodic runoff led to gullying of the watersheds, with alluvial fans growing along the floodplain margins. As aridity increased, upland ground cover was reduced, slope soils eroded, and sheets of colluvium built up along the edges of valley floors, with two peaks of sedimentation about 8500 and 5200 BP. Ground cover only improved, with stable soil development and a switch from a braided to a meandering floodplain, after 4800 BP.[14] This long-term but relative impairment of upland resources may have encouraged the population to concentrate more on obtaining food in the form of lake and riverbank plants and wildlife that characterized Archaic developments here. In the more humid Northeast, late glacial woodlands had been relatively open, typically with 15 to 30 percent of the pollen belonging to nonarboreal species. Eventually dense forests, with a lower animal population, were established and, as in the European Mesolithic record, evidence for settlement is very thin, except along the coasts.

It is therefore plausible that the increased regional differentiation of environments and human ways of life in North America from 8000 to 3000 BP was interrelated.

## Towards an agricultural landscape in the East

About 3000 to 1500 BP, economic trends that emerged during the Late Archaic period crystallized into more definite patterns. Mesoamerican cultivated crops (cultigens), pottery technology, and cultural ideas became important in the Southwest and the Mississippi Basin. The bow and arrow, a major improvement in hunting technology and warfare, were introduced from the North. Trade in food, raw materials such as copper and marine shells, and ornaments accelerated and affected economic life in the back country of the coasts and river valleys. New forms of social organization and ideology appeared and were reflected in large ritual centers in the Mississippi Basin and a general increase almost everywhere in the clarity of the picture archeologists were able to build up.

In the Mississippi, Ohio, and Tennessee Basins the period from 1000 BC to AD 900 represents the Woodland culture complex, a disparate group of proto-agricultural tribes that was interconnected by an active, long-distance trade network. Intensive gathering of wild plant and aquatic foods continued, but the array of local cultigens was increased by the addition of sunflower (an oil plant, *Helianthus*) and goosefoot (a starchy seed, *Chenopodium*), while eight-rowed "flint" and twelve-rowed "dent" maize were introduced from the Southwest and Mexico respectively.[15] Maize of both types has been verified in Tennessee about 350 BC, in the Ohio drainage after 300 BC, and in the Illinois valley by AD 650.[16] Tobacco was also introduced from Mesoamerica about AD 200, while pottery traditions of similar origin were established in the Ohio and Tennessee basins by 900 BC, spreading to the northern High Plains by AD 500.[17]

In effect, the Woodland phenomenon represents a 2000-year period of diffusion, innovation, and development: regions where humans could live expanded and productivity increased; populations grew significantly and settlements became semi-permanent. The rôle of domesticated foods also increased progressively. The stable carbon isotopes found in human bone remains indicate that maize played a small but expanding dietary rôle after AD 400, which is even true for cemetery records of Ontario and the East.[18] By this time one can speak of "supplementary" agriculture within an intensified gathering economy. But even prior to the dissemination of maize, sizeable towns with great burial mounds sprang up (Fig. 2.2). The largest of these is Poverty Point, Louisiana, a complex of artificial earth mounds and geometrical earthworks that contain nearly 1 million cubic yards of material, begun about 1200 BC. A cluster of such sites in the middle Ohio valley around Adena and Hopewell includes towns with up to 38 burial and effigy mounds about 100 acres in size, that date from between 500 BC and AD 400.[19] Trade goods are prominent in such centers, indicating a far-flung exchange system that actively linked a multitude of small villages (50–100 inhabitants) and raw material sources across the Midwest, while maintaining indirect contacts with towns in the Mississippi valley and the Southeast. Presumably trade also assured complementary food supplies, at least during years with average crop yields.

Although overall population density was low, perhaps as low as one person per square mile, the persistence of some towns with several thousand inhabitants over four and five centuries—without a true agricultural base—has no parallels in Old World prehistory. The level of political organization in the Adena–Hopewell town clusters is a matter of debate, but

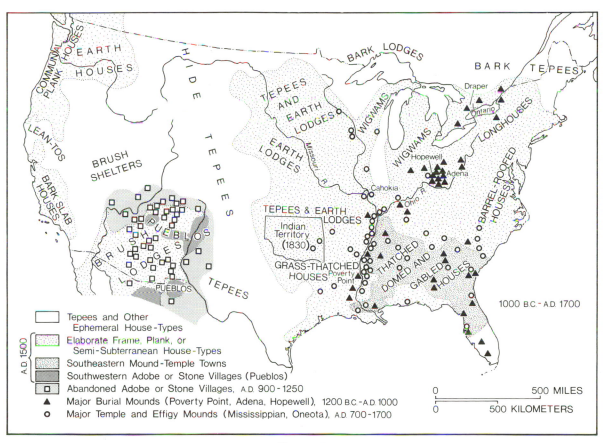

**Figure 2.2**
Indian settlement in late prehistoric and European contact times.

their resource base may have been vulnerable to environmental perturbations. Drier episodes with gullying and fan alluviation, dated roughly from 100 BC to AD 50 and AD 750 to 900,[20] coincided with the shift from the Adena to the Hopewell archeological phase, and again with the Woodland–Mississippian transition. Severe food shortages may therefore have triggered or exacerbated sociopolitical crises and ultimately stimulated incremental shifts towards agriculture.

The Mississippian phenomenon refers to the agricultural high point of native American settlement in the Mississippi and Ohio basins. Geographically, at any one time this Mississippian phase represents a dozen or so settlement clusters along different floodplain segments (Fig. 2.2). Many such clusters were short-lived, perhaps enduring a mere 75 years, while others spanned most of the 600 or so years represented by the Mississippian period (about AD 900–1500). The designation again encompassed different tribes, with varying sociopolitical complexity, but each geographical and temporal component was concentrated around one or more ceremonial centers, with conspicuous "temple mounds," that also served economic and political

33 functions. The hierarchical nature of settlement size, function, and

arrangement seems to have been paralleled by some degree of social hierarchy ("chiefdoms"). The unifying elements of the different regional components, spread from the Gulf coast to the Great Lakes watersheds, appear to have included riverine trade networks, a common system of agriculture, and a broadly shared body of ideas and beliefs.

The Mississippian phase developed from indigenous, Woodland roots, with some infusion of cultural and ideological elements, from the Gulf coast and from Mesoamerica, in part via the Southwest. The configurations emerging through archeological research took form over some two centuries, attained their maximum visibility between AD 1100 and 1300, and subsequently show evidence of decline and regional abandonment. The agricultural base was ostensibly centered on maize, but a large range of plant foods was actually exploited. Beans began to be cultivated, providing a balance of amino acids, together with squash, gourd and sunflowers. "Flint" maize was best adapted to shorter growing seasons in the northern part of the Mississippian area, but both varieties were widely grown and commonly harvested when still green. In the warmer areas, a second crop of late maize was planted lower on the floodplain, and often allowed to mature fully, after which it was parched, stored, and used for making hominy during the winter and spring. Possibly maize was intercropped with beans, but this is not supported by later ethnohistorical sources.

Yet carbon and nitrogen isotopes from Mississippian human bone indicate that beans were less important than might be assumed, and that animal protein provided about half the dietary intake.[21] This was not true, however, in dense agricultural settlement clusters, where the cemetery record testifies to a poorly balanced diet.[22] Fish and perhaps shellfish provided additional food sources, and the bow and arrow allowed more effective hunting of migratory waterfowl as well as deer, wild turkey and raccoon.[23] Thus the floodplains and their margins provided complementary environments in an annual cycle of exploitation at different seasons.[24] Finally there were supplementary, wild plant foods such as nuts, fruit, berries, and seeds. The Mississippian agricultural system was therefore highly diversified, rather than specialized, but invariably dependent on proximity to floodplains for both their fertile alluvial soils and natural pulses of energy. Nothing is known about the scheduling of fallow periods, and manure was not used, but the simple hoe and digging stick technology would have been unable to provide sustained yields on sandier soil without long fallow intervals. Overall, this method of agriculture was extensive, rather than intensive. Allowing for the absence of domesticated animals, the closest European analogy was with simple Neolithic farming.

Excavated site residues suggest several categories of settlement: (a) short-term, special-purpose sites used in hunting, plant collecting, or processing; (b) homesteads of one or several families; (c) hamlets of perhaps 10 or 20 houses; (d) villages, with an area of ½–3 acres and from 30 to over 300 houses, enclosed by a palisade or earthworks; and (e) ceremonial towns, ranging from 12 to over 200 acres in size and including anything from 200 to

1,000 houses.[25] Houses enclosed space of 30 to 60 square yards and were roughly rectangular, with numerous post impressions in the soil indicating permanence but frequent rebuilding with perishable materials, in pole and thatch style; there was a central hearth, with storage pits inside or outside. They are thought to have been inhabited by extended nuclear families of seven or eight people. Such structures were commonly arranged in rough rows, at a density of 12 to 28 per acre. A typical hamlet had about 100 people, a village between 700 and 1,300 inhabitants, and a ceremonial town 2,500 or more.

The largest settlement of the time and region was Cahokia, located on the former levee of a cut-off Mississippi River meander, near East St. Louis (Fig. 2.3). The intersecting meanders were already partially filled in, as indicated by several mounds built down within them; but the sloughs and seasonal marshes provided access to fish and fowl, while the connected waterways facilitated navigation and contact with the outside. The site was occupied by a large settlement from at least AD 1100 to 1350, but enjoyed its heyday during the 13th century.[26] Over 100 mounds have been identified in the area illustrated by Figure 2.3, with some 40 conspicuous enough to be visible within the site on the contours of the 1 : 24,000 topographic maps. Most served as platforms for public buildings or the residence of prominent people, although at other sites mounds were often still used for mortuary rites or burials. The Cahokia mounds were primarily oriented along the crest

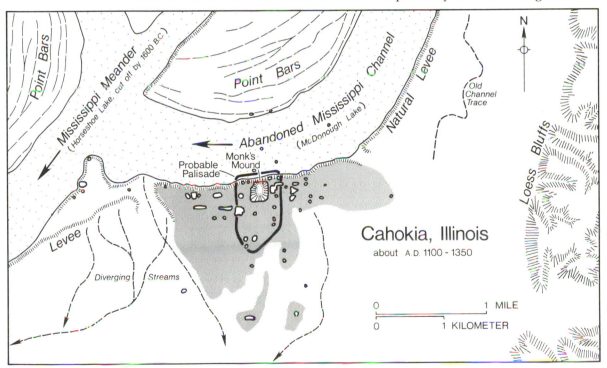

**Figure 2.3**
The large population center of Cahokia, Illinois, had 30,000 inhabitants in the 13th century. Ceremonial mounds visible in the 5-foot contours of the 1 : 24,000 topographic map are shown by strong outlines of various shapes.

of the levee, centered on the four-tiered Monk's Mound (13.5 acres, with an intact relief of 112 feet); further lines of mounds were arranged in perpendicular fashion, probably with large open "plazas" adjacent. A central area of 200 acres was once enclosed by a log palisade, with watchtowers and gates set at regular intervals. Rebuilt four times, this palisade may have served to enclose a defended refuge as well as a high-status area.

Residential land use in Cahokia was concentrated in a roughly 2,000-acre area, with several adjacent satellite clusters of houses, and an estimated total population of 30,000 people about AD 1250.[27] Goods found within such residences indicate strong differentiation according to wealth, as well as between craftsmen and farmers. Several other large ceremonial towns of 120 to 300 acres surrounded Cahokia, at least during its early stages, as did dozens of villages, suggesting some form of central place hierarchy. Cahokia was a major center, the largest settlement in the United States until it was surpassed by Philadelphia in AD 1800, and it remains prominent in the landscape today.

The demise of the Mississippian settlement clusters is poorly understood; however, the cemetery skeletal record of the 13th century indicates poor nutrition, widespread infectious disease, and high numbers of births per woman.[28] Since many potentially productive areas remained unsettled, this implicit subsistence crisis was apparently compounded by social constraints on dispersal and by unequal access to resources. In any event, large areas were quasi-abandoned and in 1673 Marquette and Joliet found the mound cities deserted and saw remarkably little evidence of settlement along the lower Illinois and middle Mississippi Rivers. However, a modified version of the "mound temple" towns and their sociopolitical system was still encountered by De Soto in the southeastern United States, and by the French north of Natchez in the period 1673 to 1682.[29]

The Mississippian economic network stimulated agricultural development and village agglomerations well beyond the direct influence of this cultural sphere, in the Northeast and on the Great Plains. In upstate New York, the Iroquois, a peripheral offshoot of the Woodland tradition, shifted from small, oval houses to great longhouses during the 13th century, indicating a change from nuclear to extended residences, with up to two dozen units; from then until about AD 1500 they congregated into increasingly large villages (Fig. 2.4), supported by relatively intensive agriculture and by hunting, fishing, and plant gathering within a large territorial radius.[30]

To the west, Woodland groups first penetrated river valleys of the eastern Plains about 2000 BP, building countless small river-bluff mounds. After AD 700 semi-agricultural villages began to appear along the central Plains rivers where maize, squash, and sunflower were cultivated on the major floodplains, complemented by bison hunting.[31] These villages frequently shifted their location, and consisted of some 20 to 30 multifamily lodges of rectangular, semi-subterranean type. These Plains Village Indians competed with the established, mobile bison hunters and berry foragers of the region,

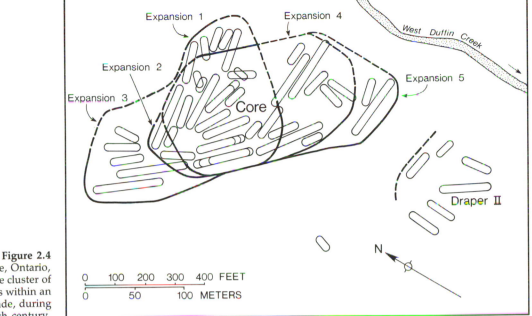

**Figure 2.4**
The Draper site, Ontario, represents a dense cluster of Huron longhouses within an expanding stockade, during the 16th century.

but they began to abandon some valleys by AD 1300, partly in response to recurrent droughts and erratic floods. This withdrawal, recalling that in the Ohio-Mississippi drainage, continued over several centuries and was accompanied by social changes, reflected in a shift to circular or oval lodges, larger villages with at least 30–100 houses, and stout palisades. Oñate visited Wichita Indians at Quivira on the middle Arkansas in 1601, estimating the number of houses in this large but otherwise unremarkable town to be about 1,200. Further retraction of these communities on the ecological limits of extensive farming ensued when both they and the neighboring Plains hunters adapted to horseback riding during the early 18th century. The Mandan, Arikara, and Pawnee peoples represented enclaves of this tradition a century later.

## Pueblo and irrigation agriculture in the Southwest

The agricultural transition in the Southwest was also gradational. Eight-row maize, squash, bottle gourd, and beans were all introduced between 3000 and 2000 BP, the timespan of the San Pedro stage, for which available sites are limited to rockshelters in the mountains of southern New Mexico and Arizona.[32] Plant gathering and hunting were, however, the staple food practices. Proto-agricultural settlements soon began to spread to the Mogollon Rim and onto the Colorado Plateau (about 200 BC) with hamlets or small villages and increasing use of semi-subterranean houses, and the gradual appearance of two different pottery traditions (Mogollon and Pueblo

**Figure 2.5**
The masonry structures of the Pueblo Bonito ceremonial and population center, Chaco Canyon, New Mexico, illustrate the durability of 11th- and 12th-century settlements. The arroyo in the background was incised after AD 1100 but before abandonment, probably impeding floodplain cultivation.

or Anasazi). Simple villages with a third pottery tradition appeared in the arid Gila and Salt River lowlands after AD 1 where, by AD 500, there was a progressive introduction of several new beans, Mesoamerican cotton (and loom weaving), and grain amaranths, their cultivation made possible by irrigation.[33] This Hohokam tradition supported larger agricultural settlements around AD 550 to 700, and new varieties of drought-resistant maize were developed to increase the dependability of the food supply.

Eventually two distinctive settlement styles, linked to different ecologies, emerged after AD 950. In the high country, increasingly large settlements were constructed of multiroom, multistory, and flat-roofed, dry-masonry houses, arranged around large, circular, masonry-lined, ceremonial pit-houses, known as "kivas."[34] These pueblos have a strikingly urban appearance (Figs. 2.5 & 6), whether they are situated in open valleys, at canyon heads, or in immense rockshelters in or below the canyon walls. Supported by cultivation of maize, wild foods such as pinyon nuts and juniper berries, as well as jackrabbits and domesticated turkey, such towns sometimes housed several thousand people. Cultivation depended on

38

rainfall and the diversion and control of sporadic flood waters, with successive checkdams slowing the runoff of small upland streams.[35] It also relied on rock lines along the lower borders of cultivated fields to prevent soil erosion. The best known emergent towns with large apartment complexes date after the period AD 1150 to 1175, when defensive situations were generally selected and satellite hamlets increasingly abandoned. At some point between AD 1290 and 1450 these settlements were either totally abandoned, or abruptly reduced to very modest proportions.

In the lowlands, the Hohokam of the Gila-Salt drainage developed a complex irrigation network around modern Phoenix that is the largest (over 250 square miles) and most elaborate of the New World (Fig. 2.7). Some of the canals were 15 to 18 miles and more in length by the time that this system achieved its maximum development (around AD 1400), and flows of up to 237 cubic feet per second have been estimated for trunk channels.[36] Feeders appear to have taken off directly at the Salt River banks, presumably when rainfall was more regular and the present erratic flooding was not a factor, and without the use of the mortared, masonry diversion dams characteristic of Spanish irrigation. Hohokam canals were not "lined," although centuries of flowing water have impregnated many with hard lime, and sluice gates were simple arrangements and involved backfilling and removal of earth, unlike the mortared counterparts in Spain, with wood or iron traps.[37] The prehistoric Salt River system remained sufficiently

**Figure 2.6**
Masonry construction and pine crossbeams, Pueblo del Arroyo, Chaco Canyon, New Mexico.

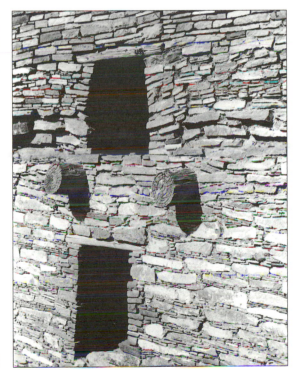

visible and logical in its arrangement that in 1878 Mormon settlers hired Pima Indians to reconstitute the 300 miles of major Hohokam canals. Interspersed within this network are at least 80 Hohokam settlement sites that have been classified into several size categories, some of which were larger than 250 acres and many of which remained occupied over a span of 500–800 years.[38] The settlement surfaces of the Salt River south bank, roughly half of the total, add up to nearly 5,000 acres,[39] suggesting a maximum possible population of 75,000 to 100,000. By any reckoning, this was one of the largest ever traditional irrigation systems in human history.

Hohokam agriculture involved a great deal of field preparation that has left visible small landforms.[40] Rocks from the stony alluvial soils were systematically piled up in small mounds or around field margins, sometimes functioning as true retaining terraces. Rocks were also removed from grids of small depressed squares known as "waffle gardens," watered by hand in the period of first European contact. Irrigation was initially practiced with partly controlled floodwaters on the floodplain, and elaborated later with water dispensed from higher-lying canals through parallel sets of tightly spaced ditches. Away from the main rivers, water was diverted out of streams to run down canals high on the valley margins, irrigating local areas of better soil. Further back into the deep valleys of the Salt drainage, rainfed agriculture was increasingly practiced on high alluvial terraces or on suitable mountain slopes, where scattered plots were somewhat protected by lines of rocks that retained water and soil (Fig. 2.8).[41] This extension of cultivation to marginal lands accompanied population expansion between AD 1150 and

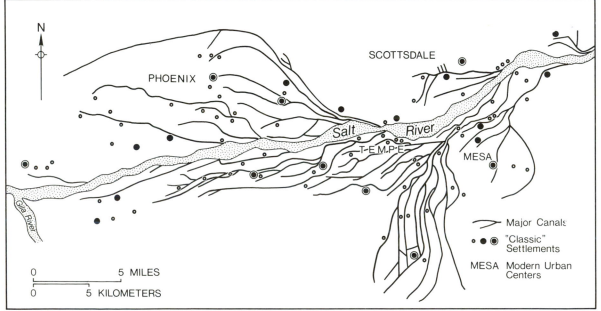

**Figure 2.7**
The irrigation and settlement network along the lower Salt River, Arizona, in Classic Hohokam times (AD 1150–1400), was the largest in the prehistoric New World.

1250, after which resources were exploited to capacity, given the available Hohokam technology. Some peripheral areas began to be abandoned by AD 1250, and about AD 1400 the Tonto system collapsed, followed by the Salt River core network some 50 years later.

House and town construction by the Hohokam was less permanent than in the masonry pueblos of the plateau. Puddled adobe was the basic building material, poured in regular courses of calcic mud that hardened to the consistency of a low grade concrete to allow the raising of multistoried, rectangular structures. Casa Grande, near the Gila River, had four floors and walls three feet thick (Fig. 2.9), and has remained a prominent, if derelict landmark since it was described in that state by Kino in 1694. Other ruins

**Figure 2.8**
A model that illustrates the diversity of agriculture and settlement strategies of Hohokam in the Tonto Basin, Arizona, about AD 1250.

Idealized Tonto Basin Settlement Pattern (Early Classic Period)

⊞ Major Settlement    / / / / / / Runoff Agricultural Fields

⊞ Village    Floodplain Agricultural Fields

Ꮾ Hamlet    Irrigated Agricultural Fields

▫ Homestead

have generally fared less well, "melted down" slowly by rain or quarried as
a source of soil in the late 19th century. But the mass of adobe accumulated
in Hohokam villages over centuries of occupation has created conspicuous
mounds similar to Near Eastern tells. Roofs were flat and supported by large
wooden beams (that allow tree-ring dating), covered by a bed of stout reeds
and then several layers of adobe. Windows were small and rare. The so-
called Spanish domestic adobe architecture in the Southwest and northern
Mexico is in fact indigenous, with the exception that Spaniards substituted
preformed, sun-dried adobe bricks for puddled adobe and then added drain
spouts from the roof. Nowhere in Spain is adobe plastered on masonry
walls, as is the custom in many surviving southwestern pueblos (Fig. 2.10),
although Spanish walls may be surfaced with a thin coat of cement before
whitewashing.

The cycle of demographic growth, settlement groupings, and eventual
abandonment evident in the late prehistoric site clusters of the Southwest
paralleled that of counterparts in the Mississippi-Ohio Basin. It suggests a
latent instability in such settlement systems that needs further exploration.

Significantly, the southwestern site clusters that appeared about AD 950 to
1050 showed a parallel but not strictly synchronous development. Such
clustering peaked as early as AD 1075 and as late as 1325, and partial or total
abandonment took place in some areas during the late 1200s, in others
during the mid-1400s. Maximum population tended to accompany or
precede congregation in large settlements, suggesting social changes,
possibly a switch from an inter-community exchange system to one of
centralized redistribution. Abandonment sometimes followed droughts
evidenced in long tree rings, or local floodplain downcutting (with lower
water tables and loss of irrigation "head"), but more commonly coincided
with periods of wildly erratic rainfall.[42] It was also sometimes preceded by

**Figure 2.9**
The Casa Grande, near the
Gila River of Arizona, was
built about AD 1300 and
abandoned during the 15th
century. Measuring 41 by 62
feet, this adobe structure was
33 feet high and had some 60
rooms. The walls taper
upwards from a base of 53
inches to 21 inches, and were
constructed with regular 25-
inch courses of puddled
adobe, poured between some
sort of formwork. The lower
wall surfaces were restored in
1891, the shelter built in 1932.

**Figure 2.10**
The multistoried, flat-roofed and adobe-faced masonry houses of Taos, New Mexico, are representative of surviving pueblos in the Southwest.

an abortive attempt to expand cultivation to marginal sites.

In one case where the population trends and available resources for one small site cluster have been reconstructed, the combination of available arable soils, water supply, and wild plant and animal foods would not have sufficed to feed the expanding population during times of declining rainfall reliability.[43] Abandonment ensued. To this one must add the inevitable depletion of indifferent, unimproved soils after decades of planting with a demanding crop such as maize. Alternate cropping appears to have been unknown and beans are, here too, surprisingly rare among botanical remains. Even if short fallow periods had been in operation, maize yields could not be maintained over time. The basic problem in the Southwest, therefore, seems to have been that productivity could not be sustained in the face of demographic growth, given a relatively static technology. Thus, the social systems appear to have been too rigid to adjust, and wholesale abandonment ensued.

The displaced populations subsequently relocated to existing pueblo centers, where a dramatic upsurge of population occurred between 1250 and 1400. At Zuñi, a cluster of six or seven archeologically documented villages was described as the "seven cities of Cibola" at the time of Coronado (1540), and in 1582 the Spanish estimated 130,000 inhabitants in 61 pueblos for the Southwest.[44] Perhaps the Old World diseases introduced by the Spaniards headed off further crises of sustainability and Malthusian "overshoot."

While agricultural economies with large, permanent settlements evolved in the East and Southwest, the productive environments of the west coast became the scene of highly successful foraging societies. In California, a vast range of wild plant foods was utilized, with much emphasis on acorns that were ground into bread meal, while tobacco was the sole cultivated crop. Freshwater and marine fish were equally important, and exchange networks bound together people of the coast and the interior.[45] Prior to European contact, a population of over 300,000 included at least a dozen centers with more than 1,200 people.

In the Pacific Northwest, by 1500 BP equally large communities lived in fortified, seashore villages of communal plank houses that were supported by salmon, halibut, and cod fishing from boats, with harpoons and nets. Small, curly-haired dogs and mountain sheep provided a form of wool for blanket weaving, while some groups planted and tended gardens of clover roots and other plants.[46] Further inland, smaller villages consisted of large, circular pithouses sunk into the ground, the roofs formed by heavy, sloping rafters covered with bark and earth. Wild, starchy roots and bulbs were roasted in earthen ovens; spawning salmon were taken in the rivers and lakes, along with beaver and mussels, while moose, deer, bear, and mountain sheep were sought farther afield on seasonal hunting forays. Because they were built of perishable materials, there is little visible evidence of the Northwest coast settlements today, other than an occasional totem pole. But early travelers left vivid accounts of their strange charm, teeming populations, and industrious bustle.

## The European intrusion

When the first European explorers and settlers reached and penetrated North America they encountered agricultural peoples (Figs. 2.2 & 11). On the mid-Atlantic coast between Capes Cod and Hatteras they found groups of small tribes practicing a reasonably intensive agriculture, with a short fallow system.[47] In the lower Great Lakes area they visited the large palisaded villages of the Huron and Iroquois. In the Southeast, they initially found temple towns recalling the settlement clusters of the Mississippian period. In the Plains they caught a glimpse of the big riverine villages, and in the Southwest they climbed up to the populous pueblos perched on mesa tops. These ethnohistorical observations, by 16th- and 17th-century European explorers and colonists, are lucidly synthesized by Sauer.[48] They complement the archeological record, but in isolation they are too incomplete and biased to provide an adequate view of the original American cultural landscape.

Estimating the population of pre-European America is intrinsically difficult, and necessarily based on assumptions of population density, early ethnographic estimates, and a few rough censuses in the period of initial European contact.

A major complication is that the 15th century was one of demographic decline in the Mississippi-Ohio Basin and Southwest. Many of the thriving farming villages and ceremonial or trade centers had been abandoned, and agriculture was retracting on the Plains, perhaps in response to increasingly frequent drought. Another factor is that the Spanish first introduced Old

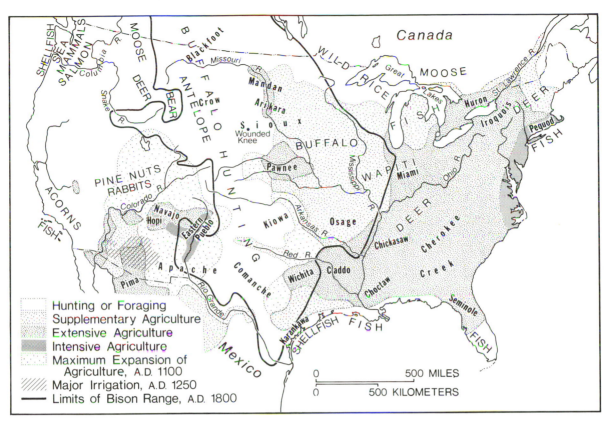

**Figure 2.11**
Patterns of Indian subsistence in Euro-American contact times, 16th to 19th centuries.

World diseases to which the native Americans had no immunity. Beginning with the early Spanish and French contacts, wave after wave of plague, smallpox, measles, scarlet fever and whooping cough swept across whole regions, killing off aboriginal populations well ahead of the explorers or soldiers.[49] After Cartier's visit to the St. Lawrence in 1535–6, Iroquois agricultural settlement disappeared, presumably as a result of disease. Before the landing of the *Mayflower*, plague introduced by French fishermen had destroyed up to 90 percent of the New England population, and during the 1630s smallpox and measles eliminated up to two-thirds of the Huron and Iroquois. Similar series of years with mass deaths affected the Southeast from the 16th to the 18th centuries, the Southwest during the 17th century, and the Plains during the 19th century.

Ubelaker suggests a pre-contact population of 1.85 million for the continental United States, a figure that successive volumes of Sturtevant's reference work would cumulatively revise upward to at least 2.5 million.[50] For AD 1500, Denevan's aboriginal number of 3.2 million is not excessive, with another 1.2 million in Canada, Alaska, Hawaii, and Greenland.[51]

The European intrusion was peaceful and violent by turns. De Soto's entry was so barbaric that the survivors were reprimanded in Spain. Already in 1609 the French were in confrontation with the Iroquois. In Connecticut in 1637, 800 Pequot Indians were burned alive after a puritan attack on their village; a Plymouth chronicler described the terrible stench as "a sweet sacrifice." And in 1680, the heavy-handed efforts of the Spanish governors and the Franciscan missionaries to abolish their native culture goaded the southwestern pueblos into bitter, protracted revolt. But until after American independence, these hostilities were overshadowed by other cultural impacts.

The native American had always been highly mobile, and tribal territories commonly were flexible as a result of tribal intermarriage and kinship ties.[52] Furthermore, complex regional trade networks were common long before the arrival of the Europeans. Marine shell for ornaments, furs, cold-beaten copper, pottery, flint and obsidian, stone pipes, tobacco, maize, and salt were all exchanged along waterways and at periodic markets within a radius of 60 miles or more. These trading patterns were intensified by European demand for furs in exchange for guns, domestic metal products, glass beads, and liquor. The Euro-American fur trade in the St. Lawrence, Great Lakes, and Hudson Bay regions consequently revolutionized the Indian economic system. By the 1640s, the French, British, Dutch, and Swedes had created a strong demand that stimulated intertribal warfare and steadily increased the radius of overintensive fur-trapping, and the drawing out of a string of strategically located European trading posts and forts along the principal waterways of the Midwest and Canada.[53]

A second factor was the erosion of Indian culture. After 1598 the Spanish introduced thousands of sheep and 1,300 horses to the Southwest, and the recently arrived Navajo Apache raided enough stock to adopt sheepherding in a significant way, with wool weaving verified among them by 1706. Spanish horses also made their way to the settled Plains tribes after the Pueblo Revolt of 1680, and by the 1720s many of the Plains hunters had become highly accomplished horsemen and deadly raiders. Equestrian hunting was spurred by the lucrative profits from trading buffalo pelts, that increased pressures on the Plains farming villages, and encouraged many Plains and Rocky Mountain tribes to turn from a settled to a nomadic lifestyle. In the Southeast, de Soto had introduced 400 Spanish pigs, most of which were promptly lost or stolen and went feral in the eastern forests.[54] In 1560 a large cattle herd was driven from Mexico to Florida, and cattle subsequently were run by the Seminole and Creek. Semi-cultivated native plums of excellent quality were tended by tribes from the High Plains to Georgia, according to the earliest Spanish reports, and several tribes soon adopted Spanish peaches as well as South American potatoes. When the British penetrated the Carolina piedmont in the early 18th century, the Cherokee were herding pigs and cattle, and growing peaches and apples;[55] by 1800 the Cherokee were shifting to plow agriculture. This abandonment of native culture by the Cherokee, and to a lesser degree, of the Creek, Seminole, Chickasaw, and Choctaw, earned them the 19th century label of the "Five Civilized Nations."

This cautiously optimistic picture of measured social accommodation through the mid-1700s was shattered by the vigorous expansion of an independent America after 1776. Hundreds of thousands of settlers poured across the Appalachian passes, placing the native Americans on the defensive. The dreary cycle of settlement or conquest, Indian cessions, government guarantees for new borders, and renewed Anglo-American advance, is summarized in Hilliard's map sequence of confiscated lands, and recounted by Utley and Washburn.[56] The remnants of the "Five Civilized Nations" were marched in chains to Oklahoma in 1831–42, despite a Supreme Court decision in favor of the Cherokee.[57] The Ohio valley was cleared out after 1811, and the upper Midwest "pacified" in 1832.

The fur trade now shifted to the Plains and Mountain West. The western woodlands were trapped barren by 1840, leaving the Plains buffalo as the last great resource.[58] When railroad construction began after the Civil War, buffalo meat was needed to supply the work crews, and robes made of buffalo hide were in insatiable demand now that transportation by railroad opened up previously inaccessible markets. Anglo-American hunters joined the Indians in slaughtering up to 1 million buffalo a year. As a result, the buffalo was extinct in the southern Plains by 1879, and the original multitude of up to 60 million head was reduced to 500 animals in the northern Plains by 1889. The Plains Indians, who had posed the major obstacle to westward settlement, lost both their prime exchange commodity and their staple food supply. As they succumbed to starvation and disease, the U.S. army destroyed encampments and winter food supplies with minimal provocation. Dwindling rapidly in numbers, the Plains tribes succumbed one by one, and their remnants were exiled to marginal reservations where they could not live by their traditional economy. In 1890 the last Sioux uprising ended when uniformed soldiers executed women and children at Wounded Knee.

The Census of 1890 enumerated only 249,300 American Indians, a bare 0.4 percent of the national population and 10 percent of the original indigenous population in 1500. The survivors were scattered on some 275 reservations, amounting to 2.5 percent of the continental United States. Through a combination of expropriation, disease, and extermination, the policy of "manifest destiny" had eliminated native Americans as a competitive minority. Except for the southwestern Pueblo Indians and Navajo, traditional subsistence and settlement patterns were defunct, and although sacred places on traditional tribal grounds may retain their significance, the built environment of the residual reservations now serves only to exhibit a legacy of impoverished Anglo-American ways of life.

## The surviving legacy

The most obvious imprint of native Americans on the landscape are the Indian place names. Of the 48 coterminous states, 25 carry Indian names, as do 13 percent of some 1300 counties, hundreds of rivers and mountains, and thousands of towns and cities. So familiar to the average Anglo-American as to be unrecognized, these toponyms serve as a constant reminder that the landscape had been humanized by the first Americans. Zelinsky in his *Cultural geography of the United States*, draws this single conclusion, downplaying other cultural impacts.[59]

There is indeed a problem of recognition and acknowledgement. From the 17th century on, the Indian has been portrayed as a brutal savage, while the litany of Euro-American provocations and atrocities was conveniently forgotten. The Indian became the victim of derogatory, racial stereotyping that remained standard fare for American movies through the 1950s. Demoralized by defeat and the collapse of their system of values, the surviving Indians lingered as government wards on desolate reservations. Romanticized alternative views saw the Indian as a noble savage, in close communion with nature; but he remained an outsider to the dominant Anglo-American culture.

The importance of the Indian legacy is, however, expressed each year in the average American home when turkey, corn, squash, pumpkin pie, and cranberries are served, and decorative gourds form the centerpiece for the Thanksgiving dinner, remembering a fleeting moment of cooperation between Puritan settlers and their American hosts. That legacy is also recalled each morning in a traditional Southern breakfast when grits are served, and in the Southwest where tortillas prevail. Indian corn became a staple of the British colonists within a generation after Plymouth Rock, and south of Philadelphia it replaced wheat in the making of bread. Eminently suited to the American growing season, maize remains one of the most productive food plants in the modern economy, and a prominent reminder of the Indian legacy in the rural landscapes of the Midwest heartland.

Not just corn, but tobacco and cotton stand today as retrospective landscape symbols of an Indianizing influence felt by early European society in the American environment. At Jamestown in 1612, cultivated American tobacco preceded commercial tobacco of West Indian origin in the development of the Virginia tobacco industry, and the original species continued to be grown and smoked by French Canadians well into the 19th century. Wild Carolina indigo dyes, long used by the Indian, were a key component of emerging plantation agriculture, and when long-fibered Mesoamerican cotton was established in 18th-century Georgia, it formed the foundation for the southern slave economy. Native plums became a standard Anglo-American orchard crop and, after phylloxera destroyed the French vineyards in the 19th century, American stalks of grapes, once semi-cultivated by the Indian, were grafted onto Old World vines; they not only saved the global wine industry but led to an American counterpart that

48

included Catawba and Concord variants. Indian medicinal plants, sassafras tea, and maple sugar remain popular in some areas.

The unprecedented success of the American frontiersmen was in part predicated on Indian customs and expertise. To clear the forest, aside from clear-cutting, trees were girdled and deadened by burning the detached bark around the base of the trunk—the Indian custom of land clearance. The stream of Anglo-American settlers advancing through the eastern forests often reutilized the open tracts or secondary growth marking old, Indian fields, both for their ease in clearing and in the knowledge that these represented the best local soils.[60] The tale of Johnny Appleseed, planting fruit trees in the vanguard of Ohio settlement, reveals the importance of abandoned Indian orchards for a balanced diet among the pioneer settlers. Early homesteaders in the Great Lakes area and northern Plains survived long, snowy winters by eating dehydrated meat ("jerky"), a mortar-crushed meat with vitamin-rich berries (pemmican), and parched corn, in Indian fashion. Their migration routes followed Indian trails, just as the French had used Huron birchbark canoes to claim the Mississippi Basin, and Euro-American fur traders had penetrated the Plains and the West.

The biological heritage of the Indian is equally real. The Indian population registered by the 1980 Census is 1.4 million, 413 percent of what it apparently was in 1950, as urbanized Indians begin to acknowledge their ancestry with pride. Only 370,000 of these lived on reservations or tribal trust lands. A similar but smaller explosion is apparent in Canada, with an increase of 170 percent between 1960 and 1980, with 375,000 now identified as Indians. In addition, the 1980 Census now includes some 5 million Americans claiming partial Indian ancestry, a figure that still includes far too few people in the Northeast.[61] The number of early settlers taking Indian wives has always been politely overlooked, but was a reality.[62] The large, French-speaking minority of the Canadian Plains, the Métis, are mixed-blood descendants of the French fur traders, and there were similar but less publicized multicultural communities in the American West.[63] Regardless of the genetic contribution to American bloodlines, these points show that Indian women played an underappreciated rôle in facilitating frontier expansion and shaping its society, well beyond the significance of Indian cultigens, technology, and landscape guides.

Physical configurations of the Indian landscape also survive directly. Apart from the abandoned or living pueblos of the Southwest, thousands of mounds in the East remain conspicuous landmarks of an earlier civilization, despite road building and mechanized plowing. The 19th-century Mississippi boatmen returned upstream to Tennessee by the Natchez Trace, previously the Chickasaw Trail, and still visible today. The Angeleno who drives over the Cajon Pass towards a Las Vegas weekend follows an Indian trail already adapted by the Spaniard. The modern irrigation system around Phoenix, Arizona, is largely a recreation of its Hohokam counterpart. The flat-roofed adobe house of the Borderlands, and its gentrified application to new architectural designs, is basically an Indian form, not a Spanish introduction

49

of a Berber house type.[64] French fur trade posts and Anglo-American forts were located at Indian communication or population nodes, and served as nuclei for civilian settlement: Kingston, Ontario; Albany, New York; Pittsburgh, Pennsylvania; Detroit, Michigan; Fort Wayne, Indiana; Peoria, Illinois; Green Bay, Wisconsin; Des Moines, Iowa; Fort Smith, Arkansas; Fort Worth, Texas; Missoula, Montana; or Walla Walla, Washington, provide some examples. Spanish presidios and missions were located next to Indian settlements or ceremonial centers in the Southwest and California, to become centers like San Antonio, Texas; Santa Fe, New Mexico; Tucson, Arizona; and in California San Diego, Los Angeles, or San Francisco.

Thousands of years of Indian settlement influenced the Anglo-American landscape in many other subtle ways. The quality of land had already been determined by generations of Indian use, a realization that may help to explain the insatiable greed of the homesteader and rancher for Indian core territory. Indian expertise in countless facets of forest and prairie living greatly facilitated British colonization and American westward expansion, preventing much costly trial and error. Determined Indian resistance by the Comanche, Sioux, Apache, and other tribes probably affected rates and patterns of settlement as much in a negative way as passive tribes or thinly settled lands did in a positive way. Although the average American might well not appreciate this legacy, cultural and historical geographers have no excuse for lacking a deeper appreciation of the American roots of the American landscape.

# Chapter three
## Spanish legacy in the Borderlands

DAVID HORNBECK

THE SPANISH LANDSCAPE of the United States is usually associated with California and the Southwest alone, yet Spain explored and colonized a much greater proportion of the United States than the small area now identified with Spanish influence suggests. A fundamental reason for the general unawareness of Spanish settlement is that the history and geography of the United States has been written from the viewpoint of English settlement on the east coast. Before English colonists settled the eastern seaboard, however, Spain had explored and occupied much of the present day southeastern and southwestern parts of the United States.

Spain's influence on the United States has both geographical and institutional foundations. Today the names of six states—Florida, Colorado, Nevada, California, New Mexico, Texas, and Arizona—have their origins in the Spanish language, as do those of scores of rivers, mountains, and towns. To this day, many Indian groups in the Southwest speak Spanish better than English. Spanish architecture appears throughout the western part of the United States. From San Francisco to St. Augustine, title to land originated from Madrid or Mexico City. Principles of mining, irrigation, water, and property rights of women stem from the Spanish regime. Yet, many believe that Spain never really occupied the land, but only explored for "gold, God, and glory," and therefore had little or no impact on the development of land and society in North America; real settlement had to await the French and English.

Admittedly Spain's occupance of North America in some areas was a tenuous, short-lived experience; however, 20 states had some contact with Spain. For almost 300 years Spain occupied the southwestern part of the United States. Between 1762 and 1800, Spain possessed the entire trans-Mississippi West, granting lands, conducting trade in furs, and building trading and military posts as far north as Minnesota. Florida was in Spanish hands from 1526 until 1821, during which time military outposts and missions were established as far north as Port Royal, South Carolina; Spain even briefly occupied the Chesapeake Bay. Today, the areas once settled by the Spanish are usually referred to as the Spanish Borderlands (a term popularized by the historian Bolton in 1921), referring to the areas' location peripheral to central Mexico.[1]

A chapter that attempts to synthesize Spanish settlement and its landscape heritage cannot hope to cover more than 300 years of exploration and settlement in detail or discuss all areas equally. However, a brief examination of specific topics and themes should illustrate the importance of Spanish settlement in North America. Much like all European occupation of the New World, Spanish settlement became complicated by political intrigue, internal bickering, war, and bureaucracy. At the outset, however, exploration and settlement were new and exciting, but foremost was the search for unknown lands, a discovery of exciting places and peoples. Spain began her search for new territories in North America from two established areas of settlement. The first push was from the Caribbean into Florida, along both the Gulf and Atlantic coasts.[2] The second area from which Spain began to explore North America was central Mexico northward into the trans-Mississippi West and along the Pacific coast (Fig. 3.1).

## Spanish exploration

The second decade of the 16th century opened the geography of Spain in North America; three decades later it closed with Spanish withdrawal from the area. During the intervening years, Spain was an active participant in exploration and colonization. In 1513, Ponce de Leon landed on the southern coast of Florida. Six years later, Alonso de Pineda explored the Gulf of Mexico, clearly illustrating that North America was a continent of its own. By 1525, Esteban Gomez had explored the eastern coastline from Florida to Labrador, passing the Connecticut, Hudson, and Delaware Rivers, and naming the region Tierra de Gomez (land of Gomez). In one of the most spectacular explorations in the history of North America, Panfilo de Narvaez set out to investigate the lands between Florida and the Rio Grande. Leaving Havana in 1527, the group finally ended its trek in 1534 at the Gulf of California. Hernando de Soto explored a vast area between 1538 and 1541, traveling through what are now the states of Florida, Georgia, South Carolina, Alabama, Mississippi, and Arkansas.

From Central Mexico, Spain began to explore the lands towards the north. In 1538, Francisco de Ulloa explored and mapped the Gulf of California. The next year, Fray Marcos de Niza trekked through the present-day Southwest, perhaps as far as to modern New Mexico. Based on Fray Marcos's report of seeing wealthy villages to the north, Francisco Vasquez de Coronado organized and led an expedition north from Mexico City to Arizona, New Mexico, Colorado, Texas, and Kansas; along the way members of the expedition explored the Colorado River and discovered the Grand Canyon. Soon after Coronado's return in 1542, Juan Cabrillo explored the Pacific coast from San Diego Bay to Oregon.

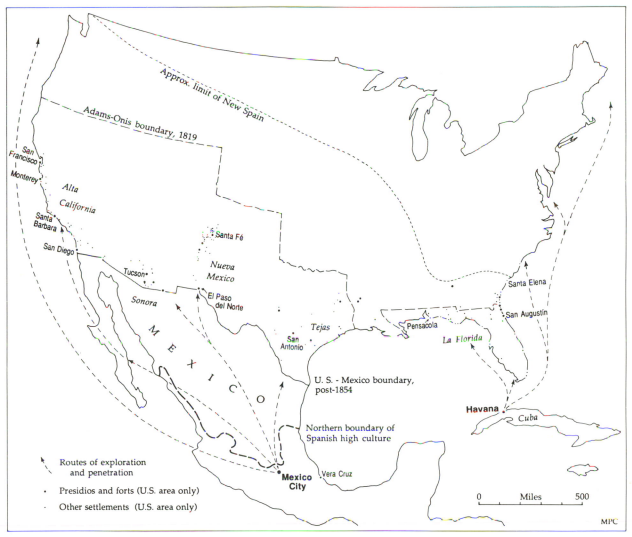

**Figure 3.1**

Spanish North America, 1600–1854. Spain considered all of North America in its possession. Dashed lines show the origin and direction of Spanish explorations of the continent.

Thus by 1550, Spain had explored and mapped a vast expanse of North America extending from Florida to the Oregon coast. During the early years of Spanish exploration, this area was perceived as a land of mystery and hope, of romantic stories and imaginative tales that somehow were believable. In Florida, explorers sought the Fountain of Youth, in South Carolina they looked for the fabulous Diamond Mountain. In Arizona and New Mexico, the Seven Cities of Cibola offered unlimited wealth for their conqueror; somewhere on the California coast could be found the Straits of Anian; and in Texas the Kingdom of Gran Quivira awaited discovery. These were extravagant tales, credible "facts" that led men to try their luck on what became known as "the northern mysteries." Bold adventurers, these explorers searched each tale to its end. Forty years of exploration revealed that there was little or no substance to the imaginative northern mysteries, but Spanish exploration gave North America its first geographical outline.

Those who sought the secrets of the northern mysteries had little to show for their efforts. Narvaez and de Soto came to watery graves exploring Florida. Coronado, searching for wealth, returned a broken man. Cabrillo was lured up the Pacific coast only to be buried on Santa Barbara Island. These men and others were the adventurers of the 16th century; although they found no wealth, their efforts were not merely idle jaunts into an unknown land, but rather the beginnings of a map of North American geography to be filled in and detailed later by the men and women of other European nations.

## Populating the land

Spain did not simply explore and then leave an area; rather, Spanish explorers established settlements in most of the areas they explored. In 1559, Spanish settlers founded Pensacola and six years later established St. Augustine (Fig. 3.2). The first of many Jesuit missions along the South Atlantic coast (from southern Florida to Chesapeake Bay) was founded in Florida in 1566. By the beginning of the 17th century, Spain had placed permanent colonies in New Mexico and had established missions in the Hopi area of Arizona.

Settlement during the 16th century was for the most part driven by economic and religious motives. Mines, stock ranches, towns, and missions were established to exploit or convert local Indian populations. But with intrusions from other European powers, Spanish settlement began to be driven by a new factor—defense. During the 17th century, defensive

**Figure 3.2**
Moated bastions guard the northern wall of the Castillo de San Marcos at St. Augustine, Florida, as seen looking east towards the Matanzas River. Although the fort and town were founded in 1565, the elaborate stone fortress dates from 1672–87.

settlements north of the Rio Grande and the Gulf of Mexico were established in response to French and British threats of incursion. Of Spain's settlements in North America, only New Mexico was not initially settled to create a buffer against encroachment, instead it was colonized to christianize the Indians. For the most part, however, new settlements throughout Spain's northern frontier during the 17th century were constructed primarily for defensive reasons. Even during the 18th century California was not occupied for economic reasons, but rather to thwart Russian expansion southward along the Pacific coast.

Spain's strategy was to protect the more heavily settled areas of the Caribbean and central Mexico from foreign intrusion by using the area north of the Gulf coast and west of the Mississippi River as a buffer zone. After the French arrived in force at the mouth of the Mississippi during the 1720s, Spain retreated and turned Texas into a buffer province. By 1750, the geopolitical maneuverings between Spain, England, and France began to have an effect on the Spanish Borderlands, causing Spain steadily to lose territory.

To carry out its settlement strategy, Spain employed three frontier institutions: the mission, the presidio and the pueblo. The missionary and the military were the primary means by which settlement was achieved, with small civil colonies established later. Short of both manpower and civilian colonists, Spain depended upon a settlement strategy that absorbed the indigenous population. To effect settlement, Spain employed a network of Catholic mission stations that were to convert the local Indians to Christianity and teach them to become loyal Spanish subjects (Fig. 3.3).[3] The type of mission most frequently used was the *reduccion* or *congregracion*. Its purpose was to attract natives who lived in small, dispersed villages, congregate them in the mission, and "reduce" them from their heathen way of life to that of Christians. After they had been successfully weaned off their native culture, the mission was to be turned over to secular clergy, with the missionaries moving on to another frontier to repeat the process. At one time Spanish missions extended from Florida and Georgia through Texas, to New Mexico and Arizona and into California. Today the remnants of these early missions serve as one of the most visible landscape elements of Spanish occupancy.

Presidios formed the defensive arm of Spanish settlement. As agents of the government, they were responsible for defending the area, subduing hostile Indians, maintaining peaceful relationships with friendly Indians, and acting as the secular authority until a civil government could be established. Presidios were scattered along a wide arc extending from Georgia and Florida on the Atlantic coast to four strung along the California coast (Fig. 3.4 & 5).

Pueblos—civil communities—were usually a later addition to the Spanish colonization scheme, after missionary efforts were completed. They were established to supplement the soldiers with agricultural products, engage in trade when feasible, set examples of Spanish life for the Indians to follow,

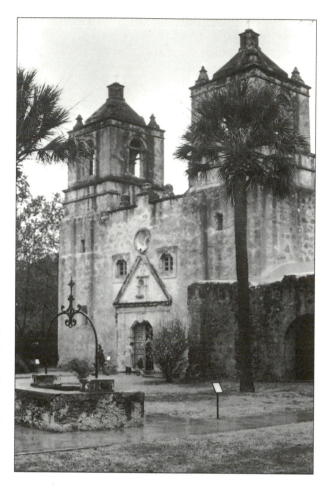

**Figure 3.3**
Mission Concepción, just
southeast of San Antonio,
Texas, built between 1731
and 1755, is the oldest
unrestored church still used
for religious services in the
United States. Twin towers
and an elaborately carved
entrance typify Spanish
mission architecture in the
Borderlands.

**Figure 3.4**
Presidio at Santa Barbara,
California, founded 1781, as
seen in a 19th century
lithograph. Mission Santa
Barbara can be seen at some
distance from the military
town.

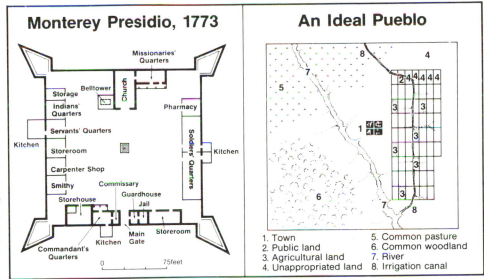

**Monterey Presidio, 1773**

Missionaries' Quarters

Belltower
Storage
Church
Indians' Quarters
Pharmacy
Servants' Quarters
Kitchen
Soldiers' Quarters
Storeroom
Kitchen
Carpenter Shop
Smithy
Commissary
Storehouse
Guardhouse
Jail
Commandant's Quarters
Kitchen
Main Gate
Storeroom

0                75feet

**An Ideal Pueblo**

8        4
7
5        2 4 4 4 4 4
3        3
1        3
3        3
6        3
7        8

1. Town
2. Public land
3. Agricultural land
4. Unappropriated land
5. Common pasture
6. Common woodland
7. River
8. Irrigation canal

**Figure 3.5**
The building plan for the presidio of Monterey, founded in 1770, shows the internal arrangement of Spain's military fortresses in North America. The idealized layout of a pueblo is drawn from the evidence of the pueblo of Los Angeles, founded in 1782.

and, in times of emergency, to act as a reserve militia for the military (Fig. 3.5).

The ultimate goal of the presidio-mission-pueblo settlement strategy was to ensure Spain's claim to a vast area extending from Florida to California. The choice of settlement sites, therefore, was an important consideration and in large measure was predetermined by the specific rôle each institution played out on the frontier. As military outposts, the presidios were located in areas that would provide maximum advantage against foreign intrusions and hostile Indian attacks. In contrast, pueblos were founded with an eye toward permanent settlement and agricultural development. Mission sites were no less planned than the presidio and pueblo but were more flexible in their location. Missions were found primarily in areas that contained large numbers of Indians and were allowed to take up and use as much land as was necessary to care properly for Indian neophytes, or converts. So the missions were able to take advantage of good sites and Indian labor to expand into large, well-developed settlements (Fig. 3.6).

## Shaping the borders

Spanish settlement was mainly for defensive purposes and thus institutionally organized.[4] Individualism was not encouraged in Spain's settlements as it was on the American frontier. Spanish settlers, soldiers, and missionaries were part of a royal play and acted rôles according to the parts sent them from Madrid. With Spain more interested in protecting her rich settlements to the south, she steadily lost much of the northern lands which she had claimed and colonized during the 16th and 17th centuries.[5] Political

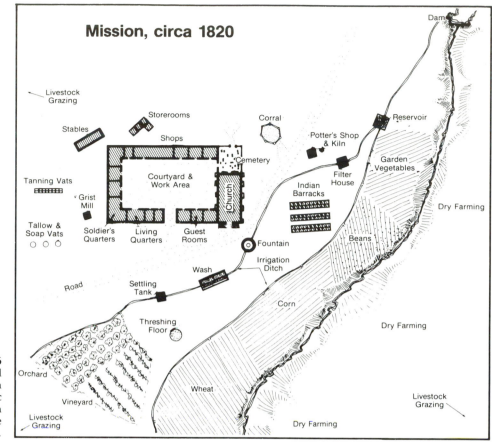

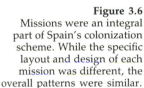

**Figure 3.6**
Missions were an integral
part of Spain's colonization
scheme. While the specific
layout and design of each
mission was different, the
overall patterns were similar.

maneuvering and war began to reshape Spain's North American borders.
Importantly, the Seven Years' War altered North America's political
boundaries.[6] French rule was ended and England pushed rapidly towards
the Gulf of Mexico and the Mississippi River. Russia, a new player in North
America, began to push southward down the Pacific coast. In response to
both Russian and English efforts to expand their settled areas, Spain
occupied California and strengthened her position in Arizona, New Mexico,
and Texas. With the fledgling United States posing yet another force to be
reckoned with, Spain's borders began to bend even more. France sold
Louisiana to the United States, creating problems along the Mississippi. The
United States took advantage of Spain's problems with her colonies to
acquire the Gulf region, including Florida. In the 1819 Adams-Onis Treaty,
which established the boundaries between Spain and the United States,
Spain yielded her claims to Oregon and British Columbia to the United
States so as to retain Texas.

Spain, however, was not to remain a major player in North America
during the 19th century. In 1821, Mexico declared its independence from
Spain and subsequently adopted Spain's defensive strategy for holding its
northern frontier. Nevertheless, during the remainder of the 19th century,

the Spanish Borderlands continued to recede in the wake of aggressive American settlement. First Texas fell into American hands through annexation, precipitating a war with Mexico, a war that allowed the United States to acquire the remainder of the Spanish Borderlands, including California, in 1848. In 1853, present-day boundaries became complete with the Gadsen Purchase in southern Arizona. In each case, the American advance stopped when it reached the line of permanent Spanish settlement. The defensive strategy of Spain had worked, but by the mid-19th century she no longer had a foothold in North America and was not able to reap the benefits of her defensive efforts.

When American frontiersmen began to push westward from the crest of the Appalachians and across the Mississippi River, they found settlements already established throughout much of the frontier. Saint Louis on the Mississippi, Poste des Arkansas at the mouth of the Arkansas, and Natchitoches on the Red River were occupied long before the Americans arrived. As the American frontier moved farther west it ran into an uneven but nevertheless defined line of occupation that stretched from Texas through New Mexico and Arizona to California. These areas were the Spanish Borderlands, the outer rim of Spanish colonization, containing a population of almost 100,000. The Borderlands, however, were not a wilderness; rivers had been mapped, towns founded, roads completed, agriculture developed, and trade routes established. The frontier wilderness of the 19th century West, as portrayed in American literature, was not entirely wild (Fig. 3.7).

**Figure 3.7**
The meeting of hispanic and Anglo cultures is well illustrated in this corner house in the El Presidio Historic District of Tucson, Arizona. During the 19th century Americans altered many traditional adobe buildings by adding pitched roofs. In this case, a later storefront has also been inserted.

## Spanish legacy

Half of the land in the present-day contiguous United States was once under Spanish control, and the most recognizable area of Spanish influence is that extending from Texas to California. Here social, cultural, economic, and legal institutions derived from Spain remain a part of everyday life. The irrigation systems of both the small market gardeners of New Mexico and the large corporate farmers of California share in a common water-rights system that is a thinly disguised copy of Spanish water law. It was in the Spanish Borderlands that Indian and Spanish culture came together, mingled and established a new pattern, a pattern that is only slightly altered today in many parts of the Southwest. The irregular land ownership patterns throughout the Borderlands remain as evidence of Spanish land tenure (Fig. 3.8). Spanish names of rivers, mountains, towns, and cities are the enduring witness in modern times to Spanish exploration and settlement that took place many centuries ago.

The more obvious remains of Spanish influence—her language, art, and folklore—exist throughout the Borderlands, but are most evident in New Mexico. There, the Spanish language as it is spoken contains many phrases and words derived from 16th- and 17th-century Spain that are in common usage. So too the legacy of Spanish art lives on in the vivid decoration of the many small wayside churches which dot the landscape, art which combines both aboriginal and 17th-century Spanish color schemes and designs. The religion of New Mexico is a strange mixture of Catholicism and native Indian belief and practice, particularly in the rural areas, testifying either to

**Figure 3.8**
A Spanish land concession, shown in an 1840 *diseño*, or crude estate plan, of Rancho Piedra Blanca, San Luis Obispo County, California. Each citizen requesting land had to prepare a sketch map, depicting the area requested. Such vernacular cartography produced the earliest maps of California.

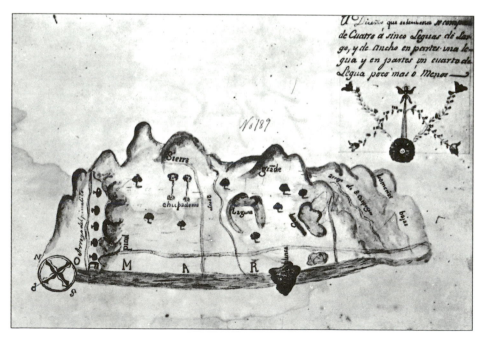

successful or unsuccessful missionary efforts, depending on one's perspect-ive. Spain also left behind a veritable wealth of folklore, much of which has become indigenous to the greater Southwest, particularly in New Mexico, where it is not uncommon for Pueblo Indians to recite traditional Spanish romances of the 16th century as if they were tales of their own forbears.

One of the most obvious remains of Spanish occupation in the landscape is her architecture. The oldest standing dwelling today in the United States is not in Boston or Virginia but in Sante Fe, New Mexico. In addition to Sante Fe's historic buildings there is a trail of what were originally Spanish outposts composed of civic buildings, houses, missions, and military fortresses extending from Florida to California, whose construction was perfectly adapted to the climatic conditions of each region. Unlike their English counterparts, Spanish settlers did not disdain aboriginal architec-ture, but rather strove to mingle and assimilate all that could be used to good account, leaving us today a blend of Spanish and aboriginal buildings that are distinctive in their artistic design. Nowhere is this more evident than in the Spanish mission ruins of Texas, New Mexico, Arizona, and California (Fig. 3.9).

One of the more underplayed and least noticed legacies of Spain in North America is her impact on modern urban patterns. As suggested earlier, Spain employed institutions to occupy new areas and peopled its land with three types of communities. Today, many of these communities have taken root and become major cities along the Gulf coast and throughout the Southwest. The major cities of New Mexico and Arizona were built upon Spanish foundations. Nowhere in the Spanish Borderlands, however, has Spanish settlement had a greater impact on the urban structure than in California. To settle and occupy that state, Spain established 21 missions, four presidios, and three pueblos along the California coast. Today, 72 percent of the state's population live in one of the 28 sites originally founded by Spain. Within these cities, many street names, roads, boundaries, neighborhoods, the orientation of street patterns, water rights, and land

**Figure 3.9**
Mission Santa Barbara in 1895. Founded in 1786 by the Franciscan order, this is the only mission in California continuously occupied since it was founded. The mission is considered the "Queen of California Missions" due to its distinctive architectural style.

tenure are of Spanish origin, to the surprise of many who reside there.

Rapid urbanization of the Southwest and California during the past 20 years has created considerable change in the landscape. Once rural areas have spawned rapidly growing communities and existing urban areas have expanded substantially, creating pressure to change the elements of the Spanish landscape that remain. Today in California, those most visible features identifying Spanish settlement, the missions, have become urban tourist attractions, luring thousands of visitors each year. In Arizona, New Mexico, and Texas, urban growth has had similar effects. It is not uncommon to see a Spanish mission next to a busy freeway in a rapidly growing community, preserved as a symbol of the past, yet modified to fit how we think a mission should have been constructed, and now used as a recreational facility for weekend visitors. Spanish mission architecture and design traditions have spurred emulation in modern times as buildings and furniture created in the mission revival style have gained national popularity.

Spanish contributions to the United States are all too frequently dismissed with the phrase, "they came for gold, God, and glory but did not settle the land." Yet the American landscape is replete with symbols and relics of Spanish colonization and influence in shaping the vast reaches of the continent. The oldest genuine historical artifacts of Spanish origin are concentrated in the Southwest, but Spain's ultimate influence upon urban design and building styles is to be found in various forms throughout the modern United States.

The legacy of Spanish accomplishments and heritage is extensive and suggests that Spain had a considerable impact on the history and geography of the present-day United States. Spain planted her institutions, language, religion, and traditions over a wide area. In our textbooks we share with Spain a common heritage: the exploits of de Soto, Coronado, Cabrillo, and de Leon. Yet we often downplay their exploits while emphasizing the childish myths that surrounded their adventures. The evolution of the Spanish Borderlands is a rich chapter in the discovery and settlement of North America.

# Chapter four
# French landscapes in North America

## COLE HARRIS

IN GENERAL FRENCH landscapes could not be transplanted overseas but elements of French landscapes, like other elements of French culture, could be. Official France, centered in the towns, was more transferable than local France, dispersed through the countryside. Everywhere the French settled in North America, French traits were rearranged; the new landscapes were North American compositions fashioned, largely, from French elements.

Of course, there never was a French landscape, least of all in the 16th and 17th centuries when French interest in North America began. France was a dense mosaic of local cultures marked off from each other by language or dialect, custom, and economy, as well as by landscape. The numerous *pays* of France each had their own character—differences from place to place that frequently emerged clearly even within a day's walk. Superimposed on this sense of locality was a more official France expressed in the great estates, the towns, the provincial governments, the church, and, of course, the royal court. Merchant capital also transcended the local worlds of peasant culture. Literary culture and high style dominated official and, to a degree, merchant France, but hardly touched the great mass of rural France where oral cultures predominated and nine out of ten Frenchmen lived. Even the towns reflected their regional cultural settings. Modern techniques of surveillance had not yet created a unified nation–state. Variety characterized the myriad, diverse landscapes of a still profoundly rural and, in many ways, medieval France.

### Footholds on the continent

French commercial capital reached out to North America at the beginning of the 16th century.[1] In 1497 John Cabot noted the abundance of cod in the northwestern Atlantic. Within the next few years French fishermen who had until then been operating in waters south of Ireland, swung west across the

Atlantic to exploit this new source of fish. Well before the end of the 16th century most of the Atlantic ports of France, great and small, participated in the transatlantic fishery with at least 150–200 ships and thousands of men crossing the Atlantic each year. Some of them fished on the great offshore banks and returned to France without landing in the New World. More made for a rocky harbor where their ship was beached for the season. Fishing took place in small prefabricated boats assembled ashore and operated in inshore waters. The men lived ashore, salting and drying their catch there. At the end of the fishing season ships were loaded with dried cod and everyone returned to France.

Work camps scattered around Newfoundland and Cape Breton Island, along the Labrador shore, and in the Gulf of St. Lawrence, were the first French settlements in North America.[2] They were utilitarian workplaces, built by migratory workers for the seasonal processing of fish, and not intended to last for long or to accommodate families. Sometimes structures from one season survived to the next; if not, they could be quickly rebuilt. There had to be a landing stage (*echafaud*) where the cod were unloaded, headed, gutted, and lightly salted. There had to be a wash cage and a large vat for cod liver oil. Commonly there were low drying platforms (*vignaux*) for the cod, or perhaps branches (*rances*) spread out for this purpose. There was usually a cabin for officers, at least one for the men, and in the larger camps there were small breweries (for spruce beer), bake ovens, and even tiny gardens. The regional variety of western France penetrated this sparse, transatlantic world. Isolated in different harbors, Norman, Breton, Gasgon, and Basque fishermen built slightly differently, piled cod differently, dressed differently, used slightly different fishing gear, and ate somewhat different foods. A sensitive eye would have identified the region of France from which fishermen in a particular harbor had come. Yet the opportunity for cultural transplantation was severely curtailed in these settlements shaped, primarily, by the technology and work of the cod fishery. In essence, fragments of European capital and labor were detached from Europe, placed on the edge of the wilderness for a few months each year, then withdrawn. The laborforce was entirely European; natives were pushed aside, their summer fishing grounds pre-empted.

Year-round fishing settlements began in a few places in the 17th century. Women arrived, cabins were slightly better built, kitchen gardens became a little larger, although in many areas climate and rock discouraged even this minimal year-round settlement. Basically, the French cod fishery remained migratory, dependent, by the 17th century, on a few fishing ports in France, traditional techniques, and a renewable resource. For more than 300 years a type of seasonal workcamp would be built and rebuilt in tiny harbors around the complex coastline of what is now Atlantic Canada.

From early in the 16th century some fishermen traded with natives for furs. Late in the century a few ships began to be outfitted expressly for the fur trade. As this happened the focus of the fur trade shifted westward, toward the St. Lawrence River, the principal conduit for the furs of the interior. In 1600 fur traders overwintered at Tadoussac at the western end of the Gulf of St. Lawrence; eight years later another group (led by Samuel de Champlain) established a post at Québec, the head of deep sea navigation on the St. Lawrence River. This time the French were on the St. Lawrence to stay. Trois-Rivières was established in 1634. Montréal, founded as a mission in 1642, soon became the most interior outpost of the fur trade. In these years French traders did not venture beyond the St. Lawrence Valley; the fur trade was in the hands of their Indian allies (Algonquian-speaking groups living around the southern fringe of the Canadian Shield, and Iroqoian-speaking Huron living in what is now southern Ontario) who brought furs to the lower St. Lawrence and traded there.

By the 1650s European diseases and heightened intertribal warfare (associated with the introduction of firearms) had destroyed most of the former native trading partners of the French. French traders themselves began to venture inland, in the process mastering the birchbark canoe, learning native languages, and, in 1670, building the first trading post west of Montréal—Fort-de-la-Baie-des-Puants on Green Bay. In this interior world of shifting military and trading alliances and declining local supplies of beaver, canoe and fur post facilitated the remarkable territorial expansion of French commerce. Before the end of the 17th century there were French posts on each of the Great Lakes, along the Illinois and upper Mississippi Rivers, on Lake Nepegon north of Lake Superior, and even on James Bay where the French captured posts built by the Hudson's Bay Company (Fig. 4.1). Such expansion soon created a glut of furs in Montréal. In 1696 the crown closed all interior posts, and did not reopen most of them until the Treaty of Utrecht (1713) returned the French-held forts on Hudson and James Bays to the British. French traders again circulated in the interior; by the 1730s there were French trading posts as far west as the lower Missouri and Lake Winnipeg.

The fur post was a palisaded, frequently garrisoned settlement in native territory. The largest—Fort Detroit and Michilimakinac—were entrepôts laid out in a grid of streets and defended by cannon mounted in small angled towers at the corners of curtain walls (Fig. 4.2). The smallest, comprising a few buildings surrounded by a palisade some 12 feet high, could be constructed in a few weeks to provide minimal accommodation for a few traders and soldiers overwintering among potentially hostile natives. White women were absent at such posts, and the traders themselves would leave after a year or two, not necessarily to be replaced. The fur post was, characteristically, an ephemeral outlier of French commerce and the French military, built to house and protect trade goods and personnel, a point of contact between native and European worlds in the wilderness. Wooden palisades and buildings made of squared timbers laid horizontally and tenoned to posts at the corners and at intervals along the walls had not been used for centuries in military construction in France.

As the French fur trade became established in North America, it drew a few settlers, not all of whom could be employed in a trade that depended

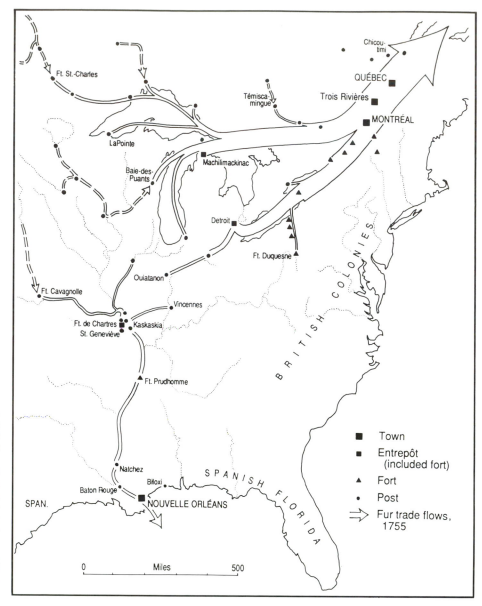

**Figure 4.1**
The French arc of settlement
in North America in about
1755. The fur trade linked the
web of settlements together.
Trading posts were the most
far-flung sites of French
presence, guarded by forts in
areas contested by the
British. The Illinois country
served as a breadbasket for
many western operations,
and the chief towns
developed at the outflows of
the St. Lawrence and the
Mississippi Rivers.

primarily on native labor. In the 1630s agricultural settlement began in
Acadia (the area centered on the Bay of Fundy between the present
Canadian provinces of Nova Scotia and New Brunswick) and along the
lower St. Lawrence River near Québec. From these frail beginnings emerged
two different French-speaking peoples in North America.

In Acadia farming began on tidal marshes created by the great tides (up to
50 feet) of the Bay of Fundy.[3] The upper reaches of these marshes could be
protected with broad low dykes made of sods, reinforced with branches or
logs, and punctuated at intervals by sluice gates fitted with clapper valves.
The marsh behind such dykes would freshen in a few years and make

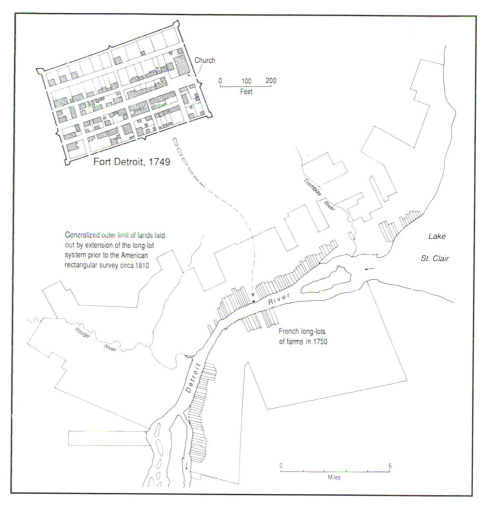

Church

0    100    200
Feet

Fort Detroit, 1749

Trembly River

Lake
St. Clair

Generalized outer limit of lands laid
out by extension of the long-lot
system prior to the American
rectangular survey circa 1810

River

French long-lots
of farms in 1750

Rouge River

Detroit River

0                    5
Miles

**Figure 4.2**
Fort Détroit and its French settlement district in easternmost Michigan around 1750. The town developed as a compact unit, but did not survive American takeover, which produced a grandiose new plan for the city of Detroit centered several hundred yards to the east. The rural long lots endured, however, and with their pre-American extensions created a framework that still controls the land parcel pattern of central Detroit and the adjoining city of Windsor, Ontario.

excellent ploughland. Acadian life depended on these dyked marshlands, a niche of New World agricultural opportunity, bounded by sea and forest, in an exposed corner of the northwestern Atlantic.

The marshes supported the crops and livestock of northwestern France and, with them, a vigorous peasant economy. There were not many immigrants, perhaps no more than 40 founding families, and little export opportunity (there was some trade with Boston and, later, Louisbourg), but for several generations there was room for young Acadians to establish new farms on the marshlands around the Bay of Fundy. The Acadian farm was a mixed operation in which wheat and legumes were supplemented as field crops by oats, rye, barley, and flax; cattle were the dominant livestock, and most farmers also kept pigs, sheep (for wool), and poultry; and every farm had a kitchen garden. The success of Acadian farming is reflected in the expansion of Acadian settlement. Girls married in their teens and the population grew rapidly by natural increase. In 1670 some 350 Acadians lived on the marshlands, by 1710 there were 1,400; Acadian settlement had spread to all the cultivable marshes around the Bay of Fundy.

When France held Acadia, the fort, garrison, and governor at Port Royal maintained an official connection with France. But this exposed colony alternated between French and British control in the 17th century, and fell to the British for the last time in 1710. Even before 1710, the imprint of traditional power on such a countryside was slight. There were no royal taxes although, intermittently, men were required to serve in the militia, and there were no seigneurial charges for land. There were a few priests, who must have received some tythe. Acadian land was not valuable enough to attract or create a landed élite, and the export economy was not robust enough to draw merchants from France. In the 17th century the few Acadian exports fell within the coasting trade from Boston. For the most part the Acadians were left to themselves. Their domestic economy, supplemented by some trade, maintained a rough sufficiency. Acadian families were better off than the rural poor in France, but none was nearly as well off as the more prosperous French peasants. The landscape created by such a people was dominated by their arable marshlands, dykes, and wooden, thatched farmhouses, built at the boundary of marsh and forest. Such farmhouses did not reflect a particular French regional style, rather the local availability of wood, and peasant ways from all over France. Over time, a common experience with a novel environment and a selective peasant memory (some memories were lost because they were environmentally irrelevant, others because not enough immigrants shared them) had created a unique peasant culture.

## The core landscapes of New France

Along the lower St. Lawrence River, a somewhat different colony, Canada, emerged.[4] Québec and Montréal were the early foci of Canadian development. Both centers of the fur trade—Montréal as jumping-off point to the interior, Québec as port and point of contact with France—they slowly developed into small towns as their administrative, military, and commercial functions expanded; and as local authorities drew up town plans and distributed lots. By 1739, date of the last census of Canada during the French regime, there were some 4,500 people in Québec and almost as many in Montréal.

Québec and Montréal were the most comprehensive transplantations from France in the New World. They performed most of the functions of French towns, and housed similar classes. There were centers of power where merchants, government officials, military officers, and important clerics lived; where instructions arrived from France; where laws were made, judgements passed, and offenders punished. Occupationally they were diverse; some 40 percent of household heads were artisans representing all basic port trades, construction, and the provision of common consumer goods. Socially they were highly stratified, culturally they were melting

**Figure 4.3**
Street scene in the upper town of Québec City. Typical urban dwellings with long gabled roofs and dormer windows reflect the strong French influence of the early period. A similar streetscape developed in the Vieux Carré district of New Orleans.

pots, their populations reflecting the many regional sources of French emigration to Canada. Visitors likened them to French towns, Québec to a provincial capital; they most closely resembled the port towns of northwestern France, from whence, in good measure, they had sprung.

The European dichotomy between a commercial lower town and an administrative and military upper town emerged very early in both Québec and Montréal. Québec's congested lower town served the activities of the port on a ribbon of land between the river and a cliff the heights of which commanded the St. Lawrence. Its upper town, far more spacious, was the location of royal and clerical officials and the garrison (Fig. 4.3). There were handsome baroque structures in the upper town, and much of the land around these buildings was laid out in garden plots arranged geometrically and walled. In the lower town, where land was scarce, buildings were contiguous along a street. Streetscapes were dominated by spare, symmetrical stone facades, large, well-proportioned and shuttered windows, narrow dormers, and massive chimneys—as in the towns of northwestern France. In Montréal warehouses and other commercial buildings lined the riverfront and a far more open institutional town emerged behind them along an approximate grid of streets. In the 1680s Montréal was palisaded for

*69*

protection against the Iroquois, and in the 18th century the wooden palisade was replaced by a stone wall.

The countryside that expanded slowly along the river from Québec and Montréal was a more original creation. As in Acadia, it was built up from the family farm and the domestic economy in conditions where agricultural land was available but markets were inaccessible. The Canadian countryside, however, was never as detached as the Acadian from towns and the power they contained.

Land in Canada, as in France, was held by seigneurs from the crown. The seigneur subgranted land to farmers (habitants) who acquired security of title in return for annual rents and charges for seigneurial services. In theory the seigneur was to behave towards his tenants as *"un bon père de famille."* In fact in France by the 17th century the seigneurial system was little more than a source of revenue for seigneurs and of financial burden for their tenants. In Canada few seigneurs produced much revenue in the 17th century, but seigneurs kept accounts and collected their due sooner or later. The bishop established parishes as soon as numbers warranted; whether the habitants wanted him or not, there was soon a resident priest and tythes to pay. The crown did not impose taxes, but did require roadwork and expected farm families to house troops and provide able bodied men for the militia in times of warfare. "The Canadians," an official in Canada explained to his superior in France, "pay with their blood." As Canadian agriculture began to find export markets in the 18th century, merchants were regularly in the countryside. Many habitants were in debt to them. In such ways traditional sources of power in rural France penetrated the Canadian countryside.

But rural Canada was not a reproduction of part of rural France, and could not be. French institutions and peasant ways had penetrated a forested valley near the climatic margin for agriculture where farm lots were available from a seigneur for no initial charge. Farm lots were laid out with a characteristic ratio of width to length of about 1 : 10 and an area of 50–100 acres. Such long-lot farms were well known in Normandy, source of many of the earliest immigrants to Canada, and suited new settlements of farmers who wanted to live along the river on their own land. The lots were easily and cheaply surveyed, and gave most farmers river frontage, a variety of soil and vegetation types, and neighbors close by (Fig. 4.2 & 4). As elsewhere in the North American forest, the pioneer work of clearing, working the land, and building, was unremitting—a farm of some 30 cleared acres was the product of a lifetime of labor. One of the sons would remain on the parental farm. The others would become pioneer farmers in their turn, usually as close to the parental farm as possible, and repeat the lifetime cycle of work and farm creation.

In this way land was available, but the local market for farm produce was small, and the export market was nonexistent until the 18th century. And under such circumstances the Canadian farm, like the Acadian, was an unspecialized, mixed operation that provided as much as possible for domestic consumption and some surplus for sale. A kitchen garden

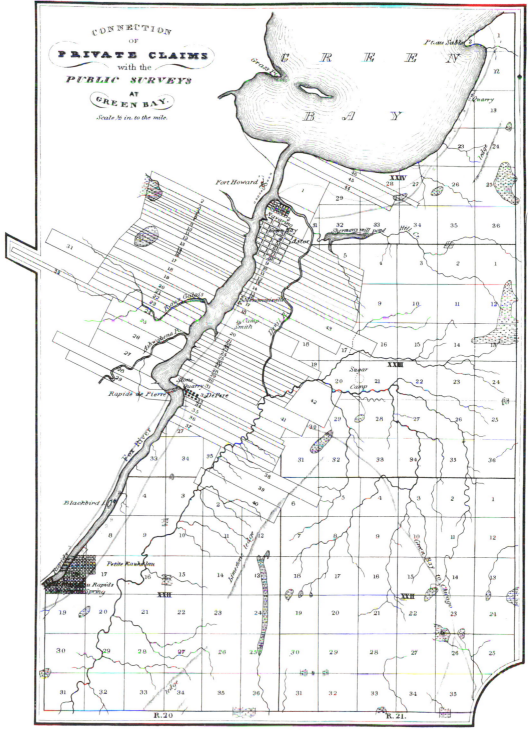

**Figure 4.4**

The pattern of long lots at Green Bay, Wisconsin, in 1809. When the United States land surveys reached the area, they gridded all land not previously laid out. Authorities honored the long lots as existing "private claims," and their outlines became embedded in the subsequent evolving pattern of land ownership, still very evident today.

produced vegetables, tobacco, and fruit; ploughed fields were planted principally in wheat, but also in barley, oats, and legumes; meadow and pasture supported cattle, oxen, sheep, and, usually, horses. Every farm raised pigs and poultry. Such were the elements of almost all established farms from one end of the colony to the other. There were a few larger farms on seigneurial domains, but the family farm was the basic unit of agricultural production. With 20 acres cleared on such a farm there was hardly a surplus for sale; with 30 or 40 acres cleared some wheat, a cow or two, perhaps some piglets, perhaps a few tubs of butter, could be marketed most years. In the longer term no farm family could be or wanted to be self-sufficient.

Compared to the French peasantry, habitant society was relatively unstratified. In a weak commercial economy there were no really wealthy habitants, and as long as land was available there were no landless families and few beggars. At the same time, the regional memories of immigrants from France were being blended along the lower St. Lawrence as an unconscious selection of remembered ways reinforced by common immigrant memories, or memories that were particularly relevant to the demands of pioneer settlement in a northern forest. Languages other than French, and many dialects of French, quickly disappeared. As in Acadia techniques of building in wood came to the fore and others were forgotten. In sum a distinctive, vibrant, Canadian culture was emerging. Because family farms were similar from one end of the lower St. Lawrence Valley to the other, and because part of the habitant population was remixed generation after generation as the young moved to new land, the rural culture of early Canada was expansive and probably fairly uniform.

By the mid 18th century farms lined both banks of the St. Lawrence for more than 200 miles. Near Québec land for agricultural expansion was no longer available. Everywhere the forest had been pushed back, replaced by tended countryside. Parish churches dotted the lines of settlement, more conspicuous than the many small water-powered grist and saw mills on tributary streams or the windmills on promontories. Here and there a manor stood out from the houses around it, a reflection of a seigneur's growing revenue as a seigneurial population rose. The predominant building in the countryside was the small habitant house, usually constructed of squared logs dovetailed at the corners and tenoned to vertical posts around windows, chimney, and doors; usually whitewashed to preserve the logs; usually roofed with thatch or cedar planks. Overlooking river or road at the front of a long-lot farm and 100–200 yards from similar buildings on either side, such houses were a measure of a New World opportunity for the poor to acquire farms and of a unique peasant culture.

## The French crescent: St. Lawrence to the Mississippi

All these French settlements in North America developed within the context of the larger military struggle between France and England for control of a continent. In this regard the Treaty of Utrecht (1713), which ended the long Anglo–French hostilities known as the War of the Austrian Succession, was calamitous for France in North America. The Treaty confirmed English title to much of Acadia, ceded Newfoundland (France retained fishing rights in the north), and returned the forts on Hudson Bay. France had bargained for European advantage with North American territory. In the aftermath of the Treaty of Utrecht, France sought to strengthen her diminished North American position by building a massive fortress town, Louisbourg, on Cape Breton Island at the entrance to the Gulf of St. Lawrence; and by encouraging trade and settlement along the Mississippi. It was hoped that a crescent of French power from the Gulf of St. Lawrence to the Gulf of Mexico might contain the British east of the Appalachians.

Begun in 1717, the fortress at Louisbourg was a defensive stronghold designed in the Vauban style to resist cannon bombardment. When completed in 1734 it was the largest fortress in North America, built on a low, exposed, frequently fog-bound peninsula at the entrance to Louisbourg harbor, and protected on the landward side by massive, low stone walls, ramparts, and angled bastions. Behind the wall was a garrison town of more than 2,000 people. The town was dominated by the military, commerce (it became the major French port in the northwest Atlantic, one of the busiest ports in North America), and the fishery. Fishing installations rimmed the Louisbourg harbor, and schooners sailed from Louisbourg to the offshore fishing banks. Louisbourg itself was laid out in a precise grid of streets. Its most imposing buildings—the barracks, the King's warehouse, hospital, and principal residences—were stone structures in the baroque French taste of the day, their exteriors proportioned and austere, some of the interiors made remarkably ornate by fittings and workmanship imported from France. Lesser buildings were mostly of timber frame construction variously infilled. Small gardens, barely feasible in Louisbourg's climate, were laid out geometrically. Louisbourg's appearance reflected what it was, an early 18th century outlier of the French state and French commerce superimposed on a far older fishery. Like Québec and Montréal it housed a mix of peoples. Many of its inhabitants, particularly its women, had been born in the New World—in Acadia, in the former French fishing settlements in Newfoundland, or in Louisbourg itself.

The year in which France decided to fortify Louisbourg (1717) she moved to strengthen her hold on the Mississippi Valley by granting a merchant company title to Louisiana and a trading monopoly for 25 years. The company was to establish 6,000 free settlers and 3,000 slaves. The next year the company founded New Orleans. It began granting large estates, assuming that they would be worked by indentured servants brought from Europe, and tried to recruit immigrants in France, the Low Countries, and

**Figure 4.5**
Jackson Square in New
Orleans, in the heart of the
Vieux Carré or French
Quarter, seen from the levee
along the Mississippi River.
Stately St. Louis Cathedral
(1794, remodeled 1851)
dominates the townscape
here, flanked by the
Presbytère (1794–1813) to the
right and the Cabildo (1795),
Spanish seat of government,
on the left. The French
mansard roof of the Cabildo
was added in 1847, long after
American takeover, but
stylistically much in vogue at
that time.

Germany. Although several thousand French convicts were sentenced to deportation to Louisbourg, few arrived and fewer survived; European labor in Louisiana remained scarce and expensive. In these circumstances the company turned increasingly to black slave labor and the model of the plantation economy as practiced on the French sugar islands. When the crown assumed control of Louisiana in 1731 there were more blacks than whites along the lower Mississippi in a non-native population of about 4,000. Plantations were the principal units of production. Rice, indigo, and tobacco were the major plantation products, together, on some of the larger plantations, with lumber and naval stores. When native groups resisted these incursions into their territory, they were overcome by French firepower. Between 1729 and 1731 the Natchez, approximately 3,000 people living along the Mississippi some 200 miles above New Orleans, were dispersed, many of them to St. Dominique as slaves.

New Orleans, like Louisbourg, was laid out in a rectangular grid of streets and, like Montréal, was walled on three sides. As local stone was not available, most buildings were of timber frame construction with brick infill.[5] Otherwise, New Orleans looked much like a smaller version of the other French towns in North America, particularly Louisbourg—both 18th-century towns (Fig. 4.5). On the other hand, rural settlement along the lower Mississippi had little in common with that along the lower St. Lawrence. The banks of the Mississippi were occupied from New Orleans almost half way to the sea, but primarily by plantations rather than by family farms (Fig. 4.6). At the core of a plantation was a small nucleated settlement tied to an export economy—the agricultural equivalent of the early fishing camps in Newfoundland. There were rudimentary quarters for workers (slaves) and much more ample ones for an owner or the overseers; in some cases a sawmill or a brickyard; the potatoes, corn, and vegetables;

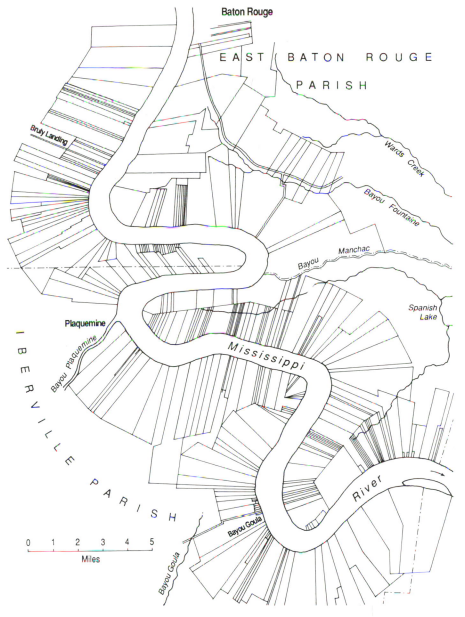

**Figure 4.6**
Mississippi long lots
downstream from Baton
Rouge, Louisiana, as they
had evolved by 1850. This
pattern reflects a long process
of selective lateral
subdivision and
consolidation since the
original French arpents were
laid out. The heritage of
French names in the
landscape is strong.

and fields planted in the export crops. These were not the large plantations
of the sugar islands, for the lower Mississippi had not established an
equivalent export staple. There were some family farms. Yet the considerable majority of the rural population was black. In fact, to the extent that
Old World folk cultures survived on New World plantations, those along
the lower Mississippi were more African than French.

There was a French garrison at Natchez, some 200 miles north of New
Orleans, and good but underused tobacco land nearby. At mid-century the
garrison at Natchez was penned in by the Chickasaw, and agriculture there

**Figure 4.7**
The French village of
Kaskaskia around 1764, the
largest of the Illinois
settlements in the mid-18th
century, with over 600
inhabitants (including
slaves). Space was plentiful,
and houses and gardens
occupied a broad river terrace
criss-crossed by informal
village lanes. The changing
course of the Mississippi
River has disrupted much of
the site since then.

was hardly feasible. At the mouth of the Arkansas River, 200 miles farther
up-river, was another fort, the most northerly French outpost on the lower
Mississippi. A few settlers had farmed there before being driven off by the
Chickasaw in 1748. Fully 500 miles farther north, in the territory the French
called the Illinois country, were several agricultural villages: Kaskaskia and
several others on or near the Mississippi south of modern St. Louis, and
Vincennes on the lower Wabash (Fig. 4.7). The first French-speaking settlers
in the Illinois country had come from Canada, from where the territory was
administered until 1717 when it was officially made part of the colony of
Louisiana. By 1750 there were 2,000–3,000 people in these villages, two
thirds of them white, the rest black or native slaves. Economically and
socially the Illinois country lay between the domestic rural economy of the
lower St. Lawrence and the plantations of Louisiana.[6] Wheat, beef, pork,
and some livestock on the hoof were sent down-river to New Orleans,
destined for the sugar islands. Corn yielded abundantly, food for cattle and
slaves. The largest landholder in the village of Kaskaskia controlled some
450 acres of arable land and owned 60 slaves (including women and
children) and many hundred head of cattle, swine, and horses. Most settlers
had very little arable land and presumably lived primarily from hunting and
the hide trade, but almost 70 percent of white families were slave owners.
Far in the continental interior, the French had reached a type of opportunity
they had not encountered before in North America—rich land for mid-
latitude agriculture *and* an export market. Some houses from the Illinois
villages of that period still survive (Fig. 4.8). Father Vivier, the Jesuit priest

who served the upper Mississippi settlements in the early 1750s, considered that the Illinois country was the pivot of the French effort to hold the vast crescent between the Gulf of St. Lawrence and the Gulf of Mexico. He may have been right, but in 1750 a few villagers far in the interior were a fragile pivot for continental ambition. The Illinois country needed more settlers and more years.

On the eve of the Seven Years' War (1757–1763) the French claim to North America extended from Labrador to Texas, including the Gulf of St. Lawrence and St. Lawrence Valley, the Great Lakes, the whole drainage basin of the Mississippi, and, except for a rim of land acknowledged to be British, most of the territory draining into Hudson Bay.[7] Britain also claimed the Hudson Bay drainage, the eastern Great Lakes, and the Ohio Valley. In fact most of this enormous territory was still controlled by natives. French claims, advanced against British counterclaims, had a cartographic and geopolitical vitality they did not have on the ground. Nevertheless, the French fur trade operated through much of the continent, the French fishery to Newfoundland and Labrador was 250 years old, and there were widely distributed patches of permanent French settlement: some 13,000 people, by the early 1750s, on or near the marshlands around the Bay of Fundy; some 5,000 or more on Cape Breton Island; just over 60,000 along the lower St. Lawrence; some 2,000 (including slaves) in the Illinois country; 1,000 scattered in dozens of fur posts; and perhaps 6,000 (including slaves) along the lower Mississippi.

These were not many settlers to hold the larger portion of a continent. There were several colonial jurisdictions: Cape Breton Island, what remained of Acadia, Canada, and Louisiana. There were several unrelated

**Figure 4.8**
Houses built in the traditional French colonial style on Main Street in St. Geneviève, Missouri. At left is the Bolduc House (c.1770), next door the Bolduc-LeMeilleur House (c. 1820), and to the right the Vallé House (1780s).

export economies: the fishery, the fur trade, and the various trades of the Mississippi. There were several isolated regional cultures. Canadians and Acadians, descended from different immigrant stocks, lived in different northern agricultural niches, and after a time were different peoples. Most of the settlers in the Illinois country had come from Canada but, on the edge of the prairie and the plantation economy, were no longer Canadian habitants. The subtropical lower Mississippi was another realm, differing in settlement history, economy, and local cultures from any other patch of French settlement in North America. A more official France was super-imposed on these scattered, varied settlements, but its impact focused on the towns and weakened rapidly away from them. The townscapes of Québec, Montréal, Louisbourg, and New Orleans all reflected the outreach of official France, whereas the rural landscapes of French North America revealed the dynamics of local cultures.

## The legacy

During the Seven Years' War France lost almost all her North American territory. The crucial military actions focused on the towns: Louisbourg fell in 1758, Québec in 1759, and the French army surrendered in Montréal in 1760. Scattered rural peoples, deprived of the protection of the state, were also vulnerable. Many Acadians were deported in 1755, and most of the rest were caught over the next several years; their marshland farms were soon occupied by others. Some Acadian refugees eventually reached Louisiana, where they formed the nucleus of the Cajun people.[8] The tiny French settlements in the Illinois country were engulfed by the advancing American frontier. Spanish, then American, influences diluted, then overwhelmed the small French-speaking population along the lower Mississippi. In much of North America placenames are the enduring French legacy. But along the lower St. Lawrence, the heart of French settlement in North America from the early 17th century, a French-speaking regional culture survived and even expanded. Eventually it would have outliers in New England, Ontario, and Western Canada. Indeed, a country, Canada, would emerge out of the French undertaking in North America. It is one of the continent's particular ironies that after the American Revolution and the border settlement, the British position in North America fell back to the lands around the Bay of Fundy and the Gulf of St. Lawrence, the St. Lawrence Valley, and the fur trade in the interior—very largely, that is, on the French position in North America at the end of the 17th century.

Today, the French imprint on the American landscape is most widely discernible in the distribution of French placenames. Not surprisingly, their density is greatest within the arc of actual French settlements, but they reach to areas widely traveled by explorer and fur trader. French patterns of land division endure with remarkable clarity in the vicinity of major settlements, such as Green Bay, St. Louis, Vincennes, and Prairie du Chien, where later American land survey studiously avoided established claims. French town planning is most evident in the cities of the St. Lawrence Valley, and New Orleans within the United States, partly in street patterns both regular and irregular, and partly in building forms that contrast strongly with standard American styles. The French imprint in the United States is sparse, muted, and mostly blurred, but in a few localities, most notably along the Mississippi River, it stands in bold defiance of patterns of later American dominance that have nevertheless failed to erase it completely.

# Chapter five
# The Northeast and the making of American geographical habits

## PEIRCE F. LEWIS

DURING THE FORMATIVE period of modern nation–states, there has been an almost universal tendency for power and wealth to accumulate in one relatively small section of the country. In England, for example, the seat of power has always been located in the Southeast, focused on London. In France, the modern nation–state was forged in the north in a small region between the middle section of the Loire and the lower Seine—ultimately focused on Paris. And, although American national history is compressed into a much shorter period, a similar geographical tendency has been at work. Ever since the United States gained its independence, political and economic power have tended to concentrate in the northeastern corner of the country. The nation's most important financial decisions were made there, and a huge proportion of America's wealth was controlled by northeastern financiers and northeastern corporations. Its most prestigious educational institutions were located there and still are, so that a disproportionate part of the country's power élite has been educated at northeastern prep schools, colleges, and universities. Through most of the country's history, most important political decisions were made there—officially, in the national capital in Washington, or informally in the clubs and boardrooms of Boston and New York and Philadelphia and Pittsburgh. And from the days of earliest European settlement, it was in the Northeast that Americans formed some of their most persistent geographical habits.

Many of those habits had very tangible results, for over the course of time they came to be etched into the face of America's ordinary human landscape. Northeastern ideas would determine where cities would be situated and how their streets would be laid out. They would determine what ordinary houses would look like and how they would be placed in relation to streets and gardens. They would determine where roads would be built, and who would build them; where farmers would live and how they would design barns to house their crops and livestock; and a host of smaller matters. In concert, these ideas and habits would produce a set of ordinary human landscapes highly distinctive in appearance, in turn underlain by a set of ethical, esthetic, and even religious ideas about how humans should treat the land.[1]

If these geographical ideas and habits had been restricted to the northeastern corner of the nation, they would be of little more than local interest today. The Northeast, after all, is only a small part of the United States. But the Northeast was the source from which most of the Midwest and West were eventually settled. In consequence, what began as a congeries of rather peculiar regional quirks was carried westward and ultimately stamped as standard patterns of human geography across an enormous part of the American nation (Fig. 5.1).

**Figure 5.1**
Westward spread of northeastern cultures. New England culture originated from a broad stretch of the Atlantic coast, but as it spread westward was squeezed into a narrow corridor between the Adirondacks and the Catskills—thence via the Erie Canal along the southern edge of the Great Lakes. Pennsylvania, by contrast, started with one small foothold on the Delaware River, but spread westward in a broadening diffuse fan that covered much of the continental interior. Even in the flatlands of the Midwest, however, the two streams of eastern settlement remained quite separate from one another.

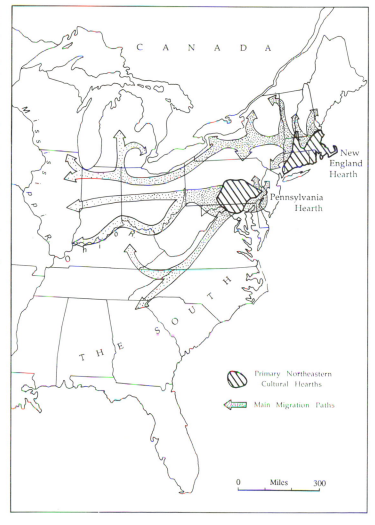

81

## An American version of England

Originally, many of the basic precepts of organized society were not American at all, but started out English. America, after all, was English long before it was American—and for most of the 17th and 18th centuries, most transatlantic settlers were content that it should remain so. The name, New England, for example, was not chosen by accident, and it announced clearly that America was not intended to become a *new* world, but instead a new version of an old one. It would be an improved version, to be sure, both physically and morally—for its founders believed that this new version of England could and should be cleansed and rid of the old country's corruptions and inquities. America would be the embodiment of the New Testament vision, they declared, a shining city on a hill, a beacon for all mankind to see and to emulate. It would be a richer version, too, for it was planted in an empty land—and had God not instructed His chosen people to multiply and subdue the Earth?

So it was that the western shores of the North Atlantic started out English, and they remained so even after the Revolution and the act of formal political separation. And, to a considerable extent, America remains English today, culturally if not politically, simply because Englishmen arrived first, and settled in sufficient numbers that they could impose their ideas and tastes on anyone who happened to arrive later—even though such later arrivals would eventually outnumber their English predecessors. And so it is that in New England today, in territory now mainly populated by folk of Irish and Italian ancestry, there are towns named York and Bristol and Plymouth and New London. Even in the parts of Pennsylvania where Germans were so numerous that English-speaking travelers in the 1780s needed interpreters to make themselves understood, counties were named for Lancaster and York, Chester and Northumberland.

Language was more than just a matter of naming things. Everywhere in British North America, if people wished to join the economic or political or social mainstream, they spoke English, or quickly learned to speak it. (French Canada remained an isolated backwater for a very long time in part because its people could not or would not speak the English language that eventually became the key to economic and political success throughout the United States and Canada.) Everywhere, people divided their land according to English measures, and settled their differences in courts under the rules of English statutory and common law.

## A different sort of place

But America was not merely a duplication of England. From the time of earliest settlement, American geographical behavior diverged sharply from that of England—in ways that often made America seem perverse, uncouth, and eccentric—at least in the eyes of European spectators.

Much of this seeming eccentricity was a matter of plain necessity. Ways of managing land that had worked in the old country often did not work in America, and Americans quickly learned (sometimes the hard way) about the virtues of keeping an open mind, and abandoning traditional ways when the new geographical circumstances seemed to call for it.

Such constant experimentation did not always produce attractive results. Judge William Cooper, the father of James Fennemore Cooper and a large-scale land speculator in New York State in the early 1800s, sold his land to new settlers with the help of a little book filled with useful tips on how to survive and prosper on the American frontier. In *A guide in the wilderness* Cooper heaped scorn on aristocratic English and Irish settlers who came to the New York frontier and then wasted energy cutting down trees and rooting out stumps in order to produce a neatly manicured, English-style country landscape.[2] Forget all that nonsense, advised Cooper. Burn the forest, and plant immediately among the charred remains. Bringing in a harvest is more important than making one's fields look pretty. If the timber was wasted and the land disfigured in the process, no matter. There was always more timber, more soil, more land—or so it seemed. That attitude toward land and resources did not end with Cooper, of course, and economics commonly took precedence over esthetics, especially in the early days. Unlike England, America was a big country, and it rewarded those who seized its riches quickly. But such ambitions did not make for a tidy landscape, and they did not encourage habits of geographical thrift (Fig. 5.2).

Nor did they make for habits of permanence. For people who had already migrated once, there was always a propensity to migrate again—and yet again. It was all very well for Englishmen to have special attachments to special places—indeed, to take their names from the places where they and

**Figure 5.2**
Newly cleared farmstead on the frontier of northern Michigan.

their ancestors had lived since the beginning of time. In England (indeed, in the Old World in general), one knew one's place, both socially and geographically. That was never the American way. Mobility—the willingness to abandon places when they had served a particular purpose—was the key to success, whether success was defined in economic or social terms. And the passion for mobility has left its distinctive marks on the American landscape: a chronic inclination to spend money on public roads; an uncritical admiration for the latest machines of transportation, whether steamboats, or speeding locomotives, or fast cars, or jet aircraft; and the unromantic willingness to abandon things that had outlived their immediate usefulness—beer cans discarded beside the highway, old farm houses, or indeed whole cities when they outlived their usefulness. But none of those habits is new. All are deeply rooted in colonial America, and in the attitudes of the English people who settled her land.

## A different sort of people

If the land differed from England, the people differed too. Americans, after all, were migrants—and, as the demographer Ravenstein observed more than a century ago, migrants in all places and all times tend to be a special breed of people.[3] So it was with the shapers of America. They were English, to be sure, but they were not ordinary Englishmen. Ordinary folk, after all, do not uproot their families and abandon their ancestral homes to cross a dangerous ocean to live in a poorly known land on the edge of wilderness. Nor, in a time when religion played a central rôle in life and thought, did conventional people publicly renounce the established church of their native land. But in the eastern part of Atlantic America, between the Penobscot River and Chesapeake Bay, nearly all the migrants had done exactly that. Taken as a whole, the migrants were a tough-minded lot, with unconventional ideas about how society should be organized, and unconventional ideas about their relationships with God, with each other, and with the land itself. It is hardly surprising that they possessed unusual ideas about organizing their new geography as well, and that they left a special mark on the American landscape.

## Two regions of the Northeast

But British North America was not a homogeneous place. Within a short time after initial settlement, major differences had begun to emerge along the northeastern seaboard of what would become the United States. Two quite different culture hearths had begun to evolve, which by the time of the Revolution had expanded to dominate the northern half of colonial America

(Fig. 5.1). One was New England, a little theocracy settled by post-Elizabethan puritans, who had broken away from the Anglican church at precisely the time when Britain's religious wars were raging hottest. Not surprisingly, these New England puritans took religion seriously, and went to great pains to organize their landscape in a way that would ensure the continuity of their ideas, and the rigorous exclusion of folk who did not agree with them. The original puritans had landed in eastern Massachusetts in the 1620s and 1630s and had imposed a theocracy so rigid that they produced their own refugees, who departed Massachusetts to settle the shores of Narragansett Bay and other nearby coastal havens. Soon thereafter others of more liberal bent arrived to settle the shores of Long Island and adjacent Connecticut. Even today those original differences can be heard in regional accents, and seen in subtle differences in folk architecture which distinguish eastern New England, settled from Massachusetts Bay, from western New England, settled from Long Island Sound and the Connecticut River Valley.[4]

In general, however, there was more agreement than disagreement among the New Englanders. They took ideas seriously, and not just religious ones. The political scientist, Daniel Elazar, has called New England a "moralistic political culture," a placed peopled by those who agreed that healthy society required strong community—a place where government would play an active, creative rôle in ensuring virtuous polity—and one where politics was not a dirty business, but esteemed as a high public calling. New Englanders took education seriously as well, and almost as soon as the first fields were planted, they hacked clearings in the forest to build colleges where young men would be nourished in mind and spirit, as well as in body. (Later on, New Englanders would be among the first to agree that women should be educated, as well as men, and New England's women's colleges came to be beacons for women's educational and political rights.)

But philosophy does not bake bread, and for all of New England's high-minded social aspirations, it immediately became obvious that New England was a meager land. The initial arrivals had expected to settle down and become farmers and, in the beginning, most of them did. Indeed, by the mid-19th century they had cleared the forests from all of southern New England and much of the mountainous north as well. But the climate was fierce, and except for the fertile bottomlands of the Connecticut River valley, soils were marginal at best, impossible at worst. New Englanders joked sourly that the most plentiful crop from most fields consisted of stones—they made fine picturesque stone walls, but backbreaking misery for a farmer who was already working close to the margin.

Thus, ambitious New Englanders could choose one of several options. They could take to the sea for trading or fishing or whaling, and many of them did so in preference to grubbing stones from sterile fields. By the mid-19th century, New England ships were trading and whaling all over the world and bringing profit to dozens of colorful ports along the rock-bound coast. Or, they could learn to manufacture things, and they did that too, considerably before most of America had thought of doing so. As a result, New England got a head start in all kinds of useful industries, and the region became a major center of America's industrial revolution. Industry was densely concentrated in places like Manchester, Lawrence, and Lowell, crowded along the Merrimac River, where waterfalls generated power for spinning thread and weaving cloth. Along the north coast of Long Island Sound, Connecticut Yankees earned a world-wide reputation for manufacturing high-quality machined products, guns and locks and machine tools—useful and highly profitable things in a country like America that was expanding by leaps and bounds. Or, finally, a disgruntled Yankee farmer could simply pack up his family and chattels and go looking for better land west of the Appalachians. By the early 19th century, New Englanders were swarming westward across New York State, first by turnpikes, then by the Erie Canal, later still by way of the New York Central Railroad.[5] Many New Englanders went as far as western New York's fertile Genesee County, liked what they saw, and stayed, ultimately converting upstate New York into an extension of New England.[6] Others, still footloose, headed yet farther west along the southern shores of Lakes Erie and Michigan, and then fanned northward to convert the upper Great Lakes states into a vast Yankee preserve, blanketed with Yankee houses, Yankee towns, and Yankee placenames.[7] Even today, rural landscapes of Michigan and Wisconsin still have a very Yankee look to them, as do the northern parts (but not the southern) of Ohio, Indiana, and Illinois. By the end of the 19th century, this "Yankee Exodus," to use Stewart Holbrook's term, had almost depopulated most of rural New England;[8] by the middle of the 1900s, most of New England had reverted to forest. Indeed, seen today from the window of an airplane, much of rural New England looks like primordial wilderness. Walking in the woods reveals another story, however, as one stumbles through a ghostly rural landscape of tumbled-down stone walls and country cemeteries overgrown with trees and vines (Fig. 5.3). The scenery is picturesque, but the facts are grim. Farming in New England was a thin and dispiriting way to make a living, and most New Englanders eventually stopped trying.

It is hardly surprising that New England was not an attractive place for non-Englishmen, and the region's population remained almost totally British in national origin until well into the 19th century. Only then did a second wave of migrants begin to arrive, chiefly Catholic Irish refugees from the potato famine of the 1840s and, starting in the last third of the 20th century, waves of Italians and Portuguese. Although all of these later migrants originally came from rural places in Europe, when they moved to New England the farmland was gone, and they consequently settled in the only places that jobs were available, cities like Boston, Providence, New Haven, Waterbury, Fall River, and a host of others. By the end of the 19th century, New England had become an overwhelmingly urban place, an archipelago of hundreds of cities and towns, set down in a vast unbroken ocean of second-growth forest.

**Figure 5.3**
Hidden in the second-growth forest that covers most of present-day New England are the ghostly remains of an old agricultural landscape, now long abandoned. Here in southwestern Rhode Island, near Kingston, circa 1967, stone walls and family graveyards are monuments to the farmers who settled this infertile place in the 17th and 18th centuries, but whose descendants have long since departed. Comparable areas in Pennsylvania are still in agriculture.

## The Pennsylvania culture region

But there was another part of the northeastern United States, and it was a very different sort of place from New England. Across the Hudson River to the south and west lay Pennsylvania—or, more accurately, "the Pennsylvania culture region."[9] Like New England and the South, Pennsylvania is seen not as a political state but rather as a multistate region with a distinctive set of cultural traits and has exercised a potent and pervasive influence on the larger national culture, on a par in importance with New England and the South. For just as New England has powerfully flavored the upper Great Lakes region, Pennsylvania's influence spilled westward in a great swath that stretches across much of the nation's midriff (Fig. 5.1).

The character of Pennsylvania was indelibly stamped by the manner of its founding in 1682, when William Penn arrived with a band of English Quakers to create his new colony, and build *de novo* his city of Philadelphia. It was a lucky time to found a new colony, for England's fiercest religious wars were finally drawing to a close, and northwestern Europe was about to embark on the unknown seas of industrial revolution. The spirit of the times was changing, and there were opportunities for political and social experimentation that would have been unthinkable only a few years before.

Penn made good use of these new opportunities, as he set about to prove that one could follow one's religious conscience, tolerate the religious view of others, and prosper economically at the same time. Penn's "Holy Experiment," therefore, started out with very different assumptions than did the early settlers in New England, where religious conformity was the order of the day, and social order was considered a higher virtue than human freedom. Pennsylvania, by contrast, would be a haven of religious diversity, but it would also be a business venture, to make money for Penn and his fellow investors, and for any settlers whom he could persuade to buy land from him.

Like any ambitious real-estate dealer, Penn mounted a large-scale advertising campaign throughout the British Isles and in parts of Protestant Europe, touting Pennsylvania as a tolerant place where settlers would be left alone by church and government—providing only that they paid for their land and obeyed the laws.[10] Thus, from the very beginning, it was a much more tolerant place than New England, and consequently more diverse, although, in fairness, one must note that it was easier for an Englishman to be tolerant in 1682 when Philadelphia was founded, than in 1620 when the Pilgrims landed in Massachusetts. But even in 1682, there were very few places in the world that offered such freedom (certainly not in puritan New England, and not in the slave-owning South either), and to many harassed Europeans, the message of a Peaceable Kingdom on the fertile banks of the Delaware must have seemed achingly attractive. From 1700 onwards, migrants flooded to Pennsylvania through the new port of Philadelphia, soon to become the biggest city in North America and the largest English-speaking city in the world outside England itself. And then, around 1740, for the first time in the American colonies, settlers began arriving from the European continent, speaking languages other than English. Overwhelmingly, these new non-English migrants were German and Swiss pietists from the upper Rhine. By that time, however, the immediate outskirts of Philadelphia had already been occupied by immigrants from England and Wales, so the Germans leapfrogged beyond them to the west, and settled in the rich Piedmont land that stretches from Allentown to Reading to Lancaster to York, a region which today constitutes the heart of the "Pennsylvania Dutch" (*Deutsch*) country. By the time of the American Revolution, those of German immigrant stock came to number more than one third of Pennsylvania's population, and they turned Penn's "Holy Experiment" into the least English of all of Britain's Atlantic colonies. More than was true for any other of those colonies, however, the promise of Pennsylvania was a portent of America's promise—a place where the highest values were freedom, tolerance, and the ability to make money. It was a quite different set of values than motivated the New England puritans; values from a different period in English history applied to a different region of America.

Pennsylvania, in consequence, took on a quite different rôle than New England in the making of American nationhood. Over the long haul, Penn's

Quaker commonwealth contributed enormously to the economic wellbeing of America, but comparatively little to its moral or political life. It is of more than passing significance that New England and New York have produced some of America's most distinguished statesmen, while Pennsylvania, just as wealthy and populous, has more often produced a succession of political hacks.[11] Pennsylvania's great men have typically been captains of industry and leaders of finance, much less often statesmen or preachers.[12]

There were other major differences between Pennsylvania and New England. At the same time that Massachusetts Yankees were struggling to root boulders from their sterile plots, Penn had stumbled across some of the most productive country in eastern North America, a place with rich soils and a genial climate—at least by American standards. A farmer could make an excellent living in Pennsylvania if he took reasonably good care of his land and, as it turned out, the German settlers included some of the best farmers ever to set foot in America. Thus, over the years, while most of rural New England has reverted to forest, the bulk of southeastern Pennsylvania remains farmland—and profitable farmland at that (Fig. 5.4).

That fundamental difference between New England and Pennsylvania survives today in popular imagery. The Pennsylvania farmer is commonly pictured as a jolly, rotund, industrious and not very brainy fellow with a music-hall German accent. His wife is very much like him—apple-cheeked and of ample girth, eternally and cheerfully preparing mountains of highly

**Figure 5.4**
Lancaster County, Pennsylvania, circa 1980. In contrast with New England, most of southeastern Pennsylvania is still farmed—a testimony to rich soils, genial climate, and a long tradition of conservative agricultural husbandry.

calorific food for her numerous apple-cheeked family. By contrast, the New England Yankee farmer is a scrawny, sallow Scrooge-faced fellow, given to laconic aphorisms, who copes with his impossible environment through miserly thrift and native guile. Like many such popular caricatures, these two are wildly exaggerated, but they reveal an important underlying truth: Pennsylvania and New England were—and still remain—very different kinds of places. It is hardly surprising. They were founded on different kinds of land, by different kinds of people, holding different sets of underlying ideas. Inevitably, those people created two very different strains of vernacular landscape.

## The two landscapes of the Northeast: differences in vernacular architecture

The appearance of domestic houses is a case in point. Until well after the Revolution, important public buildings looked much the same in Boston as they did in Philadelphia or Savannah, and so did the houses built by affluent merchants and landowners. Indeed, on both sides of the North Atlantic, power-brokers and tastemakers were all attached to the same British system of ideas and values and, not surprisingly, they often possessed correspondingly similar tastes in food, drink, clothing, and architecture. In particular, high-style buildings tended to look alike, for the simple reason that all were designed by the same English academic architects, or by a small number of American architects who had learned their craft in England.[13]

When regional differences in architecture began to appear, well before the Revolution, they came not in high-style houses but in the vernacular houses of ordinary people. Furthermore, those differences were exaggerated between the Revolution and the Civil War, a time when settlers were moving away from the coast and its Atlantic connections, into the American interior where information traveled slowly and new environments challenged the utility of traditional ways. In the new western territories of the United States during the half century after the Revolution, regional differences had grown sharper than at any other time in American history. And it was during that same time that the greatest differences emerged between the look of the Pennsylvania landscape and that of New England.

Pennsylvanians stuck to the old architectural ways longer than did New Englanders, a fact that suggests a kind of ingrained conservatism in Pennsylvanian domestic life that was not found in New England. As Pennsylvanians moved inland, they took with them the British habits of domestic building which they had contracted along the coast. The streets of inland Pennsylvania towns like Carlisle and Reading and York were lined with red-brick Georgian row-houses, much as in their English namesakes. Even today, southeastern Pennsylvania has an abundance of towns that look more British than any others in America.[14]

New Englanders, however, exhibited much greater independence of mind. Brick row-houses were built in sizeable numbers only in a few large coastal cities, Boston most conspicuously. By the time New Englanders had migrated a few miles inland, however, they had abandoned the use of brick and begun to build in wood. It was not just wood for framing, but exterior wood as well—shingles and clapboards, and a rich variety of wooden embellishments. To colonial Pennsylvanians, to build a wooden house was at best inelegant, at worst an admission of poverty. To New Englanders, it was an opportunity for exuberant experimentation and, by the time of the Revolution, even rich and fashionable people were opting to build their mansions out of wood, even in coastal towns where brick construction had until only recently been the ruling norm.[15]

Why did it happen that way? Differences in environment cannot explain it. Wood was no cheaper nor more abundant in New England than it was in Pennsylvania, and clay for making brick was available almost everywhere. One can only guess that there was some cultural predisposition for New Englanders to experiment, and Pennsylvanians to stick with what was tried and true. The reasons for that, in turn, are less than obvious.

The Yankee inclination to experiment with their common houses shows up in another very striking way. At the same time that New Englanders were shifting their favor from brick to wood, they were beginning to experiment with new locations for their houses. Only a short distance inland from the coast, New Englanders began to abandon the tradition of building urban row-houses, and instead started to build free-standing houses on spacious lots and set the buildings well back from the street. Thus, by the time of the Revolution, their towns had taken on a very different look (compare Figs 5.5 & 6). The Pennsylvanian town still seemed very European, but the New England village had begun to assume an open and rather countrified appearance. On the western frontier, with plenty of wood and plenty of space, it was an obvious way to do things—and the only mystery is why it took Pennsylvanians so long to adopt the idea. Others, however, were not so slow, and from the early 1800s onward, Americans everywhere west of the Appalachians took up this New England model— and house construction has followed this pattern in most of the United States ever since. Row-houses are scarce commodities in most American towns, except as rental units or condominiums—and, of course, in the gentrified "historical districts" of a few old eastern cities. Elsewhere, the American dream house remains a single-family free-standing house, standing independent of all others on a lot of its own, an ornamental landscaped lawn in front, and a less tidy backyard for gardens and children's play. That now familiar arrangement turned out to be one of New England's most successful inventions.

There were other architectural differences as well. Shortly after the Revolution, Classical Revival architecture had begun to make its way into the United States, a style promoted by Thomas Jefferson, who argued that 91 Greco-Roman classical architecture was more fitting in a republican

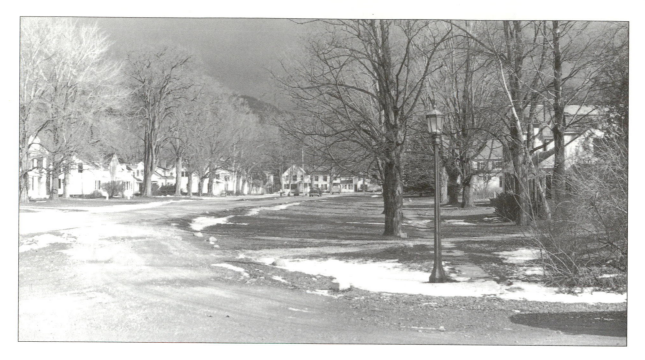

**Figure 5.5**

Village in southwestern Vermont, circa 1975. The countrified landscape of the classic New England village has become the apotheosis for suburban America: single-family houses, separated from each other, and set back from the street, with large front lawns under a canopy of shady trees. Note the extensive use of wooden construction, as reflected in the white clapboard exteriors of buildings, a sharp contrast with red-brick Pennsylvania.

**Figure 5.6**
Elfreth's Alley, Philadelphia, a well-preserved remnant of 18th century Philadelphia, is a standard bit of British urban morphology. Such brick row-houses continued to be built in Pennsylvania cities and villages until the mid-19th century, long after New Englanders had abandoned the idea.

**Figure 5.7**
Roman and Greek placenames were strewn across upstate New York in the early 19th century, as literate New Englanders migrated westward and stamped the land with names that symbolized the political ideals of classical republican democracy, and rejection of British monarchy.

democracy than traditional Georgian styles, which symbolized, after all, the most detested of British monarchs. From 1790 onward, indeed until the middle of the 19th century, important public buildings throughout the United States came increasingly to be modeled after the Parthenon or the Roman Forum.[16]

It was quite another thing, however, to incorporate classical ideas into ordinary domestic life, and the traditionally minded Pennsylvanians would have little to do with the notion. Classical architecture might serve for court houses or solemn academies, but not for houses. New Englanders, on the other hand, adopted domestic classicism with unfettered enthusiasm. From 1800 to the time of the Civil War, as they streamed westward across New York State into the upper Midwest, they gave their newly founded towns fine classical names like Athens and Sparta and Cincinnatus and Sempronius,[17] and strewed those towns with houses that were made to look as much as possible like Greek temples (Figs. 5.7, 8, & 9). Many of those imitation Parthenons are fairly crude, but they stand as exuberant testimony to the New Englander's habitual willingness to experiment with new ideas. Nor were those ideas restricted to architecture, for they flowed over into technology, politics, and even religion. In upstate New York in the early 19th century, religious revivals occurred with such frequency and immense ferocity that the very Earth seemed scorched, a district "burned-over" by the intensity of religious enthusiasm.[18] Today, classical names and classical architecture serve as hints of a wider world—tangible records of an innovative people at an innovative time. It is significant that such names and such styles are almost totally absent in the areas settled by the more sedate Pennsylvanians.[19]

**Figure 5.8**
American classical, upstate New York. Cincinnatus (pop. 600 in 1980), is 15 miles from Marathon and 30 miles from Syracuse, Rome, Utica, Ithaca, and Homer. Similar placenames occur elsewhere in the United States, but nowhere are they as frequent and as enthusiastic as in this western outpost of Yankee New England.

**Figure 5.9**
Vernacular Doric, Chautauqua County, extreme western New York. The Yankee migration corridor from western New England to southern Minnesota is thickly strewn with houses like these—some grander, some simpler, but all strongly evocative of classical ideas, and testimony to a literate self-conscious population, well connected to a larger world of ideas.

## *Barns and other rural matters*

Rural landscapes in the Northeast had also begun to take on a characteristic look. From the very beginning, American farmers everywhere had rejected the common European practice of living in rural villages, a geographical arrangement which required farmers to walk from town to field in the morning and then walk back at night. That arrangement was found on many southern plantations, of course, and in a few utopian communities in the North, but elsewhere American farmsteads were dispersed across the countryside. As a result, there came to be a sharp split between farmers and townspeople which persists in America even to the present day.

But again, significant differences had begun to develop between Pennsylvania and New England. And the design of barns is perhaps the most conspicuous sign of this divergence. Although English tradition had offered architectural guidance for domestic housing, English barns were too small to be of much use in the New World. In North America, big farms produced big harvests, and cold winters required shelter for livestock. In parts of northern New England, chiefly Maine, farmers solved the problem in a clumsy but picturesque manner by hitching a multitude of small buildings together to form "connecting barns."[20] Pennsylvanians, by contrast, shunned the British models, and imported a design that had been commonly used in the upper Rhine Valley and in northern Switzerland. This so-called "Schweitzer barn" was a capacious three-level building (animals on the ground level, threshing floor above, and hayloft above that), with a distinctive cantilevered overhang called a "forebay."[21] But its greatest utility was its size (Fig. 5.10). As harvests grew bigger, the barns did too, and even before the end of the 18th century, affluent farmers were building colossal elegant barns that often seemed more like cathedrals than agricultural outbuildings. Even today, Pennsylvania farmers are proud of those great majestic barns that still symbolize the plenty of the Pennsylvania land, the earthly rewards of hard work and a virtuous bucolic life. But it was

**Figure 5.10**
Pennsylvania barn, with its distinctive cantilevered "forebay," near Altoona, circa 1970. The ground level is for stabling livestock; the second level, entered at grade via an inclined "bank" on the uphill side, contains a threshing floor; and the upper lofts are for storing hay. Barns like these are the single most diagnostic feature of Pennsylvania German rural culture.

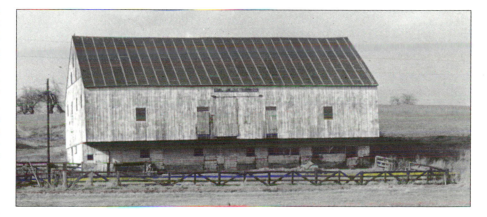

also a good workable design for prosperous farm country, based on the need to accommodate a mixture of crops and livestock. So when Americans crossed the Appalachians and needed new barns in the rich farmlands of the Midwest, it was the gigantic Pennsylvania model they imitated, although, with typical disdain for frills, they left the forebay behind.[22] The more modest English barns of New England were seldom imitated.

## Urban forms

It was in cities, however, where the American landscape began to deviate most extremely from old European forms. The most radical departure of all was in Pennsylvania, where Penn laid out the city of Philadelphia in advance of settlement, using a grid plan that called for wide streets laid out at right angles to each other—north-south streets given numbers, east–west streets named after trees (Fig. 5.11). The grid plan itself was nothing new; it had been used across the world since time immemorial—in ancient China,

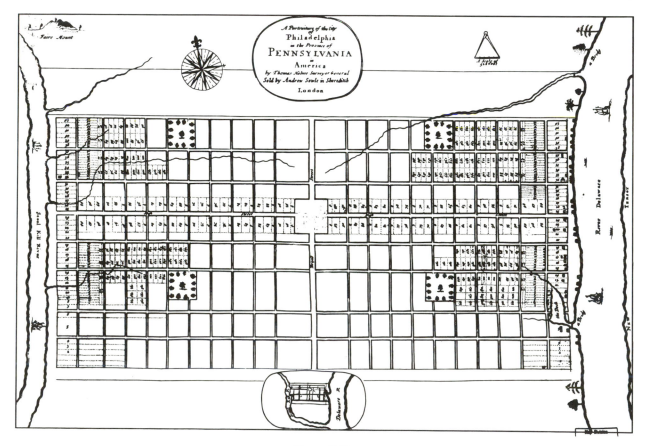

**Figure 5.11**
Plan of Philadelphia, 1682. Penn of course did not invent the grid plan, but Philadelphia's success was largely responsible for the later adoption of the grid by town planners all over the United States.

throughout the Roman Empire, and throughout Spanish America—to name but a few places. But it was Penn who introduced the idea in British America, and once implemented, the system spread across the Appalachians all over the United States. From Ohio, everywhere westward, it is the rare town where streets do not cross each other at right-angles, and any newcomer can seek out the intersection of Fourth Avenue and Maple Street in the certain knowledge that it will be there—although in many towns (including the nation's capital), even tree names seemed unduly indiosyn-cratic, and cross-streets were designated anonymously by letters of the alphabet: "A" Avenue, "B" Avenue, and so on. Whatever the names or numbers, a walk "around the block" in Columbus, Ohio, is not substantially different in length or shape from one in Oklahoma City or Sacramento.

There has been endless speculation about the reasons why Penn's Philadelphia grid plan was so enthusiastically adopted by people who were laying out towns for the new American republic. Some have suggested that Americans liked the plan because it was democratic, but that idea does not stand up under scrutiny—despite the practice of designating streets by names and numbers instead of naming them after military heroes. There was nothing in the plan to prevent rich people from buying up big blocks of land, nor were those blocks democratically uniform in slope or drainage. (More than a few unwary buyers were sold city blocks that turned out to be swampland, or even worse, located completely under water in the middle of a river or bay.) But the grid plan had several important virtues in an expanding entrepreneurial republic. Most important, perhaps, it was flexible, with plenty of room for variety within and between the presumably anonymous blocks.[23] There was plenty of room for planning, and it was not uncommon for those plans to go awry. Penn himself had expected that his big Philadelphia blocks would permit farmers to live in town and plant large gardens around capacious houses, each block a kind of mini-farm which would in combination produce a park-like "greene towne." But land in Philadelphia soon became too valuable to fritter away on mere gardens, and land speculators divided the rectangles into narrow slices, and sold them to other speculators who promptly chopped down the trees to make room for row-houses. And in Washington, D. C., when Major L'Enfant planned the street pattern for the new capital city (a grid overlain by circles and spokes), he had expected the central business district to grow eastward toward the Anacostia River. Thus, the national Capitol was built with its formal face in that direction. In fact, things turned out exactly the opposite. The Anacostia bottoms became a noisome industrial slum, while commercial and ceremo-nial Washington expanded toward the Potomac and Georgetown to the west. One curious result of L'Enfant's mistake is that for two centuries presidential inaugurations have taken place on the "wrong" side of the building. No matter. If mistakes were made, the grid would accommodate them.

Most alluring of all, perhaps, the grid made it very easy to lay out new

towns in advance of settlement, and that was a huge virtue in a booming country where population was pressing rapidly into new and townless territories. The grid also made it easy to describe rectangular parcels of land on a map, so that speculators could buy and sell those parcels sight unseen. At the same time, its mathematical regularity greatly reduced the room for surveyors' errors and consequent legal disputes over the location of boundaries. All in all, the urban grid plan was a perfect godsend for real estate speculators, not only in Philadelphia, but in all of the American towns, real and imaginary, that were strewn across the land to become new Philadelphias.

The grid was occasionally tried out in New England cities, but the effort was half-hearted. The core of New Haven, Connecticut, for example, was laid out in a grid, but New Haven is an exception. Most New England cities grew in the old-fashioned European way, with main streets following old paths, and new streets and alleys added in haphazard bits and pieces as the need arose. The street plan of Boston is typical—a tangled skein of crooked streets that looks more European than American (Fig. 5.12). And, when those crooked streets are lined with red-brick Georgian row-houses, as on Beacon Hill in Boston, the effect is very British indeed (Fig. 5.13).

Despite the unplanned street pattern of many New England cities and villages, the geographical arrangement of *towns* was very much a planned affair—and that planning reflects the way that Yankees thought about themselves and about their communities. The New England town was conceived not as a geographical thing, as most Americans think of towns, but as a religious and civic community of people. When set down in a particular geographical place, a town's natural territory turned out to be a bounded chunk of land that was large enough to support a church and its congregation, but small enough to permit all its inhabitants to attend services at the same church on a regular basis.[24]

The geographical result was predictable. New England was divided into a mosaic of politically bounded "towns," 40 or 50 square miles in area.[25] Near the center was a church, spaced 5 to 10 miles from its nearest neighbor. More often than not, villages grew up around the church, first by the building of a tavern or general store, and subsequently other commercial buildings and, usually, a town(ship) hall.[26]

The New England village center was not designed as a marketplace, although commerce usually tended to accumulate there. Visually, its most conspicuous feature was its open "green" of common land, fringed by a church or two, a town hall, and perhaps a grange or fraternal building— mostly demurely classical in design and, of course, painted white. This assemblage of white buildings around a village green has become a powerful image for many Americans, the quintessence of Yankee New England, the visual symbol of small-town simplicity and virtue.[27] One can debate whether that is true or not, but the New England village was clearly a very different sort of thing than the version that developed in Pennsylvania, where the center of town was a busy intersection or market square, suitably laid out at right-angles, with shops crowding to be near the center. Today, many

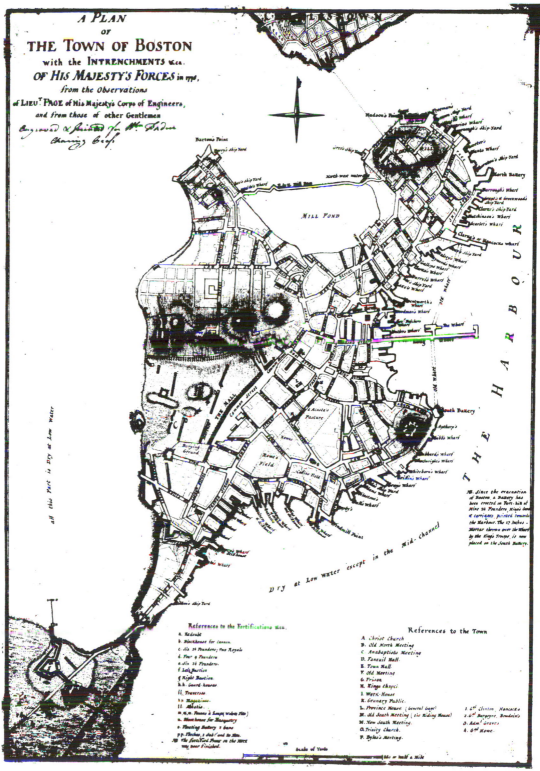

**Figure 5.12**

Street map of Boston, 1776. The streets of New England cities and villages were laid out *ad hoc*, as they had been laid out for millennia in the Old World. To Americans, accustomed to grid plans that imitated Philadelphia, Boston still looks rather foreign.

**Figure 5.13**
Early 19th-century
row-houses, Boston, circa
1975. America's political
revolution may have begun
in Boston, but there is
nothing revolutionary about
the architectural ideas behind
this staid English Georgian
street scene on Beacon Hill.
Only a short distance inland,
however, New Englanders
began building very different
kinds of town.

Americans view New England villages through a haze of nostalgic imagery, and see them as quaint vestiges of a bygone age. In one respect, they are quite correct. West of the Appalachians, when westward-moving Americans got down to the serious business of creating towns, there was no room for greens and churches in the middle of town. In most parts of the American West, the Pennsylvania model held sway. As in Pennsylvania, the business of an American town was business—only incidentally the creation of social community.

It is ironic today that the tight-packed Pennsylvania model of the American town, originally thought to be so practical and businesslike, has been routinely and unsentimentally abandoned by the practical business-men for whom it was designed. It worked very well as a commercial center during the 19th century, when people and goods were delivered to town at a central railroad station, and proximity to the station was a requisite for prosperity. But that was before the advent of the automobile. Ironically, it was commercial success that was the undoing of that businesslike town. Commerce causes traffic jams, anathema to red-blooded American motorists. To avoid that congestion in the early part of the 20th century, bypasses were built around town centers, and the traffic that supported downtown prosperity was siphoned off elsewhere. More recently, when suburban shopping centers were built to suit the convenience of motorists, Pennsylvania-model downtown commercial districts began to decay all over the country.[28] It is an additional irony that a good many New England villages, so long believed to be quaintly obsolete, have recently discovered that quaintness is a marketable commodity. In picturesque village after picturesque village along the northern fringes of megalopolis, prosperity has arrived, brought first by tourists, then by affluent refugees from urban congestion—stockbrokers and 3-day-a-week corporate executives—who were hotly pursued by purveyors of expensive real estate, expensive foreign automobiles, and exotic up-scale groceries. In sum, both the Pennsylvania town and the New England village have, to put it kindly, taken on new functions, while at the same time they have abandoned the original purposes for which they were so carefully designed. It is doubtful whether New England puritans had boutiques and stockbrokers in mind for their shining cities upon a hill! And it is equally doubtful that William Penn would have predicted the decline in the commercial fortunes of his "greene towne."

## The cultural–geographical baggage goes west

So it was that when Americans crossed the Appalachians into the interior of the continent, they carried two geographical traditions with them—and borrowed from both in highly selective ways. The New England tradition and the Pennsylvania tradition, however, were geographically separated from each other, not only along the eastern seaboard, but west of the mountains as well. The reason had to do with topography and transportation routes, for Pennsylvanians went west by a very different set of routes than did the New Englanders, and those routes led respectively in quite different directions. New England's avenue to the West was a narrow lowland that followed the Mohawk River between the mountain bulwarks of the Adirondacks and the Catskills and led to the great open plains along the shores of the lower Great Lakes—thence, as we have seen, into the northern part of the old Northwest Territory: northern Ohio, Indiana, Illinois, and the better parts of southern Michigan, and Wisconsin. Pennsylvanians, by contrast, had a wider range of choices. They could head west, by way of what became the National Road, via Wheeling, Columbus, Indianapolis, and on to Saint Louis. Alternatively, they could move down the Ohio River

**Figure 5.14**

In residential areas all over the United States houses are set on lots apart from one another and back from the street, following a New England practice three centuries old. Grundy Center, Iowa in 1940, was typical of thousands of American towns. When given a choice, trans-Appalachian Americans have overwhelmingly rejected the tight-packed row-house tradition that dominates many east coast cities.

from Pittsburgh, toward the Kentucky Bluegrass and the middle Mississippi Valley. Or they could avoid the mountains altogether, and drift southwestward down the Shenandoah Valley into western Virginia, North Carolina, and the whole upland South. The New England stream, in short, was narrow and confined until it reached the lower Lakes. The Pennsylvania stream spread out in a great fan that eventually covered much of the interior. But both streams retained a kind of cultural purity as they poured westward—and they remained separate for a considerable distance west of the mountains. Any traveler today can drive on little back roads across the state of Ohio, north from the Ohio River to Lake Erie, and see the Pennsylvanian landscape of the south abruptly change to the landscape of New England in the north. The marks of that old migration stream are still there.

But the migrants were selective about the geographical ideas they carried with them, and the ordinary landscapes of middle America include elements from both New England and Pennsylvania, both in turn much altered from ancient English models. The mixture is eclectic. The interchangeable American grid-pattern town is pure Pennsylvania, of course, and one can argue that the widespread use of the Philadelphia city plan paved the way for acceptance of Jefferson's idea of a gridded land division system for the rural lands of the whole Northwest Territory. But even that system is a combination of the two regional traditions. The basic unit of land division is a square township, 6 miles on a side, and rigidly oriented to the cardinal directions of the compass. The rectangular geometry springs from Jeffersonian rationalism, but the 6-mile dimensions are those of the ancestral New

102

England town. Towns, too, are mixtures. The middle of midwestern and western towns was consigned to business, and that was the Pennsylvania way of doing things. But the residential areas, with their widely spaced houses, big yards, and tree-shaded streets are quintessentially New England (Fig. 5.14). Farmsteads are a mix: houses are wood, as in New England, while the enormous barns are inspired by models in Pennsylvania.

Large parts of this old landscape seem obsolete today, overlaid by new technologies, new people, and new canons of taste.[29] But despite all efforts, old patterns which were etched into the landscape are not easily erased, even though Americans have a seemingly infinite capacity to redesign and find new uses for things that have apparently outlived their usefulness—the New England village being an obvious case in point. Meantime, a huge part of the United States continues to bear the imprint of geographical ideas that were imported from England three centuries and more ago, and subsequently reworked by colonial Americans in a small corner of the Northeast. That imprint is still visible today, and its patterns continue to shape our lives.

103

# Chapter six
# Plantations and the molding of the Southern landscape

## SAM B. HILLIARD

Perhaps no other image more aptly conveys the popular perception of the American South than does the plantation and, for most, that image has been created by the manifold evocations of plantation life in American literature, art, and, in our own century, film. The image is at once narrow and correct: the antebellum plantation so often portrayed as a part of the southern mystique did in fact exist, but rarely did the romanticism and allure—so readily attached to the lives of those for whom the plantation was home—become real. The plantation was far more complex than the popular image of it frequently allows; the image itself is entrenched in stereotypes that apply to but a fraction of plantations and then only in a brief period of their existence. Such preoccupation with this plantation image also obscures the fact that plantations were found throughout the tropics and subtropics, especially in the New World, and many still exist as landholdings with a specialized agricultural function.

What, then, was and remains of this powerful vision of southern life? The answer, naturally, is subjective, but perhaps not a small part of it lies in the fact that the antebellum southern plantation encapsulated two of the most potent forces in the South—the tremendous agricultural system that was that region's lifeblood, and the most disturbing element of southern life, the institution of slavery. Thus it represented an eminently successful and profitable system of agriculture, but at the cost of national and world alienation and condemnation. There is in the plantation, then, a symbolism at once fascinating, unsettling, and, above all else, powerful in the American mind. In seeking to understand the image as well as the historical reality of the southern plantation, we need to set them in the context of the regional, national, and New World development. The South expanded as Anglo-American settlement filtered southward and westward from its Atlantic tidewater hearths, seeding the plantation system in practically every hospitable locality in turn. Nowhere was it the only agricultural type, and in much of the South it was absent, but it was widespread enough to cause many to identify it with the region.

The plantation was not, however, a novel institution, for plantations had existed since the dawn of the Age of Exploration—and possibly earlier. In time, they became plentiful in Asia and Africa, but especially in the tropical zones of the Western Hemisphere. Their purpose was singular: to make a profit for plantation owners or investors through the large-scale cultivation of agricultural products. Profit reigned supreme; the human needs of the system clearly begged consideration yet merited far less attention than that lavished on the plantation ledger books. This plantation form was but an element of the larger scheme of mercantilism, and in most instances the owners and workers of plantations around the world were separated not merely by class but by race and culture. So fundamental was it to the settlement geography of the New World that one could describe the plantation system as the instrument that enabled mid-latitude peoples to exploit the agricultural potential of the tropics and subtropics. Thus, when English investors arrived on the shores of South Carolina and Virginia, the rule of profit was known and accepted.

Although plantations were among the first institutional forms to come to the New World, our understanding of them is not as clear as we might hope. But here we must distinguish between the word *plantation* and the agricultural system that has become known as *the plantation*. The word has been used for centuries within Britain to denote "something planted," be it crops or colonies, such as Providence or Bermuda plantations. Often it was used simply to describe a field that had been "planted," usage that survives today in forestry where commonly one finds reference to a "plantation" of trees. On the other hand, the origin of the landholding called "a plantation" is a bit more nebulous. Large landholdings were common in tidewater Virginia, but descriptions of their crop diversity reveal them to be more closely akin to the English estate than to the tropical plantation.[1] The word *plantation* also was used in early Virginia, but it appears first to have referred to settlements rather than landholdings. In time, of course, the two merged, and today we correctly describe tidewater Virginia as being one of the southern plantation regions.

It is at least arguable that a more likely source for the institution lies farther south. The earliest landholdings in the New World that resemble the plantation were along the northeastern coast of Brazil and in Barbados, based on sugar cane. From that core the institution spread to other Gulf–Caribbean islands and eventually on to the continent, probably at Charlestown, and in time became relatively common where southern cash crops could easily be grown.

From these early nodes of settlement, the plantation spread throughout the South, altering not only the territory into which it was introduced, but also undergoing alteration itself as adaptions to the various regions of the South demanded (Fig. 6.1). The very definition of a plantation would undergo profound change, so much so that by the late eighteenth century James Madison could write without hesitation that his 3,000 acres at Montpelier, Virginia, was but a "farm," while many a lesser holding around

him clearly preferred the more prestigious designation of "plantation."[2] For

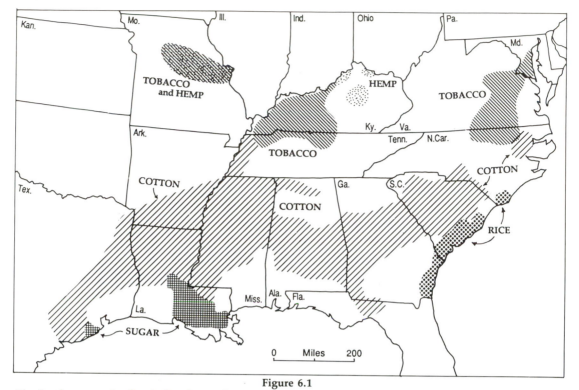

**Figure 6.1**
The Southern mosaic of agricultural specialization as it had evolved by the Civil War. Later, rice culture would disappear from the Atlantic coast and wax important in Louisiana and the Gulf Coast, and the domain of "king cotton" would ultimately shrink and move westward, centered on the lower Mississippi Valley.

American purposes, the definition did acquire some precision, and here the term plantation will refer to an agricultural enterprise composed of six basic elements: a landholding large enough to be distinguished from the family farm, generally over 250 acres; a distinct division of labor and management, with the latter primarily handled by the owner but often administered through an overseer; specialized production (monoculture), usually with one or two cash crops per proprietorship; location in the South in an area with a plantation tradition; distinctive settlement forms and spatial organization reflecting the centralized control; and, finally, a considerable input of cultivating labor or power per unit of area.[3]

Plantations, then, differed from farms in that the latter were generally worked for subsistence, hence they harvested more diverse crops, had less capital investment, and, in the antebellum South, few if any slaves. Plantations, conversely, were operated for profit, relying primarily on a single crop that was sold to be used outside the region, were more highly capitalized, and employed a large unskilled laborforce, which prior to the Civil War meant slave labor. In addition, farms were generally operated for and by their owners, typically sustained as a family venture. On plantations there existed a sharp distinction between owner, who was sometimes both operator and overseer, and the laborforce. If the owner lived on the plantation, he frequently hired one or more overseers to handle the practical

106

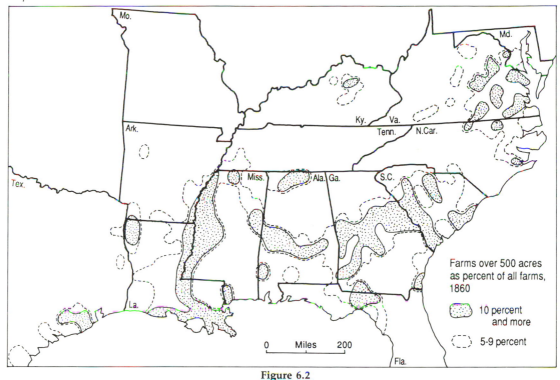

**Figure 6.2**
Large agricultural holdings on the eve of the Civil War occurred in areas of intense cotton production, mostly in the Deep South, but also in the tobacco districts of Virginia, the Carolina rice coast, and the Mississippi sugar delta.

operations of the plantation; if the owner were an absentee investor, the overseer himself assumed this head position. Either way, the laborforce was directed toward one end: the planting, cultivation, and harvesting of the cash crop. Finally, plantation crops often required some sort of processing prior to marketing, necessitating the presence of some semi-industrial functions on the plantation itself.[4]

Both farms and plantations were integral parts of the southern landscape and economy, oftentimes occupying the same areas. In many cases, farms evolved into plantations or were absorbed by them (Fig. 6.2). In many parts no plantations existed at all because the region would not support such an institution. Key factors which determined whether or not a plantation was feasible in a given area included the availability of large fertile land tracts and access to transportation routes, which early on generally meant a location near a waterway. Clearly, the mountainous Appalachians were not suitable for plantation agricultural systems.

## Antebellum plantations

In the small settlement of Jamestown, which hugged the edge of the vast North American continent in 1612, the Englishman John Rolfe assured not only the continuance of the Virginia colony, but established the commodity on which the Virginia plantation would be based. That year, Rolfe discovered the potential of what William Byrd of Westover aptly called, "that bewitching vegetable."[5] It was, of course, tobacco. Rolfe, like many Englishmen of the time, enjoyed the tobacco acquired from Spanish colonies. But because Rolfe, and his fellow nationals, disliked paying the Catholic King Philip III and his merchants for the importation of the "leaf" to England and, more importantly, because he saw that the native Americans in Virginia cultivated the indigenous *Nicotiana rustica*, Rolfe recognized the potential the Virginia settlement had for turning a profit to its investors from tobacco, a profit sorely needed. Because the indigenous variety of tobacco was considered "poore and weake, and of byting tast [sic]," to Englishmen accustomed to the Spanish variety, Rolfe planted West Indian (that is, Spanish) seeds, *Nicotiana tabacum*, starting a production that would create the wealth which supported not only the investors in England but the expansion of Virginia and the colonies to come.[6]

The early landholdings of Virginia were a far cry from the monocultural commercial plantations of the mid-19th century, for they produced a variety of food and feed crops. Indeed, to prevent another "starving time" of the likes Jamestown had experienced during the winter of 1609–10, the Virginia Company ordered that no man could raise tobacco unless he also maintained at least 2 acres of corn. By the end of 1616, in fact, only 2,300 lbs. of tobacco had been sent to England, as opposed to 50,000 lbs. of Spanish tobacco.[7] Soon afterwards, however, yields and shipments to England increased greatly, up to 20,000 lbs. in 1618, and in the following year Virginian tobacco surpassed Spanish in English imports. The large increase in production was credited to better curing methods. Previously the weed had been dried in piles, but drying on racks greatly improved the product. Although early English policy tried to discourage or limit the production of the "noxious weed" in Virginia, yearly exports reached the half-million lb. mark by 1630 and a million and a half by the following decade. After the English Revolution of 1688 the policy changed, and by 1700 there was no thought of doing away with the tobacco industry, which had spread into present-day North Carolina and Maryland as well as Virginia. The simple fact that tobacco could be grown well and sold profitably in the region of the Chesapeake Bay was the single greatest factor in the development of the southern economic, political, and social life. It alone assured that the Virginia colony, and the South itself, would survive and prosper.

## Tobacco landscapes

Tobacco growing became the primary cause of the spread of people. Its needs dictated the layout of farms, the economic interests of the growers, and, by extension, their political interests. It created the landscape pattern that was permanently to imprint the southern colonies and states and sustained the system of slavery that would mark the area for two centuries. Two types of tobacco were grown in the Chesapeake Bay region. In the area of Maryland, the Sweet Scented variety predominated. In Virginia's James and York Rivers regions, the preferred Oronoko variety was cultivated. To start a crop, seeds were sown in beds and after a May shower they were transplanted to hills set approximately 4 feet apart in the cleared fields. The tobacco had to be carefully and consistently weeded and the top of the plant was cut, with 9 to 16 leaves remaining, depending on the richness of the soil. In August, the ripe plants were cut and hung on pegs in a ventilated tobacco house to cure for five or six weeks. The leaves were then cut from the plant, tied into bundles, and prized into hogsheads.[8]

The early tobacco planters grew but a few acres of tobacco at most, since all tasks were done by hand and with limited labor available, there was little choice. Other crops had to be grown to support the colony and tobacco, as 17th-century planters stated, "wore out the soil." Typically, tobacco plots were cropped for a few years and then new ground was cleared and used. Despite such difficulties, by 1700 tobacco growing dominated the area between southern Pennsylvania and Albemarle Sound in the tidewater region, producing virtually all the tobacco grown in the British dominions. Most of the planters relied on their own labor or that of indentured servants. The latter, however, eventually worked off their terms before being released to acquire plots of their own.

Before tobacco could be grown on a larger scale, a more permanent laboring class was needed. African laborers began arriving in Jamestown by 1620, but in small numbers and generally as indentured servants. Their numbers increased until, by 1700, those entering Virginia were imported as slaves, primarily to serve as laborers on tobacco holdings. By 1790 there were 660,000 southern slaves.[9] After 1790, a rapid increase in population as well as an expansion of available land swept southern culture westward and with it the institutions of slavery and the plantation. By the time of the Civil War, over half of the 4 million slaves were owned by planters who had 20 or more slaves and one-fourth by planters who owned 10 to 20 slaves. Well over three quarters of the southern white population owned no slaves at all. Such statistics serve to place the plantation system in perspective. Although the widely recognized symbol of southern life, the plantation was by no means the only landholding type. It existed, cheek by jowl, with all sizes and types of farm.

From the original tobacco sites along the James River in Virginia, tobacco cultivation spread north, west, and south. By the end of the 17th century, its commercial production had spread to the lowlands on the Potomac and Rappahannock Rivers as well as along Albemarle Sound, which was to become part of the state of North Carolina. As settlers moved into the Piedmont in the early 18th century, they carried tobacco with them. As tobacco growth expanded into the interior, access to transport became a crucial factor. The early plantations were located on rivers, such as the

James, from which they could ship directly to England, but as growers colonized the interfluves and later the Piedmont, riverine locations became scarce, thus adding to the cost of production. By 1700 such direct trading had become more difficult and by the end of the colonial period over three-fourths of the tobacco grown in the Bay region was sold first in the colonies, then transshipped to England.[10] Between 1800 and 1860, tobacco culture had spread into all but the remotest parts of Virginia, Maryland, and North Carolina.[11] Because tobacco required constant and diligent care—most hands could cultivate no more than two acres each,[12]—it was often grown with other crops, especially grains. Corn and wheat were most common, with the latter rivaling tobacco as the primary staple.

The typical Virginia district plantation ranged in size from 150–250 acres, with many near the coast being much larger.[13] These were the backbone of the southern plantation system, although they fit poorly with the image created of the antebellum plantation. In fact, one might debate whether many were plantations at all, considering the criteria usually applied, the major point of contention being the diversity of crops and livestock products. Most grew and marketed a variety of crops and livestock products, a trait that placed them closer to the medieval manor than to the commercial sugar plantations of Louisiana.[14]

Prior to 1700 it is doubtful that any Virginia planters could afford to construct the type of manor house that can be found even on moderate sized holdings in the century to follow. The colonial mansion so characteristic of Virginia plantations did not develop fully until the 18th and 19th centuries. Many of the early and later homes, however, had broad entranceways, essentially open halls, which were to facilitate the circulation of air through the house.[15] The wealthier planters' homes, of course, were the reflection of the better plantations. These manor homes were truly spectacles to behold in a land so newly settled (Fig. 6.3). They were filled with imported furniture, many contained imported carpets, Russian leather chairs, Turkish couches, leather, and brass trunks. Porcelain dishes, silver and pewter cutlery, tin and silver plates, and fine musical instruments were not unusual in these homes, attesting to the profits to be had if one could afford the investment a plantation involved.[16]

Beyond the manor house, the Virginia plantation comprised many outbuildings, typically including a cellar, a dairy, dovecote, stable barn, henhouse, kitchen, slave cabins, sometimes a schoolhouse for the planters' children with a room for the tutor above it, and smaller homes for white workers, such as the overseer. There was also a garden to provide fruit and vegetables; water came from springs or wells. Many pigs, sheep, cattle, and horses also populated the plantation. The manor house, however, occupied the most prestigious position, frequently overlooking the land from a hill, or the waterway by which products left and entered the plantation. The slave quarters, typically wooden cabins, were generally aligned on two sides of a single street some distance from the manor house and the outbuildings were

arranged in a collection of buildings not far from the main house, especially

**Figure 6.3**
Carter's Grove, a few miles southeast of Williamsburg, Virginia. Built in 1751 in the Georgian colonial style, it is one of the grandest of the Virginia manor houses, founded on tobacco wealth. Flanked by symmetrical "dependencies" (wings), the main structure looks out over terraced lawns to the James River. The pitch of the roof and dormers of the main building were added during a 1927 "restoration."

**Figure 6.4**
Restored slave quarters on Greenwood plantation in St. James Parish, Louisiana. Extant slave quarters are more common in the sugar-producing areas than in cotton areas because cotton sharecropping encouraged their removal from their original central location to be near the cropper's plot.

the kitchen, which had to be accessible in foul weather (Fig. 6.4). The one facility somewhat removed from the main buildings was the cemetery of the planter's family, which was often placed in a secluded part of the plantation, a landscape relic that survives in many parts of the South today.

## Rice landscapes

In the lower South tobacco did not become the staple crop of planters, resulting in settlement features that differed markedly from those of the tobacco region. Following close on the heels of the Maryland/Virginia/North Carolina tidewater development, South Carolina began carving its niche in the agricultural system of the region.[17] While Virginia virtually monopolized the tobacco trade, and the West Indies early on captured the sugar trade, the coastal regions of South Carolina and Georgia discovered equally impressive profits could be had from the production of rice and indigo. Although a major cash crop for a time, the removal of the crown subsidy effectively eliminated indigo as a cash crop in South Carolina, leaving rice as a staple of the region during the antebellum period.[18] In no other agricultural region of the South was the staple crop as intensely and singularly produced or as ingeniously accommodated to the natural environment as was rice in the Georgia–Carolina rice coast.[19]

Legend has it that the first rice seeds that were to become the famed Carolina Gold rice arrived in the Carolina province around 1685 from Madagascar, when a brigantine carrying the seeds pulled into the port of Charles Town in distress.[20] While the ship was being repaired, the captain gave some of the seed to the Carolinian Dr. Henry Woodward, which he planted, and presumably this was the source of all future rice in the region, which spread both north and south of Charleston.[21] Whatever its origin, rice soon became the premier cash crop along the South Atlantic coast, and throughout the antebellum period, the region produced approximately 90 percent of the nation's crop. Virtually all rice plantations were located on river floodplains to facilitate irrigation. The principal rivers along which rice was planted were the Waccamaw, the PeeDee, the Santee, the Cooper, the Edisto, and the Combahee. Large rice plantations also flourished along the Savannah River, which serves as the border between South Carolina and Georgia. In Georgia, the Ogeechee, the Altamaha, and the Satilla Rivers supported rice plantations as well.[22] The core of the rice growing region, however, lay on the coast between Georgetown, South Carolina, and Savannah, Georgia, with South Carolina dominating; Georgetown County alone accounted for over 40 percent of the nation's production.[23]

There were two periods of rice growing in the Georgia–Carolina coastal region, each marked by a different method of cultivation. The first period extends roughly from the 1680s to the mid-1700s, during which rice was grown primarily in the inland swamps. These inland swamp fields were a phase between the earliest rice growing, which was probably accomplished in unirrigated plots, and the later tidewater plantation systems which came to the fore in the late colonial period. Inland swamp cultivation involved clearing small rice fields in the floodplains of small streams, constructing two dams, one upstream from the cleared field to impound water and another at the seaward margin of the cleared field to permit field flooding. Both dams were equipped with one or more sluice gates, known as trunks, which controlled the entrance and exit of water to the field. Irrigation depended upon the water impounded by the upstream dam.[24]

The vagaries of this situation became more pronounced as settlers in the Carolina–Georgia region in general began to push beyond the coastal region, many planting crops that increased the surface water runoff with disastrous effects downstream for the inland rice planters. Such hazards contributed to a gradual shift to the second phase of rice planting in the region, that of tidewater rice plantations. Tidewater planting required precise conditions to be effective, thus the area available for rice culture was limited. Tidewater planting differed from inland swamp rice production in that it used fresh water directly from the rivers rather than water reservoirs, depending upon tidal power to lift the level of the streams high enough for their fresh water to be diverted on to the fields. Of extreme importance was the fact that salt water, being denser than fresh, formed a salt–water wedge under the fresh water flow. The size and shape of the streams affected the degree of salt-fresh water mixing and hence the saline content of the water used to flood the rice fields. Only those areas where the river provided a distinct layer of fresh water, without mixing with salt water, were acceptable for rice growing.[25] Thus, in order to flood a rice field, the planter opened the trunk to allow successive tides to fill the field to the desired level, and to drain the field the reverse procedure was used.

The means used to clear land for rice planting were slow and arduous, requiring some knowledge of engineering in addition to planting skills. Thus the advantage lay with the planter who had a large laborforce, and slavery served these plantations as well as those in northern Virginia. Operating a rice plantation made equally strong demands on the planter. During the fall and winter the ground was "broken." In the spring the seeds were planted and throughout the growing season the fields were alternately flooded and drained. Harvesting was done by hand with a sickle in September, after which the rice was carted to mills, usually in boats or "flats," where it was threshed and milled.[26]

Rice was the dominant cash crop in the area, enabling a plantation system to develop akin to that in the Chesapeake region. Given the heavy capital investment in dikes, dams, sluices, and rice mills and the considerable personal expertise required, it behooved the planter to concentrate his efforts on producing one staple. Simply put, it was the success of the perhaps 50 percent of the planters who did engage in rice production that accounted for the tremendous rice culture which developed in this region. *113* Among the rice planters were farmers of grains and cotton and many who

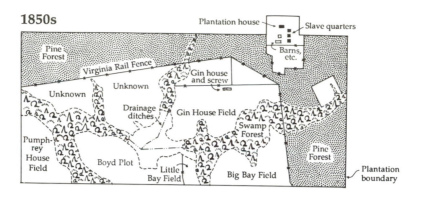

**1850s**

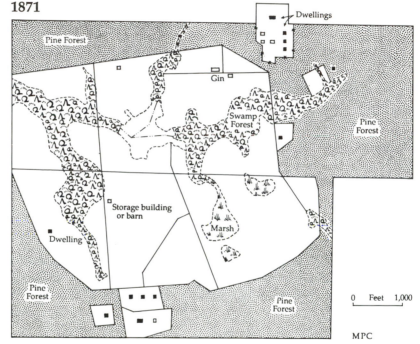

**1871**

**Figure 6.5**
The layout of a typical Georgia plantation is revealed in these plans of Birdsong in Taylor County in the southwestern part of the state. Reconstructed from the diaries of the owner, William J. Dickey, they show fields separated by ribbons of swamp forest as well as the dwelling pattern, concentrated before the Civil War, more dispersed afterwards.

engaged in a mixture of crops (Fig. 6.5).

The rice plantations themselves, although vastly different in setting and staple than the Virginia plantations, existed for the same reasons: to maximize profits from the landholding. A well-run plantation returned huge profits from the investments, and many rice planters became the wealthiest men in the region. Not all rice growers were planters, but rice plantations dominated the river landscape in the rice area to a greater extent than the tobacco plantation held sway in Virginia and Maryland. The difference lay in the enormous effort required to ditch, drain, and dike the rice fields.

Like other plantation areas, the main house (if there was one) was the center of the plantation's grandeur. In this warmer zone, it was most typical to have some type of piazza or porch about the main house. Again, the main house generally stood on higher ground overlooking the rice fields, both esthetically pleasing and as protection from flooding. Slave quarters were placed similarly to those in Virginia, at some distance from the main house. Frequently the slaves were skilled at the engineering tasks required to keep the rice field operable. All the other aspects of the Virginia plantation and all the buildings on it were present in the rice plantations, adapted to the crop and region as needed. For example, the rice mill replaced the tobacco curing barn, and boats, skiffs, and flats were used to get about on the canals.

## Southern expansion and the rôle of towns

By the early 19th century the Indian threat had been eradicated in the central Gulf states and by 1830 the entire Georgia Piedmont had been settled. Although the Cherokees were still entrenched in the "Great Valley" of western Georgia and eastern Alabama, and the Choctaw and Chickasaw Indians occupied northern Mississippi, the white enclave in central Alabama was quickly expanding and overwhelming the Indians. The cause of this expansion was the settlers' pressing need for land on which to plant cotton. By 1840 the entire Gulf area had been opened to white settlement, and by 1850 all territory east of the Mississippi had been occupied to some degree by Americans.[27] New land was in demand, for tremendous profits were to be had. Both the poor and the wealthy swarmed into the region. Farmers with all their worldly possessions crammed on to two-horse wagons camped near planters with dozens of slaves, both hoping for better returns in Alabama. By the 1840s, a similar exodus was in motion from Alabama on to Arkansas and Texas (which became a state in 1845 after annexation from Mexico) for precisely the same reasons. Since most of the immigrants came from the older southeastern states, they carried with them their ideas of farming and plantation systems to be implemented in the new territory.[18] By 1850 the western frontier of the South ran roughly from Corpus Christi, Texas, on the Gulf, through San Antonio, Austin, Fort Worth and at the Red River it ran eastward to the western boundary of Arkansas near Indian territory.

Despite a similar westward migration, the development of cities and towns in the southern United States took a different path than that of the northern and western United States. As populations moved into the interior South, into the lower Mississippi Valley, towns were created and population increased in existing towns, but this growth was slower than corresponding urban expansion in the North and in large part led to the increasing differentiation between North and South in the 19th century.[29] By the outbreak of the Civil War, the only significant towns in the South were those of the region's periphery—Louisville, Memphis, New Orleans, Mobile, Savannah, Charleston, and Richmond—and the society itself tended to discourage the type of urban growth that characterized the North and West at that time. The plantation system must have had a significant impact on this different urban development.

The influence of the planter culture on the growth of cities in the South and on the type of cities that did emerge is evident in both social and economic spheres. Although most southerners were not plantation owners, the plantation was the ideal, the ultimate goal, of most southern whites engaged in agriculture. Thus, the plantation, not the city, was seen as the location of opportunity. Furthermore, the planters themselves often set the tone in southern cities. Charleston, the earliest port city of note in the South, reflected this planter influence in dramatic tones and was considered by many to be the truest exponent of southern culture and urbanism. The buildings themselves had a different flavor than their northern counterparts, with the long, humid summers eroding the structures rapidly, giving them a "hue of age"—and to some observers a look of untidiness. Between buildings were found long, narrow passageways leading to interior courtyards, surrounded by high walls, where Charlestonians located their detached kitchens, slave quarters, and formal gardens, in much the same manner as they were arranged on the plantations themselves (Fig. 6.6).[30]

Further echoes of the planter culture were the nightly curfew bell tolls and drum rolls, reminding all visitors of the unfamiliar dynamic at work in the South, for antebellum Charleston had fewer than 13,000 white residents in a

**Figure 6.6**
Elegant town mansions built by planters and merchants between 1830 and 1860 along East Battery in Charleston, South Carolina.

116

population with 15,000 slaves and some 2,000 free blacks.[31] The planters themselves often dominated Charleston, and southern cities in general, as their money supported the commercial system that was the base of the early port towns. As planters traded their rice, indigo, and cotton through the port, they purchased many of the imports coming through it from the British Empire. At the time of the American Revolution, Charleston was the third busiest port in the American colonies, agrarian based yet quite urbane. As the capital of South Carolina, it was dominated by planters and the factors that served them; Charleston did not even have its own legislature, as the state legislature served as both state and municipal director. But it mattered little; both were dominated by the planter interest.[32]

The extent of the southern city's domination by the plantation can be seen not only in the growth of Charleston, but in its decline also. As the plantation culture spread throughout the South, especially in the 19th century with the development of the cotton gin and the spread of upland cotton plantations, planters were no longer drawn to Charleston. The westward movement of populations, the shifting of the state capital to Columbia, and the depression which followed in the wake of the dislocations of the war of 1812, all left Charleston unable to regain its colonial position. As the planters' primary interest was agricultural, not urban, there was little to prevent the urban commercial decline that followed. By 1830, New Orleans had replaced Charleston as the major southern port, and Mobile began to develop as a major entrepôt in its own right as a market for the ever increasing Gulf states cotton. These cities, like Charleston, were serving the needs of planters and the plantation system.

But what of the towns and smaller settlements in the South? As plantations often took years to create, many starting out as farms on small clearings in the wilderness, towns did emerge in the southern frontier as they had in the Northwest Territory, opening up areas to settlement and providing basic necessities to settlers. The difference between the South and the North and West was not so much in the creation of towns, for although fewer towns were established in the South, they were none the less created. Rather it was that in the South the towns did not flourish and in many instances actually decreased in numbers. The stunting of the growth of interior towns corresponded strongly to the emergence of plantations in given areas. Once again, the spread of the upland cotton plantations seemed to have played a pivotal rôle in the survival or creation of interior towns in the South. One basis for the retarded development of interior towns lay in the quasi-industrial nature of the plantation itself. Early on, in Virginia and the Piedmont, the plantations had little need of town services when the excellent river transportation facilitated trade between plantation and England with relative ease. Later, when American ports became primary destinations of planter production, each plantation formed a fairly self-contained unit of operation and life, separated from other plantations, often more closely tied to the port of destination of its crop than to local towns. Plantations themselves generally produced many of the items that in other

117

areas of the United States were available only in towns. However, with the introduction of railroads into the South, goods manufactured in the North could be bought relatively cheaply, a factor that further retarded manufacturing development in southern towns and, in fact, led to a decrease not only in town craft and industrial production but in plantation industrial production as well.[33]

Those farmers not operating on plantations, therefore, had to rely on goods available at a country store generally at a rather idle, passive county seat town. The fact that the great number of smaller farmers in the South remained at the subsistence level and the slaves were outside the economy reduced the demand for goods that might otherwise have been a spur to local urban growth. The resultant lack of rural as well as urban purchasing power, together with the absorption of capital in slaves and the rural mindedness of southern political leadership, all militated against urban growth that might otherwise have been encouraged.[34] Thus, investment opportunities were far more lucrative in the agricultural realm in the South than in the industrial, focusing primary attention not on urban growth but on agricultural production. The upshot of this was an increase in importance of the port cities, which handled the shipment of plantation crops, explaining why the major cities of the South were located on its periphery. In the South, regional urban systems were slow in developing and could fairly be said not to have existed in the antebellum period, thus the plantations not the cities, were the focal points of political, social, and economic control and influence; within the cities themselves, often the planters dominated as well.[35]

## Cotton landscapes

The introduction of the cotton gin in the late 18th century was pivotal in the development and spread of cotton culture in the South. Less environmentally demanding than sugar cane or rice, cotton was grown from Virginia to Texas and northward into Ohio, Illinois, and Missouri. But it was in the Deep South that the cotton plantation reached its apotheosis—in the Black Belt and alluvial valleys of Alabama, Mississippi, and Louisiana, the largest and most productive being the floodplains of the Mississippi and its tributaries. By the time of the Civil War, plantations could be found from the Mississippi delta to that river's confluence with the Ohio. From New Orleans to Memphis ideal conditions existed for plantations—fertile land available in large tracts, convenient transportation, and labor in the form of slaves. It was here that the plantation would reach its greatest density and importance, and from this area comes much of the popular conception of the plantation South.[36]

Cotton plantations differed little in morphology from that of plantations of the eastern South. The planter's house (if there was one) was the focal point;

**Figure 6.7**
A plantation house in
Rapides Parish, Louisiana.
The Greek Revival style was
preferred by Anglo planters,
and many such houses were
built as late as the 1890s. The
TV satellite dish in this view
is a modern artifact in an
otherwise traditional scene.

most were of wood, the typical being either a dogtrot or an "I" house, both
characterized by a central hallway and exterior chimneys at both ends. Full
length porches (verandas) were attached on both front and rear. They were
placed on the high point of the plantation facing the transportation artery,
whether road or stream. Usually the house was placed back somewhat from
the main road leading to it, and often the road was lined with large trees for
shade as well as beauty. The best of the big houses were well landscaped,
often with a fine garden surrounding them or to one side (Fig. 6.7). The
physical layout of the cotton plantation was also reminiscent of the earlier
plantations, with slave quarters neatly aligned along a secondary street, or
along shorter streets aligned in a rectangle or square, and the outbuildings
serving the various needs of the plantation. Such rectangular order among
the western plantation was enhanced by the nature of the original survey.
All of Alabama, Mississippi, Arkansas, and most of Louisiana were
surveyed under the rectangular federal system, making it more likely that
straight lines and right angles would be manifest on both field and
settlement features. Among the outbuildings were sheds for tools and
implements, offices, barns for the stock, and a blacksmith shop. The cotton
gin with its prominent bale screw press replaced the tobacco barn or rice
mill. Cotton plantations were frequently of 1,000 acres, but only a fraction of
that was improved during the early years. Substantial quantities of corn
were grown, primarily to sustain livestock and the residents. Fields were
generally not fenced, but pastures were. On many plantations, small plots
were cultivated individually by the slaves, allowing the slaves some
spending money for amenities. The sheds and barns were generally situated
approximately centrally in relation to pasture, cropland, and labor quarters,

though many plantations were large enough to have satellite building clusters. Those located on rivers obviously had a distinct advantage in transportation costs, and soon the Mississippi became the main artery of cotton transportation in the South, with New Orleans and to a lesser extent Mobile thriving off their position as rivermouth marketplaces.

## The Lower Mississippi valley and cane sugar

One region where the cotton culture was superimposed on an older agricultural system was lower Louisiana, the domain of Old-World French and Acadian French. Much of the agriculture in this region was, and is, located on the natural levees of the Mississippi and Red Rivers and their south-flowing tributaries and distributaries. To incoming Europeans, it was a marginal agricultural domain, poorly drained and lying perilously close to sea level. For thousands of years silt laden rivers had deposited layer upon layer of rich alluvium creating the natural levees that French, German, Spanish, English, and American settlers made their homes. A variety of Old and New World crops was tried, including indigo, corn, wheat, tobacco, rice, and sugar cane, but sugar was the one to dominate.

The levees of the Mississippi River were and remain remarkably productive territories. In keeping with the southern penchant for producing staple crops, sugar plantations fit nicely into the plantation pattern that had been established elsewhere in the South, but with some noticeable differences. Of all the plantation crops grown in the South, sugar cane required the longest growing season. Ideally, it should have a frost-free environment, but by judicious planting and harvesting those planters north of the 30th parallel can achieve a good crop despite the occasional winter freeze. Moreover, unlike cotton, tobacco, and rice, cane culture has shown remarkable spatial stability. Virtually all the cane grown in Louisiana today comes from the *same fields* that were used for cane in 1820 or in 1870.[37] Once established, sugar plantations remained in the region. Finally, sugar culture was the domain of the large planter. Whereas small farmers might venture to grow a token crop of cotton or tobacco, the capital investment and technological expertise involved in cane culture and raw sugar manufacturing discouraged both smallholders and outsiders from becoming sugar planters.

Cane was introduced into the colony and cane syrup produced quite early, but not until the sugar granulation process had been perfected in the 1790s did sugar become a cash crop. The hearth of cane growing was on the natural levees of the Mississippi near New Orleans, but it quickly spread both upstream and downstream from that city, until, by mid-century, most of the environmentally acceptable land was taken up in sugarcane production. The nature of this territory itself limited what land could productively be used for sugarcane growing, and sites were carefully chosen. Only the natural levees along the Mississippi and local bayous were sufficiently well drained to support the cane growth, thus settlement became riverine. Levee land was in great demand, and in time landholdings lined the waterways much like beads on a rosary. Therefore, plantations were located along the rivers. Because of the high demand for land fronting on the river, plots were laid out in long, narrow holdings with the short dimension fronting on the river or bayou. These grants were made under the French arpent system, with one arpent equalling 192 feet. A typical grant was 25 arpents or less along the river front and about 40 arpents deep. When the prime lands were taken, and if the levees were wide enough, a road was constructed behind the first holdings, and a second, less desirable range of holdings was created, some 40 arpents back from the river, in the same narrow fashion, reaching to the backswamp region.[38] With such a location, the waterways served as the transportation route to and from the market.

Despite their advantages for crop production, the levees were subject to floods that endangered both crops and buildings. None the less, plantations were established on the levees, most of them fronting on the water. The sugar plantation was similar in arrangement to other plantations, though perhaps slightly more elaborate, owing to the complex needs of sugar culture. Absentee ownership was common among sugar plantation proprietors, thus many properties did not aspire to a big house, but those that did could often boast of the finest of any region of the South. Moreover, because sugar plantations were much less likely to have been fragmented into sharecropping units in postbellum times, many more have survived, with Louisiana having a remarkable repertoire of extant examples. Where present, the main house reflected the culture of the owner; Anglo planters favored the styles in vogue elsewhere, such as Greek Revival, while those of French or Creole planters had a distinctly different look to them, unlike any others in the South, clearly reflecting the French influence. They were typically wooden, with steeply sloping hipped roofs and double verandas, on first and second floors, often circling all four sides of the house, with windows that extended to the floor and served both as windows and doors (Fig. 6.8). Other buildings flanked the big house; the slave quarters consisting of two or more rows of houses and the sugar house placed at the end of the rows. The layout of the fields was dictated by terrain and was more orderly than was the case elsewhere in the South. Being located on the natural levee in an area of high rainfall and poor drainage, the fields had to be drained. With the surface gently sloping away from the stream, fields were drained with a system of ditches and cross drains that eventually led to the backswamp creating a neat pattern of parallelograms. Because of environmental limitations on the expansion of sugar cane, it was the cultivation of cotton and not sugar that continued to spread throughout the South, carrying the plantation system west into Texas.

121

**Figure 6.8**
Parlange Plantation on False
River near New Roads,
Louisiana. Built in 1750, it
epitomizes the height of
development of the Creole
plantation house, reflecting
French influence on the
Lower Mississippi River
landscape before competition
from Anglo-American
settlement. The living
quarters and their shady
gallery are raised well above
ground level on brick piers to
avoid flooding and to help air
circulate in the subtropical
climate of the region.

## Postbellum landscape changes

Although the Civil War greatly disrupted planter markets and caused local
damage in particular parts of the South, the agricultural system emerged
from the military episode essentially intact. What had a far more immediate
and profound effect was the end to slavery and its consequences. Without a
large laborforce, the plantation system could not survive. What evolved
from that apparent chaos was an alteration of the agricultural system to
accommodate the economic and social changes of the time. A number of
management systems was tried, including the use of wage labor—essentially
gangs of freedmen and working laborers organized into squads that received
a part of the profit; but the system that eventually prevailed was one of
shared production known as sharecropping. In theory, sharecropping is
easy to describe; the landowner (planter) supplied the land, mules,
implements, and housing while the cropper supplied the labor. After
subtracting expenses, such as seed and fertilizer, the crop was divided
50 : 50. In practice, though, sharecropping was rarely so simple. A plethora
of variations might be found, ranging from 50 : 50 division of the cropping
proceeds, to cash payments for labor, or a standing charge for rent. In rare
cases, enterprising freedmen rented land from the landowner and sublet it
to others as sharecropping units.

Of particular interest here is the effect such arrangements had on the
plantation itself. At first the changes were functional only; the croppers
lived in the quarters that had served them as slaves and worked in the

gangs in the fields. But such arrangements were so repugnant to the laborers that planters resorted to subdividing the plantation into share-cropping units. Each worker and his family was responsible for cultivating a certain section of a plantation, the size of which depended on the number of workers in his family, but was generally between 20 and 50 acres.[39] The owner of the plantation supplied everything needed for crop production except labor, but included the croppers' cabins, and paid half the cost of the seed and fertilizer. Crop proceeds were normally split at the end of the season, hence the term "share" cropping. The owners' share included rental on buildings and land, equipment, and mule power. Contracts were negotiated annually and included points such as the amount of acreage to be planted, by what crop, cultivation procedures, marketing practices, and the wage rate to be paid for work off the cropper's unit.[40]

The primary differences between the sharecropper plantation and its antebellum predecessor were that the large fields were now subdivided into smaller units, each of which was typically planted in two or three crops, at least one of which was the plantation's staple. In time, the old slave cabins were discarded or moved to a site near the cropper's assigned plot, thus altering the physical layout of the plantation and necessitating the construction of more roads on the landholdings (Fig. 6.9).[41]

An essential element of sharecropping was the furnish system. Lack of reserve capital left the cropper dependent upon others for subsistence until market time. In areas where the plantation was absent, this need was supplied by retail stores located either in the small market towns nearby, or by country stores. Such institutions "furnished" the cropper with food and clothing during the year, the accumulated debt to be repaid, with interest, at harvest time. In many cases the store owner was also the buyer of cotton or tobacco. In those areas dominated by plantations, the planter often assumed the rôle of furnisher, and on very large landholdings the plantation store resembled a warehouse in both size and content. In many cases, ex-slaves worked on plantations where they had lived as slaves, lived in the same houses, and were furnished from a store that had served as the plantation storehouse during the slave era.

Given the radical functional changes that had taken place, the spatial arrangement of the plantation also changed. The nucleated settlement, so characteristic of the antebellum period, became much less notable, for the quarters had been dispersed. First the boundaries between the cropping tracts became hedgerows, then trees grew around the croppers' cabins creating the impression of a landscape consisting of small farms interspersed with an occasional big house. As whites moved to the towns and cities in the early years of the 20th century leaving the big house idle, it was easy for outsiders to gain the impression that a new social order was emerging. The plantation appeared to be fading away. But such was not the case. The plantation retained much of its antebellum vigor; the landholding remained intact, and the owners or overseers retained control of day-to-day operation by means of tightly written contracts that specified duties backed up by

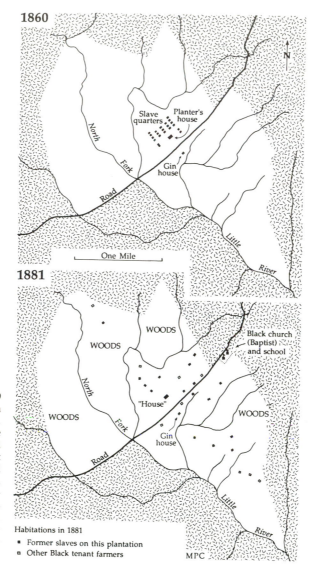

**Figure 6.9**
The Barrows Plantation, in Oglethorpe County, Georgia, illustrates the radical change from nucleated to dispersed agricultural settlement patterns following the Civil War, as black emancipation turned slaves into share-croppers, who tended fields from nearby homesteads and cabins. Much of the peripheral land reverted to woodland.

ruthless intimidation. The sharecropping system itself was not inherently evil; indeed, such arrangements have been used all over the world, but social and political conditions in the postbellum South rendered it especially vulnerable to exploitation. All too often the temptation to profit from the existence of a largely illiterate, subservient laborforce proved too strong to resist. That, coupled with the periodic hard times often left the cropper perennially in debt, converting the cropping system into a form of debt peonage.[42]

124

## The neoplantation

The system of sharecropping remained strong in the South until after World War II. The decline in sharecropping was directly related to the development of mechanical means to harvest cotton crops in the late 1940s and the introduction of herbicides in the 1950s. Thus hand picking and hoeing became obsolete. The result was that the southern agricultural system mechanized completely and rapidly, since previous technological advances were of little use if a planter had still to rely on many laborers to bring in the crops.[43] With mechanization complete, the entire agricultural structure of the South was altered, perhaps more profoundly than it had been by Emancipation nearly a century earlier. Ironically enough, however, this turn to mechanization led directly to another spatial reorganization, a return to the nucleated agricultural settlements that typified the antebellum plantation South. Mechanized farming became more efficient by eliminating the need for sharecropping labor. Within a decade the plantation area underwent radical reorganization. Cropper cabins, hedgerows, and field roads disappeared as bulldozers worked to make large fields out of the small cropper plots.[44] Tractor sheds replaced the mule barns, gins became larger and more centralized, often one gin catering to several producers, and grain bins (for soybeans) have replaced cotton houses. Thus, the neoplantation was born.[45]

The typical plantation of today's South is essentially the same as those original plantations: large tracts of land planted with a cash crop, with a spatial–functional organization similar to that of its antebellum predecessor. More often than not, present day plantations plant the remunerative soybean rather than the cotton of bygone eras, but the raison d'être of the plantation never was its crops, but rather the desire to mass produce a crop for a profit. On the modern plantation there remains an owner's or manager's house, and often close by is housing for workers (if labor is not hired from local towns), but the housing is but a tithe of what had been needed on the antebellum plantation, for labor needs are far less. Machinery sheds and buildings have replaced stables and cook houses, but the idea remains the same as with the first plantations—to secure a profit through the efficiencies of scale and specialization. The primary change has been a shift from manual labor to "machine labor" (Fig. 6.10).[46] With the increase in scale have come plantations ranging from 750–2,000 acres, often with one owner holding several plantations units, another trait in common with the antebellum era.

There is enormous variety in the human landscapes of the South, a product of the timing of population movements within the region in relation to changes in markets, agricultural techniques, and the blending of local patterns of culture. All this diversity emerged under a social system that stamped a unity upon the region that to this day shapes fundamental southern attitudes towards the land and between people. Widespread, though not universal, the plantation from the beginning symbolized the separateness and peculiarity of the South within the broader American

**Figure 6.10**
Since its invention the cotton gin has provided a focal point in the local landscapes of the Cotton Belt. Shown here is a modern gin in Franklin Parish, Louisiana. The trailers are used for hauling cotton from the fields to the gin, four bales to the load.

developmental scheme. Other characteristics help distinguish the southern landscape from those of the North and West—the southern small town, the rural cemeteries, the back-country settlements, not to mention the visual expressions of such traditions as country music, stock-car racing, Bible Belt fundamentalism, and political conservatism. But no landscape element is woven so deeply into the fabric of the region as the rich heritage of plantation land use, stately mansions, and their urban cousins in the gracious ports of the region's periphery. The southern landscape has known tumultuous change, differing subtly from place to place, but its common roots are plain to see in every corner of the territory.

# *Chapter seven*
# *Towards a national landscape*

## HILDEGARD BINDER JOHNSON

THE ORIGIN OF the United States' land survey system has been associated with Thomas Jefferson, who chaired a committee in 1784 to prepare a plan for the government of the Western Territory. His proposal divided the land into geographical square miles by "hundreds" with lines oriented north–south and east–west, crossing each other at right angles. But there was also Hugh Williamson, congressional delegate from North Carolina who had studied medicine in Utrecht, who in the same year suggested to the committee to divide the land by "parallels, dotts and meridians." He had seen rectangular field divisions in the Netherlands, some dating from the Roman era. One can readily call the first proposal the Jefferson-Williamson plan while acknowledging the contributions by others during the debate, notably Timothy Pickering of Massachusetts, who warned astutely against having straight lines represent converging meridians.[1]

Jefferson may have been influenced by Roman centuriation and the Cartesian *esprit géometrique* during the century of the Enlightenment. But people in different places at different times can find the same solution to a problem. We should therefore consider the human context. Squares, circles, and equilateral triangles are more readily recalled than figures of irregular shape. The straight line, rare in nature, can be obtained by stretching a vine between two trees; with one end tied to a tree, we can with the other circumpace the ideal form of a circle. But circles are useless for subdividing an area when complete coverage is desired. In the 3rd century AD the Greek geometrician Pappus of Alexandria considered the hexagon; but it lacks parallelism. The pervasive functionality of the right angle makes it the preferred form, and human eyes still see it when shown an angle of some degrees more or less than 90. This may be related to man walking erect, similar to his preference for the number "6" which equals our existential directions in space—up, down, forward, backward, left and right.

The square has been used for land assignment worldwide since antiquity, particularly in colonized regions. Mencius in China stipulated nine squares for eight families with the well in the central square. In 1638, New Haven was laid out as a square of nine blocks with a central green. The Japanese *jori* system has 36 *cho* in a square *Ri*, comparable to our township, but the coordinates are often tilted adjusting to topography. Roman centuriation in Italy, around Ravenna and in Lombardy, has *decumanus* and *cardo* run in cardinal directions, but not in Dalmatia and North Africa. Only the United States has a rectangular cadastral system with strict adherence to cardinal directions (Fig. 7.1). The coordinates were rarely tilted. The few exceptions include two military grants in Indiana and in southeastern Maine in NW–SE and NE–SW direction; the axis adjusted to the trend of the mountains in southeastern Tennessee; to the rivers Ocmulgee and Oconee in Georgia; toward the coast in Walkulla County, Florida; and in Gadsden County, toward the River Hurricane.

## A system to span the continent

The long and dramatic history of the federal govenment's rôle in shaping the land began with the "Ordinance for ascertaining the mode of disposing lands in the western territory" passed May 20, 1785 (commonly known as the Land Ordinance). The title reflects the legislators' major concern: orderly transfer of an immense, poorly known territory to private ownership through sales. The Treasury was heavily in debt and the country impoverished. That squares need only one measurement and thus save money was mentioned during the debate; so were some Virginians' suggestions to settle "along natural lines." But the traditional metes and bounds system caused lawsuits in Jefferson's experience. Indiscriminate

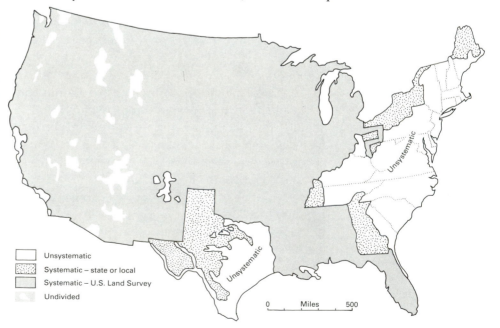

**Figure 7.1**
Types of land division in the United States. Except for the original 13 colonies, Texas, and some western mountainous areas, most of the country is parcelled out on the township and range system.

Unsystematic

Systematic – state or local

Systematic – U.S. Land Survey

Undivided

0    Miles    500

128

location would not result in coherent settlement progressively moving westward, he felt, and might jeopardize clearly defined property titles.

Townships were reduced from 100 to 36 square miles. A surveyor from each state, working under the Geographer of the United States using their chain carriers, was to run lines due north and south, with others crossing these at right angles, "as near as may be," a phrase regularly used in later legislation and instructions to surveyors. The first north–south line was to begin on the Ohio River due north of the western boundary of Pennsylvania, and the first east–west line at the same point. Along the straight north–south *township* line and the east–west *range* line, the square miles could thus be counted off as on graphpaper from the initial point (for example, T2N R3E). The lines were to be measured with a chain, marked by chaps on trees, and drawn on plats. Mines, salt springs, salt licks, mill-seats, water courses, mountains, and the quality of the land crossed by these lines were to be noted. The township plats were to be subdivided into squares of 640 acres numbered from one to 36 starting at the southeast corner and proceeding as the plow follows the ox, in boustrophedonic fashion (i.e., left to right, then right to left). Townships would be sold alternately "by lots and entire." The Geographer would transmit the plats to the board of the Treasury after seven ranges of townships were surveyed. The Geographer and his surveyors were to pay "utmost attention" to the magnetic needle and run all lines by the true meridian, and note the variation on every plat.

The beginning point was established on the north shore of the Ohio in August, 1785; a few miles of the baseline, later named Geographer's Line, were measured by fall. Surveying began again in August, 1786 and by spring, 1787 four ranges were ready for sale. Thomas Hutchins, the Geographer, resigned, and Israel Ludlow finished the measurement of the seventh range in June, 1787. Inadequate protection from the army, marauding Indians, personnel problems, and the rough terrain explained the rather ignominious beginning. But original practices like using township plats on the scale of 2 inches per mile and filing detailed survey notes endured. These notes represent a record of original vegetation along compass lines at predetermined intervals. They do not follow any paths where usage would have affected virgin growth. They allowed F. J. Marschner in 1929 using 240 volumes of surveyors' notes to produce a hand-colored composite map on the scale of 1 : 500,000 entitled "Original Forests of Minnesota."[2] As for the survey of the Seven Ranges, it left no noteworthy legacy in the environment, and surveying was discontinued.[3]

Ohio was a crucible for the United States survey but the new geometric system did not immediately become the prevailing method of land division.[4] For example, the Virginia Military District was surveyed by metes and bounds between 1810 and 1819, while John Cleves Symmes, who controlled a large land grant from the federal government, allowed settlers within it to practice indiscriminate location (Fig. 7.1). Several land acts and proposals for a General Land Office and a Surveyor General stalled in Congress. After the Constitution was rectified and the new government began to function in

1789, interest among members of Congress, now clearly opposed to further large land grants, revived. On August 3, 1795 the Treaty of Greenville was signed, which assured security for settlers.

"An Act providing for the sale of the lands of the United States in the territory northwest of the River Ohio and above the mouth of the Kentucky River" passed on May 18, 1796. It repeated the "north and south lines to be crossed by others at right angles." Surveying prior to sale was required and consisted of lines 2 miles apart with corners set 1 mile apart. This divided a township into 36 square miles—now called sections—with three corners marked. Townships were to be sold alternately as quarter townships or subdivided into 36 square miles, reflecting the persistent attitude toward land as a tradeable commodity, defined by size.

To become an effective system of land survey and division, the tools and procedures of survey had to become standard and universally applied. The scale and complexity of the American environment ensured that this would be a slow and evolutionary process. The Act of 1796 stipulated that "All lines shall be plainly marked upon trees, and measured with chains, containing two perches of sixteen and one-half feet each, subdivided into twenty-five equal links." The chain used was Gunter's chain, already widely employed in Massachusetts and New York State. It consisted of 100 links totaling 66 feet in length or 4 rods (also called poles or perches). Eighty such chains measure 5,280 feet or 1 mile. Ten square chains make an acre and 640 acres fit into 1 square mile—a fortuitous combination of the decimal with the traditional—and 640 acres can be halved six times before reaching an uneven number. We should remember Edmund Gunter, an English mathematician and surveyor (1581–1626) because of the prevalence of five-acre blocks in American cities and of the two-and-a-half-acre lots cherished by rural-minded urbanites.

The two-pole chain of 32½ feet could be replaced by a four-pole chain on level land. Ten tally pins 11 inches long with handles marked the length of five chains on the ground. For uneven ground the two-pole chain was preferable, "keeping it horizontally levelled and being careful when plumbing the tally pins on steep hills." Official instructions repeated frequently that the length of the line be ascertained "by precise horizontal measurement as nearly as possible approximating an airline." Good surveyors took accuracy seriously. William. A. Burt after a cold day warmed his chain in a fire to bring it up to summer heat and discovered his field chain differed 0.4 inch from the standard chain in his office. Burt, a deputy surveyor in Michigan in 1833, found the aberrations of the magnetic needle excessive because of nearby iron ore deposits (Fig. 7.2). He invented the solar compass, which received awards from the Franklin Institute in Philadelphia and at the World's Fair in 1851 in London, and a modernized Burt's solar compass was used well into the 20th century.[5]

The problem of using straight north–south township lines for converging meridians was solved in the field. President Jefferson appointed Jared Mansfield, a mathematician, as the second Surveyor General in 1803. He

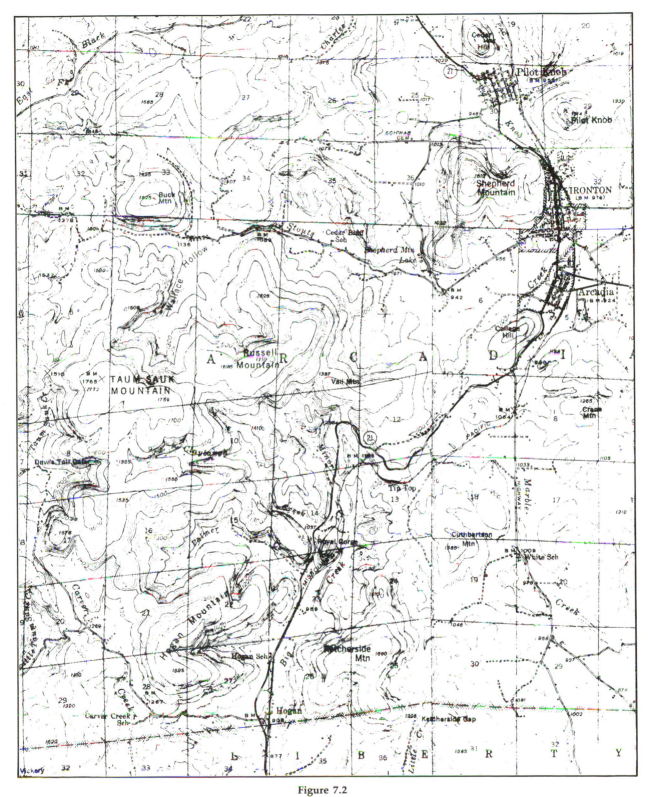

**Figure 7.2**
Irregularities stemming from faulty survey technique reach a peak southwest of Ironton in the Ozark Hills, where sections 1–6 of Arcadia Township are far from being square.

arbitrarily selected a new initial point in southern Indiana, laying out astronomically a new meridian and a new baseline. This constituted a precedent for further principal meridians with guide meridians in between for determining the degree of convergence. At every twenty-fourth township line along a baseline, called a correction line, township lines from the south are shifted and continued true north. The correction line explains a peculiar, somewhat amusing section road pattern. One drives on a straight road north, suddenly turns to the right, drives on for some yards and turns sharply left to continue straight north. Correction lines are plainly visible when flying in an easterly or westerly direction.

The meandering lines of large rivers or lakes created fractional townships, subdivided and numbered as if they were parts of whole townships. An Act of March 1, 1800 established the principle that corners set by first surveyors are held to be true corners even if later surveys proved them incorrect. Just claims from earlier English, French and Spanish occupation were honored, even when legal settlement took many years (Fig. 7.3). French lots near Vincennes, Indiana, and Spanish *sitios* in Texas and Louisiana are still easily detected from the airplane. Edward Tiffin, Surveyor General from 1814 to 1829, established the Fifth Principal Meridian and a baseline from the initial point at the mouth of the Arkansas. It deserves mention because 164 townships as far north as Minnesota's Northwest Angle refer to that baseline.

The claims of six former colonies to parts of the Public Domain in 1785 derived from charters which granted land "from sea to sea" or "from the western ocean to the South Sea," between parallels. These phrases reflect both geographical ignorance and continental vision, which Tom Paine expressed in 1775 in *Common Sense*: "The sun never shone on a cause of greater worth. 'Tis not the affair of a city, a county, a province, or a kingdom; but of a continent." Historians have not explained why delegates to the First Congress talked about *continental* currency and a *continental* army. It was perhaps subconscious awareness of the challenge presented by the virgin and unstoried western wilderness to be turned into the American landscape ideal, Improved Nature—a state between the overcivilization of western Europe and the savage frontier. The Louisiana Purchase of 1803 brought the continental dream closer to reality.[6]

Louisiana presented a greater problem of pre-survey occupance than the Northwest. Thus, an Act of 1811 instructed surveyors in the territory of Orleans to lay out tracts along waterbodies, measuring 48 poles in front and 465 poles in depth, continuing the pattern of French long lots. Claims of various sizes and forms in Missouri were also maintained. Until the 1830s the main concern, aside from rapid sale of the Public Domain, was to give the common man a chance to "improve nature."

A succession of land acts dealt extensively with administrative matters, with little or no effect on the appearance of the landscape, but a reduction of the minimum size of tracts purchasable from the government had a major effect. In 1800 the section purchasable from the government since 1796 was

**Figure 7.3**
French and Spanish private claims lie embedded in the rectangular survey pattern in St. Charles County, Missouri, just northeast of St. Louis.

Scale: 400 chains to the inch

halved. Citizens from Ohio petitioned Congress in 1803 to divide sections by six. The popular number would have meant subdivisions of 106⅔ acres and Congress declined. In 1804 the quarter section to be enshrined later in national consciousness by the 1862 Homestead Act was legislated, and in 1820, the half-quarter section. Then, on April 5, 1832 "An Act supplementory to several laws for the sale of public land" declared quarter-quarter sections available and ordered that all fractional townships also be so divided.

On December 5, 1836 the Commissioner complained to the Secretary of the Treasury of increased work "by reason of the new and minute subdivisions of fractional sections . . . into forty acre lots, as nearly as possible." Maps and diagrams had to be prepared in triplicate. Complaint of too much paperwork in Washington is understandable, but calling the 40-acre lots minute subdivisions is not fitting. The forty became the modular unit for settlement (Fig. 7.4). It was sufficient for an average family, and one man could clear it in about eight years. It was frequently "swapped" to "round out a farm" and, perhaps most important, it made it possible to

133

**Figure 7.4**
Square fields and
straight section line
roads march across the
landscape of southern
Michigan. Single
farmsteads lie scattered
within this rural grid,
highly individual
family islands in a sea
of regimented land
parcels.

adjust the shape of a quarter section to topography. Considering the
cardinal directions, a quarter section can be composed of forties in 19
different ways when "located in a body," which means the squares cannot
touch only at the corners but are adjacent to one another at one side.[7]
Railroads sold more land than was granted under the Homestead Act,
chiefly by forties. By the middle of the 20th century, the forty was preferred
in general. Developers to this day buy forties; rotary sprinkling systems are
designed to their dimensions.

The forty, never surveyed, was determined by pacing to the point
equidistant between corner and half-mile post. A *Land buyer's guide* explains
under "Pacing" that to save time, "only alternative steps are counted," for
the "40" of 250 double paces.[8] The Pre-emption Act of 1841 would not have
been functional without the squatters' ability to pace. All claim associations
made their own township plats.

## Single farmsteads

The classic American family farm of between 40 and 160 acres was typically
isolated in the forested country. A more neighborly settlement pattern could
have resulted if in 1804 selected sections had been divided into oblong
rectangles fronting the road, as happened in Ontario, Canada. Divided
again, eight farms, 1 mile long, would line the road from both sides, rather
like a street village. But such alternate platting would have entailed
complicated bookkeeping, and even at road corners the houses of four
farmsteads were not necessarily built in neighborly reach, either.

In England and Germany the countryside is open to the public. The American landscape of single farmsteads is essentially a private one. It has a history of fencing fields against animals, of spending much work and wood on rail fences and too much money on wire fences which now interfere with the turning of heavy machinery. If there is an earlier path across a field, it is accessible only via the farmyard, which one respects as private property. People do not hike, they drive through single farmstead country for recreation, or to town for social functions. Hence the early initiatives in modern times to establish park, forest, and wilderness reserves open to the public and to create trail opportunities.

After the dissected Allegheny plateau in eastern Ohio, still known as the Seven Ranges, settlement spread over existing roads toward the Connecticut Reserve and from the Ohio River bottoms inland. In central Ohio the woods opened up to prairies readily settled by landseekers, contrary to the myth that treeless land was believed to be less fertile. Much hardwood, plentiful for cabins, fuel, fencing, and for laying over mudholes in roads and across creeks, still ended up in piles for burning. Pioneers' attitudes toward the woods are described in Conrad Richter's novel *The trees* (1940), where a girl is embarrassed to mix socially with people who come to the store from open farmsteads because she is a "woodsy." Currier and Ives, purveyors of cheap hand-colored prints to hang in the parlor, presented the woodsies' dream on four prints: the first, a small cabin with a few stumps around it; the second, a Virginia snake fence in front of the house, a brush fence behind, and men working on the clearing; the third, a rectangular farmyard, flower and vegetable beds, and rectangular fields lined by woods; the fourth, a two-story mansion, barn and stables, a broad road, and fields stretching far into the background. Its caption: "The land is tamed."[9]

The homesteader could identify his plat on a map in the courthouse and recognize the surveyors' marks on the trees along his lines. Gradually he cleaned out all the brush and saw bare ground, reflected in the word "clearing." The closer he got to his property lines, the more fields and fences ran in north–south and east–west directions. It took decades before fields and remaining woods emerged as a coherent rectangular landscape.

After the log cabin or sod house on the prairie the farmsteader built a house of custom-cut boards, often selected from Ward's catalogue and shipped in by railroad. "The embellishment of the home and the planting of the yard were left mostly to the second generation."[10] Then the family could subscribe to a county atlas with a picture of their place (Fig. 7.5).[11] Because details were true and it was recognizable, it looked "natural," a word still used in this sense by old-timers in the Midwest. All illustrations are in one point perspective. By far the largest market for atlases was the Middle West where draftsmen and surveyors could easily redraw township maps with owners' names. Atlases were published at first in the East; Chicago replaced Philadelphia as their center of production between 1870 and 1880. Over 4,000 different county atlases were published before World War I. This truly American phenomenon is directly connected with the survey. Ross

Lockridge, Jr., in his novel *Raintree country*, tells of the county atlas lying next to the Bible and family photo album in the parlor. Captions under the pictures of residences show the owner's name, township, range and section number of his place, sometimes pictures have his photograph. On the illustrations houses, carriages, gardens, ladies with parasols, etc. make the pervasive rectangularity look like the necessary background.[12]

In northwestern Ohio land sales began in 1829. In northern Indiana Indians delayed settlement relative to the heavy early influx from the Ohio River in the south. On Indiana's prairies settlement proceeded fast, with farmsteads of 80 acres being the most numerous to this day. From 1820 to 1829 Indiana's land offices sold almost 5 million acres for $2.5 million. By 1900, 221,897 farms totaling 5,700,000 acres established on the former Public Domain were in Indiana.[13] In Illinois settlers began to look for wood along rivers; in upper Mississippi country, some bought wooded forties for $50, which they subdivided and resold at $5 per acre.[14] The mixed forest and prairie changed to prairie in Iowa; South Dakota, Nebraska, and Kansas are emphatically prairie states.

As one geographer asserts outright, "the Middle West is flat" all the way between the Appalachians to the east, the Ozarks to the south, and the

**Figure 7.5**
Gilbert Walldroff's
Farm, Leoni Township,
Jackson County,
Michigan, in 1874. The
artist has captured the
formality and seeming
orderliness of the farm
in this county atlas
view, accentuated by
neat fences and patches
of woodland. Note the
rectangular spread.

Rocky Mountains to the west.[15] To the west farmsteads locate within their
holdings in relation to water, because that, not land, becomes the essential
resource. Water problems in the Middle West result from the unfortunate
Anglo-American legacy of using rivers for boundaries. It left the nation's
geographical symbol, "Ol' Man River," with two different states facing each
other eight times across his shores. Only Minnesota and Louisiana occupy
stretches of both banks. New France was claimed in terms of drainage
basins, which Americans only learned to understand in this century.

## Townsites

Schoolhouses, generally four to a township, cemeteries and small churches
on donated lots dot the dispersed single-farmstead landscape. Other social
needs, however, are met by towns, which developed from trading posts,
road crossings, mill sites, river landings, and natural harbors. Town
speculators bought tracts of less than 640 acres before the 1870s.[16] Grid
pattern plats were unavoidable and often tilted so that the main street
follows the waterfront. Of 204 river places between Chester, Illinois and
Hastings, Minnesota, 193 have plats adjusted to the shoreline. One or more
blocks without lot divisions and open for public use were frequently left on
speculators' plats.

Land societies instructed their scouts to look for townsites by a navigable
river during the steamboat age. Some of these small river ports became
virtual museums after cargo shipping decreased sharply in the 1870s.[17]
Railroads and increasingly mechanized agriculture brought new functions to
rural towns, and the improved economy enabled farmers to support larger
parishes. The steeples of their churches added an attractive vertical to the
skyline, later rivaled by less inspirational but no less welcome watertowers.
The growing population needed more services and when the threshold of
2,500 residents was surpassed, small places could acquire the civic mantle of
a city. By that time the original plat had several "additions" and special
features like a fairground, hospital, baseball park, or larger courthouse.[18]

Other towns never filled the plat, lingered on or disappeared. They all
started with one wide Main Street, the "business district," with two or three
cross streets. Residential lots allowed for gardens but rarely developed city-
type alleys (Fig. 7.6).

Esthetically Main Street was off to a bad start: it adopted the false front, a
deplorable invention of the building trade. Horizontal boards cover gables
and fake the appearance of a second story; they were also used for lettered
signs. That stage was followed by two- or three-story brick buildings with
roofs sloping toward the rear and straightlined front façades.

Sauk Centre in central Minnesota, platted in 1863 near a gristmill, recently
renamed its straight north–south running main street "the Original Main
Street," crossed by Sinclair Lewis Boulevard. Lewis was born here in 1885

**Figure 7.6**
Main Street in St.
Charles, Minnesota, an
archetypical
Midwestern small town
streetscape. Late 19th-
century brick business
buildings, lining the
straight thoroughfare
for two blocks, define
the shopping district
without ambiguity.

and his childhood home is a historical landmark. He disputed that Sauk Centre was Gopher Prairie in his novel *Main street* (1920), but readers worldwide do not believe that, nor do the citizens of Sauk Centre. It took them years to forgive the first American Nobel Prize winner in literature the nearly mortal blow he gave to their main street which, in his own words, "is the continuation of Main Streets everywhere." In 1970 a reporter for the *Saturday Review* investigated social and cultural conditions in Mason City, Iowa and found them indistinguishable from those of Sauk Centre. "The village virus"—Lewis's first title for his novel—seemingly spread to Mason City, where the hut-shaped kilns, clustered around the brick and tile plant, "add picturesqueness to the surrounding farm lands," according to the WPA Iowa state guide, printed five times between 1938 and 1959.

Railroad towns were located according to plans of the companies, and they shared the prosperity and the decline of the railways. Some depots are attractive enough to be preserved. Once these towns were the middle border between eastern cities and the yet unsettled prairie. The rails respect topography and do not tolerate right-angled corners. Engravers and printers in New York could not advertise the prairies and Great Plains through popular pastoral scenes which romanticized eastern train journeys. The producers of travel literature found the public preferred Rocky Mountain scenes; so did artists. The contrasting parallelism of rails and crossties and the verticals furnished by telegraph poles and grain elevators were first revealed through photography. Surveyors had some problems with setting posts and mounting corners on the prairies, but rarely with leveling the chain.

## The section roadscape

Township platting by single lines may explain a curious omission in United States land legislation: no allowances for roads. Canada adopted the American section in 1871 with roads between all of them, 99 feet wide, changed in 1881 to 66 feet, and in 1908 to roads along alternate township lines and all range lines. Canadian surveyors do not use the word plat; "it changes to plan at the border."[19] Around 1850 the country had Indian traces, the National Road, military and territorial roads, ridge roads—still delightful to drive—and stagecoach roads.

The preoccupation with railroads led to the neglect of roads and left their maintenance to towns and individual land owners. The use of every section road under which survey markers got buried was "natural but wasteful," according to one report of 1869, but habit led to rejection of diagonals, although early market-to-town roads ran diagonally across fields. In 1935 the Highway Commission of Iowa was actually prohibited by the Iowa General Assembly from grading, bridging, and surfacing diagonal roads around Des Moines. However, the orthogonal survey landscape conceded a dramatic exception with the advent of the interstate highway system.

By 1900, the nation with the greatest railway system in the world had the worst roads. Many interests sought improvements: the military, cooperative creameries, the National League for Good Roads (organized in 1892), the Grange, citizens' groups, and the League of American Wheelmen, supported by bicycle manufacturers. After 1903, when Rural Free Delivery brought the all-American metal mailbox as a national emblem to country roads, mailmen urged farmers to keep roads in good condition. Some states aided counties to improve section roads. Finally, a major step was taken with passage in 1916 of the Federal Highway Act through lobbying by the most effective advocate, the American Automobile Association.

Most automobiles can climb straight 15 percent slopes, the upper limit highway commissioners will approve. When one drives in the heartland one can almost sense the tension between slope and section road, which keeps its straight up and downhill direction to the limit to avoid curving. After World War I states declared section roads to be public highways with only minor variations in their laws. The rural population declined consistently from then on, but road mileage increased all over the United States. Most of that increase consisted of straight section roads, increasingly paved when school consolidation required good local roads (Figs 7.7 & 8).

Since subsequent internal subdivisions are expected, township boundaries should be correct. The quarter section was never fully surveyed because defining the central point of sections was not legislated. When needed now it is established as equidistant from opposite corners. States began to legislate corner perpetuation through remonumentation (remeasurement of corners) by surveyors in the 1970s; Wisconsin and Indiana project a 5 percent remonumentation annually, the most successful rate for such programs. Sophisticated instruments now measure distances with a margin of error of 2 inches in 1 mile. One wonders if section roads need such scientific accuracy in a country where farmers are eager to contribute half of the width of a section road when public funds pay for paving and maintenance. Blatant surveying errors, such as the survey of Reynolds County, Missouri, are visible.[20] But the section roads look straight despite

**Figure 7.7**
A section road in
Antigo, Langlade
County, north-central
Wisconsin, in the early
1920s. The right-of-way
is not only straight but
wide, framed by the
double row of utility poles,
and the thin tires of many
model-Ts have plowed
numerous spoors in the
roadway.

small irregularities. "For flying, the section lines are wonderful. They make
the country in reality just what a pilot wants country to be—graph paper,"
wrote a German-American research pilot in the 1950s.[21] The overlay of
interstate highways brought some interference with the graphpaper.

## The conservation landscape

This square world is humanly artificial, it is not a pattern rooted in nature.
For all its economic simplicity, it is far from ecologically ideal. "Square
agriculture on a round earth," fulminated Hugh H. Bennett, author of the
United States Department of Agriculture pamphlet, *Soil erosion: a national
menace* published in 1928 to a rousing nationwide reception. Surveyors'
lines, which are also property lines, and fence lines, and field lines, all make
for straight furrows. Truly flat land needs drainage, widely applied in the
Middle West but rarely noticed. The prairies are seen as flat but have swells
and depressions. When slopes are steeper than 5 percent, the soil is subject
to water erosion, and clean tilled fields are subject to wind erosion. By the
turn of the century insufficient crop rotation, monocropping, overgrazing
and other widespread malpractices reduced productivity. Soil loss on
uplands, siltation in valleys, gullies on slopes, and flooding occurred in
many regions. Agricultural experiment stations began to work on counter-
measures. Bennett, first as head of the Erosion Service in 1933, then as chief
of the Soil Conservation Service from 1935 to 1951, fought ceaselessly to
promote contouring, which Jefferson had called horizontal plowing, and
Bennett's term became a household word.

Three concepts guided the change from traditional practices: watershed management, voluntary cooperation, and land use capability. Earlier endeavors toward land classification faltered. For example, the resolution of the House of Representatives of May 7, 1830 that public lands be classified by their "quality" and mapped on the basis of surveyors' notes was rejected by the Commissioner of the General Land Office because the notes represented lines, not the land in between, labor would "consume incalculable time," and "the great variety of soil embraced by almost every township would render it impractical." A century later, the Soil Conservation Service began to make such maps on the scale of 4 inches : 1 mile, showing soil, slope, stage of erosion, and erodibility. A new series began in 1974–5 and is scheduled for completion in 1995. These maps furnish the basis for planning conservation farms. The conversion to contouring could be watched on Conservation Day, which became a community event. With one day's enormous input of manpower, machinery, nursery stock, and fencing material, a farm's landscape was changed from rectangularity to curves—an impressive spectacle.

Farms have become increasingly fragmented through purchase or lease of additional forties; one farmstead no longer represents the owner's property. But survey lines endure (Fig. 7.9), still recognizable under modern practices such as stubble mulching, no tilling, terracing, use of sprinklers and combines. Section lines persist, with farmyards (sometimes abandoned) and buildings oriented along cardinal directions. Shelterbelts generally guard against northwest winds. Contours often do not mesh along property lines because the layout differs between neighbors. Seen from the air, the fields'

**Figure 7.8**
By the 1970s hard surfaced roads, such as this one on a former prairie in Winona County, Minnesota, etched the straightness of the section lines with even more finality.

tapestry of curves and colors still shows the survey's underlying seams.

Bennett wanted farms in the same watersheds to form soil conservation districts. But no watershed is delineated by straight lines. In nearly two-thirds of the United States, boundaries for states, counties, townships, and incorporated places are tied to the survey or follow rivers—a situation bad for coordinated flood control and water management. Yet by the late 1930s, soil conservation districts were organized by counties, probably because districts' supervisors needed the advice of county attorneys.

Coming from La Crosse to Coon Valley, Wisconsin, a sign by the highway reads: "The first watershed project of the nation." The Coon Valley Erosion Control Demonstration Project, started in 1933, had about 40,000 of the total 92,000 acres in the watershed under conservation practices by 1938, which extended into three counties.[22] The Turkey Creek Soil Conservation District in southern Nebraska, proposed in 1937 and organized with over 63,000 acres 18 months later, covered 96,377 acres after one more year. This does not imply conservation measures covered the whole area because data for non-cooperating farms were not published by the Soil Conservation Service. Since the Watershed Protection and Flood Prevention Act of 1954, watersheds not exceeding 250,000 acres are eligible for federal assistance provided local contributions are made first. Watershed management in soil conservation districts begins with petitions by county commissioners to the state board of conservation districts. The contemporary term for the continuing challenge of watershed management is hydrological planning.

Voluntary cooperators may neglect and discontinue conservation practices, even destroy them—for example, by pulling out shelterbelt trees that interfere with machines—leading to lost investment of public funds and labor. Modern laws contain clauses for crosscompliance, including acknowledgement of owners' responsibility for subsidized conservation measures. The Soil Conservation Service still has no regulatory power, and erstwhile

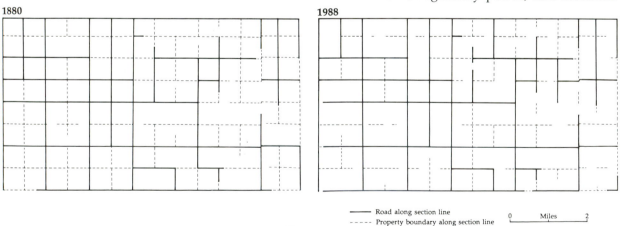

**Figure 7.9**
The land survey's grid lines remain stamped on the modern landscape. Many original section lines survive as road alignments and property boundaries, as demonstrated in a part of Jackson Township, Hamilton County, Indiana. The road pattern of 1880 is remarkably little changed today, but property lines, already departing from the primary section grid in 1880, have moved further away.

conservation farms can and do return to straight rows.

Operators change practices for economic gain and are helped by social pressure. In the Middle West, progressives used to call laggards "square-minded farmers," who returned the compliment by calling contour-stripping "crazy-quilt farming." Numerous publications preached "stewardship" of the land. A recent survey of prairie farmers in Illinois found that they ranked stewardship second, after productivity, as a criterion of "attractive" agricultural landscapes. Fifty years ago they would not have thought of the word.[23]

## Towards a national landscape

The gridiron monotony of urban America is not entirely a consequence of the survey. Colonizers contributed Philadelphia, Nouveau Orléans and other "historical" cities with geometric layouts. Brigham Young's Salt Lake City—with a monument to the Salt Lake City Meridian on Temple Square—has undifferentiated squares, quite suited for level ground. Citizens of Duluth, with streets running straight up a steep scarp, are less fortunate in Minnesotan winters. Some of San Francisco's streets are a challenge to pedestrians the year around, but they love the cable cars. Consider also the advantage of the grid pattern for numbering streets and avenues or giving them names with initials in alphabetical order, and easily finding the one-way street going in the opposite direction.

The contemporary problem is the survey-connected suburban subdivision: unregulated, extremely wasteful of agricultural land and, in the desert, ecologically destructive. When rebellion became acute, developers advertised subdivisions with curvilinear streets, providing "an environment for living close to nature" with lanes, crescents, hollows, and groves. An Illinois architect commented in 1966, "Underneath all these contemporary trappings, much of our basic thinking is geared to a gridiron block system." He believed that a significant change in platting can come only by public or quasi-public acquisition of large areas of land and complete rebuilding.[24] Replanning subdivisions is impossible because too much capital is invested underground. Besides, physical evidence of original corners is valid for property title. Resurveying and remonumentation is a formidable task. The federal government itself should resurvey about 50 million acres of national parks and federally owned land. So rectangular suburbia spreads further, not only from metropolitan areas.

Air travel has given millions of Americans in our time a glimpse of the nation's checkerboard land divisions. The idea that the survey landscape represents an airview infringes on the concept of landscape as a naïvely given reality, postulated by Carl O. Sauer. The airview puts the survey on display; it does not make it more comprehensible. It has its own regionalism which precludes a description of sights; readers must look for themselves. 143 Flying from east to west across the heartland one sees how the survey lines evenly cover most of the Northwest Territory and control the agriculturally used land until stopped by the mountains. Between their ranges on valley floors fragments of north–south and east–west lines appear, with a few buildings and roads ending somewhere, perhaps at an airstrip. The visible resemblance to the illustration of *Traces on the Rhodian shore* by Clarence Glacken is impressive. Shipwrecked Aristippus recognized geometrical figures on the sand and was cheered by these traces of men. Similarly we are reassured that the surveyors, unable to measure all the land on their advance to the west coast, will have resumed measurements in Oregon or California. Through flying, we can experience the continental spread of the United States land system.

The heartland invites driving rather than walking tours, although the latter would undoubtedly provide better communication with the country-side. The survey landscape is thought-provoking rather than enjoyable. One thinks of its attributes: relentless, sober and geometric, perhaps ahistorical. Every square mile is documented; so is its inception on May 20, 1785. The American Congress on Surveying and Mapping sponsored a two-day historical symposium in 1985 to honor the bicentennial of the Ordinance, which predates the adoption of the American Constitution and is considered the second most important piece of legislation ever passed by Congress.

We think of the grid-defined "Mainstreet of Middle America" as one of three American community types between the New England village and California suburbia, the cosmopolitan East Coast and the erstwhile frontier. Donald Meinig calls the heartland "typical America" in our auto culture. J. B. Jackson finds the grid layout of the Northwest Territory "the most imposing example" of the Great Awakening in the 18th century and considers the survey "not an easy landscape to understand."[25] The arts might help. Foremost is the Prairie School of architecture, from Sullivan's Bank in Owatonna, Minnesota, to Frank Lloyd Wright. His Broadacre City was planned "without changing the existing land system." His homes are both in a survey landscape: Taliesin East, rather neglected in lovely Spring Valley, Wisconsin, and Taliesin West, beautifully maintained but surrounded by the disheartening desert suburbia of Phoenix, Arizona. Of less renown is a bank he built in Mason City, Iowa.

Iowa's "mystique of geometry" lured a Swarthmore College professor away from "the vast reptilean suburb that writhes along the Atlantic" to spend his retirement in Iowa City.[26] In contrast, Grant Wood, after a fruitless year in Paris, returned to his home state and painted landscapes of billowing hills to convey the maternal roundness of Earth as "a gigantic reclining goddess," according to the catalogue of a recent retrospective exhibition on the artist. His fame derives from a 1930 picture, which became a national icon 30 years later. *American Gothic* is instantly memorized for its linear composition; with its religious inference, it is pure Middle West and, through its innumerable caricatures, undoubtedly at present the painting most widely known in the nation.

144   When in 1978 the National Endowment for the Humanities proposed

recorded programs "for the listening environment of the cabin," a reporter announced he would rather look down at the real landscape than hear a talk about the heartland.[27] Travelers acquainted with the genesis of the survey might feel the same way. After all, the square has the quality of firmness, and "the four Elements, the seasons, the stages of Man's life, and especially the four points of the compass are all sources of order and the stability of the world."[28]

# Chapter eight
## The clearing of the forests

MICHAEL WILLIAMS

O THER THAN THE creation of cities perhaps the single greatest factor in the making of the American landscape was the clearing of the forests that once covered nearly half the country. Clearing was the first step in the creation of new farmland. The abundant timber was a ready source of domestic fuel without which life in the northern two-thirds of the country during the winter months would have been impossible. Wood was the source of fuel for industry and transportation, and it was the major building material for houses, bridges, fences, furniture, ships, and a host of other artifacts which included even roads! The forest was ubiquitous and abundant. Wood and wooden products were central to and thoroughly permeated American life so that in 1836, James Hall could truthfully say, "Well may ours be called a *wooden country*."[1]

Several writers have explored the degree to which timber has entered into American life,[2] but the topic is much bigger than the "life from cradle to coffin" approach. It involves the whole geography, economy, and cultural fabric and ethos of America, and it resounds with grandiose themes such as deforestation, destructive exploitation, industrialization, agricultural self-sufficiency, Americanization, and environmental awareness.[3] That all these themes stem from the one great story of the clearing of the forests and the making of a new landscape is rarely appreciated and imperfectly understood.

Broadly speaking, the clearing of the forests was an outcome of three major processes—making farms and settling the land; logging to supply timber for constructional needs; and cutting to provide fuel for homes, industry, and transport. This three-fold division is valuable but it should be borne in mind that the distinction was never as clear-cut as that. In reality the clearing of the forests was a complex process. For example, the pioneer farmer not only cleared his land but he supplied fuel to the growing towns, and might even work in a mill during the winter months, or otherwise supply timber for building purposes. Likewise, while the primary object of the industrial loggers was to supply cheap timber for construction, the logged-over land, or cutover, was often sold for farming. The fuel needs of industry and transportation were often supplied by both farmers and loggers as well as specialized fuel getters. Nevertheless, for all this, the three-fold division is a useful one as it lends order to the complexity of processes and patterns that have spanned the continent for over four centuries, from even before the beginning of European settlement to the present and, inevitably, will continue well into the future, if only because trees are living, regenerating entities with the longest life cycle of any organism on Earth.

## The landscape of clearing

The conventional wisdom is that the landing of the Pilgrim Fathers and the planters in Virginia started the onslaught in the forest. The "war of the woods," as one settler called it, heightened the heroic nature of pioneer endeavor. But such a view conveniently ignores the fact that there were probably up to 12 million people in North America before European settlement,[4] the bulk of whom lived in the forests. We can never be exactly sure of the true extent of the Indian impact, but with these numbers it must have been great. Early explorers' accounts of "meadows," "fields," "openings," "flats," and "savannahs" leave one in no doubt of the extent of clearing, of the thinning out of the forests, and of the change in its composition with repeated firing.[5] One account of many must suffice. John Stratchey described the country around the present site of Hampton, Virginia, as

> ample and faire contrie indeed . . . the seat sometime of a thowsand Indians and three hundred houses, as it may well appeare better husbands [farmers] than in any part ells that we have observed which is the reason that so much ground is there cliered and opened, enough alreddy prepared to recieve corne and viniards of two or three thowsand acres.[6]

War, alcohol, disruption of tribal society, and, above all, disease wiped out most of the Indians, hence the already cleared fields which Strachey saw, and the Europeans moved easily into the clearings and cultivated the land. The Indian fields together with Indian crops such as maize, potatoes, squash, water melon, and kidney beans, and the cultivation of them in Indian fashion in mounds and rows with a hoe, enabled the European to gain a toe hold on the continent. The Europeans' debt to the Indian was immense.

Soon, however, the press of new migrants became greater and farm-making occurred everywhere in the forests along the eastern seaboard. A few acres were cleared quickly during the first year, either by clear cutting the trees—more common in northern states and hence known as Yankee

147

clearing—or by girdling the bark, which was more common in the southern states. In the former, the stumps were left to be pulled out of the ground when they rotted; in the latter the deadened trunk stood gauntly in the field and toppled over in time. Crops were cultivated in mounds between the stumps and fallen trunks, and stock were left to roam and graze in the surrounding forest. Clearing was long, hard, and gradual, and as each year passed so a few more acres would be opened up and added to the farm so that in ten years about 30 to 40 acres were cleared, depending on a variety of factors such as the size of the trees and the degree of family help.[7] More might have been cleared, but one must remember that the pioneer farmer had other tasks than simply felling trees. He had to be fairly self-sufficient and provide nearly everything on the spot from his block of land—a house, crude furniture, food, fencing, and a stock of fuel wood to bide him through the winter months. Moreover, initially there was little point in clearing more ground than was necessary to raise food for his family. In time, as settlement expanded and service centers grew up in the vicinity, a local market existed for his surplus food and fuel wood. Then it became worth his while to clear more land.[8]

The forest experience of the pioneer was the basic element in American geography and history for the first two and half centuries of settlement. Chastellux, who traveled extensively through the East in the 1780s, said that the sight of "the work of a single man who in the space of a year" had cut down several acres and built himself a house was something he had seen "a hundred times . . . I never travelled three miles without meeting a new settlement either beginning to take form or already in cultivation."[9]

Nevertheless, despite the fact that the felling of the forest and the making of a clearing in order to begin cultivation was the common experience of millions of Americans by the beginning of the 19th century, the realities of this everyday, mundane task of the ordinary people are difficult to pinpoint and to understand. Perhaps the essence of the experience is conveyed best in the series of four sketches made to illustrate Orsamus Turner's *History of the Holland Purchase of western New York*.[10] These sketches represent intervals of six months, two years, ten years and "the work of a life time" in the making of a farm in the forest. They are like four "stills" in the continuously moving picture of the making of the American landscape.

In the commercially oriented plantations of the South the slave replaced the pioneer family farmer as the clearer of the forest. Commonly, a slave was calculated to be able to clear three acres during the fall, split the timber for fences and posts, and then prepare the ground for planting in March.[11] Although clearing was done by slaves, there is no reason to think that it was done without expense as slaves had to be bought, housed, and fed, so what the northern farmers paid for in hard labor the southern planters paid for in hard cash.[12] Generally, clearing in the South was in large fields, big enough to accommodate the slave-operated crops of cotton and tobacco. But because these crops, particularly tobacco, were heavy consumers of nutrients and even made the soil toxic, and because no manure was put back into the ground, yields soon declined drastically and the planters moved on to clear fresh forest land after an interval of 10–20 years. Consequently, they rarely thought it worth grubbing up stumps because the field would soon be abandoned to weeds and the regenerating pine forest. This continual clearing and shifting on was worthwhile as tobacco yielded high returns and new forest land was cheap to buy.

It is difficult to estimate the total amount of land affected by clearing as no tally was kept because, among other things, clearing was regarded as the first step in the "natural" process of "improvement" that was not worth recording because it was so obvious and commonplace. Nevertheless, in the forested eastern half of the country the amount of "improved land" in predominantly forested counties is a good indicator of land cleared (Table 8.1). Before 1850 (when accurate figures became available), it is probable that over 113.7 million acres had been cleared. In the ten years between 1850 and 1859 there was a big upswing in clearing when a remarkable 39.7 million acres were affected. During the turbulent decade of the Civil War the amount of forest cleared and settled fell to 19.5 million acres, but rose again to its highest intercensal amount in 1870–9 when 49.3 million acres were affected. After that more acres of open prairie land rather than forest land were settled, a mere 1½ man-days labor being needed to break the sod and plow an acre of prairie compared to about 32 man-days of labor to clear an acre of forest.[13] Henceforth, agricultural clearing as an element in the making of the landscape diminished in importance compared with other processes, and the demand from the relatively treeless plains for construction timber and fuel stimulated the commercial lumber and fuel-providing trades.

In emphasizing the destruction and removal of the forest it should not be forgotten that the timber was also a resource of the highest value for housing, fencing, fuel, and, if the farmer was fortunate to have access to a ready market nearby, also for selling cordwood, making potash and pearl ash, collecting bark for tannin, turpentine, and pitch, and even for selling lumber.

**Table 8.1**  Improved land in farms, forested and nonforested counties
(in millions of acres)

|  | Forested areas | Nonforested areas |
| --- | --- | --- |
| Before 1850 | 113.7 | — |
| 1850–9 | 39.7 | 9.1 |
| 1860–9 | 19.5 | 19.4 |
| 1870–9 | 49.3 | 48.7 |
| 1880–9 | 28.6 | 57.7 |
| 1890–9 | 31.0 | 41.1 |
| 1900–9 | 22.4 | 51.6 |

*149*    *Source:* Primack 1962.

The pioneer farmers' most urgent need was to provide shelter for their families. The log cabin, the symbol of American pioneer farming life, was probably introduced into the Delaware region by the Swedes during the late 17th century, and it became universal in the forested areas of the country.[14] It was extravagant in its use of wood, but because it required no nails, holes, or shaping, it was easy and quick to construct, both great advantages on the frontier. With about 80 logs of between 20 and 30 feet in length and a few helpful neighbors gathered together for a logging "bee," a cabin could be erected in under three days.[15]

The details of the corner notching and stone chimney style varied from region to region and from one ethnic group to another to produce distinctive vernacular architecture, but the basic plan of one large room, perhaps with a division for sleeping quarters, was general.[16] Only the floorboards, doors and furniture consisted of sawn, or more likely, hewn timber. Furniture and utensils of wood were added as time permitted and need dictated, the most important of which were the two great beds that seemed to dominate most cabins and which "receive[d] the whole family." Later, as the locality became more settled, water-powered sawmills and sufficient quantities of sawn timber became available for the methods of construction to change. Elaborate and elegant clapboard houses (which had nearly always been the norm in the New England coastal settlements) built around carefully constructed timber frames became more common, and log cabins were abandoned or sometimes built over and incorporated within the clapboard house (see Figs. 8.1a, b & c).[17]

Fences were essential to keep out the free ranging cattle and hogs that roamed the uncleared and unclaimed forest. Once the trees were felled crude makeshift fences of tangled branches, rolled logs, and piled-up stumps gave place in time to more elaborate and permanent structures. The Virginia fence, also called the worm, snake, or zigzag fence because of its shape, was used everywhere in the East. It consisted of slender logs or split rails laid in a zigzag pattern and intersecting with each other at right angles. There were anything from six to ten rails in each segment and heavy bracing logs were sometimes placed at the intersections. The Virginia fence required great amounts of timber and took up large areas of land. For example, a square field of 160 acres required a ½ mile of fencing on each side (a total of 2 miles), but nearly half as much again if fenced in right-angled zigzags. Therefore a ten-rail, 10 foot length zigzag required at least 15,000 rails. The advantages of the Virginia fence were that it required no post-holes, pegs, notches, or ties, and it was easy to repair and move to new locations—an important consideration in the incremental enlargement of clearings in the North and the shifting tobacco cultivation in the South. Because no posts were embedded in the ground, it was said to last for 20 to 30 years. More importantly, it was hog-proof.[18]

Post and rail fencing was more economical in timber use—8,800 rails and 200 posts would enclose a 160-acre square field—but it meant more labor for the farmer who had to dig the holes as well as split the rails and slot the posts. The invention of the spiral augur after 1800 increased the popularity of post and hole fencing, particularly when farmers reached the treeless prairie edge after 1830 where wood was scarce and imported supplies very expensive. Not until the invention of barbed wire did the prairie farmer solve his fencing problem satisfactorily and cheaply.[19]

As the clearing expanded and coalesced, farmers were left with remnants of woodland on their steeper slopes, poorer ground, or extremities of their farms (see Fig. 8.1d). Even up until the beginning of this century, after nearly three centuries of clearing, anything up to half or more of the land in farms in the South and northern Lake States was still in woodland, as was 10 to 20 percent of the farmland in the Middle West and Middle Atlantic States.[20] To clear more would have been ecologically impossible given the regrowth rate, and economically unsound given the value of wood to the farmer. The woodlot, depending on its size, was a valuable source of rough grazing and browsing for stock (particularly in the South), a source of shelter from cold winds and heat, a source of construction timber and above all, a source of fuel.[21] The woodlot remains a prominent feature of the landscape.

The cold winter months made cheap and abundant fuel indispensable for settlement in the northern two-thirds of the country, and even in the South winters were cold enough for dwellings to require heating. The remedy was, said one settler, "not to spare the wood of which there is enough" and great blazing fires half way up the chimney were a common sight in pioneer cabins on all except the warmest summer days.

Initially, of course, fuel was the incidental by-product of clearing. Consequently, there is little evidence of how much wood was cut, gathered, or burned. Probably, the average farmer devoted between one-eighth to one-fifth of his work time to chopping, splitting, and stacking cords of wood once his initial farm-making activities were over.[22] An annual consumption of 20 to 30 cords was common for a rural household and larger farms used double that.[23]

Fuelwood was also an important source of cash for the pioneer family. Even if they did not live near a large town, such rural industries as blacksmith shops, tanneries, and iron works could provide a market. Certainly, all the larger towns on the eastern seaboard were short of fuel from the early 17th century onwards, a situation which grew progressively worse, and land haulage of timber was found to be practical for up to 25–30 miles.[24] During the colonial period firewood was moved further only if water transportation was available, either by river or along the coast. Wood for New York City came from Maine and New Jersey.[25] Merchants who cornered this lucrative trade relied on the farmers to send their cordwood downstream from the interior. After the Revolution, the scarcity of fuelwood became even more acute in the older settled areas and prices rose, making it profitable for farmers to haul cordwood from even greater distances than before.[26]

151    While emphasizing the theme of deforestation as a major formative

process in the landscape, it should be recognized that in recent years, and particularly since the mid 1930s, the forest has regenerated over vast areas where once it had been cleared. Abandonment of marginal and unproductive farms, the elimination of damaging fires, decreased dependence on wood, some aforestation, and better forest management all round have meant that in the 31 easternmost states 65.5 million acres of cleared farmland have reverted to forest between 1910 and 1959, against which can be balanced the clearing of 21.7 million acres (often for suburban growth).[27] Since 1959 another 16.9 million acres net have been lost to agriculture and inevitably gained by the forest. Some measures of these gains are shown in Table 8.2. Indeed, much of what we take to be virgin forest today in the eastern and southern states is barely 40 to 50 years old and it is growing out of old fields. The vitality of the forest is astounding and its rebirth is extensive.

## The landscape of logging

Until the early years of the 19th century lumber activity and agricultural settlement were coincident. The pioneer farmer was a part-time lumberman. The timber he cut was sold directly to consumers or more likely to small local mills; he sold cutting rights on his land and sometimes found seasonal employment working in the woods for a professional lumberman. Where rivers such as the Hudson, Delaware, Susquehanna, or Savannah and their tributaries flowed past an area of pioneering and onwards to a market, many farmers individually or in small groups cut timber and rafted the logs down stream, returning on foot with essential supplies bought from the proceeds of the sale in the urban market. Consequently, with this localized, sporadic, and uncoordinated logging, there was no distinctive landscape of logging in the early settled areas, only a landscape of farm-making.

But the situation changed with the advent of commercial, large-scale logging in New England and New York at the beginning of the 19th century. The new scale and form of logging was a response to the increasing demand for lumber from a growing population and an increasingly industrialized economy and society. From a mere 0.5 billion board feet cut in 1801,[28] the amount of lumber cut rose to 1.6 billion board feet in 1839, and the rate of cutting quickened at each successive decade to form a new and upward sloping curve which reached 8 billion board feet in 1859, 20 billion in 1880 and a peak of 46 billion board feet in 1904, an amount never reached since.[29]

The ability to supply these enormous quantities of lumber rested on a host of new inventions, techniques, methods of transportation, and forms of business organization all at a new, larger scale of operation. The lumber and forest products industry, like industry everywhere in the United States, was entering a phase of vigorous expansion in the era of industrial capitalism.[30] For example, steam power meant the concentration of industrial activity and

**Table 8.2**  Measures of forest regrowth, 1944–79

| Measure | 1944 | 1979 |
|---|---|---|
| Commercial forest (mill. acres) | 461 | 483 |
| Noncommercial forest (mill. acres) | 120 | 254 |
| Standing timber (bill. b.f.) | 1601 | 2569 |
| Annual net growth (bill. b.f.) | 6 | 36 |

*Source:* USFS (1982).

the beginnings of corporations and monopolies; steel meant better and more efficient tools; the railroad meant reliable, fast, and more flexible transportation; all meant increasing specializaton of activity, concern for efficiency in an era of cut-throat competition, tighter contractual agreements, and the mass production of a standardized manufactured end-product. In the forest the systematic cutting of large areas replaced the cutting of individual trees, and the large-scale ownership of standing timber enabled this monopolistic exploitation to take place.[31] The old scale of cutting was swept away.

In the mills, the water-powered, single bladed, up-and-down saws that cut between 200 and 3,000 board feet of lumber daily were replaced during the 1850s by steam-powered circular and gang-saws which raised output up to 40,000 board feet or even double, especially with round-the-clock operation which was now possible as the mills were released from the vagaries of daily and seasonal river flow. Steam replaced water as the major power source just after 1870. Friction feeds, edgers, drying kilns, and a whole host of inventions increased the quantity and quality of the output, and reduced waste which was usually about half the timber in a tree.[32] On the rivers, the rafting of a few logs lashed together was replaced by the log drive where the whole river was utilized as a transport network for all the logs cut throughout the basin. Logs were cut, hauled to the river's edge, and then sent downstream on the spring thaw, often being given a surging start with the release of the water pent up behind the specially constructed splash dams, to be sorted out at the pens or "booms" at the mills many miles downstream. The logs were identified and credited by an elaborate system of markings notched into them.

The log drive required a great deal of cooperation and regulation. Driving, river improvement, and boomage charges were levied, and strict laws enforced over the date of the start of the log drive, the methods of sorting, and the disposal of "strays."[33] Without the spatial system of the log drive as a part of the new production pipeline the new high output mills could not have functioned efficiently and met the demand. While the log drive operated at the "local" level, a new system of continental proportions

**Figure 8.1**
Orsamus Turner produced these four etchings of the life cycle of a pioneer woodsman in upstate New York in 1851. They represent the same scene at four intervals: six months, two years, ten years, and "the work of a lifetime." These delightful etchings teem with detail about the pioneer's life, from the arrival of children and neighbors (b) to the arrival of the railroad (d). They encapsulate the essential experience of millions of woodland's farmers.

evolved linking the areas of lumber surplus—mainly the Lake States—with the areas of lumber deficiency in the Northeast and the prairies. Most eastern seaboard states were experiencing shortfalls by the 1830s, New York, for example, importing over 500,000 tons annually by 1850, and double that amount ten years later. The shortfall was made up by imports, first from neighboring states and Ottawa, and then eventually from the Lake States.[34] Lumber was sent by lake steamer to be offloaded at Buffalo or Tonawanda, and then it went by the Erie Canal to Albany (which grew into the largest wholesale lumber center at the time), and then down the Hudson to New York. In the west, Chicago grew after about 1845 to become the gateway through which the lumber of eastern Wisconsin and western Michigan went to the prairie states to the Southwest and South. A subsidiary arm of this western transportation system was that whereby the lumber of Minnesota and western Wisconsin went down the Mississippi in enormous 4–5 acre size rafts to be offloaded at the westbank ports for milling and then distribution over the plains to the emerging settlements in Kansas, Nebraska, Iowa and even as far west as Colorado during the 1870s and 1880s. Initially, the Chicago and Mississippi subsystems functioned independently, but when Chicago's railroads splayed out across the Middle West they came into direct competition.[35] Later, during the 1880s, when the Lake States were in decline and the South came "on stream" as the major supplier of Middle America, the railroad system linked all areas and dominated the distribution of lumber.

The landscape of commercial logging reached its characteristic form and epitome in the Lake States where the assiduous application of new inventions, with the addition of steam skidders, ice roads, and logging railroads, enabled exploitation to proceed efficiently and ruthlessly. The logging landscape had two faces: there was the landscape of the processes of exploitation and the landscape of depletion.

There is no one example which one can point to of the typical logging landscape, but Figures 8.2a, b & c are a composite picture of many 19th century accounts. In Fig. 8.2a the landscape of the log drive is depicted; its main characteristics have been described in detail already. But in addition there were the ice roads, made by sprinkling water over specially graded tracks so that sleds with loads of up to 30,000 board feet could be drawn by horse and glide easily with a minimum of friction to the water's edge during the winter months. The lumber camps, specialist settlements to house the workers in the forest, are also shown. At first these were crudely built, composite, one-building structures of bunkhouse, dormitories, and stores. But in time they became more complex groups of structures, each with a specialized function, so that the lumbercamp came to resemble a village in the woods.[36] With the advent of the railroad during the 1860s the ideal site for a mill became the bank of a log-driving stream where a railway crossed it (Fig. 8.2b), and by the end of the century the conjunction of the two explained nearly all the larger concentrations of lumber activity in the Lake States and even in Maine. Adjacent to the mill was the inevitable lumber town to house the

*The clearing of the forests*

**Figure 8.2**
Distinctive landscapes in the evolution of American logging (these phases were often overlapping in any one region).

(a) Before 1850: pre-steam, using the river for transport. Characteristic of New England, New York, and early Lakes States logging.

(b) 1850–80: the addition of logging railroads, steam mills, and permanent settlements. Characteristic of later Lakes States and early southern logging.

(c) 1880–1920: integration of logging railroads with mainline carriers. Breakdown of processes at mills. Characteristic of the South.

(d) 1920 onward: logging by road, trucks, tractors, and mechanical hoists. Addition of pulp making at the mill. Characteristic of the Pacific Northwest.

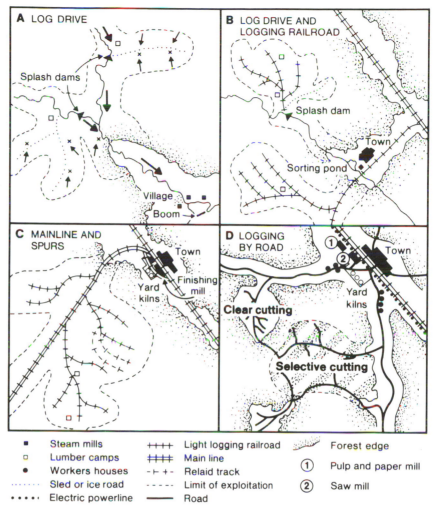

| | | | |
|---|---|---|---|
| ■ | Steam mills | ++++ | Light logging railroad |
| □ | Lumber camps | ‡‡‡‡ | Main line |
| ● | Workers houses | -⊢+- | Relaid track |
| ·····  | Sled or ice road | ----- | Limit of exploitation |
| ••••• | Electric powerline | ——— | Road |

Forest edge
① Pulp and paper mill
② Saw mill

workers. The lumber towns grew haphazardly, although in later years whole towns were created by mill owners *ab initio* in order to house their workers and retain a captive workforce.[37] In the forest above the splash dams lightweight logging railway tracks were laid in all directions, and once the immediate forest had been felled the lightweight track could be taken up, and relaid a few hundred yards further on. The final stage (Fig. 8.2c) came with the construction of spur lines from the main lines without any break of gauge. Exploitation was quickened and maximized. Mill owners found it profitable to install drying kilns to assist seasoning, and planing mills to finish off products which could then be transported directly to the customer, and they even began to produce complete ready-to-assemble wooden houses, churches, stores, and other buildings in a number of styles.

The heady boom of cutting in the Lake States which doubled production of the white pine from about 4 billion board feet in 1870 to over 9 billion in 1890 only to fall continuously from then on to a mere 1 billion board feet in

1920, left a landscape of depletion behind it. Although many mills turned to other types of wood, particularly hemlock and hardwoods, dozens of once flourishing villages and towns went into decline and the smallest disappeared. Some of the more enterprising such as Eau Claire, Oshkosh, and La Crosse in Wisconsin or Grand Rapids in Michigan for example, managed to diversify into other manufactures and a whole array of wood-using industries like door, blind and sash and furniture making sprang up,[38] but many more were like Cheboygan and Alpena in Michigan which became ghosts of their former selves. In 1886, Cheboygan had been a bustling town of over 6,000 inhabitants, 16 mills, and numerous wood-using industries, but in 1916 there were only two mills left and the number of employees in industry had fallen to barely 1,000. Alpena suffered similarly. Whereas the town had seemed "made of saw dust," it now scratched for a living with the depletion of the forests:

> Mills which formerly selected only the stoutest pine trunk now welcome the slender log, the crooked log, the rotten log, and the sunken log fished up from the river bottom. In place of beams for the western railway bridge or huge rafters for the Gothic church, Alpena busily turns out planks, shingles, spools, pail handles, veneering, and the wooden peg for furniture. It also makes manila paper out of hemlock pulp. It brings hemlock bark to its tannery. It combs its brains for inventions to utilize by-products, as does the Chicago pork-packer.[39]

In addition to the decline and disappearance of the settlements, the forests themselves had deteriorated. The great piles of slash waste left on the forest floor after the cut-out-and-get-out exploitation were ready fuel for the devastating fires that spread repeatedly through the region. The great Peshtigo Fire of northeastern Wisconsin in 1871 devastated an area of 50 square miles and killed 1,500 people, and the Michigan fire of the same year consumed 2.5 million acres. In 1885, nearly all the Wisconsin Valley was swept by fire, and in 1894 there was the great Hinckley Fire in Minnesota that caused 418 deaths, and so it went on almost annually.[40]

As the forest diminished and communities waned for lack of raw material supplies, the desire to conserve the forest in some way or another rose from being a quiet murmur of the slightly eccentric and intellectual to the loud cry of practical people who saw their livelihood threatened.

Finally there was one other outcome of forest exploitation which was manifest in the landscape—that was the cutovers; they probably totaled over 50 million acres, stretching across the middle and northern parts of the three Lake States, from the Red River in Minnesota in the west to Lake Huron in Michigan in the east. Unlike the hardwood forests to the south which had been taken up immediately for agriculture once they had been cut, these lands were marginal to farming in all senses of the word. Cutting had been careless, so that the ground was strewn with debris and massive stumps often cut many feet above the ground. Fires had been devastating, the soil was indifferent, poor, glacial outwash sands and gravels for the most part, and the climate averaged only 100 to 130 frost-free days, which was too short for growing corn but just sufficient for growing grass and hay. Most of the cutover was simply too far north for agriculture.[41]

But the timber companies wanted to wring the last penny out of the land, and moreover, they wanted to get rid of it because it was liable to state taxes. It could be abandoned, of course, but that threw an intolerable burden on surrounding tax-paying areas. The railway companies wanted settlement because new farms would increase revenues, and the state governments, imbued with concepts of progress and improvement were not prepared to allow northern portions of their states to "revert to wilderness with the passing of the lumber industry."

All three advertised the virtues of the cutover widely in America and Europe, particularly in Scandinavia. The literature was boosterish; it sidestepped the difficulties of the environment and promoted an image of a rural paradise that rivaled the Middle West or better parts of the Great Plains in its productivity. Thousands of unsuspecting migrants came and struggled to make a living in impossible conditions. There was a high rate of failure, and the remainder hung on leading a wretched life trying to eke out an existence.[42] The cutovers were (and still are in places) dotted with unpainted and sagging farmhouse structures, some mere tar-paper shacks, and derelict fences. In the deserted fields occasionally one still sees a lilac bush or a heaped-up pile of stones where a chimney once stood, both markers of an abandoned homestead, the whole scene a mute and a melancholy testimony to abandoned hopes. Only after the mid-1930s were reclamation efforts made in the cutover to return the land to the crop it grew best—trees.

The Lake States were the first region to show the degree to which man could alter the landscape by logging, but it was not the only region affected. Just as the wave of production (and firms) had shifted progressively from New England to New York and Pennsylvania by the early 19th century, so, as the output of the Lake States declined after 1880, the wave of exploitation moved on to the southern states, particularly to Georgia, Alabama, Mississippi, Louisiana, and eastern Texas. Then, when that region faltered after about 1910 production moved on to the Pacific Northwest.[43] The South was the epitome of industrial capitalism in the lumber industry. Forest exploitation was almost entirely railroad focused, except along the few rivers that penetrated the region, such as the Savannah and Alabama in Georgia, the Pearl and Pascagoula in Mississippi, and Calcasieu in Louisiana.[44] Mainline railroads were laid from southern ports to northern markets, usually in competition with the Mississippi steamboat trade, and many spur lines of 40 or 50 miles in length were laid out in the surrounding pine forests with preselected sites for mills at 3 to 5 mile intervals along their routes, the mills sometimes being built ahead of the railways so that the stock of lumber would be ready once the connection was made. Mills were generally larger than in the Lake States and exclusively steam powered. Haulage was more

159

mechanized, usually by massive steam operated skidders that ran on the railway tracks. These had long grappling arms and derricks from which steel cables could be run out into the surrounding forest and attached to logs, which could then be dragged to the railside and hoisted on to the trucks.[45] As the skidders harvested the logs in a circle around them, so they ripped out all the young growth that might have allowed the forest to regenerate and scraped the thin soil bare.

Just as the big companies owned the land, the trees—in fact whole counties—so they owned the towns and their inhabitants too. There were hundreds of little company towns, all with their center of a church or two, lodging houses and the commissary, the single department or general store owned and operated by the company where the employees bought the bulk of their food and goods, often at inflated prices, by coupons paid in lieu of wages. Most laborers were ex-slaves or poor whites coming off low-income farms. No all-male lumberjack camps with the aura of rugged and heroic individualism existed in the South. It was a docile laborforce of family men in small towns who could not protest about their isolation and exploitation.[46] They were mere cogs in the machine of industrial lumbering.[47]

With important social differences, then, the landscape of lumber exploitation in the South conformed to the pattern in Figure 8.2c, usually without the river. Additionally, because of the generally flatter terrain of the South, the felling of the forest was more regular and methodical, logging lines being laid at intervals of less than a 1,000 feet in order to strip the land bare of every merchantable tree.

When the forest was stripped of its timber the companies moved their mills and their key workers and let the town die. The mills, once the "pulsing hearts" of the settlements, sagged at their foundations and the railroads rusted from disuse. In the towns grass began "to grow from the middle of every street and broken window lights bespoke deserted homes." The mill had "sawed out."[48] The sequence of birth and death of sawmill towns in the Calcasieu basin, western Louisiana between 1895 and 1955 is shown in Figure 8.3.[49]

In the cutover what the skidders had not destroyed fires in the lumbering debris finished off. How much land was left in cutover is difficult to calculate. In 1907 it was said to be an astounding 79 million acres of which only one-fifth was restocking with trees. In 1920 the figure was revised to 55.4 million of which just over half was restocking with trees.[50] Whatever the truth, one thing was certain, logging had left a vast area of derelict land throughout the forest of the South.

In the Pacific Northwest the company lumber town reigned supreme in the logging landscape, and because there was little agriculture there were few other settlements. Initially, most of the lumber towns hugged the coast, relying on exporting their cut timber south to San Francisco and throughout the Pacific, but when the lumbermen moved inland into the broken terrain and steep slopes of the ranges other means of exploitation had to be devised.[51] Hauling could not be done easily by river or rail, and therefore water flumes were constructed to link the high ground in the ranges to the lowland mills. Stationary donkey engines and overhead skyline skidders were used to negotiate the difficulties of yarding in the forest. By the 1920s, however, significant innovations were underway in log haulage, particularly in the Douglas fir forests of the Cascades and Coastal Range, with the advent of tractors (later with great A-frame hoists behind) to snake out the logs, bulldozers to make rough tracks, and trucks to take the logs to the mills (Fig. 8.2d). The cheapness, mobility and relatively small laborforce needed revolutionized logging. While the big companies used these methods so too could individual small-scale loggers, and the landscape of heavy capitalization in equipment and permanent way was replaced by one of flexibility and few permanent features.[52] Such practices spread to most other logging regions by 1940.

On the whole, there was far less cutover land in the Northwest than in any other region. The logging companies knew that there were few farmers willing to take on the steep slopes, massive stumps, and high rainfall of the region, and they did not try to promote agricultural settlement. In any case the forest grew back so quickly and the product was so valuable, and they knew that there were no other regions to which they could move on as in the past, that they made the best of what was there. Many companies attempted to adopt conservation techniques of cutting in order to promote regrowth in time. Thus the Pacific Northwest was different to the other logging regions.

**Figure 8.3**
The creation and abandonment of lumber towns as stands were cut out in the great southern pine forests of the Calcasieu Basin, western Louisiana between 1895 and 1955.

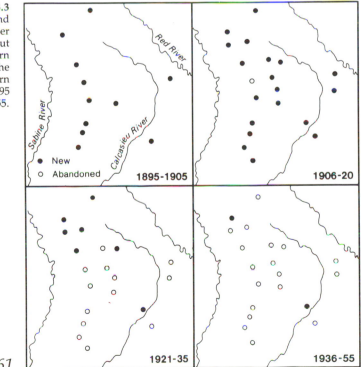

161

## The landscape of fuel gathering

While the cutting and gathering of wood for fuel has probably consumed more wood than any other use to which the forest has been put, even to the present day, it has produced few distinctive landscapes. Fuel was the incidental by-product of agricultural clearing and, to a lesser extent, of logging. It was subsumed in the bigger and and more spectacular themes of change in the forests, although occasionally we do have an example of effects of domestic cutting as when John Thomas of New York was taken by a landowner he knew to view "over one hundred acres of land, once densely covered with timber, but now entirely cleared for the sole purpose of supplying his family with firewood during the forty years he has resided there."[53]

But this was rare, and only in the cases where mineral deposits impinged on the forests, large towns made exhorbitant demands on the surrounding area, or specific routeways funneled the concentration of steam-powered locomotives or boats, can one point to definite inroads due to fuel getting.

Iron-making caused denudation and thinning of the forest on a local scale, especially as the use of charcoal for fuel lingered on in the United States well into the late 19th and early 20th centuries when it had long since disappeared in other industrialized nations.[54] The slow death of charcoal iron-making arose from the sheer abundance of wood as a fuel, but also from the fact that charcoal-made iron had positive qualities of heat resistance, toughness, yet also malleability.[55] It was a good all-purpose iron for use on the frontier which could be made into boilers, tools, and implements and could retain a good cutting edge.

In 1865 there were 560 iron furnaces in the United States of which 439, or 78 percent were still charcoal fueled, and these were concentrated in the Hanging Rock district of southern Ohio, in the Allegheny Valley northeast of Pittsburgh, in the Juniata Valley, in south-central Pennsylvania, and in the Berkshires on the New York/Massachusetts/Connecticut borders. The bulk of the remainder of the furnaces burnt anthracite and were concentrated in eastern Pennsylvania.[56] In time most of these charcoal furnaces were abandoned or converted to coal of some sort or another, but charcoal iron-making did not die out entirely and continued to flourish in the South, and particularly in northern Michigan and Wisconsin, in conjunction with the high-grade iron furnaces of the Superior ranges until as late as 1940.

Large supplies of wood were needed to fuel these furnaces, and iron "plantations" or estates of 30,000 to 100,000 acres of woodland around or near the furnaces were common. These would be cut in a rotational fashion, and there is plenty of evidence of exhaustion of supplies through over-cutting as in Scioto, Jackson, and Vinton Counties in southern Ohio or in the Ramapos Mountains in New York/New Jersey, and of the abandonment of furnaces for want of fuel as a consequence.[57] The amount of forest cleared specifically for iron-making depended upon the density of the trees and the

162

efficiency of the furnace, but at a modest estimate of 150 acres for every 1,000 tons of pig iron produced then the amount of acres affected could have been as low as 25,000 in 1862 and as high as 94,000 in 1890, although it should also be borne in mind that many forests near furnaces were cut over at 25–30 year intervals, or sometimes less. For example, a detailed survey of the 837 square miles of Vinton and Jackson Counties in the Hanging Rock district of Ohio shows that 60 percent of the forest was cut clear between 1850 and 1860 down to 4-inch diameter trees, and that the forests regenerated sufficiently for recutting to be carried out again at the beginning of this century.[58] Either way, taking the larger or smaller estimate, the amount of forest cut had relatively little impact on the forest as a whole. Even if we total all the known charcoal iron production between 1855 and 1910 (20.4 million tons) it would have only consumed 4,800 square miles of woodland, or 3,000 square miles if a 25-year regrowth had been employed. Impressive as this is, it should be compared to the amount of land cleared for agriculture during the same period. It is a mere 1.3 percent of that or 0.8 percent if regrowth is considered. Having said that, however, charcoal iron production was concentrated and the effects on the forest were noticeable; it was an industrial intrusion into the rural landscape and thus commanded special attention and comment. Locally, the furnaces and the thinned and cut forests were visually prominent, and charcoal iron, rather like fuel for locomotives, could be pointed to as a great destroyer of forests. Nationally it was a mere pin prick.

Steamboats, steam engines and locomotives also consumed large amounts of wood fuel, but how much is difficult to ascertain. Because of the relatively late start to industrialization in the United States, there was little demand for generating steam in stationary engines. By 1850, 65 percent of all mechanical work output still came from wind and water and the remainder from wood and coal, and it was not until 1870 that the proportions were reversed.

Bulkiness was an important consideration of substitution, particularly in locomotives, as 1 ton of coal could replace about 4 tons of wood, but the sheer abundance of wood along the railroad routes delayed adoption.[59] Along the major rivers, ample supplies of timber powered a complex steamboat system. The distribution of the number of cords sold and entering into commercial trade in 1840 shows that the counties adjacent to the Mississippi–Ohio account for 16 percent of the total of 5.3 million cords entering the trade in that particular year, the line of above-average producing counties paralleling exactly the course of these two rivers across the continent.[60] However, just as the wood cut for charcoal, the wood cut for fuel for mechanical purposes was a minor inroad into the forest compared to that cut for domestic purposes. It is far more probable that timber cut for railroad ties exceeded many times the timber cut for fuel on the railroads.

In 1879, domestic fuel use was 95.5 percent of a total of 147.2 million cords cut during that year, the remainder being divided between charcoal for iron *163* smelting (1 percent), manufacturing and railroads (1 percent each), steamboats (0.5 percent), and mineral operations taking up the remaining 0.4 percent.[61] Which brings us full circle. The greatest impact on the forest—domestic fuel use—is the impact that we know least about because it is the combination of millions of individual unrelated actions, and it is submerged in the bigger and grander topic of agricultural clearing. Only where there was a complex coastal trade, as between Maine and Boston and New York, or between the New Jersey Pine Barrens and New York do we know about the areas affected by cutting. Domestic fuel getting and marketing is, as the historian Arthur Cole has suggested, a "mystery" in that is was so important and ubiquitous, but that so little is known about it.[62] Nevertheless, the conclusion must be that fuel getting exceeded by far all other demands on the forest, lumber included.

## The balance sheet

At the most conservative estimate over 350 million acres of former forest have been cleared for agriculture and another 20 million acres for industry, communications, mining, and urban spread. In all, this destruction must have eliminated one half of the original forest cover of the United States, which should give us pause to think when we bewail the present deforestation of the tropical world.

But what of the landscape of clearing today? Simply, it is the normal landscape that surrounds anyone who travels in the rural parts of the United States where trees grow naturally. It requires an enormous effort of imagination to see the forests as they once were (Fig. 8.4). Unlike other activities of man in changing the landscape which leave a permanent legacy in the form of buildings, embankments, draining channels, survey lines, and roads, for example, the end-result of clearing is the elimination of the landscape feature under examination. The result is nothing, or at least, the norm; the tamed, domesticated landscape of fields, meadows, intervening patches of woodland and woodlot, of settlements, and suburbs. As for the artifacts of clearing, they have nearly all gone. The log cabins and zigzag fences are found occasionally in remote rural areas as in upland Appalachia, but increasingly they are to be found only in museums and preserved historical sites. Splash dams, booms, and logging railways are increasingly things of the past and are replaced by highways, trucks, tractors, and chain saws. Only the massive mills with their log ponds and piles of sawn timber remain as visual reminders of the logging landscapes of the past. Lumber towns still exist, particularly in the Pacific Northwest, but they are functionally and socially much more heterogeneous. The cutovers are reverting to forest everywhere (Figs. 8.5a, b, c & d). Despite the massive destruction of trees by agriculture, logging and fuel getting, the forest is still a dominant feature of the American visual scene. To imagine an America without trees is to imagine another world.

**Figure 8.4**
Area of "virgin" forest in 1620, 1850, and 1920. These were a stark and graphic portrayal of deforestation, but in a sense they were misleading. Forests are dynamic, living entities, and although the original "virgin" forest may have been cut, the new forest grew back. Therefore, the picture of 1920 is a gross understatement of forest cover, although the others were more or less correct.

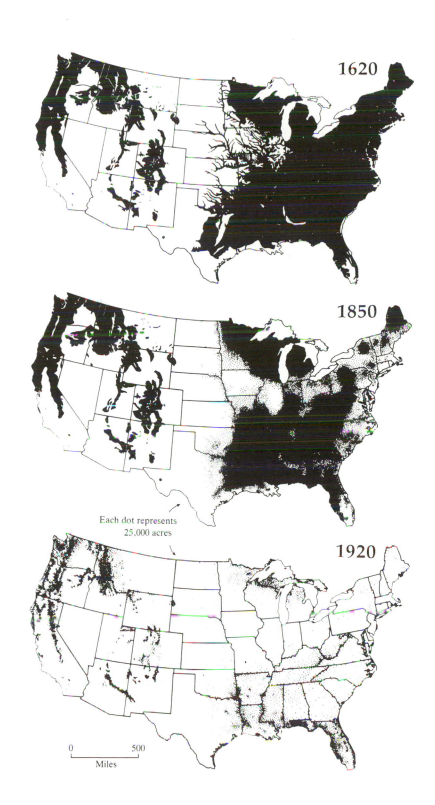

**Figure 8.5**
Natural regrowth is far more vigorous than most people realize so that today the United States probably has about 60 million acres net more forest than it did in 1910. Shown here are four scenes somewhere in the Pacific Northwest, taken at roughly ten-year intervals between 1930 and 1960.

If we try to draw up a balance sheet of the positive and negative aspects of forest clearing then the following is clear. The forest supplied the raw material for industrial growth during the late 18th and most of the 19th centuries. The forest that was cleared supplied the land that has supported the agriculture that has made America the foremost food producer in the world, and the lumber has provided cheaply the houses and helped the means of transportation that are major features of American life. The forest has other attributes. It and the pioneer farmer or backwoodsman have provided potent symbols of American life and ethos, in terms of self-sufficiency, effort, and practicality. It is a great esthetic and leisure resource, for to indulge in recreation out-of-doors means going into the woods for most Americans.

Balanced against these immense benefits have been many, but less tangible, losses. The subtle relationships between forests and runoff, floods, rainfall, soil formation, erosion, and micro- and macro-climatic occurrences have never been clearly quantified, but it is certain that rivers have filled with sediments, floods have been more frequent and greater, and that large areas of fertile land and sloping ground have been degraded. Wild life has been lost—in fact the whole ecological balance has been upset. But even out of this has come some good. Trees produce strong emotions in most of humankind, and the wholesale destruction of the past centuries was not done without protest. The first stirrings of the conservation and environmental movement as we know it in the Western World today began in the American forests in the years just prior to, and just after, the Civil War.

# Chapter nine
# Settlement of the American grassland

## JOHN C. HUDSON

THE GEOGRAPHY OF settlement in the American grassland reveals two fundamental relationships. The first is that the largest share of its area is devoted to crop production because the grassland offers the most fertile, least hilly, and generally most suitable farming country found anywhere in the United States. The proportion of land in crops increases markedly as one moves from forested areas to grass, and the contrast is even stronger if the comparison is made in terms of the acreage simply in grain crops. Second, the economic potential of these prime farmlands was well known during the railroad-building era of the latter 19th and early 20th centuries. As a result, there developed within the grassland a strong correlation between the number of miles of railroad and the number of acres in crops. The better the land the greater the value of its produce and the more money railroads stood to earn hauling it to market. Each new line of track was dotted with new towns, most of which were built at the time of railway construction. Thus, the better the land the greater the crop acreage and the finer the "mesh" of the town-and-railroad network. Each organized county had to have a seat of government; the location and spacing of the county seats, most of which are the largest towns in their respective counties, create a striking general pattern of towns (Fig.9.1).

These linkages define the settlement system of a broad area beginning along the western edge of Indiana and spreading fan-like west from there to include nearly all the land between the Red River of the North and the panhandle of Texas. The largest number of towns within this region was sited by railroad companies whose purpose was to create linked chains of marketing points where farmers would deliver crops for the railroad to haul to distant urban centers. Competition between railroads led to a uniform spacing of towns along a line as well as a uniform placement of the lines of track. This was the process that produced the "central place" network of states such as Iowa in the latter half of the 19th century. Because of the comparative recency of these developments and the lack of sweeping changes that might have produced newer forms, the landscape still has this

organization.

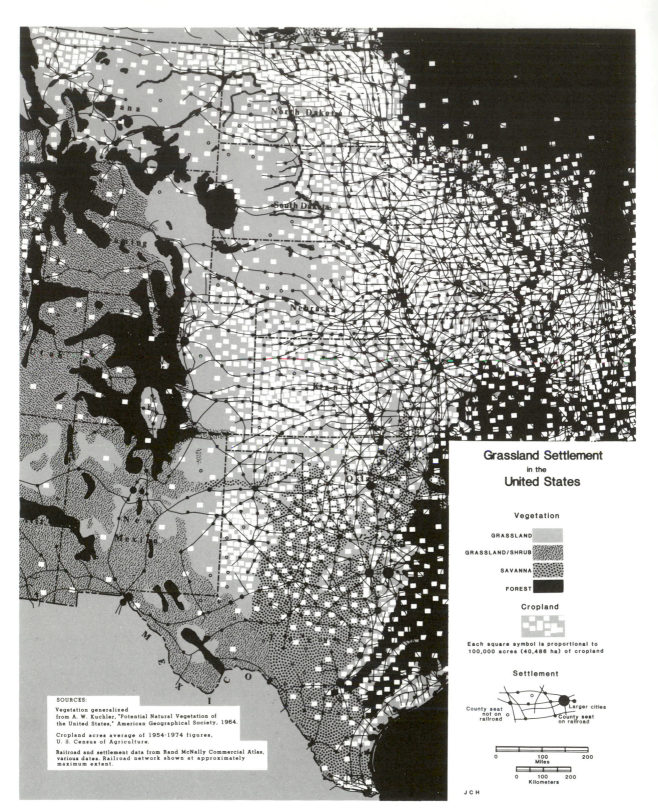

**Figure 9.1**
Grassland settlement in the United States.

In central Montana, western South Dakota, south-central Colorado, and most of Wyoming and New Mexico grasses dominate, but they grow on soils so marginal for agriculture, and which receive so little rainfall during the growing season, that crop farming is not economical in most years. Although these western short-grass plains have been plowed up and planted during periods of high prices and strong demand for grain cereals, the land is devoted largely to stockraising today just as it was a century ago. Only transcontinental or other long-distance railroads ever served such areas; towns are few in number, small in size, and spaced like beads on a string. What differentiates this region from that to the east is its poor prospects for crop farming which, in turn, discouraged westward extension of the railroad-settlement grid beyond the crop-producing areas.[1]

The grassland settlement pattern is also demarcated on the northeast and southeast by clear boundaries at the forest margin.[2] Deciduous forest occupies a wide swath across Wisconsin, but it narrows practically to disappearance in northern Minnesota. North and east of this, in turn, lies the coniferous forest, a land almost totally unsuited for grain crops. Hilly lands southeast of the grassland region, especially the Ozark Highlands of Missouri, define another sharp transition in settlement systems coinciding with the prairie–forest border. In south-central Missouri, as in northern Minnesota, Michigan, and Wisconsin, lands that would not support commercial grain farming did not attract railroad builders except for purposes of resource extraction.

## Vegetation and settlement

The grassland settlement region can be delimited with reference to vegetation, croplands, and railroads because the linkages between these three explain more than does the usual schema in which precipitation and population density are compared. Nevertheless, after more than a century of scholarship on the American grassland and its mode of human settlement, "rainfall determinism" remains dominant in much of the literature. This explanation claims that grasslands result from a deficiency of precipitation; semi-aridity restricts agricultural options; and thus limited economic possibilities set a ceiling on population density.

In truth, however, moisture deficiency alone cannot even explain why the grassland exists, let alone reveal why it is best used for some things and not others, or account for why people built certain kinds of settlements there. More than four decades ago, Carl Sauer wrote that the "climatologic description of grasslands is not at all satisfactory," and in a few paragraphs demolished the circular reasoning that had led to concepts such as "grassland climate."[3] Sauer, following the works of Shaler and Hilgard half a century before, identified fire as the primary cause of the central North American grassland. Sauer's hypothesis has remained controversial, perhaps because he insisted that fires on a scale necessary to produce the grassland must have been set by early man. A recent survey of Holocene vegetation history in the Middle West concludes "that topography, fire, and soil are proximal factors controlling the exact timing and local expression of vegetation change."[4] Although fire remains the best explanation we have of why grass vegetation became established on gently rolling uplands, climatic factors offer a convincing explanation of the regional limits of this vegetation type, especially the grassland's wedge-shaped penetration of the continent as far east as the southern tip of Lake Michigan. John Borchert demonstrated correlations between this "prairie peninsula" and the relative dominance of adiabatically warmed Pacific air east of the Rocky Mountain front during the growing season.[5] Drought is particularly common in the area most dominated by this Pacific air stream. Thus, climate alone does not explain the grassland, but neither should climate be omitted from the explanation.

The grassland is less extensive today than it was just before Euro-American settlement began. It has shrunk because the practice of extinguishing fires has allowed trees to survive farther and farther away from protective crags and crevasses. More important in the disappearance of the treeless grassland has been the habit of tree planting that white settlers brought to the plains. Shelterbelts and plantations of various sorts have been made throughout the region; accidental fire or deliberate removal, rather than dessication, has caused the demise of some of these plantings.

The American grassland contains remnants of another human modification of woody vegetation. Wood for fencing was in short supply on the prairies. Experimentation with hedges, ditches, and embankments began in Illinois in the late 1830s and continued until the late 1870s when economical barbed-wire fencing was introduced.[6] This period, which covers the dates of initial settlement as far west as central Nebraska and Kansas, was characterized by mixed crop and livestock farming over most of the region, and thus the need for confining animals was widespread. The most popular of the hedge varieties was the Osage orange (*Maclura pomifera*), a tough, hardy shrub that grew well as far north as central Iowa, and its survival along fencerows from Illinois to Kansas can be observed today (Fig. 9.2).

It is the forest patches on steep valley sides and isolated buttes that hold the key to landscape history, however. The gorge of the Niobrara River in northern Nebraska, the buttes of the western Dakota, and the abrupt breaks of the Canadian and Cimarron Rivers in northeastern New Mexico are examples of places receiving precipitation of approximately 15–20 inches per year, well within grassland norms, yet these sites support healthy, spreading forests. Such sites have offered sanctuary for more than trees. It was in the woodland of Palo Duro Canyon, along the Prairie Dog Town Fork of the Red River south of Amarillo, Texas, that Francisco Vasquez de Coronado and his party rested in the spring of 1541 (Figs 9.3 & 4). Their long trek across the flat and featureless Staked Plains (*Llano Estacado*) in search of the mythical city of Quivira produced no riches, but in the sheltered canyons they found the more or less permanent settlements of

**Figure 9.2**
A relict Osage orange hedge marks a field boundary along a sectionline road in Lyon County, Kansas. Rail, or worm, fences dominated this county in the 1870s when as much as 10 percent of the county's area was in timber; by 1880, more than 60 miles of hedge fencing was reported here. Barbed-wire fencing dominated Kansas after 1885. A barbed-wire fence was added along this hedgerow (lower right in photo) and a hog-wire mesh fence is also visible; both wire fences are attached to posts cut from Osage orange.

**Figure 9.3**
The *Llano Estacado* in Randall County, Texas. Coronado and his party crossed here in 1541 and reported marking their route across the featureless plain, "a land as level as the sea," by using buffalo bones and dry dung, "there being no stones or anything else." Men became lost from the party and disoriented if they were drawn apart by as much as half a league (about 1.5 miles). The edge of Palo Duro Canyon lies just beyond the horizon.

Texas Indians who cultivated beans and gathered the wild grapes and plums that grew there in abundance.[7]

The "unbroken sea of grass" is a powerful image, and there were no doubt many places where the early Euro-Americans could view such a scene, but few chose to live at such sites unless there was some sort of nearby woodland. The exploitation of isolated forest patches took place on a broad scale in the settlement of North Dakota, for example. Open-country homesteaders who came there in the 1880s from the upper Middle West, eastern Canada, or Scandinavian Europe took trips of up to 60 miles to reach the aspen-covered Turtle Mountains along the Canadian border. Protected valley walls along the Sheyenne and James Rivers and the forested moraines south of Devils Lake also attracted settlers from every direction. Wood cut one autumn was corded for drying, while that from the previous year was loaded aboard wagons or sleds for the trip home. Some North Dakota pioneer settlers recalled that a week or two was allocated for this annual activity.[8] When those same settlers built their first dwellings, the overwhelming choice of building material was sawed lumber brought in by rail from Minnesota. The typical house was of simple frame construction and it was covered with tar-paper on the roof and sides.[9]

The habits of two other groups of North Dakota settlers offer a marked contrast to this pattern of behavior. The *métis* (French-Ojibwa) who lived in Manitoba and northern North Dakota were accomplished parkland (prairie–forest mosaic) dwellers who often made a living selling firewood. They hauled wood long distances in their high-wheeled Red River carts for sale to Anglo settlers unwilling to break their long-standing habit of woodburning.

**Figure 9.4**
Palo Duro Canyon, where Coronado found Texas Indians practicing agriculture in the sheltered valley bottoms (downstream from this view near the head of the canyon). Pinon (*Pinus cembroides*) and juniper (*Juminperus spp.*) are found on steep slopes such as these throughout the western plains.

174

**Figure 9.5**
Rammed-earth house constructed after 1900 in Morton County, North Dakota, an area of heavy Russian-German settlement. The sod house (extreme left) probably was the original dwelling; a small sod barn, incorporating a four-pane window sash, is visible behind the rammed-earth house.

The typical *métis* dwelling was a log structure that was often covered with willow branches and then plastered with mud to keep out the elements; it was topped by a sod-and-pole roof. A third group, the Russian-Germans, arrived in the northern plains after several generations of grassland experience in south Russia. They brought to North Dakota the practice of sod and rammed-earth house construction (Fig. 9.5); their common fuels were *mist* (a compacted brick of dried livestock manure) and tightly twisted marsh-hay bundles; and they seem to have been attracted to southwestern North Dakota by the presence of lignite, a resource that few others recognized as valuable.

The contrasting practices these three groups exhibited in a single climate–vegetation zone suggest the possibilities, rather than the restrictions, that "treeless" conditions presented. Sod houses, far from being necessary, were viewed with contempt by Germans and Anglo-Americans who did not know how to build such structures and harbored no desire to live in something that dripped water inside for days after a rain. The Russian-Germans, many of whom were recruited to the plains by railroad and state immigration agents, had few adjustments to make. They expected a hard life and they neither modified nor modernized their farming practices as much as their German, Scandinavian, or Anglo-American neighbors did. The *métis*, who had resided in the parkland for generations, made no attempt to live beyond easy access to wooded patches and they used the prairie mainly for seasonal hunting. Human ingenuity, habits, and preferences, rather than environmental limits, are most obvious in these glimpses of early grassland settlement.

175

## Migration patterns

The history of American agriculture has been witness to an almost constant shift of farmers toward the flattest, richest, grassiest lands available. Since the grasslands were the product of fire, and because fire spreads rapidly across a flat to gently rolling surface, grasslands tend to be gently rolling and practically never steep. Fertile soils (typified by the order of Mollisols) on undulating prairie define the best cropland existing in the United States today. The "prairie peninsula" is thus also a cropland peninsula bordered by hillier, forested lands to the north and south. To this zone of vegetation types there corresponds a region of pioneer settlements based on settlers' birthplaces.

The prairie/deciduous forest border across Illinois, Wisconsin, and Minnesota was settled by westward-migrating Yankees between 1840 and 1870 (Fig. 9.6). They made the prairie fringe a wheat specialty zone, just as the area of their birth, in western New York State, had been earlier. The early Yankee settlers assembled their farms by choosing a variety of land types, ranging from open prairies to upland copses or wooded valleys, and thus made use of the full range of ecosystems (environmental types) available to them.[10] The wheat frontier moved rapidly along the prairie–forest transition zone in Wisconsin and Minnesota in the two decades centering on the Civil War and, by 1870, Yankees were firmly established frontier wheat farmers in western Minnesota's prairies. The Red River Valley of the North, in turn, became a wheat specialty region in the 1880s.

**Figure 9.6**
Upright-and-wing, Greek Revival-style farmhouse in Rock County, Wisconsin, along the prairie–forest margin settled by wheat farming Yankees from New York in the 1840s. This style of house, found on farms as well as in villages, is common in the Middle West's Yankeeland.

**Figure 9.7** Headquarters of a wheat ranch in Choteau County, Montana, part of the Wheat Triangle near Great Falls, a region devoted almost exclusively to wheat and barley production. The area was settled in the decade centering on 1915. The farmhouse follows the bungalow style popular in American cities at that time. The cluster of small buildings includes grain and seed storage sheds and several machinery sheds but no livestock barns. The absence of fences also is typical of a cash-grain operation.

The wheat frontier moved west with the tide of New York-born pioneers until 1870; from then until the 1880s its westward push resulted from the children born to this population and to the westward migration of first-generation Norwegians and Germans born in southern Wisconsin or Minnesota. Wheat monoculture was a frontier practice that could not be sustained for many years because of the inevitable appearance of wheat rust and other crop diseases that followed a few years behind the frontier itself. The introduction of more disease-resistant European wheat varieties, plus the constant experimentation to acheive new and hardier strains, enabled northern North Dakota and Montana to become stable, long-term zones of spring wheat production (Fig. 9.7). The old wheat frontier from Wisconsin across Minnesota eventually became part of the dairy region.[11]

A second culture hearth for the grassland's pioneer population was southeastern Pennsylvania. Ideas about farming that spread west from there were based on crop rotation and livestock husbandry practices which the Germans, Scotch-Irish, and others who first settled the Pennsylvania (or Midland) hearth had brought from Europe. Whereas Yankees tended to favor wheat and dairy farming, Midland farmers raised both corn and wheat in rotation and fed part of their grain to fatten meat animals (Fig. 9.8). This particular combination of crop and livestock production was carried west to the Miami Valley of Ohio by southern Pennsylvania-born farmers early in the 19th century, and from there it spread rapidly westward across Indiana, Illinois, and Iowa.[12] The Corn Belt, as this region became known, was characterized by prosperous farms of substantial size centered around a cluster of specialized-function buildings (Fig. 9.9).

Midland or Midland-stock settlers dominated the prairies south of a line running from Chicago to Omaha, although northern Illinois and northern Iowa had a substantial Yankee minority as well. Within this zone there were extensive areas of wet prairie—lands that would eventually produce large grain crops, but which first had to be artificially drained.[13] Eastern Illinois evolved as a cash-corn specialty region: cash-crop oriented Yankees

177

**Figure 9.8**
Feeder livestock barn
near Weeping Water,
Nebraska. Probably the
most typical of Corn
Belt farm buildings,
this barn may have
originated in the
Upland South. It
resembles the
Appalachian-style corn
crib with shed wings
added. The feeder barn
is found in areas of
beef (as opposed to
dairy) cattle production
in the Middle West.
Hay is stored in the
upper story, ear corn at
ground level; animals
and machinery are
sheltered in the wings
at the side.

**Figure 9.9**
Buildings belonging to
a mixed crop–livestock
farm, Sibley County,
Minnesota. The large
barn on the left is a
typical "basement"
style that housed dairy
cows on the lower
level; the large hayloft
has a protruding gable
to allow easier loading
of baled hay. Flanking
the barn are silos used
to store chopped, green
corn (ensilage). The
corn crib in front of the
barn stored ear corn;
today, corn is more
often shelled before
storage and the corn
crib has largely been
replaced by round,
metal bins.

abandoned wheat in favor of corn, while corn-livestock Midlanders abandoned meat animals to concentrate on crops. The cash-corn specialty region of Illinois was established by 1880 and it remained unique in this rôle for the next century (Fig. 9.10). Today, however, a cash-grain region (based on corn and soybean production) extends from northern Ohio to western Iowa, a product of recent agricultural trends that have made crop production more profitable than livestock in much of the Middle West.[14]

The association between wheat and the Yankee's frontier and grain-livestock and the Midlander's frontier extended west of the Missouri River into Kansas and Nebraska. A combination of political and economic factors projected the Midland agricultural complex into eastern Kansas by 1860. The

Missouri Compromise of 1820 had made that state an extension of slave territory, while the Kansas-Nebraska Bill of 1854 allowed slavery to be an open question west of the Missouri border. The first of these two developments made the grasslands and forested valleys of northern Missouri a frontier with deep southern roots; many of its first settlers were born in the Bluegrass region of Kentucky which was, in turn, a late 18th-century extension of Virginia. North–South tensions were strained nearly to the breaking point by 1854 when Kansas and Nebraska were opened to settlement. By then population growth in the early Corn Belt of Ohio and Indiana had produced a substantial population that was ready to move to the next frontier. Midlanders thus jumped across Missouri, which had already been settled, and took land in eastern Kansas.[15]

The wheat belt of Kansas runs through the central portion of that state, just west of the lands settled initially by Midlanders. The winter wheat region emerged in the 1880s where Yankees had been settled by railroad companies and where Mennonites and others of German stock who had come from the grasslands of south Russia began to establish farms and villages of their own. Wheat continued to move west in Kansas under the influence of this already diverse mixture and with the addition, after 1890, of northern Missouri-born farmers whose parents and grandparents had settled that state after 1820.[16]

After 1900 grain farming was extended into the grasslands of western Oklahoma and Texas. Settlers were lured to both of these areas by Chicago-based railroad companies and this produced a stronger component of men

**Figure 9.10**

October corn harvest in Bureau County, Illinois. A century ago, this county already had more than 200,000 acres in corn, but farm income depended heavily on hog production. Today, corn acreage is somewhat larger, production per acre has more than tripled, and nearly two-thirds of Bureau County's farm income now comes from crops, predominantly corn. The present number of farms in the county is half of what it was in 1880; the average size of farm has doubled.

bred in the North than would have been true had the trend of westward migration within the South continued unchallenged. The result was an unusual grain and cotton mixture in the Texas panhandle that reflected a merging of regional agricultural practices. There was a brief period of optimism that began when the large cattle ranches were subdivided for agricultural settlement, but optimism turned to despair during the droughts of the 1930s. Billowing clouds of dust kicked up on the surface of these red, sandy soils spelled disaster for thousands of farmers. Some predict that another Dust Bowl, just as in the 1930s, is possible; wind erosion remains a problem in western Oklahoma and the Texas panhandle, barely held in check by modern conservation tillage practices. The region specializes in grain sorghum (raised for cattle feeding) and irrigated cotton. The meat-packing industry, which moved west with the expanding Corn Belt, continues its westward shift toward the supply of fed cattle and is now well established in western Kansas and Texas, the heart of the former Dust Bowl.

## The western plains

Yankees, midlanders, and southerners moved into the American grassland following routes that are roughly predictable given the overwhelming tendency for settlers simply to "move west." None of the three groups paused noticeably at any particular precipitation level or line of longitude—including the 98th meridian which Walter Prescott Webb claimed as a cultural "fault line."[17] Familiar crops were taken west, as would be expected, but experimentation also occurred when the old cultures proved unsuited.

One of the most successful adaptations to semi-arid conditions was dry farming.[18] In its fullest development it was a complex series of soil and moisture conservation procedures involving deep plowing, subsurface compaction, and frequent cultivation; but dry farming came to be recognized best by the practice of sowing alternate, parallel strips of land in alternate years thus creating striped patterns of fallow and cropland. The idle strips store moisture and are cultivated to control weeds. Dry farming was widely adopted in the northern plains, where railroad companies and agricultural colleges stressed its benefits, and in Montana the techniques became practically coextensive with the wheat and barley growing areas of the state (Fig. 9.11).

Precipitation declines steadily (at a rate of approximately 1 inch per 16 miles of westward distance) across the central grassland, although there are few areas where a lack of moisture alone has prevented agriculture; soils and topography are just as important a limit. For example, wheat has been raised for 80 years in the short-grass plains of western North Dakota and eastern Montana; but in western South Dakota, at the same level of precipitation, wheat is confined to a few, narrow upland strips where soils

**Figure 9.11**
Wheatland County, in the
Judith Basin district of
Montana, is true to its name.
Fallow strips on the
dry-farmed wheat fields are
kept free of moisture-robbing
weeds by a combination of
summer tillage and chemical
weed control.

permit cropping. The Nebraska Sand Hills have a tallgrass prairie vegetation like central Iowa, but their dune sand surface cannot be broken if wind erosion is to be prevented. These sections of the plains have long been the domain of the cattlemen.[19]

The range cattle industry originated in two distinct regions of Texas, the better known of which is hispanic south Texas where large ranches were established early in the 19th century. The word, "ranch" itself, along with such terms as "corral," "lariat," "lasso," and "rodeo," are of Spanish origin and their common usage down to the present indicates one measure of hispanic influence.

Recent research shows that, at the same time as the hispanic cattle industry was beginning in south Texas, there also took place a migration of Anglo cattle raisers from middle Tennessee to northeast Texas.[20] The Anglo cattlemen contributed traditions such as the use of open range, large herd sizes, branding and annual roundups. The two groups began mixing after 1850 and, as the industry grew and spread northward, the two complexes became one. Northward cattle drives were undertaken for the purpose of reaching summer pastures and distant markets. Railroads were extended east to west across the plains beginning in the 1860s, and where the lines of track met the south-to-north cattle trails a series of "cow towns" grew up—places like Dodge City and Abilene, Kansas. By the mid-1870s, the Texas-style ranching complex had reached north to the Dakotas. Overstocking of the range, blizzards, and drought in the mid-1880s and the steady westward push of agricultural settlement brought an end to the open range by 1900.[21]

## Town settlement

The creation of towns in the American interior began during the era of water-borne commerce, prior to the arrival of the railroads. Most towns founded up through the 1840s were speculative ventures, the work of one man or a small syndicate of investors who hoped to create thriving commercial centers along the navigable streams.[22] The first railroad across the grassland was the Illinois Central Railroad's Illinois main line constructed in the 1850s. This, and all subsequent lines, instantly placed the formerly inaccessible prairies within easy shipping distance of major cities. At the same time there emerged a new set of procedures for the creation of towns. No longer the isolated and uncoordinated attempts of small-time investors, towns along the railroad were sited, planned, and sold under the watchful eye of the railroad itself.[23]

Railroad companies (or their designated townsite affiliates) sometimes made substantial real estate profits from lot sales in the new communities, but a railroad's principal goal was to increase the volume of traffic moving over its lines. Towns in the grassland region were thus uniformly spaced, often after careful calculations had been made as to the trading volume each town might sustain. The railroad's purpose in town-founding was to create trade centers for the surrounding farm population, a fact reflected in the internal structure of the towns.

Land along the tracks in a town generally was not sold, but rather it was leased for grain elevators, lumber yards, and fuel dealers who needed direct rail access. These businesses themselves were often owned by line-chain companies whose headquarters were in major cities. Some Minneapolis-based line elevator companies, for example, owned more than 100 country

**Figure 9.12**
Elevators dwarf the few business buildings along Main Street in Chaffee, North Dakota. The town was platted in 1893 to handle business from the Amenia and Sharon Land Company's 14,000-acre bonanza wheat operation in southwestern Cass County. Bonanza farms, similar in scale to southern cotton plantations, originated with massive purchases or railroad-grant lands in the 1870s, but proved to be too large to manage effectively.

**Figure 9.13**
Corning, located on the
Burlington Northern Railroad
in southwest Iowa, exhibits
the typical T-town design.
Most of the town's
businesses began on this
street and remain there
today.

elevators along the tracks of a single railroad company. Each town thus acquired several grain elevators as a result of the railroad's practice of leasing adjacent elevator sites to competing line chains (Fig. 9.12).

Commercial and residential lots on the townsite were sold by railroad townsite agents. It was the agent's task to lure to each new town the proper mix of businesses that would make a viable trading point for farmers. The town's main street was divided into strips of narrow business lots, 12 to the block-face. The result was a series of identical-looking, false-front store buildings each housing a small, specialized business such as a hardware or grocery store, a bank, or a print shop. Grain elevators and railroad depots were often the first town buildings, followed by an infilling of structures along the business street.

Because railroad-town real estate was sold before the town started to function, the town had to have a plat that looked convincingly like a town ought to look in order to give prospective merchants an idea of where to locate. Two plat designs were common. The earliest idea was a symmetrical arrangement with business buildings lined up to face the tracks on either side. In time, however, railroad companies realized the limitations of locating tracks in the busy center of town and the railroad-centered plat lost in favor. The most common railroad town design was a T-shaped configuration in which the main business street met the tracks at a right angle, with the railroad depot itself located at the intersection (Fig. 9.13).

Common to both the symmetrical and T-town designs was the priority of the railroad as a formative element of the plan. While the surrounding countryside remained ordered according to the township-and-range checkerboard, the railroad town was an obvious exception; its own internal geometry of rectilinear streets invariably followed from the location of the

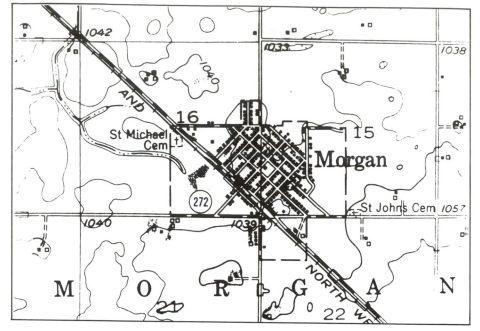

**Figure 9.14**
Morgan, Minnesota, as
shown on a 1 : 62,500
government topographic map
published in 1953. Morgan's
orientation to the Chicago &
Northwestern Railway's
tracks was retained even in
subsequent additions to the
town. Only its recent
"suburban" streets depart
from the railroad's geometry
and return to the township-
and-range grid.

tracks (Fig. 9.14). Because commerce was concentrated in the heart of town, railroads rarely set aside any of this valuable property for parks, squares, or other amenities of urban design. Lots for churches, schools, and court-houses, as well as for parks were donated by the townsite company and were taken from unsold land at the margins of the initial plat. All the functions of a town were thus incorporated into the designs provided by the railroad.

## Conclusion

The landscape of the American grassland today reflects the history of its human occupance in nearly every stage. The past can be read with accuracy, perhaps better here than anywhere else in the nation. Rolling grass-covered hills that stretch toward unbroken horizons suggest a natural landscape, one that humankind has not altered much less dominated, yet we know that even the plant cover itself owes much to human occupance. The sparse look, too, reflects human designs rather than neglect. A gigantic plain of unequaled productivity, the grassland was parceled into farms and laced with routes of trade and commerce by governments and railroad corpora-tions whose broad-scale plans for the region envisioned a settlement fabric that has endured to a remarkable degree. White settlement in the region is comparatively recent, even by American standards. In hundreds of towns and on thousands of farms one can find some of the first, substantial structures still in productive use. The region's past is so suffused into the present that deliberate attempts at historic preservation often seem out of place, literally. It is a region that has caused worry from time to time: the land and its people have not always seemed to live in balance; technological change and shifts in world commodities markets have produced severe shocks to the system. Yet compared with the Northeast, the South, or the Far West, landscape changes in the grassland have been more in degree than in kind. Whatever the future holds for this region, it is likely that continuity, rather than change, will offer the more enduring perspective.

# Chapter ten
## Challenging the desert

JAMES L. WESCOAT, JR.

THE DESERT CONVEYS important lessons to "those who see." This message pervades both ancient and modern accounts of desert experience. Current American fascination with Sunbelt living, "Marlboro" men, and Monkey Wrench activism carry forward the 19th-century lore of irrigators, cowboys, and desert rats. The rhetoric in that lore draws in turn upon biblical images of paradise and prophetic traditions to portray the promise and perils of desert landscapes. In literature these traditions have been enlarged over the years by a rich body of western fiction, history, and nature writing; and in visual terms by western films, art, and photography. Idealizations of the desert have swirled through the national consciousness, influencing public perceptions and policies.

Of particular interest are stories about how, with proper tending, the desert will bloom as a rose.[1] Reclamation enthusiasts see desert cultivation as an esthetic and technological triumph over nature, a previously inconceivable extension of the national frontier. It was alleged that irrigation would produce small farms, cooperation, and a mode of rural life that would transcend the social ills of rural isolation and urban industrialization.

These portraits of reclamation are countered by warnings about the risks and improprieties of arid zone development.[2] Deserts place limits on human settlement to be ignored only at great consequence. Suffering and death stalk alongside desert romance and utility.[3] In the "True West" deserts provide refuge for those who fail utterly in society.[4] Cynics remind us that few American desert settlements have endured long enough for assessment of what has been achieved. Quite enough time has passed to point to the apparent failures: abandoned settlements, depleted resources, social conflicts, and degraded environments that mock the rhetoric of challenging the desert.

But the emphasis on success and failure in the desert may be misleading. Marginality, constraint, and intensification occur in most environments. Arguments that "water is different" and that irrigation projects reclaim otherwise useless lands have come under increasing criticism.[5] Even granting the special significance of water in desert environments, it is sometimes difficult to recognize when the challenges of aridity have been successfully met. Historical endurance and geographical spread do not necessarily mark great achievements, nor abandonment an unqualified failure.[6] Indeed, the dramatic spread of desert settlements in one period may later prove a great folly. And then there are projects, such as Glen Canyon Dam on the Colorado River, that are simultaneously regarded as heroic or horrible by different social groups.[7]

In light of these problems it is tempting to put aside the desert rhetoric; to travel through arid landscapes without prejudice; and to try to observe the material forces and situations that have shaped what one can see. From this point of view, the lessons for "those who see" are to be gained by "those who look." It would be a mistake to think, however, that a landscape approach can operate entirely without prejudice or that it can stop short of making critical judgements about the history of desert development. Using the word "desert" immediately invokes the full vocabulary of challenge, accomplishment, and failure just noted. Desert rhetoric can only be abandoned when we discover that people in places such as Phoenix, Arizona have at various times not thought of themselves as living in deserts at all.

The intuitions brought to this chapter revolve around the notions of challenge, success, and failure in desert water development. In exploring the prehistoric, hispanic, and modern landscapes of water control, one encounters surprisingly similar desert irrigation features: ditches, wells, and dams. There is at the same time great variety in the geographical configuration of desert water features and institutions. Patterns of growth and decline in these varied contexts remind us that deserts pose a fundamentally agrarian challenge to society. Where are the American deserts and their oases? How have they been shaped by irrigators? And what implications do they carry for those who see? These questions call for an overview of the places considered to be deserts, with an emphasis on obstacles and enticements for human settlement. The greater part of the chapter then explores four contemporary landscapes that reflect major processes of desert water development.

## Finding the desert

The term desert, like wilderness, has been applied to a broad range of places in the United States, including midcontinent grasslands during the early 19th century and cities at various times. Although this chapter limits itself to areas of extreme moisture deficit—where short-grass prairies give way to xerophytic shrubs (i.e., those adapted to arid conditions) and succulents—there remains a significant semantic problem.

In physical terms, the most arid areas of the United States are found in the shadow cast by the mountains of the Pacific coastal ranges. Continentality,

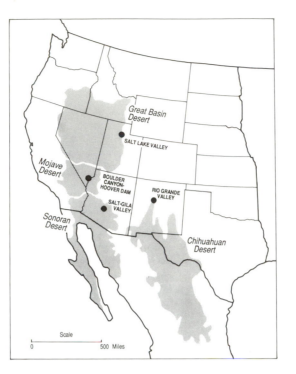

**Figure 10.1**
Major desert provinces and
case study areas.

cool Pacific Ocean currents, and high atmospheric pressure systems help explain the aridity of the southwestern and intermountain regions (Fig. 10.1). The culture histories of these regions reveal a keen appreciation of variations in aridity, however, from prehistoric times onward. Initially this meant an understanding of streamflow and channel patterns on perennial tributaries; familiarity with how large rivers innundate their floodplains; discovery of seeps, springs, perched water tables, intermittent creeks, and other favored niches; and, lastly, a knowledge of native plant and animal habitats outside the oases. Prehistoric groups occupied the full range of natural desert landscapes, modifying nature and varying their mix of subsistence activities in tandem with environmental and social change.

Experimentation in desert environments continues in various forms during historic times. In each period, deserts are re-explored in light of contemporary human interests, and their nature rediscovered. Early surveys focused on territorial and agricultural opportunities; ways of traveling between and enlarging the oases of the West. Delineations of the desert have often employed crop production indicators, reflecting national interests in agricultural settlement (e.g., the 10-inch rainfall boundary, Thornthwaite's aridity index, and the Palmer drought index). Modern maps testify to the timing of social interest in river basin development, transportation, mineral exploration, military testing, groundwater development, and desertification.

Political partitioning of the West has also had profound impacts on the distribution of water resources from the 17th century onward. The historical unfolding of hispanic and Anglo systems of water rights established complex local patterns of water surplus and scarcity.[8] The incongruity between political and river basin boundaries has led to protracted struggles over regional entitlements to the Colorado and Rio Grande.[9] Federal water claims for public lands and Indian reservations represent the most recent processes of redistribution in overappropriated basins.

These natural and cultural dimensions of desert waters come together in four major provinces and their outliers: (a) the Sonoran Desert of Arizona (and the associated Colorado Desert in southern California); (b) the Mojave Desert of southeastern California; (c) the Chihuahuan Desert of west Texas and the Rio Grande Valley; and (d) the Great Basin Desert of Nevada, Utah, Wyoming, Oregon, and southern Idaho (Fig. 10.1). Each arid province shades into grasslands, mesic shrub communities, and montane forests—gradually in most areas but sharply in the vicinity of oases. The four deserts and their oases have distinct personalities, traceable in large part to the historical processes operating within them.

## Transforming the desert: looking at dams and ditches

Landscape changes during the 20th century, when a common formula of federal irrigation subsidies, river impoundment, highway development, and defense expenditures stimulated oasis expansion throughout the West, can be considered in broad national terms. A more focused perspective is needed, however, to understand how these national processes have been played out in specific desert arenas.

### The prehistoric legacy in central Arizona

What were the prehistoric water systems like that thrived along riverine corridors in central Arizona? Riparian (riverbank) vegetation and wildlife today are drastically modified; farms have little relation to the predominantly urban economy of the region; streams appear unpromising.[10] The route from Tucson to Phoenix follows one of the northward trajectories that characterized southwestern settlement up to the mid-19th century (Fig. 10.2). Modern travelers along this path are likely to pass by the Snaketown site near Florence, Arizona and to arrive in downtown Phoenix with little grasp of what has arisen from the ashes and what has been buried beneath them.

Although not limited to perennial streams, large prehistoric canal sites such as Snaketown lie along the northeastern fringe of the Sonoran Desert, the moist rim of a basin which wraps around the Gulf of California up into the lower Colorado River watershed. Debate rages over the relative importance of indigenous innovation and Mesoamerican influence on prehistoric Hohokam irrigation.[11] Somewhat less controversial is the rough sequence involving early canal systems around the confluence of the Salt and Gila River basins, an outward spread of increasingly complex canal networks along riparian corridors during the Colonial and Sedentary periods; regional retraction during the Classic period; and then abandonment in the mid-14th century. The onset of Hohokam irrigation is also under dispute, with estimates ranging from 300 BC to AD 500. Puzzling questions have arisen over changes in settlement distribution, size, architecture, burial practices, and ceremonial features during the Sedentary–Preclassic transition. Particularly troubling, however, is the collapse of Hohokam settlements from some unknown combination of forces.

Excavators at Snaketown have inferred that Indians used brush dams to divert water through earthen canals to fields lining the river terraces. Canals extended as much as several miles in length, with cross-sectional dimensions up to 20 feet in width. Very few of the ancient irrigation works remain visible today. Canals have been realigned, reshaped, and paved over in urbanizing areas; brush dams have long since disintegrated; and few settlement sites have been excavated.

**Figure 10.2**
Water development in central
Arizona and the lower
Colorado River Basin.

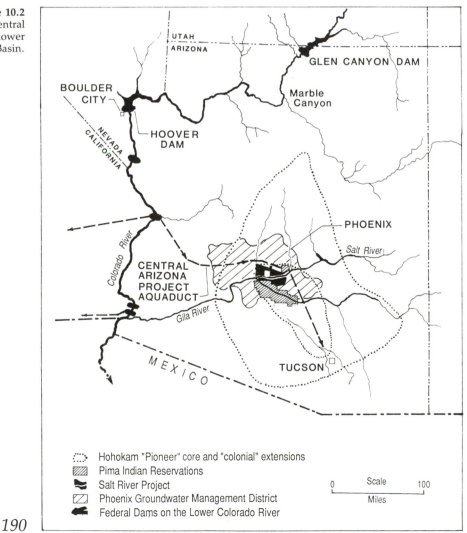

190

Nevertheless, prehistoric canal patterns provided the tracery for an irrigation revival by Pima Indians in the early 19th century, and later for the Phoenix of Anglo settlement that rapidly displaced Indian irrigators. How did 19th-century Pima irrigators revive the prehistoric canal technology and infrastructure? Pima Indian *rancheria* (settlements) were described as few in number, small in population, and widely dispersed at the time of Spanish contact in AD 1700.[12] Spanish missions penetrated no further north than Tucson and thus had limited influence on Pima irrigators in the Salt–Gila area.

Pima renovation of prehistoric water systems marked an entrepreneurial response to the fledgling food market that was expanding with east–west travel across the Sonoran Desert during the mid-19th century. Canal renovation proceeded in a fragmented and incremental manner. Although associated with population growth and tribal social stratification, irrigation did not radically overturn the dispersed *rancheria* pattern of settlement.[13]

Pima irrigation systems exhibited a functional continuity with subsistence in the surrounding desert. In drought years and drought-prone locations, the Pima drew upon the strikingly rich plant resources of the Sonoran desert.[14] In moister years and locations irrigated crops were substituted for gathered foods. These fluid modes of desert occupance reduced vulnerability to geographical and historical fluctuation.

Few elements of Piman irrigation remained in operation after the rapid inmigration of Anglo irrigators into the upper Gila during the late 19th century. Some Indians moved from the Gila River reservation to the Salt River, but the reservation there suffered similar problems. Depletion of Indian water supplies predated Arizona's adoption of a water code that assigned water rights on the basis of seniority (the prior appropriation doctrine).

Between 1860 and 1900 Anglo grain production increased in direct proportion to the Pima decline.[15] Agricultural production then escalated rapidly throughout the Salt and Gila River Valleys with transportation improvements and the growth of national and international markets for cotton, citrus, and field crops. In addition to historic Pima and Hohokam canals, large-scale diversions were made from the Salt River. Although some roads and field patterns followed the alignment of prehistoric and Piman canals, the broader grid of urban streets and platted blocks bore little relation to earlier settlement patterns or canal networks.

The expansion of Anglo irrigation during the last decade of the 19th century, coupled with a severe drought, drew one of the first projects under the Reclamation Act of 1902. The federal project included construction of a large masonry dam on the Salt River, modifications in the historic canal network, and hydropower production (Fig. 10.3). Federal projects have several distinct landscape characteristics. Power production and generous repayment rules subsidize irrigation, promoting a larger scale of agricultural production than would otherwise occur. Water on federal projects is also appurtenant to the land, meaning that water rights remain attached to

**Figure 10.3**
Citrus fields on the Western
Canal, Salt River Project
south of Phoenix, looking
west.

specific parcels of land regardless of changes in land use. With the rapid pace of urbanization in the Salt River Project after the 1940s, irrigated fields have been converted to lawns, pools, golf courses, and such urban recreational curiosities as the artificial surfing complex in Scottsdale. Conflicts have arisen between farmers and suburbanites,[16] but the process of reallocation is projected to be completed by AD 2030.

During the past three decades surfacewater features have gone through a process of technical elaboration as ditches are lined, diversion structures are automated, and measurement devices are installed physically and legally to monitor agricultural water use. Furrow irrigation now employs siphon tubes or gated pipes that deliver water to individual furrows. Many orchards have been converted from basin irrigation to sprinkler and low-pressure trickle irrigation. Although these technical innovations have decreased ditch seepage and improved crop water delivery efficiency, their most significant social impact has been on farm labor.

Groundwater pumping is pushing irrigation into areas with limited physical or legal access to surface water. Groundwater levels in Arizona have dropped precipitously since the 1950s, producing ground fissures and chronic well deepening. The Central Arizona Project, an ambitious diversion from the Colorado River and the most recent catalyst for growth in the region, was not approved until Arizona adopted a law to "manage" groundwater withdrawals. In an ironic twist, Central Arizona Project waters originally intended to augment Anglo irrigation will instead be employed to fulfill Indian water claims and to offset groundwater mining. Anglo irrigators may purchase whatever is left over.

Thus, for the third time in 2000 years an irrigation system has grown in an impressive fashion only to dissolve under some combination of stresses. A rich array of hypotheses has been explored for the Hohokam collapse of the mid-14th century: climatic variability, river channel incision, warfare, population pressure, disease, salinization, and internal social change.[17] In addition to this litany of explanations for agricultural collapse, there is an intriguing link between Preclassic settlement changes, foreign inmigration, and the possible subordination of agricultural activities within Hohokam social organization.[18]

The Piman irrigation crisis is far clearer. Decline stemmed from an upstream–downstream conflict in which downstream Indian canals were dried up and food gathering was enframed within reservations subject to increasing ecological disturbance.

The contemporary irrigation decline exhibits, at first sight, a quite different set of processes. The growing urban economy easily overshadows agriculture in the competition for land, water, and labor. If anything, the process has been slowed by institutional constraints on the transfer of land and water rights, as well as by governmental subsidies to irrigators.

And yet these three periods of irrigation decline may share a common characteristic. Inmigration of foreign populations initiated radical shifts in settlement patterns and agrarian stability. Given the declining significance of agriculture within contemporary Arizona, the dwindling proportion of the population engaged in agriculture, the pressure for reducing groundwater withdrawals and continuing urban growth, there seems little doubt that irrigation agriculture will decline in scale. The important question is whether and how it might be meaningfully transformed in response to contemporary landscape forces in central Arizona.[19]

*Hispanic settlement in the Rio Grande Valley*
Spanish explorers threaded northward through the Rio Grande Valley during the second half of the 16th century. From its semi-arid and montane headwaters in Colorado flowing south to El Paso before angling southeast to the Gulf of Mexico, the Rio Grande River passes through the northern extension of the Chihuahuan Desert. This corridor represents the most enduring region of hispanic desert occupance in the United States (Fig. 10.4).

Spanish explorers encountered concentrations of Pueblo settlements in the upper Rio Grande Valley of northern New Mexico. They observed Indian farmers employing small canals, check dams, and flood irrigation.[20] In contrast to central Arizona, however, what the Spanish saw in the Rio Grande Valley did not constitute the prehistoric center of Anasazi irrigation.[21] More extensive water control systems had existed in the upland sites such as Chaco Canyon until the mid-13th century. Unlike Snaketown canal irrigators, Anasazi cultivators developed technologies of runoff control

**Figure 10.4**
Hispanic village near Taos, New Mexico. Adobe residences surround a plaza and its church on three sides; small irrigated fields usually under ten acres are irrigated by surface ditches and laterals off the Rio Hondo. This centralized settlement pattern stands in contrast to the dispersed pattern of modern ranches and farmsteads in the Rio Grande Valley.

with distributaries on to irrigated terraces. But like those of the Hohokam, these upland and tributary systems were more sophisticated than those flanking the major river corridors of the Rio Grande and Colorado.[22]

Spanish administrators avoided settling in the Rio Grande Valley, establishing their headquarters at the start of the 17th century in San Gabriel and later at Santa Fe (Fig. 10.5). The mix of indigenous and Spanish architecture in the Rio Grande Valley took place instead through the construction of mission churches in *pueblos* such as Sandia and Isleta, and smaller *visitas* at Puaray and Alameda. Indian converts constructed the earthen ditches (*acequias*) at missions, while Spanish rural land grantees used conscripted Indians and slaves.

The Rio Grande riverfront remained an unfavored location for hispanic settlement until the 18th century, due in part to the problems posed by large floodflows and heavy sediment loads. During the late 17th century, individual rural land grants (*estancia*) began to fill in the riverfront between the Sandia and Isleta pueblos. This process and the material landscape culture of the Rio Grande were radically disrupted, however, by the Pueblo

194

**Figure 10.5**
Water development in the
middle Rio Grande Valley,
New Mexico.

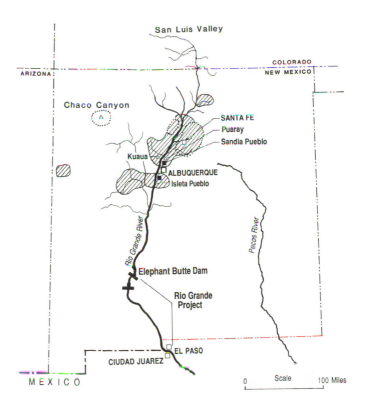

 Concentrations of Anasazi Sites
 Centers of Pueblo Indian land grants

Revolt of 1680. *Estancias* were sacked, churches desecrated, and in
retaliation the pueblos were burned. The Spanish return to New Mexico in
1691 was officially a return to Santa Fe, but several attempts were now made
to settle the Rio Grande Valley. Larger-scale *ranchos* replaced the estancia
settlement system, substituting hispanic for forced Indian labor.

Finally, the *villa* (village) of Albuquerque was officially founded in 1706.
There seems some doubt, however, that Albuquerque had fulfilled the town
planning requirements of the *Recompilacion de Leyes de los Reynos de las Indias*
at its founding. When the city sought a land grant on the basis of its status
as a villa, and more recently "pueblo water rights" which automatically
increase as water demand increases, its claims were denied.[23] At the time of
its founding Albuquerque was little more than an assemblage of ranchos
located near a main irrigation canal (*acequia madre*) that had been started
before the Revolt.[24]

Whereas insecure tenure plagued the water systems of central Arizona up
through the 19th century, Spanish settlers in the Rio Grande Valley began
with an institutionally sophisticated system of recorded titles to land and
water.[25] Irrigation of Spanish settlements (*viz-à-viz* individual ranchos) was a
community undertaking that introduced a mix of Roman and Islamic water
institutions to the Southwest. The *acequia madre* and its distributaries were
195 public works, constructed by a community, and supervised by a ditchmaster

or *mayordomo*. The *acequia madre* generated long, narrow field patterns which, unlike the *arpent* long lots of the Mississippi River Valley, were tied into canals rather than to river frontage.

The hispanic irrigation network physically impressed early Anglo explorers such as Zebulon Pike, who in 1807 compared it to the irrigation works of Egypt (hardly an apt comparison). Mexican independence in 1821 further opened the upper Rio Grande Valley to Anglo contact and trade. Then in 1848 the Treaty of Guadalupe Hidalgo established an international boundary at Paso del Norte where only vague upstream–downstream competition had previously existed. In principle, hispanic land and water uses were to be respected after 1848, just as Spanish law had called for respect of Indian resource uses.[26] In practice, the tensions between hispanic water claims and those which preceded and followed have given a multifaceted character to irrigation in New Mexico.

Anglo settlement transformed the Rio Grande Valley during the second half of the 19th century, as it had central Arizona. The railroad station at Albuquerque led to the construction of a new town—separate in form, location, and character from the "Old City." This "dual city" pattern characteristic of 19th-century southwestern cities marks a transition away from agricultural production for local markets toward a more diversified trade economy.[27]

The delineation of boundaries between New Mexico and Texas and Colorado, coupled with agricultural growth in Colorado triggered inter-regional conflicts over the Rio Grande. A riot between American and Mexican farmers at El Paso revealed that there was little understanding of the upstream origins of the problem as late as 1877, but after the drought and depression of the 1890s, this had changed. It was in this geographical context that the Harmon Doctrine was formulated by United States Attorney General's Office, asserting that an upstream country had no obligation to let water pass to a downstream country. Demands for equity and comity led, however, to a series of actions formally allocating the Rio Grande waters among various political entities, including: a preliminary treaty with Mexico in 1906; a state water code adopting the prior appropriation doctrine in 1907; pathbreaking state groundwater laws in 1931; the Rio Grande interstate compact in 1935; and a more concrete water delivery commitment to Mexico in the Treaty of 1944. These broad policies laid the groundwork for massive federal projects such as Elephant Butte Dam, as well as an expanding process of state bureaucratic administration.

Regional growth and politics continue to generate water conflicts. Most recently, the city of El Paso has filed for hundreds of well permits in southwestern New Mexico. New Mexico's rejection of these applications was discarded in a federal court decision as a violation of interstate commerce. If approved, water pipe lines will traverse the desert toward El Paso and a new chapter will be written in transboundary resource transfers.

What makes the Rio Grande Valley distinctive is its combination of hispanic and Indian settlement forms and its enduring hispanic water institutions. This tradition of collective water management contrasts sharply with the individualism of Colorado and Arizona, and even more deeply with the barbaric "rule of capture" in Texas groundwater development.[28] And yet the New Mexico landscape displays a separation of cultures— between pueblo and hispanic, villa and rancho, Anglo and hispanic—that has not been fully bridged by the general commitments of dominant communities to recognize the claims of those that preceeded. Adjustments in the New Mexico landscape show how past and present can grapple alongside one another.

### The Mormon desert

Mormon emigration to the semi-arid eastern fringe of the Great Basin Desert fueled town development in tiers of intermontane valleys and in more distant outliers across the West.[29] Taken out of their landscape context, Mormon irrigation ditches display few distinctive features. What sets these ditches apart from others is how they fit within the fabric of Mormon town planning and resource management.

Unlike migrants to the Salt and Rio Grande Valleys, Mormon settlers could not draw upon local irrigation precedents. They had minimal capital and virtually no irrigation experience. Thus, what one sees in Mormon irrigation are the physical manifestations of a remarkable vision and of the social organization that realized it. Upon entering the valley in 1847 Brigham Young made the powerful pronouncement that, "This is the place." Just four years earlier explorer John C. Fremont had described the Great Basin as a wasteland. Although by no means a retreat to solitude, for Salt Lake City was conceived rather as a hub for expansion,[30] the desert here did offer insulation against the types of harassment experienced in Illinois and Missouri.

What then was the physical and social context of Mormon irrigation? The "Zion plan" established at Salt Lake city in 1847 revolved around a temple set within a grid of large blocks and wide streets, cardinally oriented. Street names and numbers marked the location of a block in relation to the temple (e.g., 6th West St. is the sixth block west of the temple). Town blocks were subdivided into large residential lots on which garden homesteads were built and watered by ditches taken off from local creeks (Fig. 10.6). A belt of larger irrigated fields surrounded the town. This geometrically ordered rural town plan stood in marked contrast to the dispersed farmsteads of Anglo settlers and Spanish ranchos.

As one plat was settled, new plats were added following the same plan until the Avenues Area of Salt Lake City broke with tradition.[31] New towns followed a similar sequence. Church elders would issue a "call" to selected individuals to found a new town, and in this way settlement proceeded southward and into the higher valleys.

Land and water were allocated by the church leadership on the basis of "stewardship," labor contributions to ditch construction, and "beneficial use." Although resources were allocated to individuals, they initially

**Figure 10.6**
Mormon settlement of Snowville, Utah. Poplars mark the grid of individual family plots; these are surrounded by larger irrigated fields.

remained under collective control. The beneficial use rule represents an important contribution to western law; for it insists that resources claims must not be speculative or wasteful.[32] Although widely adopted in western water law, Mormon application of this criterion to land was unique, and it helps explain the relatively small farm sizes in Utah.

Equity and sharing governed the allocation of resources. This carried over into irrigators' responsibilities during drought. In principle, the prior appropriation rule places the entire economic burden of a drought on junior appropriators. In Mormon practice, severe droughts called for proportional sharing of water deficits. Charging market prices for water was regarded as profiteering; and overappropriation as water hogging.[33]

The Mormon town plan also specified wide roads and sidewalks. It was in these unmown sidewalks that the town irrigation ditches were constructed. Ditches flanking the main residential streets were narrow with primitive wooden headgates and weirs. The ditches initially served a full range of domestic and agricultural water uses. They were charged with esthetic as well as functional significance. Brigham Young had encouraged tree planting, garden plots, and attractive houses. Interestingly, roadside ditches and sidewalks were not always kept clear of vegetation or debris.[34]

By the start of the national irrigation movement of the 1890s Mormon irrigation was being described as technologically primitive.[35] As cities grew and water quality declined, ditches were restricted to irrigation uses, lined with concrete, buried in pipelines, or replaced with conventional curbs and gutters. Even if relatively primitive in the 1890s, Mormon irrigation retained its responsiveness to hazards and conflict. Church members were encouraged to resolve disputes voluntarily. When they could not, the church bishop decided the dispute. If disagreement persisted, the central church leadership rendered a final decision.

When the settlement of one area was well established, however, the central church would focus on other areas, leaving the operation of local water works and settlements to local leaders. Thus, an initially centralized authority was replaced by a highly diffuse pattern of locally controlled canal networks. As early as the 1850s the territorial legislature of Utah sought to shift the locus of water control to various civil arenas, e.g., the county court, the county board of selectmen, municipalities, and public irrigation districts.[36] In spite of increasing heterogeneity and water conflicts in Utah's population, early efforts at civil water control were largely unsuccessful. Water rights were regarded as the legacy of the community and only reluctantly sold or placed in the control of higher levels of government. When civil courts did enter the fray, it was usually to ratify an arrangement already arrived at through private negotiation. State legislation codified customary practice. Finally, in the late 19th century Utah adopted a state water code and administrative bureaucracy marking the transition to higher levels of regional water administration.

Federal reclamation canals followed along similar lines as those in central Arizona and the Rio Grande Valley. Established irrigators resisted subsidies to new users and release of their senior water rights to large-scale federal ventures. This tension led to a visibly weak coordination between simple on-farm distribution systems and highly engineered diversion canals constructed by the Bureau of Reclamation.

Arrington and May have asked, "Is Mormon irrigation a model for other regions and cultures?" The question can be turned around to ask, "How did Mormon irrigation become increasingly like that of other areas?" Some distinctively Mormon settlement features have gradually disappeared; others have been adopted by non-Mormon groups. Irrigators have surpassed their original goals of a simple life-style, sharing, and equality—and have moved closer to the individualism and quest for prosperity that is pervasive in the West. The old social institutions for resource allocation have less force. And yet early Mormon irrigation remains a model; if not one that is directly copied, at least one that reinforces the importance of collective action for successful desert settlement. The Mormon example inspired both utopian experiments, as at Greeley, Colorado, and civic institutions such as the beneficial use rule. Egalitarian and religious values no longer govern the Mormon ditches, but the ditches remind us of those values.

### Federal transformation of the Colorado River

The federal reclamation program was initiated in 1902 to stimulate homesteading on arid lands, to develop water projects beyond the financing capabilities of local groups, and to promote agrarian settlement free from speculation, monopoly, and water shortages. There has been a continuous retreat from these ideals (which had been materially expressed in the 160 acre limitation, the appurtenancy rule, and farm residency requirements) to the point where there is now little that enables one to distinguish federal from other modern irrigation projects. Federal control over irrigation projects is also less than might be expected. Canals constructed at the national expense are generally turned over to local organizations which operate them.

The reclamation program has had dramatic impacts, however, on major rivers such as the Colorado (Fig. 10.2).[37] Countless travelers drive across the northern edge of the Mojave Desert, often from an urbanized area in California or Arizona, to see Hoover Dam. They travel from an oasis across the desert to a structure that makes the oasis what it is. What do they see? The concrete arch dam is visually overwhelming, no more so than when floodwaters ripped through its spillways in 1983. The reservoir behind the dam attracts waterskiing and other forms of flatwater recreation. One can look downstream from the dam to imagine the canyon terrain drowned beneath the reservoir and its silt; but there are few who can recall from experience that lost landscape. A short trip west into the hills reveals the extent of the reservoir and a view of Boulder City on the other side of the ridge (Fig. 10.7). Turbines, generators, and ganglia of power lines symbolize the regional extensions of the dam.

The Colorado River was officially viewed as a "national menace" during the first half of this century.[38] Efforts to divert the river into the Imperial Valley had triggered an accidental refilling of Salton Sea in 1905. Flooding and increasing demand for water and power in southern California had stimulated early plans for reservoir projects on the river. At the same time there had been mutual apprehensions between the upstream and downstream states. Downstream states feared that their water supplies would dwindle in the event of upstream development, while Colorado, Wyoming, and Utah feared that a prior appropriation rule would require them to pass "their" water downstream without using it. A compact was negotiated among the seven basin states in 1922 that divided the basin into two halves and ambiguously apportioned the waters between the upper and lower halves, but approval of the compact was blocked by Arizona. Eventually, Congress broke the deadlock by passing the Boulder Canyon Project Act of 1928, of which Hoover Dam was one part, ratification of the compact another, and quantification of the California and Arizona shares a third.

Thus, Hoover Dam has a complex institutional context that guides its operation.[39] The Boulder Canyon Project Act was a synthesis of several innovations in federal water resources planning, the most important of which was to design large dams for multiple purposes. Hoover Dam was authorized on the basis of flood control, power production, and water supply benefits (as well as the obligatory but absurd navigation objective on federal projects). While this may seem less than radical, earlier federal dams generally had a single official purpose with any other benefits regarded as incidental.

200    Control over Hoover Dam is held by the United States Secretary of the

**Figure 10.7**
View of the planned federal construction town named Boulder City, Nevada, an unusually compact town in the modern West. Lake Mead and Hoover Dam lie in the background.

Interior. In a major deviation from western water law, the Secretary also has the power to allocate reservoir releases among the lower Colorado Basin users during droughts. Although the rôle of Colorado dams in delivering water to federal irrigation projects is limited, they are sometimes referred to as "cash register dams" because their power revenues subsidize new irrigation projects that would otherwise not be feasible.

The one settlement directly associated with Hoover Dam is Boulder City, Nevada. Initially built to house construction workers, Boulder City had the odd institutional status of being a federal municipality.[40] The closest comparison would be the Tennessee Valley Authority's model town at Norris, Tennessee. The aerial view of Boulder City in Figure 10.7 reveals an uncharacteristic compactness for towns in the American West. Street level comparisons with its nearest urban neighbor, Las Vegas, could not be more striking in contrast.[41] Liquor, gambling, and prostitution were all strictly prohibited in Boulder City, despite their legality under Nevada state law.

Boulder City brings together elements of suburban and company town planning. Its plan is structured around two main diagonal streets that converge heroically on the Bureau of Reclamation Administration Building. Street trees and lawns were planted throughout the town. Eventually the problems of spatial constriction, municipal financing, governance, and land ownership led to a transition toward ordinary municipal status—but not without assurances that certain forms of recreation and urban ways of life would continue to be prohibited.

Urban and agricultural settlement have proceeded most slowly in the Mojave Desert, Las Vegas and Boulder City being two of its larger towns. The Mojave supported virtually no irrigation agriculture outside Owens Valley.[42] Nevertheless, it now faces the heaviest urban pressures of the American deserts. Proximity to the Los Angeles conurbation, long distance water diversions from the Owens and lower Colorado Rivers, traversing highway and rail corridors, luxury resort complexes, and modern vehicular recreation have all drawn the public out of its oases and into the desert.

To appreciate the precedent established by Hoover Dam, one needs to proceed downstream through the succession of dams and reservoirs that culminates with Morelos Dam in Mexico and the Yuma desalination plant's last-ditch effort to remedy the water quality impacts of river development. Upstream travel toward Glen Canyon Dam carries one through the history of social reflection on this mode of river development. It was in Marble Canyon just north of Grand Canyon National Park, for example, that a proposed dam was halted by a shift in public attitudes during the 1950s—away from water control and towards wilderness protection. Further upstream at Glen Canyon Dam environmentalists failed to stop its construction, but they altered the way that monument is viewed.[43] Criticism of the reclamation ideal gained its strength from conflicts over the positioning of dams in scenic locations and then spread out to deal more comprehensively with the environmental impacts of western agriculture and river development.

## Conclusions

We have swept broadly through space and time, sketching out a key mode of landscape transformation in the American West. The four cases examined stayed as close to the climatic deserts as possible. Even so, it is apparent that desert oases lie on desert margins. Oasis development obscures the desert over time as agriculture and urbanism separate society from aridity. A long-term view reminds us that the separation can be dramatically reversed by various types of collapse. The rôles of climatic fluctuation and environmental degradation are of course prominent in this regard, and they receive the active attention of some contemporary desert dwellers. Yet one cannot point to a major settlement that has self-consciously sought a "sustainable" mode of desert occupance. The record of groundwater development in the Southwest indicates the remoteness of this ideal.

At least as significant are the social dimensions of oasis development. Cultural contact has destabilized irrigation societies from prehistory to the present. Community organization played a crucial rôle in the "success" of hispanic and Mormon irrigation and the "failure" of Pima irrigation. Local collectivities have on the one hand given way to more individualistic patterns of water control, but on the other have been overlain by progressively larger water organizations and bureaucratic frameworks for water allocation and administration. The "community" of modern water control is both complex and factious. There is little question, however, that the modern vision of reclamation has faded in each of the desert provinces surveyed here. This raises important questions about the future of irrigation in the West. This future depends as much upon the cultural meaning and social structure of water use, as upon the volume, cost, and techniques of use—which have been the preoccupation of research thus far. Until the agrarian challenge is radically reconceived, the lessons for those who see will continue to shift from accomplishment to failing, and the most inspiring desert experience will lie outside the oases.

# Chapter eleven
# Democratic utopia and the American landscape

## JAMES E. VANCE, JR

THE OBVIOUS CORRESPONDENCE in time of proposals for utopian settlements advanced by European thinkers and the early plantation of European migrants in the New World has often been noted, leaving the impression that such proposals clearly played a major rôle in the shaping of the American landscape. Yet a search within that landscape seems to produce little to support any enduring impact of philosophical utopian schemes, leaving intellectual and social historians who seek to demonstrate a utopian background to retreat to the fastness of a thin scatter of religious villages of a generally communitarian organization, places that had no appreciable influence on the way Americans came to live. Nevertheless, there is a very strong utopian quality to early European settlement in what is now the United States, a quality that has been experienced, if hardly well perceived, by generations down to the present. Perception has eluded most observers because the literary and intellectual view of utopia has been largely élitist, as the views held by such observers are all too frequently found to be. The aristocracy of the informed has normally taken its rôle to be that of advocating, from its elevation of understanding, particular solutions to present ills through creation of rather rigid patterns of social behavior and settlement form to be introduced on a vacant site and within an immigrant population. Reduced to essential qualities, utopias envisioned by the élite normally are both digests of laws for social engineering and also plans for the exercise of a sturdy physical determinism. Most utopias had both a concrete physical shape and a rigid custom to be demanded of residents. Improvement in life was the goal, but there was to be little free will or chance risked in its attainment.

To understand the utopia that did come about in the United States it is useful to make clear the two design components that had become part of most literary proposals for the improved state of living, as well as the state of Europe at the time when the earlier utopias were sketched for a small literate audience. The 16th century was the end of the Middle Ages; at the same time it was the beginning of modern times. Society for the mass of Europeans was still largely medieval, even widely feudal. In a number of countries feudalism was still the structure of rural society and in most cities the now sclerotic guilds hung on tenaciously. The custom observed within cities and the feudal practices enforced in the countryside were rigid expressions of social engineering before there was formal recognition of the force.[1] It is not surprising, therefore, that utopian proposals tended to share that rigidity and sense of enforced conformity to a carefully specified practice. Less widely appreciated have been the impact that the highly constrained spatial structure of the medieval city exerted on the nature of urban life, and the legal fixity of persons living under serfdom experienced as rural provincialism. It would be entirely natural to argue that lifting those constraints, by creating new physical provisions for housing and work, would improve the nature of daily life. New morphologies would be conducive to the transformation of life in ways that the intellectual élite thought desirable. Thus, utopian plans sought to use quite concrete architectural and settlement patterns to gain their social objectives. And because a reformation of social custom was also thought to advance those objectives, individualism and the expression of free will were normally banished through the clustering, even communalization, of settlement.

Utopianism is a general force with diverse expressions and a plenitude of assumed satisfactions: what it is not is the certain attainment of a set of goals that lead to an actual improvement in the human condition. Utopianism is, instead, mainly sensed socially and advanced societally, because society was in the 17th century seen as the institutional outcome of a determined application of custom and local practice, the observable expression of which, in the morphology of the city or of the countryside, was assigned an acknowledged rôle in the shaping of society. In the 16th century it was reasoned that a societal modification could be brought about through a physical transformation. Many physical planners, social engineers, and architects still believe strongly in such a physical determinism. Even at the present time it can be argued that most North Americans, as well as many Europeans, would seek to improve the general lot of human beings through what are mainly concrete physical transformations of our societal environments rather than through the lessening and remaking of social practice alone. Accepting that, one can regard early European-Americans as exercising pragmatic wisdom in paying little attention to the élitist utopias already devised by self-conscious thinkers of the time. By crossing a dangerous and culturally vast Atlantic they risked the full nature of their existence, not merely the outcome of clever mental speculation. Those who died in large numbers trying to reach North America were still survived by individuals whose collective experience, as contrasted to mere speculations, did create a new society in a new landscape and one that reasoned and acted inductively and incrementally rather than doctrinally and deterministically.

Those settlers, most specifically the puritans of the several New England colonies, were in their own lights as "high minded" as any of the largely literary utopians of their time. No puritan shied from practicing social engineering any more than does a modern Swede: what they did seek to do, however, was execute changes along strongly social lines expressed in terms of religion, ethical precepts, and societal organization. Puritanism in 17th-century New England emphasized the involvement of the individual both in the responsibility for his own fate and in any decision relating to the introduction of practices seeking particular goals. Individual participation was the root and trunk of any undertaking toward human betterment: congregational organization of religious practice, covenential association in the political community, cooperation of independent individuals in economic activities, and representative and responsible colonial government, all in varying degrees, exemplified individual responsibility and participation in life. In no significant sense could any New England utopianism be either devised or imposed by outsiders or advanced through a physical determinism absolving the individual will and spirit of responsibility for meeting those goals.

There might be determinism but any that would apply must be based on social influence rather than physical constraint and must rely on individual commitment rather than societal constraint. The sort of determinism represented in much of modern structuralist thought could apply to these early European settlements in North America; the sort of continuing physical determinisim represented by the efforts of architects and physical planners even today, as well as the literary utopians of the 17th century and later times, would have been personally irresponsible in the mind of the New England puritan.

In this context of individual responsibility for the nature of life and the condition of grace, what were the characteristics of a logical native American utopianism in the 17th and 18th centuries? The best answer is to consider briefly the meaning of freedom of person and possession in the late medieval times that immediately preceded the European settlement of North America. In northwestern Europe, particularly in England and Wales—the area whence came most of the earlier settlers in the 13 British colonies—feudalism had been the basis for both personal status and property holding for a number of centuries. That feudalism had been waning for several centuries by the early years of the 17th century when the earliest settlers arrived on the American shore, from Britain in what became the United States and from France in early Canada; but the vestiges of feudalism were still numerous and compelling, particularly in rural areas. Landholding was still mainly in large estates leaving the bulk of the ordinary population as small tenant farmers or, more frequently, as farm laborers on those estates. Serfdom may have been extinguished as the basis of that labor but economic fixity on the estate was little less geographically constraining. In cities, small in their populations, there was, however, increasing disenfranchisement and decreasing personal liberty at this time. The spread of the urban fabric into areas formerly held in large landed estates tended to supplement the medieval burgage plots of individual holding from a lord by new urban holding mainly at leasehold. The narrowing proportion of freeholders of land was fully understood by the group Carl Bridenbaugh has designated as the "vexed and troubled Englishmen" who showed the greatest inclination to cross the Atlantic in the 17th century.[2]

Although many factors pushed the migrants out of England, certainly religion among them, it seems that feudal practice, in both its social and economic manifestations, serves well as a summary term to encompass these forces. Feudalism had determined landholding, geographical mobility, the passing on to children of property and position, the form and practice of religion (casting it in an episcopal and caste-bound mold), the creation of a hierarchical society, and the dominance of rural political power over urban economic power among the many facets of English life that created that troubled state. Those actually leaving the Old World of Europe for the New World of North America wished, among other hopes, to escape the still compelling relics of feudalism in the settlement pattern and practice of the New World. Often they sought to modernize that feudalism by proposing utopias divested of hierarchy, narrow landholding (tenancy and leasehold), property qualification for political participation, bestowed social engineering, and devolved government (in contrast to evolved participatory democracy).

The specifically utopian settlement proposals came in America to be most directly associated with the least popular or democratic colonies. Those latter terms must be understood in their 17th-century context: no North American colony was very popular or democratic when first settled, still some were germinally more so than others. The New England colonies established by the puritans were controlled from the New World, were considerably less hierarchical, possessed far broader landownership, and tended to substitute personal social structuring for social engineering from the mother country. The church was powerful in New England but it was geographically congregational, certainly subject to more variation and potential evolution than was the episcopal church in the Middle Atlantic colonies. And, despite the diversity of religion that grew up in New England, there were no important physical–utopian developments there. In contrast, the Middle Atlantic and southern colonies were initially the site for several important physical–utopian schemes proposed by English proprietors who had emerged as the favored under the remnant feudal society of the motherland. In Maryland the Roman Catholic Calverts, possessed of social and economic elevation under the reigning English practice, had sought to transport the manorial system of rural Ireland to their Chesapeake proprietorship. And in the Carolinas the proprietors, the elect of the traditional rural English system, sought to create an ordered and stratified society of ranks of nobility, a practice subsequently sought according to a plan by John Locke in the seeming base metal of the Georgia colony of the 18th century. That none of these physically deterministic plans for the proprietorial colonies worked out in practice tells much about the general conditions in the North American plantings of settlers. A practice of settlement did become widespread and conducive to a new landscape and society in the New World. But to find its roots and the basis of its nurture we must look at the example where the original practice was most determinedly and openly anti-feudal; for it was in the deliberate and forceful rejection of the relics of feudalism that America found its first utopianism.

The Middle Atlantic and southern colonies were the scene of efforts to employ the traditional rural economic and social structure of contemporary England to create a "greater Britain" where there might be new players engaged, but little actual transformation of society or landscape. The rural nobility and squirearchy would be introduced alongside the manor, the notion of the conferal of elevated status through the ownership of large units of land, and the practice of rural wage labor and tenancy. From the Hudson Valley, after the 1660s English, through the Penn colonies, Calvert's Maryland, royalist Virginia, and the slave-owning and socially stratified Carolinas and Georgia, efforts were made to enlarge the realm of traditional, rural England, but rather little interest was shown in abolishing the practices of feudalism that still survived in the original model. Where there was any utopian aspect to the use of that semi-feudal model in the American colonies it showed up as attempts to retrieve those persons who had fallen foul of that traditional society—debtors who had been thrown in prison, dissenters to an established religion, younger sons of an élite where primogeniture ruled widely—rather than create for them as a group or American settlers as a class a new and utopian land and folk. Widening the geographical spread of what was still thought by the political and social élite of Britain to be an enviable settlement form and well-ordered social structure was utopian enough.

## New England: cradle of American utopianism

Only in New England did utopianism become the general practice, though it was in the form of social structuring that the perfecting took place. The object was to do away with the vestiges of feudal social structure and landholding practice. To the extent a physical change had to be made to rid English society in America of feudal components, there was indeed a consequence in terms of physical development. It is not that a particular settlement morphology was used as a means of enforcing social engineering, but rather of analyzing various elements of the settlement morphology to distinguish between those carried overseas from England as representative of traditional feudal landholding and those still a necessary part of rural agricultural or an urban mercantile economy and society. The physical changes that took place in New England resulted mainly from doing away with those vestiges of feudalism unnecessary in a society of greater personal freedom and a much wider freehold possession of land. The central factor in this is the evolutionary nature of the emergence of the individual, family farm of freehold possession among New England agriculturalists. It seems clear that the method of settlement morphology was not the instrument of social change but rather the consequence of what began as a social objective—certainly with utopian aspects. Only after use by several generations of New Englanders did it come to be possessed of a particular and characteristic landscape expression. This was social determination of physical settlement pattern.

In the colonies that became the United States physical instruments for the accomplishment of utopian objectives were almost wholly missing. What physical instruments there were resulted from the attempts to transfer directly to the colonies the social and landholding practices of the England of the early 17th century. In sharp contrast, however, was the experience with social utopianism, though what constituted a utopian change was viewed rather differently on the opposite sides of the Atlantic. Britain saw such a program of human betterment mainly in terms of expanding the cultural realm of the established British Isles, Great Britain as well as Ireland. To the west of the Atlantic a very different view emerged quite quickly when control of the local destiny was transported along with the early settlers, a situation that was fundamentally true only in New England.

Because the puritan colonies of the 1630s were established at a time when puritanism was widely accepted in Britain, but vigorously suppressed by the monarchy, a large movement of often quite prosperous city merchants and freehold farmers took place as "the Great Migration of the 1630s." The numbers were sufficient to translocate a society more or less in the completed state of development, certainly more than was the case at any other place or time in the long span of overseas British migration. Furthermore, the charter to the Massachusetts Bay Company, which had been issued to a mercantile company by the crown, as had the other charters to proprietorial companies that guided most English settlement overseas in this century, was exceptional in that it was taken by the leaders of the Great Migration to their new capital in Boston and effectively retained there for the formative period when social experimentation was likely to have the maximum effect. And for complex reasons, that translocating "Commonwealth" sought vigorously to stamp out the social vestiges of feudalism in this new land. And with that abolition went much of the landscape of traditional northwestern Europe, requiring in its place the creation of a North American landscape engendered by the special political and social conditions of New England in the 17th century. Over the succeeding centuries that model was also found to fit better in most parts of North America, even in the strangely vestigial Kingdom of Canada where the New England puritan transformations of the period of the Great Migration came to guide the laying out of most landscapes west of Québec and the shaping of a society mostly as free of medievalism as is that of the Great Republic.

Why then did the puritans come rather quickly to seek the extinction of feudal social practice, and thus to shape the main and most expansible American utopia? The answer lies deeply embedded in the precept of

puritanism that made the individual family, if not initially the precise individual (given the status of women in this society), responsible for its salvation. The medieval practice of commendation was not individually responsible enough for the stern thinkers of Boston in 1630: if one might shift off responsibility for security, salvation, succor, and sovereignty to others, as medieval practice had decreed, then the individual's responsibility directly to God was fatally weakened. More must be expected of the true Christian, and to gain that end the perfectionists must reject the timidity, absence of free conscience, and restraint of the expression of true volition found in the untransformed transfer of traditional (medieval) British society and landholding to the New World colonies.

There were other reasons for the creation of a post-medieval practice, perhaps the most dominant of which were the notions of the beneficent use of land and the substitution of "God's grace" for simple inheritance. There was a strong belief in the productive use of land rather than in the possession of land to confer a hierarchical position. Feudalism had to be done away with to accomplish the effective shift to this beneficent use of land. The puritan idea was that one held land because he could effectively use land, and in philosophical and religious terms he should hold land only to the extent he made that effective use of it. The agricultural system supported that notion; general farming for subsistence was virtually forced upon New England just because it was that new mother country, productive of crops and kind that could generally be raised as well or better in England. The plantation system of the American South, distinguished from England by its expansive subtropical climate, was missing to the North (which could not thus quickly become commercialized, providing a seemingly ever expansible appetite for land). In the South the "headright" system allowed large landholdings to grow, but at the expense of the separation of land use by individuals (through indenture, tenant farming, and rural slavery) from the freehold ownership of that land. In the South the individual free to move could gain access to land mainly by removing himself well beyond the immediate frontier of settlement. And frequently, even thus isolated, squatting tenure had to be resorted to or else submarginal purchases made from speculative landholders who tended to view land as wealth and thus to be capitalized as highly as possible.

In contrast in New England the ideal of beneficent use of land as the basis of a full freehold ownership gained ascendency along with a number of other anti-feudal practices. Massachusetts in the 1630s forbade the private ownership of game and of fish, certainly for the first time in the British world. The Commonwealth of Massachusetts also created a general court of non-hierarchical if not democratic provision, and made local governance of both town and congregation of broad if again of not fully universal suffrage through the operation of the local covenant. Ownership of land became the measure of acceptance into the covenant in the "daughter towns," and also of God's grace. Under the social engineering of New England only through starting anew could that grace be assessed and made operative, in the working of what Max Weber termed "the Protestant ethic" to equate grace with prosperity. At first land could provide little beyond subsistence, so those seeking to expand the commonwealth tended to turn toward fishing, fur trapping, and trading, and mercantile activities to demonstrate that measure of prosperity. Thus, not only was land of only modest financial utility but also, and of even greater significance, for the first time in feudal British practice, land was of little symbolic worth as to political and social distinction.

In this practical, religious, and social environment land became a basic measure for participation in the community: in the town even increasingly important shipowners still kept their cow, their orchard, and their kitchen garden, as the Boston Common attests; in the countryside the country merchants and timber producers similarly had a family farm operated alongside the most subsistent of agriculturalists. To a surprising degree the subsistence freehold farm was to be found equally in farm villages to begin with (later in dispersed farms for those serious about seeking grace from rich and commercially productive acres), and in the trading and shipowning ports of the coast (with their carryover of the burgage plot from the earlier Middle Ages with its "urban subsistence" structure). These family farms and subsistence burgage plots were fundamentally utopian derivations from the destruction of feudal landholding practices. It seems that the two clearest examples of "utopias in America"—the *family farm* and the *American suburb*—grow quite directly from the first impulse toward social betterment.

## The first utopia: the family farm

If the expression of utopia among the North Americans came in the rejection of the last vestiges of feudalism, it was the abolition of any suggestion of servile tenure that would be among the first expressions of the change. Thus, freehold ownership of land would stand as an instrumental act regardless of actual settlement form. The agricultural village, whose form was brought quite directly from England, need not immediately have been transformed; instead a straightforward shift from leasehold or even tenancy to freehold would have done away with socage (feudal terms for holding land not involving bearing arms) without forcing the immediate creation of a new settlement form. As Sumner Chilton Powell has shown, the agricultural village did stand as the earliest rural settlement in New England but that village, even in its first Massachusetts expression, was held in fee simple ownership once participation in the community covenant was established (Fig. 11.1).[3] Not all forms of servile duty were abolished, however, but the main forms to continue—participation in a militia and in the corvée to build and maintain roads—were those associated with collective action as necessary for the support of all individual families as they had been for maintaining medieval manors and their lords. Market rights, the require-

211  ment that grain be ground only at the local mills, and many other privileges

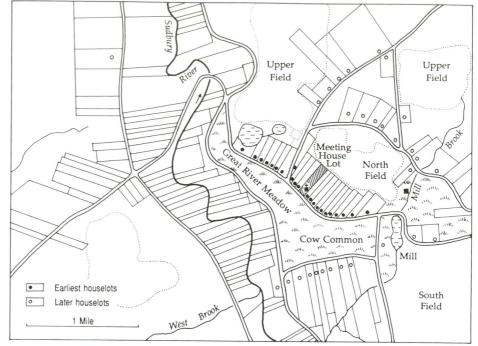

**Figure 11.1**
Land parcels in Sudbury,
Massachusetts, in 1640. Early
settlers were granted
individual landholdings
arranged in relation to
common pasture land and a
central meeting house. This
represented already a spatial
loosening of the bonds of
compact villages in southern
England whence the settlers
came.

and regalia were dropped. It became common to abolish trading and
occupational monopolies replacing them with home production of a wide
range of goods and services. The Yankee farmer was conceived of as ever
ingenious and constantly engaged in the thrifty domestic manufacture of
most of the things he needed. This wide productivity, when combined with
a comprehensive subsistence farming, seems to have led rapidly to the
shaping of the building structure as granary, shelter for animals, workshop,
housing for an occupational household, and almshouse for an extended
family, among other things, producing thereby the elongated New England
farmstead (Fig. 11.2). The manorial village was no longer an operational
necessity as that broad farm household was normally as close to self-
sufficiency as can be imagined for a single living group. Large families with
one or several "hired men" and "hired girls" could survive quite well in
considerable isolation.

There were great advantages to the dispersed farmstead as the settlement
unit, something we tend to overlook because isolation has come to be
viewed as anti-social and stultifying. In the puritan society of 17th- and 18th-
century New England isolation was always contained. Even though farms
might be widely dispersed, they were always part of a community. There
was no such thing as being outside a town, with its religious, political, and
economic organization. Distances between farms always were such that a
sense of community was maintained. For the dispersed family farm of New
England, which created the derived settlement form growing out of the
rejection of the late feudal farm village, group settlement was at first an
*212* entirely essential practice. No farmstead might lie more than a half mile or a

mile from a meeting house, or else a new meeting house with its clustered farmsteads must be formed. Only much later in time and far to the west was the truly isolated farm or ranch introduced into American life.

It is highly instructive that when a group quite used to the New England dispersed farmstead, the Mormons, found themselves no longer part of the *broad American covenential community*, they turned away from the open settlement pattern and toward "the City of Zion" where the wagons might metaphorically be formed into a circle to lend support to these separatists. And as those Mormons moved truly beyond the European-American frontier into the Great Basin they retained the plat of the City of Zion not against neighbors of other religious belief as before, but simply against isolation in a vast wilderness (Fig. 11.3). As this Mormon town spread widely over the Great Basin and even beyond its precise boundaries into the Snake River Plain, the inner sections of the Los Angeles Basin at San Bernardino, and into Palliser's Triangle of southern Alberta, the Latter Day Saints' frontier was always advanced by the covenential group settlement, just as had been the puritans' frontier of the 17th and 18th centuries.[4] There was the same notion of the self-sufficient freehold—possession of land— now the town smallholding with free-standing house, kitchen garden, barn, and extended family household as well as the true agricultural farmstead (equally held in fee simple with associated farm buildings and extended family), though in the Mormon town the dispersed pattern typical of early New England was clustered into 2.5 acre essentially agricultural "small-holding" properties characteristic even of Salt Lake City after 1847.

It is significant that the derivative settlement evolutions of the two widely

**Figure 11.2**
Characteristic of the New England connected farmhouse is the Byron Kimball farm in North Bridgton, Maine, pictured here as it had evolved in 1889. Note the fieldstone walls made of boulders cleared from the improved land.

RESIDENCE OF **BYRON KIMBALL**, NORTH BRIDGTON, ME.

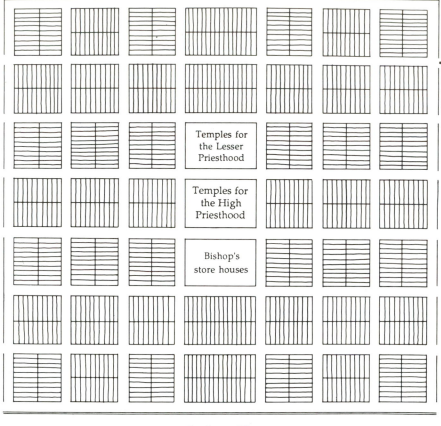

Temples for
the Lesser
Priesthood

Temples for
the High
Priesthood

Bishop's
store houses

One Quarter Mile

**Figure 11.3**
The Mormon prototype town
plan: Zion, Missouri, 1833.
What distinguishes this
1-square mile plan from
standard American
speculative urban layouts is
the alternating orientation of
many block axes, leading to a
more open character when
built up with houses, and the
three central blocks reserved
for religious buildings. The
layout of Salt Lake City and
other Mormon towns
followed the main principles
of this model plan.

adopted American utopias, the freehold family farm and the rather spacious American suburb (clustered smallholding in the later Mormon context), were so similar in landholding practice, family association, freedom from vestigial feudalism, and fundamental origin in the British North American colonies. Also they both came so clearly from the conception of improved life and its resultant settlement structure as envisaged within the most independent of American colonies. All of the social theorists, contemplating in Europe the nature of a utopia, envisaged some form of specific and elaborated physical design that would reinforce the social engineering they had in mind. Among the Europeans actually settled in the New World in the 17th century, and those persons in the 18th century who should now be thought of as American, the proposals were very different: they urged fairly abstract social, religious, and economic goals, but left the enabling settlement forms to emerge over several generations and mainly in response to an objective of family ownership of land and a personal freedom born of the notion of personal independence founded on personal responsibility. Religion was the individual's responsibility, as was his government, his occupation, the location of his residence, his security, and his mobility (both in the provision of local roads and in the decision about where he wished to live in a highly mobile society). Many individuals made significant shifts in residence during their lifetime and most American families progressed geographically with the advance of the American frontier.

At first clustered and formally communal, farms rapidly took on a truly North American dispersed pattern, normally within a generation of the original settlement. Similarly in the Middle Atlantic region and South, where strong efforts were made to shape a large estate pattern for a semi-feudal America, the dispersed family farm became the norm only for the white population in the back country outside the highly commercial plantation areas. As both the New England–New York agriculture and the back-country South farming spread westward (following a rapidly advancing frontier) that broadly utopian family farm became so nearly universal as to constitute a perceived fundamental element of American life and landscape.[5] The exceptions to this rule, isolated experiments in communitarian settlement designs, were extremely few and far between, both in time and space, and cannot be said to have influenced the American pattern in any appreciable way. Such examples as Robert Owen's New Harmony in Indiana, or the Amana colonies in Iowa, represent minute and isolated cases of social plantations in the American landscape that failed to reproduce, and stand now as picturesque oddities rather than emulated models (Fig. 11.4).

Constantly harking back to our assumed Cincinnatian philosophical roots, presidents from Jefferson to Eisenhower extoled the family farm and have undertaken costly programs of support for its maintenance on the emergence of any sign that might suggest that its utopian sap was failing.[6] The Homestead Act of 1862 saw the survival of a then divided America through encouraging the landless to side with the Union in return for free

**Figure 11.4**
A notable communitarian village experiment was the Janssonist colony of Bishop Hill, Illinois, which lasted from its founding in 1848 to 1861. The Colony Hotel, built in 1854, now used as a residence, is indicative of the several large communal structures erected in the early years of the colony.

land. So long as unoccupied land of agricultural utility remained, as it did into the interwar years of this century, the dispersed family farm on previously public land remained the main instrument of any considerable geographical expansion of the American settlement domain. But eventually this assumed bedrock fundament of American existence could not suffice to accomplish utopian aspirations for most Americans.

Already at the end of the 18th century the American economy, always commercial and trading in its support, needed more than this commercial agriculture. When the Treaty of Paris was signed in 1783 Britain not only gave political freedom to the United States, it also had to grant economic freedom to those 13 colonies to engage in manufacturing, something they had largely been forbidden to do before independence, and in world trade, again widely denied them before their military defeat of Britain with significant French assistance at Yorktown. Once free to manufacture and trade goods widely, along with traditional farm products and raw materials, the country obtained the basis for a rapid urbanization. The traditional rural utopians of the Jeffersonian stamp saw little virtue in this broader settlement freedom, but fortunately their narrow patrician social engineering was rejected by ever larger numbers of proletarian Americans. The city grew both in size and in geographical distribution to the point that by the time of the Civil War the trading and even the manufacturing city came sometimes to precede the edge of the family-farm belt as the national frontier spread, a return to the conditions found on the earliest English settlement frontier in North America when, as Carl Bridenbaugh noted 50 years ago, it was cities in the wilderness that first housed Europeans on our shores.[7]

## The second utopia: the American suburb

The cities in the wilderness were hardly utopian: instead they were medieval forms brought from Europe by the earlier settlers. The medieval town of organic growth and the bastide (fortified colonization town of French inspiration) that came into broad use in western Europe starting already in the 12th century were the two forms which the early settlers used as models for the town in America.[8] In the initially semi-feudal Middle Atlantic region and South attempts were made as well to found English Renaissance towns with their pretentious assertion of a narrow hierarchy of privilege and power. All these transfers were, however, replaced with an "American original" first evolved after 1681 in William Penn's Philadelphia, a city he sought to use to advance his own élitist conception of social engineering through the recreation in America of a class-ordered society. Anti-feudalism in America was, however, far too strong. Leasehold and peppercorn rents might survive in a vestigial form, but the town as a physical entity became an instrument of land speculation on a broad scale. As the Philadelphia model of town settlement was quickly adopted and almost universally used for subsequent town foundings in the United States, landholdings were privately and individually owned so that any speculative increases in land values flowed to actual settlers rather than to distant landowners as Penn seems to have intended.

This is not the place to expand on the failure of these initially medieval cities in America; instead we should note this attempt to bring to America traditional urban forms, even that partially utopian physical and social structure the bastide, new and reformist in the 12th century. We might say that from Boston in 1630 on, the European settlers in America sought a derivative pragmatic improvement of the European city just as they had tried to improve the agricultural settlement through the shaping of the new dispersed family farm. One of the reforms sought was the extinction of urban vestiges of medieval practice to match the destruction of those survivals in the countryside. Because towns were small in colonial America and largely dominated by the merchant and maritime classes, at first there was little transformation of the European town forms brought by the 17th-century townsmen. But with the spread of the freehold family farm in New England, where trading and mercantile marine towns were best developed, the practice grew up whereby seagoing men often had their homes in the countryside on such farms or else in small wooden houses scattered along the back coves of their home ports. Certainly, many such cottages were rented but many as well were not and the practice of occupying small detached houses even in cities arose in this country where land was vast and ownership highly diverse.

The colonial ports began to have streets of "captains' houses" as well as those of sailors and clerks. Merchants frequently had large houses used both for trade and for residence. Distinctions among buildings existed but they were far less socially and economically stratified than were those of Britain, and landownership was much broader. That ownership came to be seen as a bedrock on which family security was based, in the city as well as on the family farm. In a mercantile port such as Boston there remained a strong attachment to the land on the part of both manufacturing workers and those employed in trade. So long as the laborforce remained reasonably small and relatively well paid, as it was before about 1840, the detached house on its own small plot of land served to shelter families, while boardinghouses lodged the single women widely engaged in the emerging textile manufacture under the Waltham system of hiring. In fact the setting up of a textile mill based on water power, as most were until the 1840s, forced the employer to build reasonable worker housing in a mill village. These, however, began the sundering of residence from landownership causing concern among the workers housed there.

In an attempt in part to return to the bedrock tradition of the separate house possible under individual ownership, a new form of settlement then largely distinctive to the northeastern United States was devised. This was the second of our indigenously designed utopias, the American suburb. At first these were still located quite close to the centers of large-scale employment, in South Boston, Dorchester, East Boston, and Cambridgeport around Boston, places within walking distance of shipyards, docks, factories, and the merchants' warehouses of the increasingly complex and enlarging city. In the areas adjacent to larger cities, where the increasing use of steam power was allowing factories to grow large, similar worker suburbs could lie in a band around the earlier mill villages. Not all houses were occupied by owners—the small builder and investor often owned a few buildings let out as houses and tenements. These differed from the earlier mill villages built and rented out to their employees by manufacturers in being part of the generalized housing market of the city, let for a rentier's profit, and not dictated as to location by a single factory. The residential town came into existence, first based on a walking journey to work, but with the introduction of railroads in the 1830s and 1840s possibly based on railroad commuting. As early as the 1850s there were railroad commuting journeys made not only by the middle-class workers, as came at least a decade earlier, but as well repeating trips by those engaged in heavy and physical labor.

The development of the geographically detached suburb was encouraged by a number of basically utopian objectives. Perhaps strongest among these was the search for health based on the observation that residents of open areas and the countryside normally fared better in the repeating epidemics of the last century. There was as well a strong belief that the social asylum offered by the countryside, beginning with the family farm, could be enjoyed as well in the more open urban housing possible on the cheap land of the suburb (Fig. 11.5). Suburbs did provide cheaper housing along with the possibility of vegetable gardening to help reduce living costs. Air was commonly sweeter, space more generous, rest less disturbed, and sport and recreation made simpler in the suburbs. Unlike the utopian proposals put forth by European social thinkers, ranging in time from the 16th century of Rabelais to the present day of Paulo Solari, the American settlers starting with the puritans of the 1630s practiced a geographical rather than a physical determinism. The dispersed family farm had a physical expression, and so did the American suburb, but these expressions were locational—geographical—rather than architectural. The forms that the family farm and the suburb assumed were the results of a social objective, the abolition of vestigial feudalism, rather than the result of an operative social engineering.

The early development of the American suburb was facilitated by several aspects of life in the Great Republic. Landownership was wide and largely divorced from standing as a requisite for a hierarchical division of society. Living standards were normally higher, occupation by occupation, in the United States so the introduced mechanical transportation of the last century came into earlier and wider use in America than in Europe. Entail, primogeniture, and leasehold were largely missing in the United States, so land around cities was normally a property widely and repeatedly traded, making the creation of suburbs much easier. In American cities there was an earnest and early effort made to widen the class use of public transportation.

**Figure 11.5**
As this aerial view attests, today's suburbs emerge as often detached subdivisions sprouting among farm fields far out on the urban fringe. In time this south-suburban Chicago housing tract will be surrounded by others and become part of a new municipality.

This came through the creation of the street railway with its horse cars first in New York City in 1832 (the wide spread of that form to stand as the *chemin de fer Américain* when later adopted in France), the invention and wide application of the electric trolley car to these street railways in American cities (allowing a very cheap unit fare to be adopted that removed the economic cost of expanding commuting distances), and finally the development in the United States of the first automobiles that were mass produced and thus cheap enough to be purchased and used in commuting by blue-collar and clerical workers. All these stand as the backstays of the democratic suburb.

Much of the reasoning behind the massive development of American suburbs came from that settlement form as a solution to improvement in housing.[9] While Germany, and later Britain, sought housing improvement through adoption of the public provision of rental housing, the United States turned instead to a geographical solution. By bringing cheap land and more widespread private ownership of suburban housing into existence the utopian ideal could be gained. Where the European notion was that there must be an architectural reform, with widely used social engineering, the American idea continued to focus largely on private and individual ownership of land, in the family farm and in the family suburb, as it had from the earliest years of the settlement of Europeans in North America. To continue that traditional practice a high level of human mobility, geographical as well as economic and social, was necessary. In that situation there was great pressure on Americans to devise and apply widely successive improvements to transportation. The test of that need is furnished by the history of transportation improvement in the last century. It was strongly oriented toward the development of technologies of transportation that were most cheaply operated and most widely applicable, both socially and geographically.

In conclusion it should be clear that utopianism was in no way lacking in North America; rather it was expressed in the native idiom here. The deterministic physical and social engineering proposals of European thinkers held little appeal, and even where introduced were soon abandoned. But the utopian practices slowly developed within North America, notably the dispersed family farm for rural settlement and the clustered family suburbs that grew up around the cores of colonial towns (developed first on older European models) produced two utopian settlements that became almost universal in the New World. In a real sense these American utopias are hard to perceive because they are so widespread. Yet they stem from a single utopian ideal, the final abolition of medieval practices in the country and in the city.

# Chapter twelve
## Ethnicity on the land

## MICHAEL P. CONZEN

AT FIRST GLANCE the human landscapes of modern America seem remarkably uniform from place to place. Vast stretches of countryside are dotted with isolated farmsteads—islands of habitation in a sea of cultivated fields, grasslands or forest clearings—linked by an indefatigable web of roads and trails to each other and to distant urban centers. On closer inspection the farms might vary in the number and variety of building structures they display: large barns where dairying or fodder crops are important, small ones where cash crops prevail; silos and storage bins numerous or absent; equipment sheds large or small, depending on the importance of mechanized activity; special purpose buildings for raising tobacco, orchard fruits, poultry, or a host of other particular products. But in general the rural farmscape of America, if it varies at all, seems more adjusted to regional economic specialization than to any surviving visible distinctions that could be ascribed to cultural pluralism. True, farmhouses differ in their size and modernity—from up-to-date bungalows, split-levels, and urban-looking ranch homes to proud Victorian frame houses, modest wooden shacks, and the occasional log structure in remote and late-settled fringe areas. But regardless of building material or size, there is a general sameness to the farm scene that suggests the historical triumph of an evolved American norm, born of a desire for independent farming and universal access to the architecture of technological improvement over time.

In towns and cities the story seems to be the same. In America people have been used to towns growing fast, so buildings have become standardized for speedy replication. No matter that distinctive house types became common in many places—row houses in Baltimore, bungalows in Los Angeles, six-flats in Chicago—the standard long ago became the detached residence on its own lot, on a tree-shaded street in a grid setting, with businesses clustered along downtown thoroughfares and suburban arterials. If houses display an infinite variety of small architectural features it is because they reflect that timeless search for individual acceptability within a crowded community, offering constantly changing symbols of status and fashion in an urban world of rapid communication and sensitivity to

221

pancultural crosscurrents. But even in the city it is easy to assume that the American way of building emerged early in the nation's history and has governed the look of most urban landscapes at the expense of any ethnic expression, stamped even more firmly now with the ubiquitous imagery of budding skylines of skyscrapers downtown and outer rings of countless suburban subdivisions.

Yet the central human fact in the country's history is the near-constant immigration from all over Europe and periodically from parts of Africa, Asia, and Latin America, contributing millions of new inhabitants to the settled regions of the expanding United States over more than three centuries. If this diverse infusion of peoples resulted in landscapes displaying only a vigorous American commonality then the "cultural baggage" of individuals and groups of particular ethnic background would appear to have counted for little.[1] Whether assimilation came sooner or later, according to this view, it simply entailed adopting prevailing techniques and landscape features. But on the other hand to downplay cultural antecedents, while it may promote the notion of a new order and bolster the ideology of American exceptionalism, does little to clarify the means by which the old ways were superceded. Nor does it help uncover the mechanisms by which strongly held ethnic values helped negotiate the transition to American life and even perhaps influence the course of American cultural development itself.

A more fundamental objection to such a conformist view of American landscape evolution, however, is the widespread relict evidence of pluralism to be found in so many localities around the country. Often this imprint is now muted by the ravages of time as modernization and the cycle of replacement have substituted massproduced buildings and other landscape features for the more ethnically distinct accoutrements of the past. But 40 or 50 years ago the American landscape was far more richly endowed with local ethnic flavor than is apparent today. How, then, can this heritage be recognized, and what meaning does it hold for our understanding of the American cultural landscape?

## Early ethnic encounters

The cultural landscape of the United States contains traces of perhaps the most diverse array of ethnic influences to be found anywhere in the world, because immigrants have settled there from so many distant parts at one time or another.[2] They may not always have produced the most intricate cultural contrasts or stunning juxtapositions in space, for the cultural reshaping of groups has occurred over the period of only a few hundred years—and much less for many—and has been influenced by a strong tendency to adapt to an American way based early on English precedents. And yet the enduring contrast between the ways of life and landscapes of the Amerindian population who have long occupied the continent and those of Europeans arriving from the 16th century onward could hardly be more dramatic. And any view that considered the triumph of English-derived norms in cultural development and landscape formation in America to be near complete would ignore the extraordinary range and power of numerous competing immigrant cultures to adapt without totally disappearing, and indeed to transform the national culture, not to mention the many regional societies where they have been numerically strong.

The impact of the Amerindian, Spanish, French, English, and, obliquely, the forced African settlement on the early development of the American cultural landscape has already been recognized in earlier chapters. These were by no means, however, the only major ethnic and racial groups that shaped the human landscape of America, and the interplay of immigrant cultural heritage, evolving national culture, and changing environmental resources offers a Protean context in which processes of landscape formation can be seen. The result has been that the landscape is studded with numerous local examples of the ways in which immigrant traditions have been incorporated into it with differing success and permanence and with varying influence on the development of American vernacular practice. Often this has led to multiple ethnic imprints in the same regions, varying over time as early groups were joined or succeeded by others. Sometimes an early and clear imprint was softened or erased by a pervasive impact from a later majority, or isolated as an "ethnic island" within an otherwise prevailing landscape, and sometimes a cultural mixing occurred that created a powerful new force as population spread across the continent—such as the adoption of the log cabin as an ideal tool of colonization throughout the eastern woodlands.

Countering the ingrained urge to build from memory would be an often undeniable need to build from experience.[3] If conditions in the new land were far more critical in explaining the formation of the American landscape than was cultural background, as has often been argued,[4] then ethnic influence should not be much evident and have little historical consequence. The first condition was the nature of the environment newly encountered. Since the Atlantic seaboard was richly forested, wood was in so plentiful a supply that Englishmen there could reinvigorate a frame building tradition long in decline in Britain with the disappearance of the woodlands. However, when later settlement reached the treeless plains and deserts of the West, attachment to wooden construction would be of no use—to Englishman or Norwegian alike. Hence sodhouse construction and adobe walls gained value, at least for a while, regardless of the ethnic background of the builder.[5] But then, as craft techniques gave way to mechanized methods of producing building materials, and as advances in transport spread such materials over wide distances, the natural endowment of local environments would become less restricting. Thus it can be argued both culture and environment each had their potency and their limits in explaining the regional character of the American landscape.

223

Early illustrations of these possibilities appeared in the 17th-century tidewater settlements of the Dutch along the Hudson River, the Scandinavians in the lower Delaware Valley, and the Germans who settled in southeastern Pennsylvania. Although destined to fall under British colonial administration, these populations established in America ways of life and approaches to landscape development that were to have in some cases profound influence on subsequent national experience.

All groups when they first arrived settled in discrete localities along the seaboard and in relative isolation from each other, with the result that they attempted to modify the lands they occupied in ways they were used to. While farming sometimes included adaptations to native crops and cultivation practices, the habitations they came to build normally followed Old World precedent, at least in form if not always in materials. The first structures were often of log, given the immediate circumstances of colonization,[6] but soon many groups built more substantial houses that reflected their customary notions of what houses should be. Hence the Dutch built urban houses on Manhattan Island with typical proud crowstep gables facing the street while in New England the English built frame houses according to regional traditions in England.[7] Swedes, Finns, Welsh, Scots, and Irish, where they settled in exclusive clusters of any size, tended to build also in vernacular forms familiar to them.[8] If there had been no hinderance to the process, each group might well have recreated English, Dutch, German, Swedish, and other landscapes as extensions of the Old World over large portions of eastern America. But complete replication over large areas for most groups was not to be. For one thing, colonization by most nationalities never approached the population levels, speed, and capitalization needed to shape the land thoroughly in their culture's image.

Over time the early settlements became merged in a continuous zone of settlement stretching all along the Atlantic seaboard and into the piedmont interior.[9] Ethnic identities blurred somewhat in the face of heterogeneous immigration and increasing settlement densities. Philadelphia was particularly noted for its multi-ethnic population by the early 18th century, and it would soon be largely in the countryside that individual groups would have the best chance to develop and sustain distinctive landscapes. There are two eastern cases in which the ethnicity of groups other than the three great American colonial powers has been supposed to have had widespread influence on the development of the cultural landscape.

First, there is the matter of the ubiquitous log cabin and its possible European origins. There is general consensus that three broad Anglo-American subcultures—New England, Midland, and Plantation South—developed during the colonial period, and all expanded to other parts of the continent through the process of American woodland colonization, employing log building as an adaptive strategy. This is not the place to consider the varied log construction techniques found across the land and the problems of their dating and attribution,[10] but it is worth noting that debate over credit for the introduction of log building to the continent continues to rage.

224

Many writers regard the tradition as having Germanic roots, although Swedish scholars have long argued a Nordic origin.[11] Recently it has been suggested that the westward expansion of the woodland colonization was driven by a syncretic "Midland backwoods culture" originating actually among the "preadapted" Savo-Karelian Finns of the lower Delaware Valley in the 17th century.[12] Whatever the case, there is little question that log construction was in widespread use in most districts in which the forested wilderness was being pushed back, and that several folk traditions of log building flourished in northern Europe around the time of American colonization. Any claims for a specific ethnic contribution to what became so widespread a building convenience for families on the active frontier, however, must acknowledge that in most parts of the country log construction represented a temporary expedient for groups and individuals who saw it as rudimentary and sought, as soon as resources allowed, to create more elaborate, conventional dwellings. The fragmentary survival of log structures in many localities, nevertheless, is one of the most evocative elements in present-day landscapes, given the epic imagery associated with countless forebears who once lived in them.

As the frontier colonization zone—the "periphery" in much discussion of historical regionalism—moved inland, through and around the Appalachian barrier, the developing seaboard "core" acquired its patina of English ways, aided by the early political hegemony and commercial ties of Britain.[13] This provides a second instance in which ethnicity exerted an influence—albeit more localized—on landscape development. Notwithstanding the emerging dominance of broadly Anglo-American landscape habits, local ethnic traditions did flourish. For example, a Pennsylvania German landscape emerged in that state's southeastern corner during the course of the 18th century (Fig. 12.1). This "best poor man's country" produced a wide variety of log and stone houses of varied form depending on familiarity with different regional house types in central Europe, but leading to very substantial houses with four-room plans and central chimney, and large forebay barns.[14] Today, farmsteads in that region often contain a second dwelling, called the grandfather house, reflecting the sometimes remarkable stability of family generations on particular farms. Unlike that of the Dutch in the Hudson Valley, the Pennsylvania German landscape was more significant over the long term in not only surviving to the present with much greater clarity but also in influencing the shaping of landscapes further afield.[15]

Given the pervasiveness of Anglo-American landscape traditions since the colonial period, it is not surprising that only very few non-British influences seem to have survived from that time. But as the volume of immigration increased hugely during the 19th century, many other ethnic traditions were carried in the minds of migrants to American shores and to numerous inland locations where open frontiers beckoned. If local circumstances led such traditions to find expression in the new landscapes being created, what kind of imprint might be expected?

**Figure 12.1**
Pennsylvania German farmscape. This view of the Daniel Schultz farm near Hereford, Berks County, Pennsylvania, displays a mature ensemble of farmstead structures.

## Ethnic landscape signatures

Ethnic influence in the landscape takes many forms. A brief list of elements includes placenames, different land division systems and road patterns, building traditions, farm layouts—including farmstead, field, and fence—nucleated villages, communal facilities, religious signatures, and such other special purpose structures as were needed for festivals and musical and athletic activities. Beyond that, partiality to certain agricultural practices, particular crops, urban occupations, and locations within neighborhoods also suggest ways in which ethnicity is interwoven with the fabric of the landscape in general—although sometimes as much as consequence as cause. All the possible elements with respect to all American ethnic groups in all places where they are to be found cannot be considered here,[16] but some leading examples can give shape to the notion that the ethnic imprint is more widespread than often thought.[17]

A key distinction can be made between those influences that stem from the largely vernacular habits and preferences brought by immigrant groups actually settling in different places in the United States, and those influences that reflect landscaping styles imported from time to time from other parts of the world as a product of trends in fashion, adopted by those willing to follow national and international arbiters of taste.[18] The first type will be examined here; the second is taken up in a later chapter.[19]

### Houses and farmyards

It is at the level of the individual house or farmstead, designed and constructed in ways different from those of the vast majority of American buildings, that the most obvious ethnic influence in the landscape is usually to be seen. This is because the individual freehold farm property has reigned supreme in the American ideological pantheon and the land system, whatever its specific geometry in any region, has been designed for acquisition by individuals more than groups. Thus, it has been up to individuals, if they were going to replicate to some degree their Old World building habits at all, to do so as individuals, even if this was accomplished within the context of a larger group settlement around them.

By far the commonest American form from the 19th century onward is the wooden frame building, more often than not painted white. Brick houses come a distant second in frequency. Many regions have traditions of building in stone that cut across ethnic groups and have more to do with local availability and income differences among families, but there are cases where stone, even where it was widely available, was favored only by certain cultural groups. German, Irish, and Cornish settlers, for example, from provinces in Europe where stone houses were common by the 19th century were certainly predisposed to build stone houses in America—at least up to the 1880s—especially if the immigration included trained stonemasons.[20] Scandinavians, on the other hand, were used to wood construction, by and large, and building in stone was an acquired taste and only in some localities.[21] Often houses of ethnic origin, enlarged and much altered, stand now in the landscape barely distinguishable from later construction, and it takes a knowledgeable eye to pick out the details of floor plan, roof pitch, or window placement that may link such buildings to particular regional Old World antecedents. There are numerous examples of ethnically distinctive house types in rural America, but a few distinctive illustrations must suffice.

Half-timbering was a traditional building form in parts of Europe where the woodlands were scarce, and is much more recognizable in the United States in light of its unusual appearance and modern-day rarity. It was carried over to America by German groups more than any other and this *Fachwerk* style was planted in numerous localities—Pennsylvania, Wisconsin, Missouri, and Texas, to name a few—even where wood was in abundance,

227

though relatively few good examples remain on their original sites. Notable instances include the Single Brothers' House in Salem, North Carolina; the Beckmann-Obermeyer farmhouse in Gasconade County, Missouri; and the Koepsell farmhouse in Washington County, Wisconsin (Fig. 12.2).[22]

A different case is provided by the traditional Luxembourg house in the Middle West. This is a substantial stone house, sometimes with jerkin roof,[23] finished on the outside with stucco and featuring symmetrical fenestration, with the main entrance on the eaves side, and, like its German cousins, sporting a vaulted cellar below (Fig. 12.3). Interestingly, immigrants from neighboring Belgium settling in northeast Wisconsin chose to build mostly brick houses with gable front entrances and decorative two-color patterns in the brickwork.[24] In both cases, the preponderance of these special styles stands in marked contrast to Anglo-American houses in the vicinity.

Another example is provided by the Finns of the upper Middle West, who settled the American shore regions of Lake Superior. The Finnish log houses feature close-fitting squared logs requiring no chinking, one- and two-room house plans as well as Nordic pair houses, and a variety of log notching designs reflecting many of the types known in Finland.[25] Yet other distinctive ethnic house forms include the German-Russian house (single-story dwelling, often in stone with hipped roof, central or offset chimney, an occasional "black" kitchen, and *Vorhäusl* or small enclosed entrance porch) found in such states as Kansas, North and South Dakota, and the Norwegian farmhouse in eastern North Dakota with its two-story porch mimicking the grandeur of the *Herrgard* or squire's house in the old country.[26]

Farm layout also provides a basis on which ethnic differences can be discerned in the rural landscape, although the effect is often subtle. Most evident are those cases where remnants of the compact courtyard arrangement of farm buildings were transplanted to America. Chief among

**Figure 12.2**
The Koepsell farmhouse, originally in Washington County, Wisconsin, features a half-timber frame construction filled with brickwork, and a central chimney, reminiscent of buildings in Pomerania, the North German province from which the family came. Built in 1858, the house is now preserved at the rural ethnic museum of Old World Wisconsin.

**Figure 12.3**
Luxembourg houses on Main Street in St. Donatus, Iowa. With their jerkin-style roofs, stuccoed walls, and symmetrical fenestration, these stone houses reflect the building traditions of the Grand Duchy.

these are the exceedingly rare instances of housebarns—where living quarters were combined with livestock pens and barn storage areas. Occasional housebarns have been identified in Pennsylvania, Wisconsin, Missouri, and South Dakota, associated mostly with German and German-Russian settlers, and perhaps intensive research will reveal other areas with a significant number of cases.[27] Their rarity can be ascribed to the spaciousness of American farms and the risks of fire. A looser quasi-courtyard arrangement of farm buildings has been noted for a number of ethnic groups.[28]

Special purpose farmyard buildings present less ambiguous evidence of ethnic presence in the landscape. For example, summer kitchens have long been associated with areas of German settlement, from Pennsylvania to the Middle West. They are small, single-story buildings adjacent to, and sometimes attached to the main house, and emerged in response to the growth of family accommodations in the main dwelling and the need to keep it cool during long hot summers.[29] In areas of stone construction, summer kitchen as well as main house were of stone, although frame kitchens also occur in German settled areas. Interestingly, traditional summer kitchens are generally unknown in Europe, and largely unknown on Anglo-American farms in the United States. A related structure is the bakeoven, occasionally attached to summer kitchen walls for access from within but more commonly a separate small building in the farmyard.[30] Also once common in areas of Germanic settlement is the free-standing smokehouse with its centrally positioned flue. Perhaps the most discriminating facility of all is the Finnish sauna, or steam bathhouse, because of its association with one particular group. Usually of log, the sauna consists of two small chambers, the dressing room and the steam room, where water is poured over stones covering a stove to produce the steam (Fig. 12.4). Wherever Finns settled in any numbers vestiges of the sauna are to be found.[31]

229

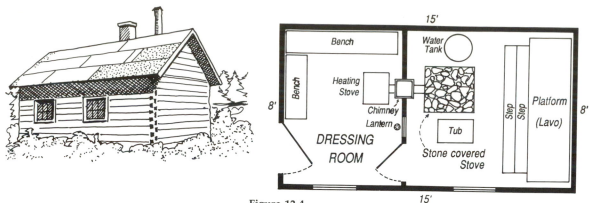

**Figure 12.4**
Finnish sauna plan. Built of close-fitting squared logs, the sauna is a small, two-room building with few windows. Not to be confused with the summer kitchen found in German-American areas, which generally has more windows, the sauna typifies Finnish settlement in northern Michigan and Wisconsin.

There are many other specific features on individual farms that bespeak an ethnic imprint, although the exclusivity of their identification with a particular group may vary. Just as the log cabin was adopted by most American pioneers, so too was the Swedish rail fence widely accepted.[32] Other constructions, however, were more narrowly implanted, as was true of the casement, or hinged window. The universal type before the innovation of the American sash window around 1700, the casement window can still be found in older parts of the Middle West, favored as it was by new German settlers well into the middle of the 19th century. Examples have been found in Missouri and Iowa (in the river town of Guttenberg, in particular).[33]

*Village patterns*

The imprint of ethnicity on the American landscape reaches beyond the individual structure, however, to encompass the broader land patterns of property ownership, the form of whole villages, and the buildings that signaled communal values. This more community-wide scale of ethnic expression has understandably been harder to establish, given the American stress on freedom of individual action. Nevertheless, one can often discern evidence of cultural preferences in the organization of the landscape that stemmed from concerted action, notwithstanding the prevailing individualism all around.

Following American independence the most grandiose schemes of ethnic colonization involved various attempts to establish a German state on American soil—Missouri being the favored locale. Such ideas came to nought. A contributing factor was the openness of the land system and the freedom of anyone to settle almost anywhere, thus in practical terms preventing any group from appropriating too large a continuous tract of territory. However, many groups managed by sheer numbers to colonize small and medium-sized areas in sufficient density to affect the patterns of

230 landholding and therefore institute a contrasting village and district layout

where the urge to reproduce a distinctive and more communal society appeared. The patterns of colonial French and Spanish land grants in the Mississippi Valley have already been noted,[34] but there were occasional instances of other implantations that stood at variance with general practice. One observer has detected relict Dutch and French Canadian field systems in the present-day Vermont landscape,[35] and another the Salzburger long-lots of colonial Georgia.[36] When settlement moved into regions surveyed under the national land ordinance, the grid imposed a spatial discipline rarely challenged. Still, some groups from time to time circumvented the system. A small Welsh community in a northern Illinois township, for instance, managed to buy contiguous river valley land, dissolve the internal grid boundaries, and then resurvey the land to produce irregularly shaped parcels that ensured each new owner access to the river (Fig. 12.5).[37]

A combination of the grid survey and the pre-emption and homestead laws encouraged dispersed family settlement across the rural landscape and thereby strongly discouraged nucleated farm villages of the type common in many parts of Europe, in which farmers lived together on village lots and "commuted" to their farm land. So strong was this reorientation to dispersed living that most American hamlets and villages have developed as commercial crossroads settlements with few or no farm inhabitants.[38] Only in a few circumstances have settlers managed to re-establish nucleated village forms in America. There are a few cases of *Strassendorf* (street village) development in the Middle West. In Altenburg and Westphalia, Missouri, for example, German settlers more or less consciously planned linear village forms complete with long narrow houselots fronting on a single street with the dwellings at roadway's edge without front yards.[39] Other examples are Kirchhayn and Hubertus, northwest of Milwaukee, Wisconsin. There are doubtless more elsewhere, though distinguishing them from casual American ribbon development requires study of historical lot patterns. In Texas, while the German Hill Country towns were laid out on a grid principle, the isolation of rural ranchers led to a unique "commuter" feature—the Sunday house. This was a tiny house for overnight accommodation in connection with church attendance in the town.

The most striking cases of planned nucleated villages of farmers are those in which communal organization was ordained and maintained through religious precept. The best known of these is the Amana Colony in Iowa County, Iowa. Set up between 1855 and 1865 by the Amana Society as a communitarian place for settlers whose forebears had broken away from an increasingly dogmatic and formal Lutheran church in Germany, the colony purchased a compact tract of nearly 18,000 acres straddling the vale of the Iowa River and adjacent gentle hillslopes (Fig. 12.6). Six sites on the lower slopes were laid out as nucleated villages, to which were added two villages close to the railway. Each village had its own communal lands around it, to which villagers repaired for work decided on by a manager. All colony members lived in one village or another, and many economic functions were

231  tied to common facilities, such as the huge village barns and small

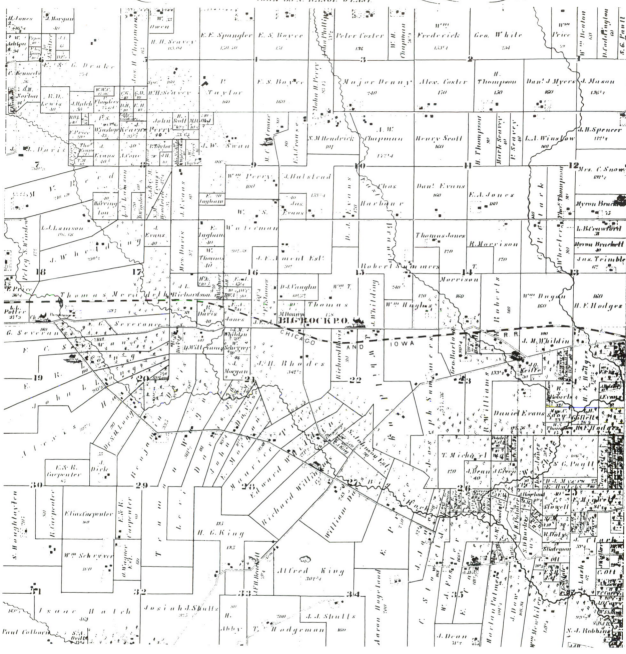

**Figure 12.5**
Big Rock Creek in Kane County, Illinois, attracted a small colony of Welsh settlers in the 1830s. When the U.S. Land Survey subdivided the area in 1840, the Welsh cooperatively bought all the square units necessary to retain their original lot boundaries, hence the oddly fused parcel systems that remain to this day.

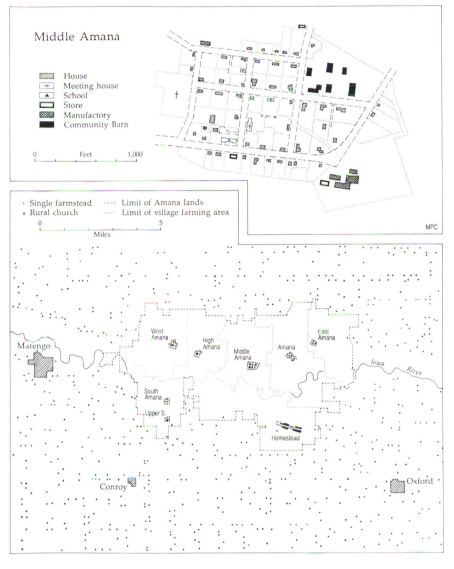

**Figure 12.6**
The Amana Colony bought a tract of land a few miles west-northwest of Iowa City and established seven nucleated villages with specific farm territory around each. An eighth, Homestead, was purchased later for its rail connections. The communal organization of farming in villages, as reflected in the spatial layout of Middle Amana, contrasts strongly with the standard American individual farmstead pattern of the surrounding district.

factories.[40] This system lasted until 1932, but the landscape created has changed remarkably little since the 19th-century heydays.

There were numerous other communitarian settlements sprinkled across the country, though very few lasted into the modern age. The Swedish Janssonist colony at Bishop Hill in western Illinois, founded in 1846, was dissolved in 1860, but not before an impressive village of imposing community buildings had been built, including a church, hotel, dairy building, blacksmith and wagon shops, stores, mills, a school, hospital, and several enormous dormitory buildings. Many of these remain today, the largest Swedish ethnic monument outside Sweden.[41] A further example is offered by the German Catholic community of St. Nazianz in eastern Wisconsin, founded in 1854 by a renegade priest, that developed a compact mixture of private and communal and religious buildings, including several lay cloisters for celibates as well as a church, seminary, convent, monastery, and way of the cross.[42]

Even if these communitarian villages were the great exceptions in the ethnic landscapes of America, they shared with most other settlements a focus on religious buildings that most directly reflected an Old World imprint. Few ethnic districts failed to produce a scatter of churches and other religious symbols that punctuated the landscape. Although church edifices were often replaced by larger structures of later date, design traditions continued to mirror local heritage. This is most apparent in Roman Catholic communities where sometimes extraordinarily complex precincts of church, school, convent, parish hall, cemetery, hospital, and even grotto could develop. Often, garden shrines to the Virgin Mary abound in such villages.[43] It is rare for the wayside cross common on country roads in Catholic districts of Europe to appear in America, but in at least one area, the Belgian district of northeastern Wisconsin, local families built quite numerous devotional chapels along roadsides bordering their property, creating a definite regional landscape accent (Fig. 12.7).[44]

### Urban house types

If ethnic flavor appears in the nooks and crannies of the American countryside, the same can be said, more strongly, for the cities. It is most evident in older neighborhoods where signs advertize business names with ethnic roots, but that tends to reflect current or recent residence in neighborhoods that may once have been home to quite other communities. Vernacular housing in cities tends not to have strong ethnic peculiarities

**Figure 12.7**
Ethnoreligious diversity discouraged wayside crosses and chapels along public highways, but this Belgian roadside chapel in Kewaunee County, Wisconsin, declares a family's piety on the edge of the farm property.

**Figure 12.8**
Double shotgun houses on a
New Orleans street in the
Vieux Carré district. Each
door and window next to it
represents the front of one
dwelling. Floor-length
windows and shutters allow
maximum air circulation in a
hot climate while maintaining
privacy.

because the density of urban living has usually integrated immigrants quickly to majority social aspirations and architectural norms. Further, the pace of urban growth and neighborhood change have accustomed urban ethnics to move easily between neighborhoods and participate in a potentially citywide housing market in which house types are valued by their functionality rather than their cultural associations.

Still, there are clear instances where ethnicity has stamped its presence on the evolving character of urban areas. Perhaps the most extensive example is the shotgun house found in towns throughout the American South, as far north as Louisville. A simple rectangle averaging 13 feet by 65 feet, the basic shotgun house type is a narrow one-room-wide, and three- or four-room-deep building with a gable front and small porch extension (Fig. 12.8). Though mostly built in frame construction, the form has been traced back through its New Orleans diffusion point in the United States, via free black migrants in the early 18th century to Haiti and half-timbered antecedents there, and further back to Yoruba wattle-and-daub precedents in Africa.[45] While not by use an exclusively black house type, it found favor as a solution to cheap housing on expensive city land (adapted for use on very narrow lots), and formed the basis for variants such as the camelback house and the more upscale "North Shore" house type in the Garden District of New Orleans.

Another way in which urban vernacular houses display ethnic influence is through features that hark back to old country forms, even if the American house is of contemporary design and construction. An example is afforded by the German traditions visible in Milwaukee, historically one of America's most German cities. Here, while many small homes reflect speedy adoption of the balloon-frame construction method begun in Chicago, there are numerous neighborhoods of generally middle-class housing in which large, comfortable-looking gable-fronted houses bear a striking resemblance to proud street gable styles in German cities (Fig. 12.9). The materials may be different and the styles may be provided by local architects and even lumber supply firms, but the esthetic is Germanic. Among the mansions of the bankers and beer barons in well-to-do districts, such as Shorewood along Lake Michigan, the partiality for architect-designed, overblown, Teutonic monstrosities is hard to miss.

More often, however, the ethnic signature in towns is found at a smaller scale. Decorative treatment of otherwise plain, standard house types sometimes shows a link to ethnic expression. The best known of these cases are the several Chinatown districts of large cities such as New York, Boston, Philadelphia, Chicago, and San Francisco. One or two buildings, usually including the Chinese Merchants' Association headquarters, are built as conscious replications of more or less complete old country forms, but most houses are of standard American shape, placed there before the street became an ethnic district. Many buildings, however, over the years acquired decorative ornamentation of roofline, window and balcony that intensified the Chinese look to the district. Add to this the persuasion of city officials to contribute street furniture in suitably Chinese motif—street lights, street signs, telephone booths and occasional triumphal gateways—and the overall effect is one of an intense ethnic stamp on the local urban landscape.[46] The visual vocabulary of Chinatown is well known through tourism; less easily recognized are decorative traditions that blend more easily with the general esthetic of the underlying functional architecture, such as the geometrical patterns on a church rectory in Chicago's Ukrainian Village (Fig. 12.10).

**Figure 12.9**
Germanic-looking gable houses grace a street on Milwaukee's north side, an area of solid German middle class residence. Although American in design and construction, the similar choices home owners made from a wide range of available standard house designs suggest a common memory of old country forms.

236

**Figure 12.10**
Slavic decorative motifs on
St. Nicholas Church
buildings at Rice and Oakley
Streets in Ukranian Village,
Chicago.

Other examples include hispanic decoration of front yards, with particular emphasis on yard fences, and a predilection for colorful murals on neighborhood walls.[47]

*Community buildings and precincts*
The ethnic imprint is perhaps most consistently shown through community buildings in towns. Houses of worship are usually the largest of these and express cultural character very easily. While many different ethnic groups may define part of their culture through their tie to a particular religion, for example Roman Catholicism or Lutheranism, variations emerge in terms of saints' names chosen for local churches, architectural style of the church itself, and often interior furnishings.[48] The onion domes topped by three-barred crosses that grace the towers of Greek Orthodox and Byzantine Rite churches in Shenandoah and other coal towns of Pennsylvania, for instance, accent the urban skyline in dramatic fashion. Concentrations of ethnic churches in particular neighborhoods, especially when they are of different denominations and within sight of each other, can vividly reflect ethnic mixing in and sharing of urban space. The juxtaposition of large parochial school buildings and convents for the teachers with the churches themselves makes for religious precincts in the urban landscape of southside Chicago or New York's Brooklyn almost as imposing as those around cathedrals and monasteries in Europe.

Besides churches, ethnic occupance shows up in the nature of neighborhood retailing. Not only do ethnic names leap out from store banners proclaiming their cultural orientation, but many signs are written in the old

237

country language for those not yet acculturated to America. In addition, many neighborhoods feature shops offering consumables, especially food fare, that is peculiar to particular groups, or where their very survival is a tribute to an ethnic loyalty not matched in districts served nowadays by modern supermarkets. Ethnic bakeries and meat markets still flourish in communities where old style bread, cookies, cakes, and German or Polish sausages retain special appeal. Mexican groceries are the only reliable places to obtain the hottest of hot peppers. Sometimes, the stores reinforce the ethnic imprint through national colors: at least two bakeries in Chicago's once heavily Swedish Andersonville district still sport a storefront design in light blue and yellow hues.

Besides food, recreation has long been central to the cohesion and flourishing of urban ethnic culture, and different groups have left different marks on the streetscape. Heavily Italian neighborhoods to this day sport storefront social clubs that provide locales for men to gather and pass the time of day. Boston's Italian North End, though now feeling the press of gentrification from its edges inward, is still a bastion of such clubs, where strangers and women are hardly welcome, though it could be said that multiple functions accrue to these establishments. One club "guards" a nearby alley by parking cars at both ends of it to create safe play space for neighbors' children, while patrons of a Bronx club in the Belmont neighborhood clearly monitor the streetlife passing within view (Fig. 12.11). Among Germans in America beer has always been a *cause célèbre*, a social pleasure to enjoy and defend. The landscapes of cities where Germans have been numerous are still dotted with reminders of the great breweries once in their midst: even small Port Washington, 30 miles north of Wisconsin's

**Figure 12.11**
Bronx Italian men's social club on Belmont Street, New York City. Ostensibly a public place, only men of the neighborhood are warmly welcome.

238

metropolis, boasted a brewery that once made "the beer that made Milwaukee furious." Beer gardens were often attached to these establishments or simply as summer appendages to local taverns. There are not a few small parks in Milwaukee—innocent-looking municipal green spaces today—that had boisterous, music-filled careers as private beer gardens up to Prohibition!

In a few instances the ethnic presence in some cities was dominant enough to influence the great public architecture of the city at large. Chicago, Cincinnati, Milwaukee, and St. Louis contained sizeable German populations throughout the second half of the 19th century that easily infiltrated or even defined the business and cultural élite. Thus, talented architects of German extraction would gain commissions for major buildings in town, and through interest in both traditional designs from their homeland as well as following modern design theories flowing from Germany at the time—particularly with regard to romantic revivals—did much to give the public landscape of these cities a decidedly Germanic caste.[49]

## The variable imprint of ethnicity in the landscape

There is no doubt that many ethnic traditions have left their mark on the American landscape, rural and urban, and a number of ways has been suggested in which this has occurred. It remains to account for how variable this historical imprint has been from place to place, and what that implies about the conditions under which ethnicity has or has not found local expression. How strong was the urge to replicate traditional Old World ways in a new arena? What conditions encouraged and sustained it? And what led to its abandonment or transformation? Put another way, how much "cultural baggage" was actually unpacked by the immigrants in their new homes? The interest and success in reproducing landscape forms drawn from memory of the Old World were in fact much affected by time and geographical circumstance. Where and under what conditions could that heritage find fullest expression, and where be most muted and transformed?

*Factors in the re-establishment, survival, and modification of Old World forms*
The most important influence was the volume of immigration in relation to time and place. Large migrant flows to a common destination encouraged an ethnically distinct landscape to form. When settlers sharing a common cultural background congregated in significant numbers to occupy the majority of land in a given district, then a second basic prerequisite for the emergence of an ethnic landscape was met—they formed a significant spatial cluster. This was true in portions of southeast Pennsylvania during the 18th century when ethnic Germans, although from various regions in

239

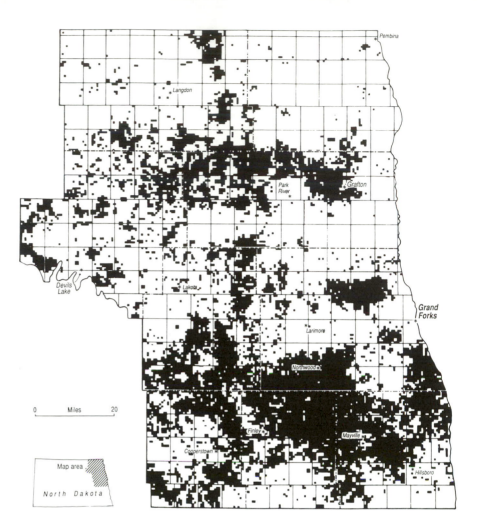

**Figure 12.12**
This eight-county area in
northeast North Dakota
shows land owned by
families of Norwegian birth
or descent in 1913–14. It
illustrates the power and the
limits of a single ethnic group
in settling densely and
contiguously enough to
dominate certain districts to
the exclusion of others. Many
settlers ended up in zones of
more or less mixed ethnicity.

central and eastern Europe, including Switzerland, Silesia, and Moravia, concentrated sufficiently to create whole neighborhoods of the same general culture, with a network of small towns to service the districts. In the 19th century, with its much larger volume of migrant flows from the same source areas to the same destinations, ethnic concentrations became widespread in parts of the Middle West and the Great Plains. In North Dakota large clusters of Swedes and Norwegians, among others, could be found in several localities (Fig. 12.12),[50] and they did replicate significant building features of their ancestral homes.[51]

Besides volume and spatial clustering, the economic experience of groups also played a rôle in the formation of ethnic landscapes, at both ends of the spectrum of economic success. In rich agricultural districts, such as southeast Pennsylvania, the growth of wealth through farming bred security and confidence that through emulation spread some landscape habits far and wide, where they contributed to a wider cultural evolution: witness the popularity of the Pennsylvania German barn. On the other hand,

240

subsistence in economically marginal areas such as the Appalachian Mountains created tenacious local cultures, most notably among the Scotch-Irish, loyal to an environment that conserved their values as much through isolation as anything else.

Indeed, location in settled areas or on the frontier was important to ethnic imprint. When immigrants entered already settled districts and filled in the remaining open land they were not likely to create separate landscapes. Isolation on the frontier was often critical to the chances that an immigrant group would do so. If isolation lasted long enough to see the community well past the log cabin stage, and if the region's fertility generated sufficient wealth, then its members were more likely to build their first substantial homes in the old styles. The breakdown of isolation would soon bring the group into contact with the convenience, price, and modern features of standard housing offered through the national commercial economy that proved so attractive to American society at large.

A last major factor was the strength of shared values among immigrants with the same background. If they came from the same areas back home, spoke the same language, followed the same religion, held the same beliefs and shared the same outlook—whether it be politically conservative, socially stubborn, or financially hardnosed, for example—they would more likely favor outward forms that reflected these traditional orientations. Group migration, especially under the leadership of charismatic clergy or lay visionaries, often displayed strong commitment to maintaining the old ways, including their reflection in building styles.

By contrast, a list of factors least likely to produce an ethnic imprint on the land is easily made: heterogeneous migrant streams, dispersed destinations, little tendency to cluster, lack of success in colonization (leading to geographical mobility), and the pull of the new culture. Where survival has been less evident the circumstances have favored greater assimilation into the American mainstream. Proximity to large urban centers, access to higher education, industrial employment opportunities, and modern recreational pursuits have redefined the relations between farm families and the national culture.

The survival of ethnic landscapes has generally required some combination of large size and extent of ethnic settlement, recency of arrival, relative geographical isolation, or strongly maintained set of community values favoring tradition over change. The growing visibility of black, hispanic, and Asian landscapes in American cities in the last quarter century is beyond dispute a function of size, spatial concentration, and replenishment. Other groups in cities have created clear and sometimes lasting cityscapes for similar historical reasons.

In rural areas the imprint is often more subtle. The more an ethnic group kept a measure of isolation from the majority culture—and this was often achieved by a kind of spatial solidarity, not allowing members of other groups to buy or marry in and minimizing outside contacts—the more they held their landscape intact. Prosperity under these conditions, indeed, could foster the fuller elaboration of an "Old World landscape" in the new place rather than the lack of it. Freedom from competing values and alternative ways would prolong adherence to traditional ethnic landscape preferences. Some of the most enduring cases involve groups sharing strong commitments to a rural way of life that incorporates active maintenance of certain religious precepts. The Mennonite and Amish communities of Pennsylvania, dedicated to a simple life-style supported almost exclusively by their own labor, are well known for this. Their landscape has survived *in situ* for about two centuries and has had time to mature and consolidate its distinctive appearance.

But rarely did any group manage to insulate itself from change in the outside world. Industrialism and modernism during the 19th and early 20th centuries progressively diminished the likelihood that earlier ethnic distinctiveness in the landscape be retained. In the preindustrial age of handmade tools and artifacts and time measured by the speed of craft production the proportion of buildings and products locally produced would be high, drawing on knowledge and skill from within the community. In such a setting traditional Old World concepts and practices could still have value, especially when knowledge of outside ways was limited. As the 19th century wore on and an increasing number of industrially produced consumer goods and building materials was fabricated outside the community and brought in at lower cost, local skills narrowed and declined, and the trend toward regional and national standardization in the landscape gained strength.

In the face of these trends, ethnic communities often responded with a progressive modernization of their local landscapes. Although immigrants might embrace wholeheartedly the influx of the majoritarian culture and its physical trappings, more often, it seems, they adopted some elements—often the large ones (such as standard American house forms, because of their conveniences), but retained or only slowly adjusted a range of less obvious ones—such as the use of rooms, types of heating, cellars, and other domestic spaces.[52] Sometimes, "investment" decisions created an opposite pattern: retention of traditional house forms coupled with ready installation of massproduced components that modernized the dwellings. Fitting a clapboard exterior over log homes and inserting sash windows were common examples.

### Ethnic islands and archipelagos

It is inescapable that in the United States in the late 20th century the geographical outcome of these large processes has been the evolution of numerous ethnic "islands," scattered in an ocean, as it were, of standard American countryside or urban territory.[53] A cluster of German Catholic communities in central Minnesota, established around the time of the Civil War, illustrates the pattern. The persistence of German farm culture in that region has been remarkable. For decades large families have amply fed the cityward movements beloved of demographers while at the same time placing new generations on the land with farms of their own. And so integrated has the region been under the dominance of the Roman Catholic church that the area has been dubbed the "Minnesota Holy Land" (Fig. 12.13).[54] Consequently, a zone with a radius of roughly 30 miles north and west from St. Cloud contains 20 places named after saints and other religious subjects, 84 public shrines—including 16 wayside shrines—and a general population at least 70 percent Catholic, reaching 90 percent in some parishes. The frequency of Germanic-looking church edifices, parochial facilities, cross-festooned cemeteries, and garden statues of the Virgin Mary in the region's landscape simply cannot be missed.

The ethnic imprint on the American land should be seen, however, as more than just a mosaic of cultural islands. The landscapes they have

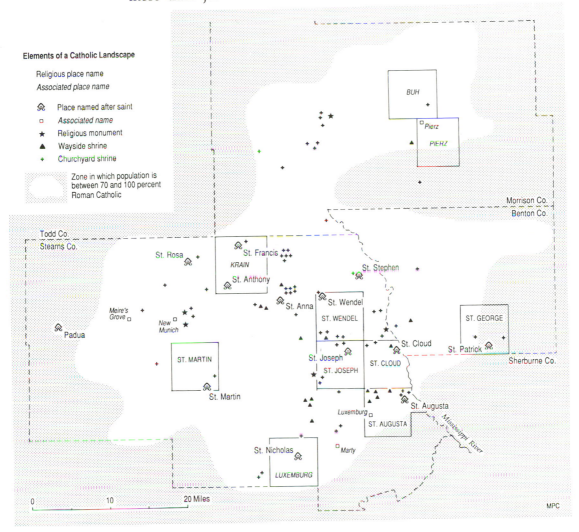

**Figure 12.13**

Minnesota's Holy Land, centered on Stearns County. Composed mostly of Germans, but with Poles in the northwest and Luxembourgers in the south, this region displays the Roman Catholicism of its inhabitants with many religious signatures in the landscape.

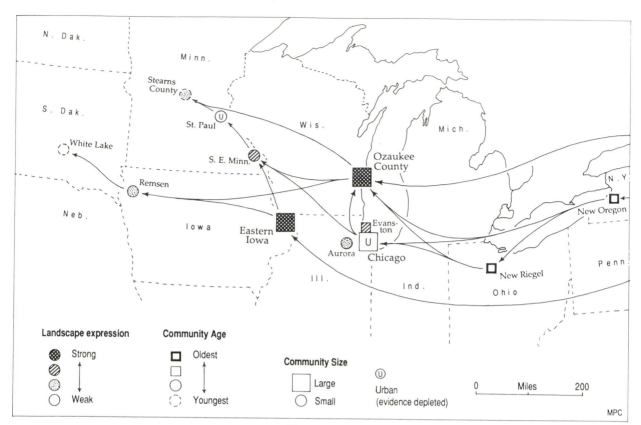

**Figure 12.14**
Luxembourg landscapes in the Middle West. Their differing intensity is a function of timing, location, and generation.

engendered vary considerably in the range and intensity of their distinct ethnic features. While little comparative work has been done to account for the variations between regions and between groups, there are some systematic differences that point towards considering many such islands as forming chains or "archipelagos." Just as it is now common to recognize that immigrant communities developed in widely scattered locations through a process of chain migration and the sequential establishment of daughter colonies, so we can begin to speak of landscapes linked in terms of such bonds of migration and also their degree of ethnic expressiveness. The case of the Luxembourgers is suggestive.

The first small wave of Luxembourgers settled in New York State near Buffalo in the 1830s and a subsequent colony settled around New Riegel, Ohio, but in neither case was a clear ethnic imprint maintained (Fig. 12.14). Few in numbers, they settled in districts occupied also by many Americans. In both areas, though stone was available, they chose not to build with it but used the handsome red brick common to Yankee settlers alike. But when later Luxembourg migrants found the open land frontier in Jackson County, in eastern Iowa near the Mississippi River in the late 1830s, and Ozaukee County, Wisconsin, near the Lake Michigan shore in the 1840s, distinct

244

ethnic landscapes resulted, symbolized most prominently by their stucco-covered stone houses (Fig. 12.3).[55] Not only were they the first group taking possession of farmland in these areas—confirming Zelinsky's Doctrine of First Effective Settlement[56]—but their relative isolation until the railroad came in the early 1870s helped nurture the replication of familiar Old World building forms. These communities and some in and around Chicago spawned daughter settlements in Minnesota and western Iowa. The Minnesota settlements were half a generation younger, peopled largely by Luxembourgers who had already spent time in America and were perhaps more acquainted with American building styles. Consequently, the traditional Luxembourger landscape vocabulary was present but adopted by a smaller proportion of the Luxembourg settlers. By the time Luxembourgers settled around Remsen, western Iowa, and White Lake, South Dakota, in the 1870s and 1880s, a combination of greater interethnic mixing and easy availability of massproduced housing during the railroad era perhaps explains a reduced ethnic imprint. While the Old World repertoire was gloriously present in religious buildings and markers, the traces of ethnic vernacular in residential buildings was faint indeed—floor plans and interiors rather than façades and outbuildings.

To visualize ethnic settlement areas not just as islands but as parts of whole archipelagos is to relate them mutually, at least within the context of each ethnic group, in terms that help explain their variable landscape expression. Many other groups could probably be viewed in similar fashion. Even the replication of Mormon landscapes throughout the arid West, for example, fits this sequential notion well.[57] The Mormons, of course, to the extent that they qualify as an American ethnic group—forged by religious conversion and significant early geographical isolation and intermarriage—do not share the long history of most European or Asian groups. But they produced a distinct variant within the general American pattern by selecting and making uniform certain building types (notably their temple architecture), town planning principles, and agricultural features suited to their early environment. The Mormon landscape was "invented" in relatively short order, but was still indigenous to the group in its time and place. There are other instances of ethnic expression, however, where the invention seems more immediately a product of the commercial culture of modern times, and yet deserves note.

## Invented and ersatz ethnicity

Ethnicity has become fashionable in late 20th-century America and this is producing some brand new forms of ethnic landscape. For most of the nation's history the major social institutions, such as government, the schools, and many churches have been dedicated to the principle of assimilating immigrants into the majority American culture, assuming that this was both essential and feasible, and a function of time and effort. The largest group, the German-Americans, was propelled along this path at least in part through the cultural complexities of two world wars. However, by the 1970s it was clear that America's "ethnics" have remained to some degree "unmeltable," and today ethnic pride is newly resurgent. Not only are ethnic pageants and parades increasingly assertive, but there has been an explosion of interest in cultural roots among "hyphenated" Americans, and a new viability to ethnic expression in the landscape, in no small measure due to the economic gains recoverable from stimulating local ethnicity-based tourism.

Ethnic reassertiveness has roots that reach back often many decades. Most groups long ago spawned their filiopietistic historians, eager to chronicle their community's "contribution" to American life. In landscape terms, however, interest then developed for some groups in museums as a means of preserving the richness of their ethnic customs, including buildings and decorative traditions. The Swiss of New Glarus, Wisconsin, established an open air museum of pioneer log cabins as early as the 1930s to commemorate their settlement in the area. As popular interest in the multicultural diversity of the nation has spread, local ethnic communities have been emboldened to halt the deterioration in the ethnic distinctiveness of their localities, especially in small towns. Where landscapes came close to losing ethnic identity completely, or actually did so, there have been strenuous efforts to reverse the trend by reinventing the signs and symbols of that presence. Hence, New Glarus, which two decades ago, aside from its open air museum up a side street, displayed no obvious Swissness in its streets, now groans under the weight of Swiss chalet balconies (many added to perfectly functional-looking American commercial buildings), cantonal coats of arms on street lightpoles, chalet-style public phone booths, and a glockenspiel-bedecked, half-timbered drive-in banking facility. A "balconied" bar on the main street has even painted its roof-mounted TV satellite dish with the Swiss flag!

Even more energetic, the good burghers of Solvang, California, have left no opportunity unexploited on Main Street to remind the visitor that this is a town with a Danish heritage (Fig. 12.14). Gift shops, restaurants, ice cream parlors, and cheese shops line the tourist thoroughfare, and of course Danish bakeries abound. Buildings are clothed in natural wood suggestive of the impression locals have of what a Danish town looks like, and the streetscape vista is closed by giant windmills that would do Hollywood set designers proud. A similarly memorable impact is afforded by the remarkable modern recreation of a Norwegian *Stavkirke* (stave church) in Rapid City, South Dakota, its four wooden, tiered façades set off dramatically by the conifer-covered hillslope behind it. Where there is a market, there is a way, and ethnicity pays. It also pays the "sending" culture sometimes to get involved. To San Francisco's long-established Chinatown north of the city's commercial center has been added recently a magnificent triumphal gateway, gift of the Chinese government of Taiwan. America's

**Figure 12.15**
Main Street in Solvang, California. Note the intermingling of Danish and American flags in the street, and the architectural detail of ancient and medieval Danish building forms most 19th century immigrants would never have built, even had they stayed in Denmark. This street scene evokes an idealized past, consumed eagerly enough by the madding tourist crowds.

Chinatowns, of course, have long been accustomed to outside visitors flocking to their businesses. More remarkable now is the breadth of ethnic reawakening among countless small communities across rural and small-town America as the depredations of decades of dilution and neglect are countered with campaigns to reinvigorate, at least commercially, the ethnic presence in the American landscape.

## The legacy

The United States is a fundamentally pluralistic society, so an ethnically diverse cultural landscape is to be expected in a land where freedom of expression is so highly valued. It is also a highly dynamic society, in which material progress and modernization can be expected to replace much of the existing physical fabric in the course of time. The balance between these two tendencies has been weighted in favor of the standardization and cultural homogenization that mass production yields. And yet, the landscape is as ever a faithful recorder of the way the totality of conflicting social influences has been accommodated in space. The ethnic imprint still survives in numerous localities, though much threatened by the primal American urge

247

for renewal through replacement, and not necessarily protected by the new enthusiasm for rediscovering ethnic pride.

The ethnic survivals in the landscape carry multiple meanings. They are a muted but often poignant reminder of the original transplantation of Old World cultures to the new continent, sometimes now centuries old. They are a tangible reminder that past generations came to the country with an overwhelming desire to begin the business of personal lives all over again in an environment of often strange people and places in which familiar ways of doing things played an important part in their adjustment. That ethnic traditions became at all embedded in the American landscape reflects the opportunity people felt for recreating a fairly familiar world, a negotiated accommodation on the way to being a new people in a new setting. The territorially limited scale of ethnic survivals in today's landscape is testimony to the power of assimilation over hundreds of years to a not particularly entrenched majority Anglo-American culture. The location and strength of each particular manifestation of ethnicity in local landscapes reveals unerringly the power of geography and history to mold a specific response to a unique set of circumstances in cultural transfer and confrontation. Although the surviving stock of houses, neighborhoods, villages, farms, and fields that speaks of an ethnic past has been diminishing relentlessly, a modern enthusiasm for that past has slightly slowed the rate of loss and led to the restoration of many eloquent examples of structures and settings recalling that heritage. Nevertheless, the many other as yet unacclaimed ethnic building and landscape elements face an uncertain future because many vernacular features are merely regarded as too ordinary and out-of-date to be recognized as significant by their owners. Nevertheless, for those with eyes to see, the American scene is yet teeming with reminders large and small of the extraordinary enrichment that each successive generation of immigrants has contributed.

# Chapter thirteen
## The new industrial order

### DAVID R. MEYER

AMERICAN INDUSTRIALIZATION HAS produced a landscape of specialized activity and mechanical integration, of growth and decline, and of abandoned and reused relics. Mineral processing plants, lumber mills, and factories are highly specialized production centers that can exist only if linked by transportation and communication systems with suppliers of raw materials and markets for finished products. The increasing specialization of production centers requires more elaborate means of both mechanical and spatial integration. In their turn cycles of specialization and integration contribute to change as new ways of organizing production occur and as old ways become obsolete. Places which acquire the new ways grow while the losers stagnate or decline. Growth leads to new landscapes as well as a reuse of past ones. Industrial decline combined with an inability to acquire new industry, however, creates an abandoned landscape.

The manufacturing process is the most prominent feature of industrial landscapes: factory buildings with machinery, chimneys, furnaces, power sources such as water wheels, dams, boilers, and warehouses.[1] Because the process requires that materials be assembled in one place and products widely distributed, transportation systems are the second most prominent feature of industrial landscapes: canals, rail lines and yards, bridges, docks, and highways. The remaining features in these landscapes, which are by-products of the process, include pollution of water and air, destruction of vegetation, and discarded products such as slag heaps, saw dust, and obsolete equipment. Immense changes in America's industrial landscapes have occurred between the colonial period and the present.

## Colonial beginnings

Although there are few physical vestiges of the pre-1860 landscape, the earlier industrialization did determine, in part, where and how the later landscape emerged. The remnants of the colonial industrial landscape are well-nigh invisible, except to the knowing eye. The few and small industrial enterprises in colonial cities were obliterated by 19th-century growth. Households produced simple furnishings and clothes, while other goods were purchased from craftworkers—blacksmiths, coppersmiths, shoemakers and the like. Their shops are recreated in colonial museums such as in Williamsburg, Virginia. Most manufactures were imported from England.[2] The exceptions were tied directly or indirectly to natural resource extraction: naval stores (pitch, tar, and turpentine) from North Carolina; timber products from New England; iron products (pig and bar iron, and castings such as pots) throughout the colonies; and ships built in two major centers, Boston and Philadelphia, as well as in villages the length of the colonial coast.[3]

These manufactures were the most important in the colonies for three reasons. First, the British restricted manufactures based on advanced industrial processes to those established on British soil, though this was easily circumvented. Second, the colonies had a comparative advantage in manufactures that processed local resources either because this reduced their weight in processing or because their low value in relation to weight warranted immediate processing. Third, British manufactures which were high in value per unit weight such as textiles and drugs could easily withstand extended but cheap transportation to the colonies. For most of the colonial period the market in the colonies was small and the population lived at a low density; indigenous producers of high-value goods simply could not compete effectively with England. Slowly, the American home market grew. The colonial population did not reach ¼ million until 1700; by 1750, however, it had quadrupled to slightly over 1 million, and by 1770 the population reached 2 million.[4]

Near the close of the colonial period, therefore, expanding local markets, plus access to British, West Indian, and other Atlantic Basin markets, combined to provide a major stimulus to industrial development. The iron industry was a significant beneficiary. Collectively, the colonies were a major global producer; as a percentage of world output, it has been estimated that they accounted for 7 percent in 1750 and 14 percent in 1775.[5] Domestic consumption of iron quadrupled during this pre-Revolutionary period. The iron goods were made on large rural iron plantations close to iron ore, surrounded by large timber acreages (numbering up to several thousand) for making charcoal fuel, and located at water-power sites. The largest ironworks, oriented to export markets, were in Virginia and Maryland. In southeastern Pennsylvania, in contrast, ironworks produced for local urban markets in Philadelphia and to a lesser extent in York and Chester.[6] Economic growth during the late colonial period, therefore, created a small but important base for subsequent national industrializaton, even though visible remains of that era are insignificant in today's landscape.

## Emergence of the manufacturing belt

While the period from 1790 to 1860 left more remnants in the modern landscape than did the colonial period, the significance of the antebellum years, instead, is that they set the framework of the industrial landscape created between 1860 and 1920 which is so prominent today. The largest industrial landscape features were iron plantations and lumber and flour mills, although their rural location hid much of their activity. Numerous small mill villages emerged in the East. Some city factories remain today as small appendages to large buildings built after 1860. However, the most widespread features still present are probably the canals, although many are unused and resemble gentle streams.

During the antebellum years the genesis of the American manufacturing belt was established.[7] This vast industrial landscape of about half a million square miles was occupied by discrete industrial cities, mines and lumber areas, separated by the dominant landscape of farms and forests. The belt can be thought of as a set of regional industrial systems, rather than as a uniform undifferentiated landscape. Each industrial system included a regional metropolis, which provided specialized financial, wholesaling, and transportation services for economic activity within its surrounding region and served as controller and coordinator of economic exchange with other regions. Smaller industrial cities surrounded each metropolis. Examples include the regional center of Boston surrounded by its industrial satellites of Lowell, Lawrence, and Worcester; Cincinnati and its industrial satellites of Hamilton, Middletown, and Dayton; and Chicago and its industrial satellites of Joliet, Elgin, and Rockford.

Regional industrial systems emerged successively with the westward shift of the frontier. The east coast regions industrialized first by 1840 while those in the Middle West emerged by 1860. The region focused on Boston industrialized by producing textiles and shoes early on for the national market. Agriculture and the extraction of other natural resources such as lumbering (except in Maine) and mining were not significant there. In other industrial systems in the East and Midwest the growth of manufacturing was stimulated initially by demands from within each region. Broad-based demand for manufactures derived from household consumers (furniture, stoves, food), urban infrastructure (bricks, glass, pipes), the natural resource sector (farm implements and machinery, flour and sawmill machinery), and intra- and interregional trade (steamboat engines, locomotives, barrels). Iron foundries, machine shops, and machinery producers emerged simultaneously with other manufactures, providing essential equipment for other factory production. That so many tools and products came to be made of metal also spurred the growth of iron firms. These remained as rural for most of the antebellum years because charcoal was the chief fuel, requiring about 3,000 acres (and sometimes as much as 10,000 acres) to supply the wood.[8] In eastern Pennsylvania, however, anthracite coal began to be used in the 1840s and rural sites declined; the iron mill town was born.

**Figure 13.1**
An S-bridge built in the 1840s
to vault the National Road
over a creek in western Ohio.
The zig zag permitted a
simple, symmetrical stone
arch to be constructed
perpendicular to the axis of
the stream, and thus save
time and materials. The
generous road width
permitted oxcarts,
stagecoaches, and animal
herds to pass in safety.
Present-day U.S. Highway 40
can be seen to the left.

Transportation improvements were critical to the growth of each region. Navigable natural waterways provided the lowest cost movement. Coastal sailing vessels connected the east coast metropolises of Boston, New York, Philadelphia, and Baltimore. Steamboats, however, were important on the inland waterways such as the Hudson River, the Ohio and Mississippi Rivers, and lake steamers on the Great Lakes. Overland transportation improvements were essential to link areas because navigable waterways limited development to narrow corridors. Local communities built roads, but these were poorly constructed and maintained. Wagon transport was prohibitively expensive, averaging 10 to 30 cents per ton-mile (cost to ship 1 ton 1 mile) until about 1830.[9] Turnpikes, which charged tolls, were built from 1800 to 1830, but their high building cost and poor maintenance substantially failed to lower costs of overland transportation. The legacies of the turnpikes, however, are the highways which follow the old turnpikes such as along the Boston–New York route in New England or the National Road which started west at Cumberland, Maryland, and was completed eventually to Vandalia, Illinois; later, U.S. Highway 40 and its successor, Interstate 70, followed this route (Fig. 13.1). This re-etching of old routes was common throughout the country.

Canals proved more satisfactory in augmenting accessibility in areas not served by navigable waterways. The period of major canal construction occurred from 1815 to 1844, although it extended to 1860. The immensely successful Erie Canal crossed 364 miles of New York State and linked the Hudson River with Lake Erie. It was completed in 1825 and became the model for others; by 1860 American canals boasted a total of 4,254 miles.[10] Other long canals included the Mainline, connecting Philadelphia and

Pittsburgh, the Miami and Ohio, connecting Cincinnati and Toledo, and the Wabash and Erie, connecting Evansville and Toledo. Before 1850 most canal traffic moved within regions, but thereafter long-distance traffic in commodities grew significantly. Most canals, however, were not particularly profitable. The few highly successful ones were the short coal canals that linked the eastern Pennsylvania anthracite fields with New York City and Philadelphia. Although most canals are disused today, many still are visible as slow moving water courses in the landscape (Fig. 13.2). Canals were superseded by railroads which provided increased speed and all-weather travel and spun networks that ultimately linked all major cities.

Railroads constructed before 1850 formed regional webs that tied a metropolis to its hinterland with radial strands. In 1835 only 1,098 miles of track existed, but during the 1840s the pace of construction accelerated. By mid-century the total reached 9,021 miles and by 1860 it had surged to 30,626 miles.[11] Although continuous long-distance journeys such as from New York to Chicago did not become feasible until after 1860, during the 1850s goods and people could and did travel by rail between the East and Midwest.[12] Major trunk-line railroads existed by 1853: the New York Central, Erie, Pennsylvania, and Baltimore and Ohio.

Improving transportation within regions helped manufacturing to grow on the strength of regional demand for goods of all types. Manufacturing favored the large city in each region as the largest single market and the site with the best access to the region as a whole. The factories built before 1860 are seldom visible today because subsequent development in these cities has usually obliterated the early mills; at best they remain as small appendages to large factory buildings constructed later (Fig. 13.3). Near the waterfront were the warehouses for storing commodities and the wharves for the steamboats, steamships, and sailing vessels. After 1840 railroad terminals appeared, which attracted warehouses to locate near them. In the interior of each region small towns along railroads and canals, or easily accessible by wagon to the metropolis, also grew as industrial centers.

**Figure 13.2**
The Whitewater Canal was dug in the late 1830s to promote Cincinnati's northwestern hinterland trade and paralleled the river of the same name between Cambridge City, Indiana, and the Ohio River. Seen here passing through the small town of Metamora, it was bought by a railroad company in the 1860s, which promptly ran its tracks unceremoniously down the towpath.

The improvement of long distance transportation between 1840 and 1860 allowed a growing number and volume of manufactures to be shipped far afield.[13] Some industrial towns thus became specialized producers for multiregional and national markets. The most prominent remains of these pre-1860 manufactures exist in the small towns in the East which once produced many of the earliest national market manufactures such as textiles, shoes, gloves, and clocks. New England had innumerable such mill villages, well exemplified in Florence, Massachusetts, Harrisville, New Hampshire,[14] and Collinsville, Connecticut. Many small mill villages, however, produced only for local, or at most regional markets. Because water power was used by the early factories, the essence of these mill villages lay in the mill, the dam, the canal, and the workers' housing. The physical remains of these features have mostly disappeared, but the sites often can be identified by place names ending in "ville."[15] Some large-scale factory complexes existed in small cities, especially cotton textile manufacturing which offered widespread employment before 1860. Lowell, Massachusetts, was the earliest large textile mill city. Founded in 1823 by Boston capitalists, it boasted 36,827 residents by 1860. These financiers also founded other textile cities in New England, including Chicopee and Holyoke in Massachusetts, Nashua and Manchester in New Hampshire, and Saco-Biddeford and Lewiston in Maine. They were examples of planned industrial communities; each included large mill buildings, a great dam and upstream millpond, and canals.[16]

By 1860 regional industrial complexes stretched from the east coast to the Mississippi River Valley and north of a line from Baltimore to Louisville. Although the growth of most industrial complexes was spurred by demand within local regions, the increasing number of manufactures produced for multiregional and national markets within established industrial districts

**Figure 13.3**
An early textile mill on the Charles River in Waltham, Massachusetts. Several generations of buildings are evident on this site, and today they are all occupied by small replacement industries, since textile production moved out of New England.

eroded the bases for the emergence of industrial complexes in newer regions. The result was that the areal expansion of the belt ceased by the 1870s.

## Specialization in core and periphery

The integration of the United States economy across regions increased significantly between 1860 and 1920, based on an enormous extension and improvement of the railroad network and on the construction of a national telegraph system. The railroad network provided low-cost locations for factories; the railroad line and factory zone became inseparable features of the industrial landscape of every city (Fig. 13.4).[17] Each metropolis had a large terminal for switching long-distance freight trains and for collecting and redistributing local shipments. Cities in the manufacturing belt became highly specialized in different manufactures. Outside the belt natural resources were processed for manufactures in the belt; by the late 19th century the nation had a core (the manufacturing belt) and a periphery (resource production).

The railroad network tripled from 30,626 miles of loosely connected lines in 1860 to 93,262 miles of highly integrated tracks in which almost 81 percent was standard gauge in 1880.[18] The eastern half of the nation was blanketed by railroads, and two transcontinental lines had been completed, the Union/Central Pacific and the Southern Pacific. By 1900 the mileage totaled 258,784, and by 1920 it increased further to 406,580 miles, a mere 23,000

**Figure 13.4**
Factories along the rail line in Hartford, Connecticut. The industrial rail corridor became a ubiquitous feature of cities between 1860 and 1920. The factory on the right is late 19th-century, while that on the extreme left was built in the first decade of the 20th century. Rail passengers were long familiar with these corridors, but the decline of rail travel has obscured their potent imagery.

miles short of the maximum mileage achieved in the 20th century. The amount of total mileage comprised of yard tracks and sidings increased significantly from 17 percent to 27 percent between 1890 and 1920. A host of technological and organizational changes in railroads resulted in a large decline in freight rates from about 2.6 to 0.75 cents per ton-mile between 1859 and 1910.[19] Steel rails replaced iron rails which permitted heavier loads to be carried on the tracks, and locomotive power increased. By 1880, organizational changes allowed railroads to coordinate effectively the rapidly growing volume of freight traffic.[20] Railroads used the telegraph to coordinate train movements, and the telegraph provided a national network for business communication. The telegraph became a nationwide network along with the railroad, the lines were strung out along rights-of-way. To this day, telephone wires can be seen marching along old railroad grades that have lost their tracks, mute testimony to an abandoned symbiosis.

Transportation and communication improvements enlarged the market areas over which industrialists could sell their products. Demand grew for machinery to increase production and it, in turn, lowered production cost and allowed firms to ship to larger market areas. Machinery, therefore, was a key late 19th-century industry. The national rank of the machinery industry by value-added increased from seventh to first between 1860 and 1910.[21] Although average firm size increased during the late 19th century as firms produced for larger market areas, the increase in plant size was not dramatic in most industries. Firms increased production by adding more plants. Three industries, however, which had significant increases in the scale of production involved the processing of natural resources: distilling, flour milling, and iron and steel.[22]

The iron and steel industry was a most prominent symbol of industrialization between 1860 and 1920. Plant size increased significantly, beginning in the 1860s.[23] Coke made from coal replaced charcoal in the regions from central Pennsylvania westward, with dramatic effects. Rural iron plantations declined because the vast adjacent timber acreages were no longer necessary to provide fuel for the blast furnaces. Iron and steel mills could agglomerate at sites where iron ore and coke could be assembled cheaply and where markets were accessible. Rolling mills had located in cities such as Pittsburgh, Cleveland, and Chicago, but with the use of coke the blast furnaces and rolling mills could be integrated in one plant. These plants were among the largest in existence during the period. The sites also had to be large to store the iron ore and coke (Fig. 13.5).

By 1900, major clusters of iron and steel mills were located in the east near Philadelphia, in Pittsburgh and nearby towns, along the river valleys of the Mahoning (eastern Ohio, around Youngstown) and Shenango (western Pennsylvania, near Sharon), and in the vicinity of Cleveland, Chicago, and St. Louis.[24] By the late 19th century the large iron and steel mill, therefore, was the pivotal point in a complex interregional collection of inputs and distribution of outputs. Outside the East the mills used Connellsville coke made at numerous ovens on the coal fields of West Virginia and western

**Figure 13.5**
Iron and steel mill at Steelton, outside Harrisburg, Pennsylvania. These mills continue to be among the largest industrial facilities in existence. This plant contains a bar mill (left), rail mill (center), rail storage yard (foreground), rail lines along the Susquehanna River, electric furnace meltshop (upper right), plus various other operations including the splice-bar and tie-plate shops, maintenance shops, and power plant. A late 19th-century multistory building remains (center). Note also the workers' housing flanking the works (left background).

Pennsylvania. In 1890 it is estimated that 15,000 ovens, mostly beehive, were in operation.[25] The coke was transported by barge and rail car to the mills. Iron ore was mined in the Lake Superior district of upper Michigan and Wisconsin and later in the Mesabi Range of northern Minnesota. In the latter mines, large steam shovels worked open pits, railcars transported the ore to the docks, and ore carriers moved the ore to lower Great Lakes ports to be used either by the mills in Chicago, Cleveland, and other cities or transported inland by rail and barge (Fig. 13.6). The output of the mills, such as steel rails, structural plates, and girders, was used locally in the large metropolises or sold elsewhere in the Midwest.

The emphasis on iron and steel in centers such as Pittsburgh, Chicago, and Cleveland, and in smaller cities such as Johnstown, Pennsylvania, and Youngstown, Ohio, was but one example of the growing specialization of cities in different manufactures. Cities became identified in the popular mind by their industrial specialities: iron and steel from Pittsburgh, beer

257

**Figure 13.6**
Heavy cranes and loading
equipment flank the Calumet
River in South Chicago,
home to numerous steel mills
since the early 20th century.
Many mills are now closed
and some have been
demolished, leaving the port
facilities largely idle.

from Milwaukee, furniture from Grand Rapids, silk from Paterson, cash registers from Dayton, electrical machinery from Schenectady, and watches from Elgin. Some manufactures also had distinctive sites which reflected their industrial processes. In Minneapolis the flour milling plants had multistory mill buildings juxtaposed with grain elevators. The brass firms of Waterbury, Connecticut, had large sheds for casting and rolling brass.

Many industrial cities, however, shared a common landscape of mill buildings and workers' housing. Most common was the rectangular, three-to-five story brick factory building along a railroad line or siding, many thousands of which were built throughout the manufacturing belt between 1860 and 1920. In one-industry towns the mills typically were clustered. The textile cities of New England were distinguishable chiefly by their size differences, from the large agglomerations of identical buildings of Holyoke, Lowell, and Fall River, Massachusetts, and Manchester, New Hampshire, to the single mills of Slatersville, Rhode Island or Wauregan, Connecticut. The workers' housing clustered near the mills. In smaller mill towns the firms built one- and two-story duplexes, and in the larger cities entrepreneurs built two- and three-decker houses. Railroads spun webs that linked these specialized manufacturing centers with both their suppliers and their markets.

By 1880 firms in the existing industrial areas could reach markets in other regions cheaply over the railroad network. Later growing regions in the Great Plains, Rockies, Pacific coast, and Southwest were settled too late for this. Hence, factory zones along the rail line in these regions' cities are small. Opportunities for new firms to manufacture for regional markets had been reduced. Their chances were better in goods for multiregional and national markets, but potential industrial entrepreneurs had difficulty acquiring manufacturing knowledge to compete with those in earlier settled regions. Most firms producing basic industrial equipment for other factories were located in the established belt; entrepreneurs in late-settled regions, therefore, could not easily equip factories with custom-built machinery. The South did not develop a significant manufacturing sector before 1860 because demand for manufactures in the cotton economy was too low; and after the Civil War it was too late, because northern regions dominated manufacturing for multiregional and national markets.

Although the manufacturing belt ceased expanding areally by the 1870s, the late-settled regions and the South did acquire manufactures based on processing natural resources. Lumber mills, pulp and paper mills, mineral smelting, and oil refining located near the raw materials because inputs were low value, bulky, and lost much unneeded weight in processing. Between 1860 and 1920, therefore, American regions fell into two broad groups. There was a core centered on the manufacturing belt, concentrating on the manufacture of finished products together with some raw material processing. And there was a periphery—the remainder of the nation—that produced and processed raw materials both for the periphery and for the manufacturing belt.[26] The railroad was the chief link between core and periphery. The lumber mills, mines and smelters, and oil refineries were specialized extensions of the manufacturing belt.

Lumber mills were always features of the manufacturing belt in Maine, New York, and Pennsylvania, but the depletion of timber required exploitation of virgin or regrown forests for new supplies. The margins of the belt in the Great Lakes states of Michigan and Wisconsin contained important lumber centers from the 1870s to the mid-1890s, such as Saginaw, Bay City, and Muskegon in Michigan and Eau Claire and La Crosse in Wisconsin. The rivers leading to the mills often were clogged with logs, ponds surrounding the mills were used for storing logs, and large buildings housed the saw equipment. Because the mills drew timber from the surrounding area, most lumber cities were not large. Each lumber center was isolated from the others and surrounded by cutover land.

The Pacific coast supplied lumber to the national market after 1890, having served the west coast and markets around the Pacific Basin since the 1850s.[27] The northern California redwood industry was a major supplier to these markets, with large lumber mills at Humboldt Bay and the city of Eureka. By the late 1890s lumber towns along the lower Columbia River and around Puget Sound, including Seattle and Tacoma, were shipping lumber east by railroad (Fig. 13.7). The forested mountain slopes were reached by logging railroads which hauled the logs to the mills. The Michigan and Wisconsin lumber areas declined because the forests were cut over. By 1900 the southern lumber industry also was supplying the national market, in addition to its own region. Pulp and paper mills also located in the West and South (Fig. 13.8). They produced mostly low-value materials such as newsprint and wrapping paper. High-quality papers were specialities of northeastern cities such as Holyoke, Massachusetts.[28]

Western mining developed because of national demands for precious metals (gold and silver) and through demand in the manufacturing belt for industrial metals (copper, lead, and zinc). Beginning with the California Gold Rush of 1848, successive gold and silver mining booms swept back and forth across the West. The term "mining district" was coined to describe rather dispersed areas where numerous mines were operated, several towns developed, and political incorporation of the district could occur; the

**Figure 13.7**
A rail yard of the Northern
Pacific in Tacoma,
Washington, hard against the
bluffs that rim the southern
edge of Puget Sound.
Lumber, grain, and minerals
pass through this
transshipment point. In the
background is an elevator
with ship-loading equipment.

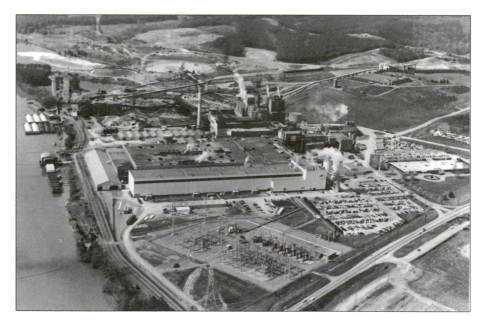

**Figure 13.8**
Paper mill on the Hiwassee
River near Calhoun,
Tennessee. The timber
resources of the South
continue to supply vast paper
mills, often in rural
surroundings. Note the
electricity apparatus
(foreground), legacy of
Tennessee Valley Authority
dam projects.

districts sometimes covered as much as 30 square miles. During the 1860s, the Comstock Lode at Virginia City, south of Reno, and the Butte district in Montana started production. Colorado had several mining booms that hit the Central City district in the 1860s, the Leadville district in the late 1870s, and the Cripple Creek district in the 1890s.

Once the initial information about a gold or silver strike spread, as many as 5,000 or more miners, retailers, and service people would arrive in an area over a short period of several months.[29] The mountain and valley landscape was transformed instantaneously. Towns sprouted "overnight" and miners swarmed over the area, housing themselves in tents and crude shacks. Within several years or less the easily mined ores in the streams, on the hillsides, and in shallow mines were exhausted. Large, highly capitalized firms supported by financiers in major metropolises such as Chicago and New York City took over the mining and extracted most of the gold and silver.

The large mining operations in the districts left indelible marks on the landscape. Hydraulic mining—blasting hillsides with high-pressure water—stripped the vegetation and topsoil. Dredges worked stream beds and piled rock along the edges, and the smelters left mountains of waste rock. Surrounding forests were used both as fuel for the smelters, although coal was used by the end of the 19th century, and as lumber for construction. Because gold and silver were valuable, their mining began before the transcontinental railroads crossed the West. Once these railroads arrived a large network of feeder railroads branched into the mining districts beginning in the 1880s.[30] Each of the districts today has abandoned towns. Other towns have populations that are miniscule compared to their peak and look hopelessly overbuilt with streets and structures only partially in use now. The Cripple Creek district had over 50,000 people at its peak and electric interurban trains joined the towns, but today it has under 1,000 inhabitants. Some towns, however, such as Central City near Denver, have revived as tourist attractions while others such as Breckenridge, Colorado, have become resorts.

Industrial minerals could not be mined in the West until the transcontinental railroads were completed and feeder lines to the deposits were built; the value of the smelted or refined ores was too low for them to be shipped by expensive wagon transport (Fig. 13.9). Upper Michigan was a major supplier of copper before 1880, but during the 1880s the Butte, Montana, and Arizona copper districts emerged. Underground shafts were used in Butte, while Arizona mines developed large, open pits. Lead and zinc were mined in the Tri-State district of southwestern Missouri and adjacent Oklahoma and Kansas beginning in the 1870s. In the 1880s the Leadville district in Colorado and in the 1890s the Coeur d'Alene district in Idaho emerged as lead producers.

Oil was both a consumer and industrial mineral from the beginning of important oil production in the 1860s near Titusville in northwestern Pennsylvania.[31] It was sold quickly in interregional markets because oil

261

**Figure 13.9**
Climax molybdenum mine near Leadville, Colorado. Situated at an altitude of 11,000 feet, this classic strip mine was first developed around World War I when molybdenum became recognized as a useful alloy to harden steel. The Climax mine accounted for a majority of global production of this mineral for a time.

fields often were distant from major markets. During the 19th century oil was used chiefly for lighting and machinery lubrication; not until 1910 was it processed in significant amounts into fuel oil and gasoline. Because oil was bulky, difficult to handle, and low in value relative to its weight, low-cost oil transportation in either refined or unrefined form was essential. Although railroads always have been used, the pipe line was the preferred solution for bulk shipment. Already by the 1880s long-distance pipe lines linked the Appalachian oil fields with Cleveland, Buffalo, New York City, and Philadelphia. From its birth, oil refining has been located both in the oil fields and in the large metropolitan markets. Urban as well as rural dwellers, therefore, have observed the typical large oil refinery with its cracking towers, storage tanks, and flames atop pipes for burning excess gas. The Appalachian oil fields remained significant producers until 1910. The Ohio–Indiana fields became important in the mid-1890s, while the Gulf coast of Texas and the California fields emerged as producers after 1900; the Kansas–Oklahoma and Illinois fields were important by 1910. By the early 20th century large refinery districts were established in northern New

Jersey, along the southern shores of the Great Lakes, the Texas–Louisiana Gulf coast, and southern California. Beginning in the 1920s these same areas became the first sites for the growth of petrochemical plants based on oil and natural gas. The vast refinery and petrochemical complex with large economies of scale, therefore, became a fixture of the industrial landscape in the manufacturing belt and on the periphery.

The greatly improved accessibility provided factories by the railroad contained the seeds for change in the industrial landscape. The railroad had allowed firms to reach large market areas, and the response was to build large, multistory factories around which employees could cluster their housing within walking distance of work. By the 1890s, the greatly increased density of railroad lines in cities and extensions into the suburbs, however, opened low-cost land to industrial development. Simultaneously, workers increasingly made use of the expanding electric streetcar system for commuting. Fire insurance companies began to advocate building the "slow-burning factory" which had safety features to inhibit fires; one of these was the one-story factory.[32] As manufacturing shifted to mass production in some industries, experimentation with continuous assembly lines began to demonstrate the advantages of one-story factories.[33] Finally, electric motors attached to machines increasingly became the preferred power mechanism, replacing the group-drive and the belt-and-shaft driving system inherited from the steam-power era. Production machinery and assembly lines could be arranged in any configuration.[34] The coincidence of these changes between 1890 and 1920 laid the basis for the shift to the one-story factory on large sites in the suburbs. These production changes were well established before the truck became efficient for industrial transport after 1910. The truck, therefore, accelerated an existing trend, and the car added to it by providing greater ease of commuting for the workers.

The switch to the one-story factory in the suburbs has had a dramatic, cumulative effect on the industrial landscape of cities. The multistory factory has become obsolete; new firms and existing firms that expand have built one-story suburban factories along major highways and expressways (Fig. 13.10). The corridors these roads create offer the preferred sites for modern factories just as the railroad lines did in the 19th century. Although the old multistory buildings have remained in use for many decades, especially by the firms originally in them, demand for the buildings has declined. The long-term effect has been a gradual abandonment of multistory factories and warehouses which had been built in the pre-1920 city. This abandonment reached such a critical level that it became one of the stimuli for the urban renewal programs initiated by planners during the 1950s and early 1960s. Many factories and warehouses located near the city center and in the inner railroad industrial zone have been torn down and replaced by parking, public housing, convention centers, and expressways, or the sites have been left vacant. Numerous multistory factories and warehouses, however, remain. In cities such as Boston, New York, Baltimore, Chicago, and St. Louis, some buildings have been renovated for commercial activity, offices, and housing. Manufacturing belt cities, therefore, look substantially different from cities outside the belt which grew essentially after 1900. The former cities retain large numbers of their 19th-century multistory factories scattered about the inner parts of the city and in the railroad industrial zone, and in the suburbs are the one-story factories. The latter cities have "suburban" factories in the inner city as well as in the suburbs.

## The blend of old and new

The American manufacturing belt was established over a century ago, but it retains a significant rôle in the industrial landscape. Within the belt, new landscapes have emerged, while the old decay or revive. Outside the belt resource processing remains important, but a new feature is the growth of the aerospace and high-technology industries. The belt also participates in these industries; the distinctions between belt and nonbelt, therefore, are no longer as sharp as in the 19th century.

The years since 1920 have witnessed a gradual decline in the proportion of United States manufacturing housed in the belt. From highs of about 85 percent during the late 19th and early 20th centuries, the proportion had declined to just over 50 percent by the 1970s.[35] The redistribution of manufacturing, however, has not been as dramatic as these figures suggest.

**Figure 13.10**
Textile mill at Cordova, Richmond County, North Carolina. Just as the three-to-five-story textile mill dwarfed the workers' housing in a New England textile city in the 19th century, the modern one-story Southern mill overwhelms the adjacent housing. In contrast to the earlier textile mills that spun and wove natural fibers such as cotton and wool, this mill uses polyester fibers. Also in contrast, this mill is without windows, permitting no natural light into the workplace.

Three-fourths of the relative decline has consisted of a southward expansion of the belt to an east–west line extending from northern Georgia to Oklahoma City. The much noted claim that the manufacturing belt is declining, while the South and West are gaining, is overstated. Although the physical form of the industrial landscape has changed from multistory to one-story factories, the regional changes are modest.

The resource processing landscape of smelter, lumber and paper mills, and oil refineries and petrochemical plants has not changed significantly from the early 20th century in its broad regional distribution in the West and South or in the manufacturing belt. At a local scale, however, as resources are depleted or new ones develop, the processing industries decline or emerge. The result has been the continual abandonment of resource sites and the use of new processing facilities, often larger than previously because of scale economies in handling and processing raw materials. The old industry of textiles has shifted from the Pennsylvania–Maine corridor to the Piedmont region extending from Alabama to North Carolina. This redistribution began in the late 19th century, but over half of all textile production was still in the northern area as late as 1940; and by the 1970s, however, about three-fourths was in the South.[36] Because the textile industry was so large, numerous abandoned, large mill buildings exist throughout the Pennsylvania–Maine corridor in such centers as Paterson, New Jersey, Fall River, Massachusetts, and Manchester, New Hampshire. In the South, in contrast, only early textile cities such as Augusta, Georgia, have old multistory factories; most southern mill towns have large, one-story factories (Fig. 13.10).

The productive capacity of the steel industry has increased over ten-fold during the 20th century, but the industry remains concentrated in the belt while some changes internal to the belt have occurred.[37] A few large mills were built outside the belt before 1900; the notable ones were at Birmingham, Alabama, and Pueblo, Colorado, during the 1880s. Two other large mills were built during World War II at Geneva, Utah, and at Fontana near Los Angeles. Other large mills, especially pipe plants to serve the oil and gas industry, have been built along the Gulf coast such as in Houston, Texas. In spite of these changes, as well as the proliferation of minimills using scrap as raw material, the large, integrated steel mill remains a dominant fixture in the manufacturing belt cities. This concentration has been reinforced by the enormous demands for steel from the automobile industry which localized in the midwestern part of the belt. Recently, however, the steel industry is shrinking drastically as cheap foreign imports capture a growing percentage of a stagnant steel market. The result has been the abandonment of old mills. The impact of these changes is most noticeable in the Pittsburgh area. Here, the formerly smoke-filled, noisy valleys are pollution-free and quiet; what remains is an eerie river valley landscape of huge, empty mills.

Explosive growth of automobile manufacture during the first two decades of the 20th century established a sprawling belt of plants assembling cars

265

and making parts, stretching from northern Illinois to eastern Ohio but focused on Detroit and southeastern Michigan.[38] This core contained the earliest successful large-scale car builders such as Henry Ford and Ransom Olds. The year 1903 was the first time automobile manufacture surpassed 10,000 vehicles, but by 1910 it reached 181,000 vehicles and by 1920 almost 2 million were produced annually; by the 1950s the typical number built was 5 million annually.[39] Most auto parts factories were not noticeably different from other 20th-century one-story factories. The assembly plants, however, were different. Because enormous economies of scale are possible in automobile assembly, these one-story plants are some of the largest in the nation, often employing between 5,000 and 10,000 workers. These scale economies have limited the spread of assembly plants from the original belt of auto manufacture, although a few plants were built in cities such as St. Louis, Atlanta, and Los Angeles. The entry recently of Japanese assembly plants has not greatly altered this original auto belt. Their plants are located in Michigan and Ohio with an extension south into Kentucky and Tennessee.

The quintessential "modern" industries today are aerospace and high technology, but both have strong roots in the manufacturing belt while forming the basis for the expanding industrial landscape outside the belt. The cavernous buildings for airframe assembly house thousands of production workers, similar to auto assembly plants. Aircraft assembly is a specialty of "new" metropolises such as Los Angeles and Seattle, but it also occurs in old metropolises such as New York and St. Louis. Although southern California has numerous parts plants, others are scattered nationwide because production requirements draw on traditional manufacturing belt skills in metal fabricating and machinery. The largest component of modern planes, the jet engine, is manufactured in the Hartford and Boston areas.

High-technology manufacture, especially of computers and semiconductors, is often cited as a symbol of the demise of the manufacturing belt. The Silicon Valley south of San Francisco is considered prototypical of manufacturing derived from science and engineering (Fig. 13.11).[40] A leading engineering university such as Stanford is considered essential for founding and supporting new firms. The heavy emphasis on research and development, employing highly educated workers, dictates locations with high amenities, it is thought, with low-slung buildings set in a garden-like environment. These so-called ideal locations lie in the carefully designed California landscape or on the front range of the Rockies between Colorado Springs and Boulder. This standard characterization, however, is misleading. The old manufacturing belt has a large high-technology base, as is well exemplified in eastern Massachusetts, which originated in part with firms started by Massachusetts Institute of Technology faculty and graduates. Numerous computer and related equipment firms are located here in "campus" settings along Route 128. In addition, new and old high-technology firms are renovating 19th-century mill buildings for research and

**Figure 13.11**
Silicon Valley, California, looking northeast from a point above San Jose. At the southern edge of San Francisco Bay (upper left), much of Silicon Valley lies between Palo Alto, home to Stanford University (off left) and the city of San Jose. Many high-technology firms have sprouted here, ranging from small specialized producers of semiconductor chips and equipment to large diversified computer firms.

development and production facilities. The New York metropolis extending from northern New Jersey through southern New York State into Connecticut also is home to many high-technology firms including the world's largest, International Business Machines. Similar to eastern Massachusetts, this area combines the one-story factory in the garden with the 19th-century renovated factory.

267

The American industrial landscape is a dynamic blend of the old and the new. Each specialized component, factory, smelter, paper mill, and refinery, participates in complex linkages of transportation and communication. New landscapes are being created while old ones are abandoned or reused. In the past the separate components were individually owned and managed, but today many are linked by chains of ownership and information flows quite invisible in the landscape. These chains, however, are real in the lines of authority in the organizational structures of large corporations.

*The making of the American landscape*

# Chapter fourteen
## The Americanization of the city

### EDWARD K. MULLER

A TRAVELER TO AN American city in the 1980s encounters an urban landscape that proclaims its newness alongside the vestiges of its past. American cities appear to be in motion, almost cinematically changing before one's eyes, even those struggling with the ravages of industrial decline. Because growth is gospel in America, change is commonplace and admired. "New" in the landscape presents a dynamic image, while "old" represents a hindrance to growth except where preservation enshrines cherished symbols or finds support in investment incentive policies.

Forests of new office towers in the largest downtowns crowd out smaller 19th- and early 20th-century streetscapes. Huge public housing projects and blighted inner-city slums slowly recede against the press of expanding gentrified historic districts and condominium developments. Obsolete central wholesale districts and waterfronts with abandoned tracks, terminals, piers, and warehouses court rediscovery by entrepreneurs anxious to establish upscale retail, residential, and office complexes.

At a distance from this central redevelopment, in older water and rail corridors, massive factories of former smokestack industries gently rust alongside their shrinking working-class communities graying with age. But beyond these idle zones, around expressway interchanges and airports, spacious office and industrial parks, enclosed shopping malls, and satellite business centers anchor a vast automobile-spawned sprawl, virtually independent of the mother city.

This American city of the late 20th century is a vast, restless, multi-focused urban region, a collection of employment and consumption centers scattered over numerous political jurisdictions. Yet a web of capital investments, electronic networks, and highways knits them together. Relatively new and low in density, these cities roll on expansively with a rectilinear geometry unsympathetic to the physical environment and interrupted only by misaligned subdivisions. However, the visual monotony of gridiron planning belies the differentiated social patterning of this urban milieu. Variations in wealth, duly reflected in the age, quality, and appurtenances of housing, distinguish neighborhoods in this immense mosaic. Moreover, new generations of oriental and Spanish-speaking immigrants exist uncomfortably alongside older European ethnic and racial migrants in an economy perceived as dividing the population increasingly into two extremes.[1]

Despite their great variety, the continual transformation of American cities is to be understood in terms of society's persistent and often contradictory values, its enduring political and economic system, and the inertia of past geographies. The original urban settlements in North America were derivative transplants of European societies, but with each passing era they diverged further from these roots and progressed along an increasingly independent course in step with the flowering of the nation-building enterprise.

American society developed a unifying consensus founded on a capitalistic economy and liberal social philosophy.[2] Economic activity and change were vested in private enterprise working through private markets with success measured in financial profits and higher material standards of living. The business community, wealthy landowners and the socially established, controllers of capital and its economic institutions, garnered considerable power, especially over public priorities. The public interest has long been defined in terms of the private economy because successful businesses, it has long been believed, redound to the benefit of the entire community.

In concert with this, the liberal social philosophy, stressing the freedom and rights of the individual, complements the individual's (or organization's) economic latitude in the capitalistic system and has long relegated local government to protecting individual rights, nurturing economic interests, and maintaining civil order.[3] Value attaches to individual performance, equality of opportunity, tolerance, and political democracy. Formal social distinctions have been few, and fair chances for material advancement, especially in the form of land, or in cities home ownership, undergird an essentially democratic society.

Substantial infusions of diverse immigrant groups have tested this social vision, but a general adherence to the liberal philosophy in a growing economy has militated against rigid class stratification, effected a sharing of power and wealth with upwardly mobile generations, and produced a dynamic, yet untidy social geography. With the increasing complexity of American society, governmental responsibilities have necessarily expanded and undergone redefinition, but the *laissez-faire* conception of government has endured, providing a constant check on public policies seeking to manage the economy or effect social engineering. Americans doggedly adhere to this national framework in the face of technological change, foreign immigrations, recurrent communal impulses, disturbing social inequities, and alternative European political models. As centers of economic activity and power, American cities reflect the geographical consequences of the national political economy and have displayed increasingly marked contrasts with their European counterparts.

## The economic landscape

Although the earliest settlers along the Atlantic seaboard concerned themselves with the demands of survival in the frontier and carried with them the directives and models of their European origins, they also worked assiduously towards the success of their economic pursuits and adapted their towns to fit with their aspirations for the New World. By the middle of the 18th century as settlement moved inland and new town founding accelerated, an American urban tradition began to unfold, and its forms have shaped the urban landscape right down to the present.

Towns were initially places of colonial administration and religious community, but trading functions, free of feudal-style obligations, increased their economic value. Individuals viewed land as not only a site for work and residence, but also a source of speculative profit. Thus, land was a commodity and a basis for rising material expectations, though it was neither universally owned nor equally distributed among the citizens.[4] Property owners exercised freedom from governmental control over the use of their land, except for instances that created a pronounced public nuisance. Formal plans for streets, property, and public spaces preceded the development of most new towns, but they had little influence over the land uses that eventually emerged. Far from the anarchy that such an individualistic economic emphasis might imply, common patterns characterized the urban landscape, because of English origins, market forces, and the diffusion of the new tradition.

Although Spanish and French settlers established distinctive colonial town forms, the more numerous English who brought various town concepts with them eventually established the characteristic American plan. Irregular organic forms oriented to the town's functional focus, usually a waterfront, developed in many of the earliest settlements, as seen today in the tangle of streets of central Boston and lower Manhattan. Rectangular gridiron plans with small lots and little open space also appeared frequently along the Atlantic coast. However, William Penn's plan for his colonial capital of Philadelphia seemed best suited to the requirements of American urban growth. Its formal rectilinearity and broad spatial extent accommodated the city's growth long after its founding in 1682, allowing the orderly and speculative sale of land by absentee investors or prospective settlers. Throughout its 18th-century prosperity, Philadelphia maintained the appearance of order and egalitarianism, so appealing to evolving American sensibilities, with its straight streets and regularly aligned and reasonably uniform houses. A few elaborate aristocratic plans for colonial Williamsburg, Annapolis, Savannah, and later Washington presented alternative models. Nevertheless, the simple egalitarian, speculative, and orderly features of Philadelphia's gridiron, the nation's premier city at century's end, appealed to Pennsylvanians as they moved west and merged comfortably with the developmental orientations of New England and southern frontier migrants.[5]

271 The gridiron was easily understood and facilitated investment, rapid

**Figure 14.1**
Residential tracts south of central Los Angeles. In keeping with the American sense of order, rationality, and expedience, suburbs sprawl in extensive, rectilinear developments across the urban periphery, similar to the repetitive gridiron plans of new towns in the 19th century. Here, even the modern freeway cuts through the area in alignment with the grid.

development, and geographical mobility. Quite simply, it worked and fitted with the American rational and egalitarian vision. While grandiose plans such as those of Buffalo and Detroit dotted the 19th-century urban spectrum, the gridiron's rectangular geometry, embellished with market spaces of central squares, spread monotonously across the continent, paying little heed to relief and barely inhibiting cultural aspirations (Fig. 14.1).[6]

Despite Penn's intention to create a spacious town, Philadelphia grew into a compact settlement of narrow lots, dense housing, and little green space. In part, the high density of early cities reflected the geographical constraints of a walking city, but it also resulted from the imperatives of a commerce-oriented economy that revolved around the waterfront (Fig. 14.2). Trade powered the early American city, and access to the marketplace for merchants and shopkeepers drove up central land values. The expansion of commercial land use in the early 19th century occurred outwardly along the waterfront and incrementally away from central markets, driving out residences and often usurping public open spaces. Social and public institutions increasingly competed with difficulty for central locations and often shared the city center uneasily with business activities.

Changes in transportation means and building technology late in the 19th century maintained peak values at the center until after World War II when automobiles, circumferential expressways, and electronic communications reoriented longstanding traditions. The resulting distribution of land values with a central peak and gradual decline away from the center, though elongated along radial transportation axes, significantly ordered the land use patterns of American cities. The initiation of urban planning and zoning in the early 20th century rarely interfered with existing land uses, because planners carefully observed the prerogatives of private property owners and protected existing values. Even as planning became more aggressive after 1950, the goals were often to re-establish the traditional peak valuations, centrality, and vitality of downtown.

The congested central business areas of the early 19th century evolved into prestigious downtowns that became hallmarks of the American metropolis.[7] The low skyline of two- to four-story buildings, broken only by shipmasts and steeples, the homogeneous architecture of brick rows or some other regional vernacular tradition, the occasional punctuation by Greek Revival monumental buildings, and the intermingling of all manner of activities (Fig. 14.3) gave way during the mid-19th century to increasingly specialized functional subdistricts, pretentious buildings that conveyed business importance, and determined elegance to attract retail consumers.

**Figure 14.2**
Tenement buildings on North Street in Boston's North End, near the waterfront along Atlantic Avenue. High land values in this central district stimulated cycles of rebuilding that ended in these very dense, turn-of-the-century living quarters.

Commodity brokers, financial houses, and bankers withdrew from the cacophonous mercantile quarters into ponderous stone edifices befitting their solid respectability. Retailers also left the congeries of warehouses, dressed up with stone and ironfront buildings, and innovated in mass-marketing techniques that promoted consumption habits, appealed to female shoppers, and made shopping a downtown event (Fig. 14.4). Perhaps more than any other institution, the department store with its vast array of goods and broad social appeal signified this transformation of central areas into downtowns.[8]

With the retail and financial districts entrenched as the bedrocks of downtown by the 1890s, the steel skeleton building frame, hydraulic elevator, and electric trolley intensified downtown's centrality by concentrating white-collar workers in tall office buildings. The emergence of corporations with national orientations multiplied administrative functions that were headquartered near sources of capital but distant from sites of production and markets. The subsequent expansion of corporate bureaucracies and legal, financial, and business professions ballooned office employment at the time the new trolleys offered mass transportation for middle-class workers and shoppers. By stacking offices a dozen or more stories high, the skyscraper solved the constraints of earlier walk-up buildings, but it also unleashed the businessman's burgeoning sense of power and importance. Originally a profitable solution to spatial demands, the skyscraper in its awe-inspiring verticality and behemoth scale became the symbol of corporate prestige and a means of competition for status among the captains of industry. By the 1920s shining towers soared dozens of stories above the street, many aspiring to be the tallest in the world. The traditional boosterism of America's businessmen focused during these years

**Figure 14.3**
Baltimore's inner harbor and downtown in the early 20th century, looking north-northwest. The old warehouses, shipping services, and docks of the original harbor contrasted with the rising modernity of the central business district only a few blocks to the north. After World War II, this and other harbors would attract urban renewal interest.

**Figure 14.4**
Lit Brothers Department
Store on Market Street,
Philadelphia, designed to be
ostentatious and appeal as a
consumer's palace. At the
focus of trolley lines coming
from the suburbs,
department stores anchored
the retail district within
American downtowns.

on the skyscraper.[9] If the department store made going downtown an exciting event, the office tower trumpeted the city center's power in the metropolis and beyond (Fig. 14.5).

The explosive growth of downtowns spawned a series of subsidiary functions that contributed to their dominant position. Despite high central land values, massive and grand railroad stations usurped downtown space where they coordinated the voluminous daily circulation of commuters and intercity travelers. The tumult in the terminals' cavernous waiting halls epitomized downtown's breathless pace and vitality.[10] Outside traffic congestion and pedestrian pandemonium heightened the sense of being at society's center. Expensive hotels, elegant theaters, movie palaces, fancy restaurants, and less pretentious mass amusements made downtown the entertainment focus as well. Clearly, the era's fashion and modernity were

275

**Figure 14.5**
The Woolworth Building in New York City (center right), completed in 1913 and an important early skyscraper, captured the American imagination and symbolized urbanity. Today it shares the skyline with other tall buildings, notably the twin towers of the World Trade Center, as seen southwesterly from City Hall.

captured by the towers, terminals, and shops, which signified downtown to urbanites, and for many symbolized the American city at large.

Even as downtown flourished in the 1920s, forces were at work to destroy its centrality and vigor within a few decades. Motor vehicles captured the American imagination and roadways, exacerbating central congestion, cluttering curbspace, and extending urban development miles into the countryside. After World War II, governmental policies stimulated highway building and suburbanization that accelerated the challenge to mass transit and inner-city neighborhoods. By 1960 retailers were following the flight of home owners and industries to distant suburbs. Deteriorating transit facilities, blighted central industrial districts, adjacent minority slums, declining railroad service, and closed department stores tarnished the once glittering image of downtown.

In the 1950s coalitions of public and private civic leaders with economic interests in maintaining central land values and business activity formulated renewal programs that leveraged private investment with federal subsidies for highways, slum clearance, parking garages, and office developments.[11] Expressway construction bored through older neighborhoods and split them into separate communities, leveled buildings in great bands around downtown, and usurped blighted waterfronts, cutting the water bodies off from pedestrians. Sprawling interchanges, cement retaining walls, and immense swaths of pavement surrounded downtown redevelopment. Modern Bauhaus architecture, carefully segregated land uses, and super-scaled projects signaled renewal and a vigorous future, but these features and the new highways also froze out pedestrians and squashed an active streetlife (Fig. 14.6).

While urban renewal arrested the physical decline of downtown, in the 1970s a new generation of planners and developers stressed rapid transit, spectator sports, cultural entertainment, streetlife, and waterfront redevelopment. Small parklets with leisure programing, outdoor cafes, pedestrian malls, and linear parks along waterfronts injected open space into downtowns almost for the first time. Retailers now eschewed older practices in favor of combining small vendors in festive markets that strove to convey excitement. While more people-oriented downtowns emerged, the rejuvenation depended on a new generation of even taller office towers. Today, downtown remains the city's premier locus of skyscrapers, regional entertainment, and civic institutions.

In the largest cities, however, downtowns no longer were the only major business district. Suburban centers of offices and stores also flourished, rivaling the size and complexity of downtown.[12] The junction of radial expressways with circumferential beltways and interstate highways created ideal locations for assembling large numbers of workers and shoppers who resided in postwar suburbs. Some corporations tired of downtown's excessive costs and congestion and retreated to suburban sites. Others carved out routine office functions and relocated them within convenient access to a low-paid suburban female workforce. Developers built landscaped office campuses in direct opposition to the unruly atmosphere of downtowns, while retailers collected in all-weather malls that became suburban entertainment centers (Fig. 14.7). By the 1970s, a new generation of consumers was maturing, who had never experienced downtown in its heyday and looked upon it as only one of several axes around which to organize their activities. Suburbia's expansive scale required individuals to use automobiles and consequently diminished employment prospects for central-city residents dependent on mass transportation.

While downtown was historically the beacon of the city, manufacturers and wholesalers comprised its energy source. Originally dominating the central waterfront, these industries followed the water and railroad corridors that grew outwardly in ribbons from the center in the 19th century. Early in the century, waterpower sites beyond the city's limits attracted large mill operations, complete with company housing and stores for the workers and their families. As the expanding city overwhelmed these early satellites, some industries again sought large and self-contained sites beyond the urbanized area, this time served by railroads. By 1900 the U.S. Census recognized that traditional city boundaries failed to capture the complexity of the urban region and called it a manufacturing district (later renamed metropolitan).

Location in the city, architecture, building size, and type of industry demarcated the eras of economic development.[13] Artisans, ship-oriented tradesmen, and piece-work manufacturers packed the lofts of narrow brick

**Figure 14.6**
The Lower Hill Redevelopment Area, Pittsburgh, in a 1956 planners' demonstration photograph. Containing over 1,500 households and 400 businesses, the buildings within the area marked out by the proposed new roads, Civic Arena, and Crosstown Boulevard, were eventually demolished. When completed, the renewal project effectively created a barrier between downtown and the adjacent black ghetto.

walk-ups throughout the central waterfront of the early 19th century. Nearby, wholesalers and processors of trade goods such as textiles, leathers, or foodstuffs built three-story structures that consumed an entire city block. The manufacturers of the mid-19th century required more space for storage, assembly, and production. These iron, machinery, or railroad car manufacturers built on the open lands of the expanding industrial corridors, amassing several buildings into complexes employing several hundred workers. By the early 20th century, factories became massive, emphasizing horizontality in one-story structures where automobiles, electrical machinery, or consumer appliances were fabricated. Thousands of workers streamed into these giant complexes through secured plant gates. Beyond the surrounding fences, trolleys, vast parking lots, taverns, and grimy mill towns served the workers. One mill town followed after another, the names often synonymous with corporations—Sparrows Point with Bethlehem Steel or East Pittsburgh with Westinghouse Electric. These corporate giants paid little heed to the environments of the industrial corridors, dumping wastes into adjacent waters and lands, belching soot and toxic chemicals into the air, and sometimes ignoring the needs of dependent communities.

After World War II technically advanced businesses, research divisions, and wholesale distributors chose the flexibility of truck transportation and suburban amenities on the urban periphery. Industrial parks offered cheaper land, access to interstate highways, and landscaped sites near suburban communities. Clustered at interstate interchanges that sometimes coalesced into new industrial corridors around the city, such as Route 128

**Figure 14.7**
Regional shopping mall in suburban Baltimore, 1972. This view shows the mall, an office plaza (upper left), and a small shopping center (lower center) sharing access to the intersection of two freeways via the road leading off to the left. Surrounding suburban housing tracts would later engulf the farm at lower left.

near Boston, these new industries complicated the simpler spatial pattern of center, corridor, and satellite that characterized the earlier city. Blight, technological obsolescence, and economic restructuring shut down first the central waterfront, then the downtown loft manufacturers, and finally after 1960 the heavy industries of the railroad corridor. As demolition clears these areas, their centrality and often waterfront sites have encouraged imitative or adaptive reuse into industrial parks or entertainment and residential developments (Fig. 14.8; contrast with Fig. 14.3).

## Social landscapes

The vision of America transcended purely economic aspirations, however, complicating the forces shaping the urban landscape. Pervasive beliefs in individual liberty, equal opportunity, social justice, and political democracy combined with the nation's rôle as a haven for oppressed peoples to create a culturally plural and socially dynamic society. Behavior, however, did not always conform with belief, generating charged, contentious, and often contradictory social relations in the city. The ever-changing social landscape of the city reflected both the vision and reality of American society—jarring extremes of economic inequality that disrupted the endless middle-class residential blocks, privatized suburban dwellings that contrasted with explicitly demarcated "turfs" of ethnic and racial groups, ceaseless social and geographical mobility that mocked the persistent despair of slums, and the signs and institutions of the contest for economic and political power.

Beginning with the earliest settlers to this New World, immigrants sought an improved standard of living as well as freedom from Old World encumbrances and injustices. As ports of entry and hubs of unskilled jobs, cities retained large numbers of the newcomers. The colonial seaports of Philadelphia and New York contained peoples of diverse religions and languages. Subsequent waves of northwest European immigrants in the mid-19th century and southern and eastern Europeans at the turn of the century complicated the social composition of most cities, except in the South where black Americans contrasted with the white Anglo-Saxon majority. During the initial half of the 20th century blacks moved to northern cities in large numbers, while small hispanic and oriental populations in southwestern and Pacific coastal cities foreshadowed their migration across urban America in the second half of the century.

The cultural plurality resulting from these migrations charged American cities with an incredible social dynamism and tension. Immigrants struggled at menial jobs scattered throughout the city, living in nearby rooming houses, barracks, or other arrangements not always intended for residential purposes. Attracted by the assortment of unskilled jobs in downtowns, recent arrivals, transients, and other poor residents also collected in polyglot central quarters composed of old building stock much subdivided and run

*280*

**Figure 14.8**
Harbor Place in Baltimore, viewed from the World Trade Center. Extensive land clearance made way for new hotels (upper center and right), a festival market at water's edge, and a sanitized brick plaza—compatible tourist accoutrements for the U.S.S. *Constitution*.

281   down. There were few neighborhoods dominated by a single nationality before the Civil War. In this walking city, workers lived near their job sites or the main loci of employment opportunities. Moreover, the scarcity of housing forced diverse immigrant workers to reside side by side or in clannish pockets that together formed a residential mosaic.[14] Social tensions between foreign and native born workers, protestants and catholics, and racial groups occasionally erupted in violence in the dense quarters, redeveloped with purpose-built tenements at the turn of the century (Fig. 14.9).

**Figure 14.9**
Pittsburgh, 1950. By the
middle of the 20th century,
the built environments of the
older neighborhoods
displayed generations of
incremental adaptations and
modifications.

When conditions permitted, immigrants preferred to reside in their own neighborhoods, where kinship, social networks, and community organizations mitigated the tribulations of foreign identity and retail demands created entrepreneurial opportunities. In the second half of the 19th century, the large laborforces of factories and increasing ethnic division of labor fostered the concentration of nationality groups in industrial neighborhoods about the city. Simultaneously, the accelerated suburbanization of middle-income residents freed up a substantial housing stock in older central neighborhoods, where immigrants fashioned self-conscious communities.[15]

Overcrowded, poor, and transient, these immigrant neighborhoods exhibited the exotic sights, sounds, and smells of older world, alien quarters in the midst of the New World. Immigrant churches, parochial schools, fraternal orders, and foodstores catered to their countrymen (Fig. 14.10). Rarely was the housing distinctively ethnic, except in the signage and decoration of commercial and community buildings. Employment linkages to nearby industries, economic hardship, and self-conscious ethnic identity more than outright discrimination, generated these separate neighborhoods. Nevertheless, even at their peak, such districts usually harbored members and institutions of other nationalities. Often, a majority of immigrants did not reside in the neighborhood of their compatriots, since many worked and lived throughout the urban region.

By World War I most cities housed several immigrant groups distinguished by their varying longevity in the region, size, economic achievement, and self-conscious ethnicity. With the 1920s restriction on additional immigration, assimilation, and new generations eventually diminished traditional nationality loyalties. The divergent paths of economic mobility and assimilation to American life taken by immigrant children further differentiated the social landscape.[16] Long-term employment stability underlay the persistence of some traditional neighborhoods well past World War II, when successful union contracts propelled workers into middle-class consumption and leisure behavior. In contrast, the precocious economic successes of other groups rapidly dismantled the original immigrant community through either assimilation with the American mainstream or movement into more prosperous neighborhoods, where residents retained some ethnic and religious affiliations but no longer identified closely with immigrant origins. This rise, decline, disappearance, and reformulation of immigrant and ethnic neighborhoods produced a dynamic, patterned social geography in which neighborhood composition could change within two generations or persist for several.

Even as rising incomes and changing social identities reshaped the residential landscape in the 20th century, the influx of black migrants markedly increased social tensions and separation. Southern blacks fled rural poverty and racial discrimination for perceived economic and civil

**Figure 14.10**
Philadelphia, around 1910.
This street scene in Little
Italy undoubtedly appeared
exotic to middle-class
American residents of the
city.

283

freedoms of northern cities.[17] While the benefits of migration were often tangible, most blacks were relegated to the lowest paying and least secure jobs and still faced discrimination in the city's workplaces, union halls, housing markets, and other institutions. The early migrants before World War I established small communities alongside central immigrant neighborhoods, but the thousands who arrived in the 1920s encountered stiffening resistance from white neighbors. Segregation became institutionalized in governmental policies, real estate practices, and financial lending programs. Hemmed in by discriminatory barriers, blacks piled up in racial ghettoes and slowly extended residential beachheads into older, declining immigrant quarters. Built on weak economic foundations and overwhelmed by new migrants, ghettoes developed the pathologies of impoverished slums. Extreme deprivation during the Depression and unrealized expectations for World War II's economic opportunities occasioned some racial violence, but the real combustion awaited postwar developments.[18]

Migration resumed after the war and could not be contained in the original ghettoes. Suburbanization, especially white flight, opened more inner-city housing to blacks, and soon additional neighborhoods were attached to the ghetto. The advancing black population inflamed white working class residents, who were unwilling or economically unable to flee to the suburbs. White resistance, urban renewal, and entrenched discrimination confined expansion of blacks to inner-city areas. This growing minority population changed the demography and power structure of the older city, polarizing it from the white middle-class suburbs that recoiled from the city's problems. Grinding poverty in the ghettoes, where dilapidated housing and declining job prospects beleaguered the poor and frustrated the aspirations of the black middle class who could not escape racial stigmatism, exploded under the leadership of civil rights activists in the 1960s. The violence and property destruction starkly demonstrated that black migrants had not been following economic and social trajectories similar to those of European immigrants.[19] This landscape of racial polarization contrasted sharply with the dynamic mosaic that had attended European adaptation and assimilation. Boarded storefronts, vacant lots, abandoned buildings, crowded tenements, littered roadways, and street corners of idle men marked the most desperate districts (Fig. 14.11).

While descendants of European immigrants inhabited a patchwork of working- and middle-class communities and blacks struggled for survival and justice, during the 1970s Latin Americans poured into inner-city neighborhoods as the latest urban migrants. Working at low paying service and manufacturing jobs, establishing their own institutions, creating barrios alive with Latin sounds and outdoor artwork, and participating in local politics, these hispanic newcomers scrambled the economic and racial polarity that had emerged after World War II. Oriental immigrants also carved out niches in several cities, adding an exotic, often economically successful, and sometimes contentious element to the unfolding social geography. While vestiges of European ethnic institutions remain in many

**Figure 14.11**
Surviving buildings on East
46th Street in Chicago. This
gaptooth cityscape hints at
the process of past
neighborhood disinvestment
as torchings and demolitions
for health and safety reasons
depleted the housing stock of
the worst affected districts.
Sweat-equity renovation and
black gentrification are taking
hold of this precinct after
years of neglect.

older neighborhoods, especially in the northern manufacturing cities, the
distinctive economic rôles, politics, and community institutions of hispanic,
oriental, and black groups have maintained, but reformulated, the
traditional variegated landscape of the inner city.

Along with long-term economic growth, the enduring faith in individual
liberty and a tolerance of diversity enabled American cities to withstand and
absorb the periodic influx of immigrants. While advantages of élite lineage
and nagging cultural discrimination persisted, this creed, however
grudgingly, recognized meritorious performance and rising wealth as
worthy attributes. The corresponding emphasis on materialism, reinforced
by protestant beliefs, became one means of displaying success and extended
middle-class status to a broad spectrum of society (Fig. 14.12).

**Figure 14.12**
Flashy residence in
Oklahoma City, built during
the oil-boom days of the early
1970s. Manicured lawns and
a palatial driveway set off a
home struggling with its
mixed French Empire, Greek
Revival, and California
Modern inspiration.

285

Blessed with immense land resources, Americans believed that property ownership both imbued owners with status and security and formed democracy's foundation. Although renting shelter was a longstanding practice, home ownership in the city became not only an obtainable goal but also increasingly widespread among the populace. The building fabric of cities reflected regional vernacular traditions, whether composed of wood or brick, row-houses or separate dwellings, or myriad other features. In the earliest cities, small lots, modest and little differentiated domestic architecture, and socially mixed neighborhoods presented an egalitarian appearance that masked social inequalities, except for those of the wealthy or severely destitute.[20] By the mid-19th century, the deteriorating environment, worsening congestion, and increasing foreign immigration rekindled an anti-urban bias and fueled an emerging domestic ideology among middle-class Americans, which stressed the family's moral rôle in nurturing order amidst urban chaos. A separate dwelling on a landscaped lot set apart from the city's clamor solved the agrarian ideal and the family's moral imperative. Families with the time and income to afford commuting to work undertook the suburban trek that emphasized a private familial existence. While architectural individuality and bucolic community planning appropriately accompanied this process in the 19th century, mass transportation and construction increasingly made suburban developments accessible to middle-class families, paradoxically homogenizing the appearance of these new residential areas.[21]

When the city's well-heeled residents relocated in newer suburbs, their old elegant houses, indeed their former neighborhoods, often filtered down to less prosperous buyers and eventually faded into the general landscape. But some wealthy neighborhoods like Philadelphia's Society Hill or Baltimore's Bolton Hill either maintained their social identity, aging with a genteel patina amidst inner-city decay, or avoided complete decomposition long enough for the architectural rescue of today's gentrification (Fig. 14.13).

The autonomy and privacy of the automobile embodied the suburban expression of individual freedom and economic mobility. Suburbanites incorporated the automobile into their life-style before World War II. However, increases in blue-collar incomes and leisure time, inexpensive automobiles, and governmentally subsidized highways and home financing after the war brought suburban living in reach of working-class families. Residential developments with minimal visual variety sprawled monotonously across gigantic swaths of land, broken only by highways, shopping centers, and factories until the major suburban commercial developments of the 1960s. Although the low density and institutional sterility which distinguished these neighborhoods from the city invited social criticism, the middle-class inhabitants evolved lifestyles that paradoxically combined voluntary participation in leisure and special interest organizations with an obsession for familial privacy (Fig. 14.14). Freedom from close community supervision blended with conservative concerns for neighborhood norms to yield only superficial demarcations of individuality such as in color or

**Figure 14.13**
Rutter Alley in Baltimore. In some cities, gentrification has reached into lower-income areas, displacing former residents who must find alternative housing in a tight market. Note the trim shutters, coach lamps, and painted cornice of these renovated row-houses.

**Figure 14.14**
A mass-produced suburb in
Pennsylvania, around 1960.
In this inexpensive
residential development note
the uniformity of bungalow
design, lack of garages, and
undisguised utility provision.
The spare quality of new
suburban subdivisions may
soften after a generation of
plant and tree growth.

decoration on the otherwise massproduced landscape.

The suburban landscape reflected the prevalence of automobiles in its organization, architecture, and land use. Expansive and horizontal suburbs shunned a pedestrian scale for complete dependence on automobile movement. Isolated stores and shopping centers were surrounded by massive parking lots or strung out for miles along highways. There were dozens of automobile-oriented stores and drive-in services from restaurants to banking. Residential blocks no longer had service alleys, so that garages and paved driveways obscured house façades. Adolescents designated streets for "cruising" in their cars as a form of entertainment. Regional shopping malls offered entertainment programs but provided limited community-wide integration. Only public schools, churches, sports organizations, and local crises, such as the prospect of an unwanted development or resident, created community involvement beyond home and personal networks. Sprawling one after another, the suburbs came to form a bewildering array of communities, maintaining identification with the metropolitan region through employment linkages, the media, and professional sports teams.[22] In the larger metropolises, the original cities' hold over suburban sentiments diminished with each generation.

## Governance and the landscape

This America, in which the emphasis on individualism often became excessive materialism and tolerance crumbled under the weight of nativism and racism, included nevertheless an abiding belief in basic rights for all its citizens. The plight of the disadvantaged in the competitive, capitalist economy and often intolerant social milieu periodically stimulated reform movements for social justice. Aggrieved groups and organizations acting on behalf of the underprivileged have used the legal system, political power available in a representative democracy, and organized protest to redress social inequities. In the years before massive industrialization and immigration transformed the cities, municipal governments tended to support business concerns for economic growth, civil order, and infrastructure, leaving social issues to the individuals involved or to private organizations.[23] The city's increased social and physical complexity after the mid-19th century forced local government to become more involved in social welfare and allowed established immigrant groups to compete for political power. But, the inclusive political spectrum did not benefit the city's newcomers and poor.

In a spurt of reform at the turn of the century, private organizations worked to improve housing, environmental quality, and health and social services through both the prodding of local government and private sector initiatives. Extensive parks, playgrounds, settlement houses in immigrant neighborhoods, sanitation and water systems, housing codes, and philan-thropically bestowed cultural institutions ameliorated the harsh inner-city world of the industrial metropolis. Unfortunately, the reluctance to tamper with the private enterprise system or pre-empt private property prerogatives limited reform results. Despite the creation of imaginative master plans, new professional urban planners only minimally influenced private development in the early 20th century and performed meek advisory rôles for municipal government, which focused on technical issues like traffic flow. Instead, civic leaders and architects orchestrated the display of the industrial city's rising status around planned civic centers composed of new public buildings, nonprofit institutions, and official monuments.[24]

The devastating Depression of the 1930s finally forced government at all levels to become more active in urban issues. In a partnership with city authorities, the federal government financed new highways, bridges, airports, and other municipal services, underwrote slum clearance, and subsidized private redevelopment projects.[25] Low-income public housing especially signaled the departure from strictly private sector proclivities. Massive housing projects, promising decent housing for all Americans, replaced decrepit tenements with spare, but modern low and high-rise buildings arranged in compounds of several blocks. By the 1960s the large number of these housing projects dramatically altered the inner-city landscape, contrasting in scale, texture, and spatial arrangement with the previous century's extant neighborhoods (Fig. 14.15).[26] These housing policies joined with other social programs to redistribute some income to the urban poor, but did little to release them from the separate world of the inner city.

The new directions in social policy only initially aggravated the racial polarization between city and suburb. They provided meager handouts, instead of meaningful economic opportunities, that confined poor blacks to segregated public housing in already segregated areas, while whites either benefited from governmental programs that promoted suburbanization or resented governmental largesse targeted for inner-city blacks. Civil rights pressures for open housing and fair employment practices, along with the rioting of the 1960s, finally riveted white society's attention and obtained

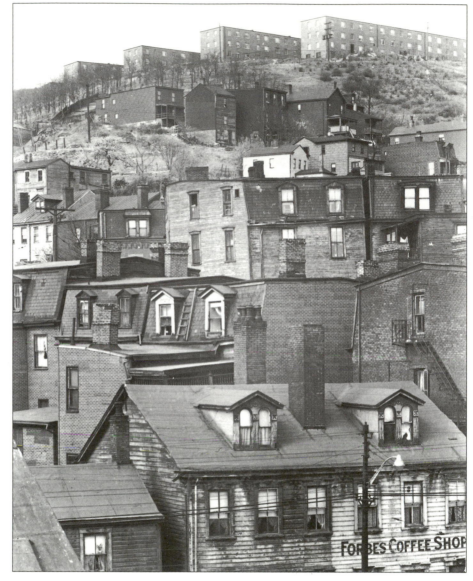

**Figure 14.15**
Terrace Village, Pittsburgh,
in 1951. Although some of
the nation's earliest public
housing exhibited
architectural merit, after
World War II most projects
added little of redeeming
value to the landscape,
except for replacement of
substandard buildings that
were no longer habitable.
Here, the visual contrasts
between old and new are full
of irony.

legislation for an integrated society. While race continued to separate neighborhoods and schools within the urban region after the 1960s, economic abilities came to provide a more important distinction in the social landscape. With legal support, more members of America's distinctive racial groups enjoyed economic success and moved beyond their former neighborhoods into integrated areas, leaving behind a tragically isolated and deprived racial underclass in central ghettoes.[27]

National concerns for air and water quality after World War II also embraced cities where automobile pollution, industrial dumping, waste production, and sewage disposal presented awful problems. Protest, regulatory legislation, and finally recognition of developmental implications

slowly led to the improvement of urban air, water, and land usage. By the
1970s improving environmental conditions and governmental subsidies
stimulated development of waterfront amenities and residences on older
blighted properties, which espoused outdoor life-styles for middle-class
consumers who would replace former poor residents. For middle-class
residents, the city as a place to live emerged alongside the traditional
perspective of the city as a place of work.[28]

## The American way

Ever since Coca Cola signs began appearing in the farthest corners of the
world, commentators have bemoaned the Americanization of the world's
landscape. American cities originated from European roots and measured
their progress for a century or two against European standards. Nevertheless, they eventually developed a self-conscious identity and associated
form, which reflected the society's particular ideology, economy, and social
composition.[29] By the mid-20th century the almost single-minded devotion
to economic pursuits had produced the dramatic profile of downtown
skyscrapers that overshadowed weakly defined cultural and administrative
spaces, the spontaneous patchwork of monotonous grid plans, a paucity of
open public space in central areas, and the fascination with newness and
large size. Boosters trumpeted growth, progress, modernism, and size as
hallmarks of greatness. Growth occurred largely within the limitations of
investment prudence and without much in the way of governmental
oversight. The freedom vested in private enterprise and property ownership
created landscapes filled with contradictory, sometimes conflicting, land
uses, frequent change, and uneven sprawl into the countryside. Embracing
individual privacy and eschewing high urban densities, middle income
residents chose home ownership, maximum personal space, and landscaped
lots in the suburbs. Immigrants and lower-income residents crowded into
tenement quarters, separate from the middle class mainstream; they too
were free in theory to make their own choices.

The repercussions of privatized growth and excessive materialism, as seen
in deleterious environments, suffocating traffic congestion, spotty infra-
structural services, visual chaos, and unattended social needs, became the
responsibilities of governmental officials, planners, reformers, and business
leaders, fearing a declining investment environment, a negative city image,
or at worst social upheaval. In early America, civic leaders had attacked
issues that affected the city's economic growth, presented an immediate
crisis, or were within the narrow purview of private charity. However, the
problems resulting from rapid immigration and industrialization generated a
debate that progressively redefined the public interest and responsibilities of
local government. The ability in a political democracy of new economic,
ethnic, and special interest groups to enter this debate broadened the scope

of municipal concerns and actions. The more active rôle of government since the early 20th century softened the harsh edges of America's economic and social privatism.

Increased governmental regulation, coordination, and initiative and the private sector's public service programs carefully work within a political and ideological framework of partnership that preserves private enterprise's independence and protects the rights of individuals, property owners, and exotic social groups, albeit within circumscribed limits of freedom prescribed by the expanded conception of public interest. The contradictions in American society generate vacillation over the merits of public and private initiatives, responsibilities for fostering economic growth, and means for providing municipal and social services. Nevertheless, the abiding faith in individualism, private enterprise, and equal opportunity maintains an American distinctiveness amidst the internationalization of many urban technologies, policies, and landscapes.

# Chapter fifteen
# Landscapes redesigned for the automobile

## JOHN A. JAKLE

No other technological innovation has so transformed the geography of the United States as the automobile. Landscapes inherited from pre-automobile times have been remade to suit highway-oriented technology and new landscapes have emerged shaped strictly in its image. The roots of this revolution lie deep in the American experience, for the automobile has enabled Americans to act out long established dreams. The motor car has not imposed new values so much as it has reinforced old. Underlying the love affair with automobiles is an American drive for individual fulfillment through freedom of mobility, the love of newness coupled with a naïve belief in change as progress, the embracing of privatism fueled by competitive rather than communal impulses, the pursuit of the utilitarian that embodies profound disrespect for the environment, and the belief in equality whereby a tyranny of the majority often rules. These social values can be observed in the processes of geographical change for which automobile technology stands symbolic.

### Automobiles

The motor car was at first a sporting device used by the very rich both as a recreational diversion and as a symbol of status. The approximately 300 motor vehicles owned by Americans in 1895 were European imports, but the next year the Dureyea Brothers began to market an American product and by 1899, when about 2,000 cars were operating in the United States, some 300 factories were in production.[1] The early automobile was a hybrid creature combining a buggy, a bicycle, and an internal combustion engine. Requisite technologies included the atomizing carburetor, as perfected on gasoline engines used on boats, and cold-rolled steel, accurately machined gears, ball bearings, and pneumatic tires, all perfected in bicycle manufacture. The buggy, or more appropriately the wagon, inspired the light, high-wheeled cars necessary to negotiate America's primitive roads. The

American automobile did not suddenly blossom into existence. Rather, it evolved out of pre-existing forms of transportation.

The automobile industry's growth was steady through the first decade of the new century. By 1908 there were nearly 200,000 automobiles among a population of 90 million people. Some 700 automobile factories were active, most of them small shops producing a few hundred high-priced cars a year.[2] Thereafter, growth was explosive as Henry Ford and other manufacturers pioneered mass production using moving assembly lines. Pointing toward an inexpensive car affordable to many, Ford wrote in 1909:

> I will build a motor car for the great multitude. It will be large enough for the individual to run and care for. It will be constructed of the best materials, by the best men to be hired, after the simplest designs that modern engineering can devise. But it will be so low in price that no man making a good salary will be unable to own one.[3]

Ford's Model T declined in price from $950.00 in 1910 to $290.00 in 1924. Whereas it took the average worker 22 months to buy a Ford in 1909, by 1925 it took only 3 months.[4]

By 1914 the output of motor vehicles exceeded that of carriages and wagons. Two years later there were 2 million cars on the road, 8 million in 1920, and 10 million in 1923.[5] Kansas had more cars registered than France or Germany, Michigan more than Great Britain and Ireland combined. By 1930, when automobile registration reached 23 million, the United States was building some 80 percent of the world's automobiles.[6] The number of manufacturers shrank in the competition. Only 87 firms exhibited at the New York City automobile show in 1921, and only 46 in 1930.[7] For surviving firms the task at hand took on the dimensions of a crusade. Hudson's Roy Chapin could write in 1926: "When I sold a car, I sold it with the honest conviction that I was doing the buyer a favor in helping him to take his place in a big forward movement."[8] Americans thrived on the increased mobility. Travel by car held implicit freedom of choice and it increased personal control over the physical environment denied by other forms of movement. Cars took owners door to door by routes owners chose, and by schedules they arranged. The automobile not only enabled but it symbolized progress through widened horizons and enhanced opportunities.

Automobiles changed. The Model T with its light-weight, high-torque engine, two-speed transmission and three-point suspension was ideal for pulling rural people out of the mud. Indeed, farm and small town Americans were the first mass adopters of automobiles, especially in the Middle West and West. Model T owners could handle most of their own repairs and, with fixed prices on spare parts, which were readily available through mail order catalogs, the car was a populist's ideal engendering a sense of self-sufficiency in transportation. With such innovations as closed sedans, electric lights, and four-wheel brakes, automobiles became increasingly complex and less easily serviced. On the other hand, they became more comfortable and easier to drive. With the introduction of electric starters the market opened wide to women who generally had found it difficult to use handcranks. Increasingly, Americans of both sexes demanded style as well as performance, for the automobile provided not only transportation but came to serve as status symbol signifying those who were tied into the emerging modernism. In his Model A, even Henry Ford acquiesced to the new demand for glamour.

Only during wartime did government seek to control automobile production. The rôle of government became one of subsidizing automobile technology through road construction. The courts, in failing to uphold George Sheldon's patent on the gasoline engine, broke a private attempt to license car manufacturers and impose production quotas. This decision favored those who saw a victory over monopoly capitalists who put short-term, high-unit profit ahead of long-term, low-unit profit which could translate into mass use of the automobile. The decision reinforced, as historian James Flink notes, public belief that technological innovation ought to compete freely in a democratic market: a caveat emptor to *laissez-faire*.[9] Those manufacturers who fought the Sheldon patent presented themselves, like crusaders, as champions of an idealized free enterprise system.

## Highways

New automobiles demanded new roads. Street and road improvements were integrally linked to the evolving automobile in a path of circular causation. Better cars and trucks demanded better highways, but better highways invited faster and larger motor vehicles.[10] Finally, the very settlement fabric of the nation was rent assunder. The scale of things changed to accommodate the speed, flexibility, and bulk of the automobile. Patterns of accessibility were changed and land uses were rearranged. People were put into new and novel spatial arrangements with profound social implications. Old proximities were destroyed and new proximities developed. The federal government played a central rôle in this unwinding drama, an involvement which matured by stages. From a complete lack of concern prior to 1897, the government began a policy of accommodating the automobile within the existing geographical structure of the country. After World War I emphasis was placed on redesigning roads to promote automobile technology, an emphasis which accelerated after 1935. After 1956 a goal emerged of national automobile dependence in landscapes fully oriented towards the automobile.

With the railroads dominating long-haul transportation, the nation had earlier seen little need to develop its highways. Rural roads served only to tie together localities and were administered by township and county officials with limited powers to impose the taxation necessary for their maintenance: officials sometimes solely dependent upon corvée labor.

Invention of the bicycle and the banding together of cycling enthusiasts in the League of American Wheelmen in the 1880s encouraged the macadamizing of rural roads outside cities, especially in Massachusetts and New York State.[11] In 1900, when there were only 4,000 automobiles, there were 10 million bicycles in the United States. Out of various farmer alliances, and out of the Populist Movement generally, there came a demand for improved roads to counter railroad dependence, part of the reaction to abusive freight rates and the monopolistic powers which rail corporations held in many localities. In 1891 the Post Office established the first rural free delivery service making improved rural roads more essential. In 1893 an Office of Road Inquiry was established in the Department of Agriculture to disseminate road building information.

Early in the century the automobile fitted easily into the American scene. Motor cars simply moved somewhat faster than horse drawn vehicles, albeit less dependably. Only when automobiles and pedestrians conflicted, or when automobile traffic became congested, were changes imposed on streets and roads. After 1910 stop signs and traffic signals were introduced in cities. Speed laws were formulated, some excessively restrictive, against which the newly organized American Automobile Association lobbied. The first concrete highway was built in 1909 with brick and asphalt also promoted as paving surfaces. Automobile manufacturers launched a massive lobbying effort to improve the nation's roads. Early effort formed around the Lincoln Highway Association, headed in its most active period by Packard's Henry Joy.[12] Not only was a route marked from New York City to San Francisco, but the automobile makers financed the building of "demonstration miles" to prove how carefully engineered highways of ribbon concrete could speed and ease long distance travel. Joy's purpose was "a quickening—an awakening—a national revival" which meant "a bigger, better, more prosperous, and more agreeable America."[13] The Lincoln Highway was the precursor of a host of named trunk roads (the Dixie Highway, the Jefferson Highway, etc.) which predated the numbered highway system.

The federal Highway Act of 1916 required states to establish highway departments in order that they might obtain, on a matching basis, federal subsidy for highway construction. Although it elevated control of highway improvement from the local to the state level, it did not call for an integrated network of trunk routes connecting cities. Rather, states could allocate monies as they saw fit (usually in response to political leverage), for Congress was as yet reluctant to impose a strong federal presence in an arena traditionally of state prerogative. During World War I when the railroads proved incapable of meeting the nation's material and troop movement needs, a clear rationale for federal involvement emerged. In 1917 the Council for National Defense appointed Roy Chapin to head a Highway Transport Committee. Motor trucks began to move freight in convoys from the Middle West's manufacturing cities to eastern seaports, especially Baltimore. Roads, such as the Lincoln Highway, suffered extensive damage and Maryland, in order to regulate traffic and generate income for road repairs, began the first licensing of motor vehicles, and imposed the first weight restrictions. In 1919 Oregon levied the first gasoline tax as a more expedient way of garnering road repair dollars.

The euphoria of patriotism that survived the Great War was traced by the highway lobbyists to the creation of a national defense highway system. The 1921 Highway Act required each state to designate 7 percent of its road mileage as "primary." Only these roads were eligible for federal aid on a 50 : 50 matching basis. The overall highway network, intended to connect every city over 50,000 in population, was expected to cover some 200,000 miles. A federal tax on gasoline charged at the pump was intended to fuel the program.[14]

The automobile's popularity as a thing to be owned and enjoyed could not be denied. The automobile promised release from the crowded cities for urbanites flocking to the countryside searching for relaxation. For rural people it promised access to city excitement and culture. Newton Fuessle,[15] an apologist for the Lincoln Highway, argued that automobile tourism would teach patriotism and "sew up the remaining ragged edges of sectionalism" thus revealing and interpreting America to its people. The new highways would give "swifter feet to commerce" and thus bind Americans "into one highly organized, proficient unit of dynamic, result-getting force electric with zeal" (Fig. 15.1). Americans were staunch highway supporters, not so much for implicit military rationales, but for the excitement and promise of the open road and the economic implications of increased mobility and ease of connections. By 1930 the automobile had affected all aspects of middle-class life in the United States. Robert and Helen Lynd's (1929) sociological analysis of "Middletown" showed that private cars played either a contributory or a dominant rôle in all areas of social life: getting a living, making a home, raising the young, using leisure, engaging in religious practice, and participating in community activities.

While state highway departments were rushing to tie the nation's cities together, municipal authorities were struggling to accommodate automobiles on streets designed for slow moving horse-drawn vehicles. Street widening began, especially on the major thoroughfares serving central business districts. Lesser streets near downtowns were made one-way in order to increase traffic carrying capacities. Residential streets that once had served as open spaces conducive to neighborliness and recreation, as well as travel, were re-engineered exclusively as arteries for automobiles and trucks. Streetcar efficiency declined in the press of traffic and in many places automobile lobbyists succeeded in replacing rail transit with buses, arguing that they were more flexible and cheaper to operate. General Motors Corporation, through subsidiaries, left nothing to chance, buying out the streetcar companies of over 100 American cities. Omnibus Corporation reduced New York City's 1,344 miles of streetcar line to only 337 miles by 1939.[16] City streets would not be people-oriented so much as they would be machine-oriented.[17] This impending change was explicit in Futurama, the

**Figure 15.1**
Along California's Mokelumne River. Here the new road will soar above the valley as if to deny topography. Below, the old road winds where once ferries operated across the flood.

General Motors exhibit at New York City's 1939 World's Fair. The model, portending American cities of the 1960s, showed miniature multilevel superhighways linked by sweeping cloverleafs. Utopian in alabaster white, the roads connected tall skyscrapers across parklike spaces of green.[18]

The American freeway was born in experimentation. The Long Island Motor Parkway, the first road anywhere constructed exclusively for automobiles, was completed in 1911 by William Vanderbilt to speed the wealthy from Long Island estates toward Manhattan. The Bronx River Parkway, a multipurpose public endeavor completed in 1923, eliminated water pollution, checked flooding, and provided recreational space along the abused Bronx River north from New York City. New Jersey pioneered the use of road cuts, viaducts, grade separations, and controlled exit and entrance ramps at bridge and tunnel approaches outside New York City and Philadelphia. Under the direction of Long Island Park Commissioner Robert Moses, in 1934 New York completed the Meadowbrook Parkway to Jones Beach State Park. It was the first divided, limited-access road built to European "autobahn" standards. Four years later the first long-distance intercity expressways opened, the Merritt Parkway and the Pennsylvania Turnpike.

Road standards were adopted by the American Association of State Highway Officials (10 foot lanes, 8 foot shoulders, a minimum surface thickness of 6 inches, and a 1 foot crown on a 2 lane pavement) and national speed limits were set for the new highways (70 miles per hour in open country and 50 miles per hour in urban areas). These decisions determined the physical layout of the new roads and, indeed, of the landscapes they passed through.[19] Lines of sight would be long and uninterrupted, grades would be moderate, and a wide sweeping geometry would prevail dictated by the gentle curves of interchanges. The roads would consume much space and thus would prove especially disruptive in the cities. The first urban expressway, Los Angeles' Arroyo Seco or Pasadena Freeway, was opened in 1940.

Limited access highways were at first special purpose roads, as the word "parkway" connotated. They were rationalized as recreational environments, means by which city people might escape the crowding, dirt, and noise of urban places. They would be the "lungs" of the city, as parks had been justified earlier, offering city dwellers access to open space. A new model for basic urban design resulted. With the central business district the hub, untouched by freeways but surrounded by an inner belt, expressways would radiate outward like the spokes of a wheel, giving access to garden suburbs and surrounding countryside.[20] Once built, the new roads quickly came to serve multiple functions: freight haulage, commuting, and long distance travel. After World War II recreational pretenses were dropped.

In 1949, the Bureau of Public Roads was reconstituted in a new Department of Transportation. In 1954, President Dwight Eisenhower asked General Lucius Clay, then a director of a large oil company, to chair an *ad hoc* committee (the Committee on a National Highway Program) charged with assessing the transportation needs of the nation. Not surprisingly, the committee, which included the Teamster's Union head, a road machinery manufacturer, and the head of a large construction firm, called for the immediate building of a new dual-lane, limited-access highway system to be separate from, but complementary to, pre-existing roads. The 1956 Highway Act formalized a plan for some 41,000 miles of road, 5,000 miles of which were to be within cities.[21] A Highway Trust Fund was established through which federal taxes on motor fuels, tires, new buses, trucks, and trailers, as well as a use tax on heavy trucks, would be channeled to road construction. The federal government would pay 90 percent of all construction costs, an irresistible inducement to the various states to build highways. The president gave four reasons for building the new system: existing highways were unsafe, too many roads were congested, poor roads inflated transportation costs for business, and, finally, existing highways were inadequate for the evacuation of cities threatened by nuclear attack.

No real consideration was given to the railroads or to public transit as
299 alternative forms of transport. No consideration was given to linking

highways, new or old, with other transportation modes. No thought was given to how highways might affect the established geography of the nation. What was transportation for, asked critic Lewis Mumford?[22] The purpose of transportation, he wrote, was to bring people or goods to places where they were needed, and to concentrate the greatest variety of goods and people within a limited area. A good transportation system minimized travel in this regard. But to Mumford the proposed highway system, which would spread things out and increase travel, could only be justified as a stimulus to automobile, gasoline, rubber, and concrete manufacture. "The most charitable thing to assume about this legislation," Mumford concluded, "is that they hadn't the faintest notion of what they were doing." Planner Robert Goodman[23] was not so circumspect. "That Washington's spending to help states build highways is one of the most expensive budget items is hardly unrelated to the fact that seven of the nation's ten largest corporations produce either oil or cars." Year after year the Highway Trust Fund pumped billions of dollars into highway construction. Earnings could not be spent for any other purpose, not even, after the 1966 Highway Act, for highway beautification.

Between 1947 and 1970 the federal government spent $58 billion on highways. Federal expenditures on airport construction and airline subsidy reached $12 billion during the same period, and $6 billion for waterway development. A meagre $795 million was spent on urban mass transit.[24] In the 1960s the average automobile carried 1.6 persons per trip into the nation's central business districts each day. Thus less than 5,000 people traveled the average freeway lane per hour. Rail transit, on the other hand, could move 50,000 passengers per hour.[25] In Chicago six rail transit lines and eight commuter railroads carried nearly 120,000 passengers away from the downtown "Loop" between 4:15 and 5:30 pm each workday.[26] By automobile such movement would have required 70 lanes of freeway in addition to the 29 already in use in 1970. Only Chicago, New York City, Philadelphia, and a select few other metropolises continued to support existing transit systems. Even in these places transit suffered from a vicious cycle of deteriorated equipment, declining use given increased automobile competition, declining revenue, and inability to recapitalize for needed renovation. Travel on commuter trains fell from 32 billion passenger miles in 1950 to less than 8 billion in 1970. In cities, the elimination or decline of transit actually crippled the automobile as an effective transportation mode as the new freeways and surface streets congested with traffic for longer periods. Freedom of action was greatly reduced when urbanites found their choices in travel restricted to a single alternative, the automobile.

## Landscapes

### Rural places

Evolution of the automobile as machine, and the highway as its container, altered rural and urban landscapes dramatically. In rural areas it accelerated the dismantling of commercial infrastructure focused in hamlets and villages as farmers could now buy and sell readily in distant towns and cities. In bigger places more goods and services were available from larger establishments that could offer, because of their size, lower prices. Mechanization in agriculture (especially the tractor and truck) increased labor effectiveness and farms grew larger with fewer laborers. Declining population wrought diminished tax revenue undermining support of public services. Rural communities were impoverished everywhere. Where lack of fertile soil, flat terrain, or other resources discouraged large-scale commercial agriculture, the automobile hastened conversion of abandoned farmland to recreation or other city-oriented uses. In 1930 the farm population of the United States numbered 30.5 million or roughly one-quarter of the total population. In 1980 it numbered only 6.1 million or less than 3 percent.[27] The rapid spread of the automobile was a catalyst in this change.

A new kind of road, the freeway, came to dominate intercity travel in rural areas (Fig. 15.2).[28] The old roads had been, as they continue to be, a definite kind of place: the geography of the roadside as important as that at the end of the road. Direct access to highway margins encourages social contact between locals and strangers and rural lifeways can be observed close up. But limited-access roads isolate and contain the motorist in an environment divorced from its surroundings. These new roads exert a

**Figure 15.2**
Ohio's Interstate 70 near Old Washington. Where once the National Road and later U.S. Highway 40 ran, the landscape has been configured anew. The car-bound motorist, confined to a ribbon of pavement, is distanced from the world beyond. Not only has the landscape changed in rural America, but the American experience of landscape through high speed freeway driving has also changed.

tyranny on what motorists see with the countryside reduced to background. Interaction between locals and strangers is impossible except at freeway interchanges. Both the rural freeway, for its monotony, and the encompassing countryside, for its distance, can be safely ignored in high-speed driving. Thus the new highways have not only changed American rural landscapes, but the manner in which Americans view and experience those landscapes as well.

### The suburbs

American cities have been remade in recent decades. Although automobiles and highways have not been the only factors in operation, they have been key elements in precipitating metamorphosis. As automobiles encouraged commuting, commuting excited city growth outward: not the ordered growth previously restricted to railroad and streetcar lines, but an explosive mutation that produced a new, amorphous, sprawling suburbia oriented to highways (Fig. 15.3). As the suburbs boomed, inner-city neighborhoods declined under the assault of freeway construction and related urban renewal. During the 1970s the nation's suburbs grew by 12 percent while its central cities lost 5 percent of their people.[29] In the largest metropolises (those containing more than 1 million residents), approximately 62 percent of the people now live outside the central city. Today, suburbia accounts for approximately 40 percent of the nation's total population, and is fast becoming the predominant place type in the American experience. Some 80 percent of the nation's population growth between 1950 and 1970 was located there.[30]

Whereas cities had been highly compact places with high building

**Figure 15.3**
A Chicago suburb. Automobiles and the highways that serve them have encourged urban sprawl, creating a spread-out city of look-alike houses in look-alike subdivisions. This aerial view symbolizes the middle-class response to an aging inner city, namely, to escape to pastoral Edens of broad streets, double driveways, and two-car garages.

densities, they now sprawled with substantially lower densities. For example, the urbanized area of Washington, D.C. grew from 181 to 523 square miles between 1950 and 1970, and Miami from 116 to 429 square miles.[31] Multicentered urban agglomerations evolved. Southward from Los Angeles in Orange County, California, some 2 million people now live in some 26 cities, several approaching a quarter million each. To the north, San Jose, with 70,000 people in 1940, now exceeds 600,000 and is larger than nearby San Francisco. Such development portends what Peirce Lewis calls the galactic city comprised of loose, separated urban clusters "rather like galaxies floating in space."[32] Other terms, like "megalopolis" and "conurbation," describing these new realities, have entered the American lexicon.

The spread of the automobile did not cause urban decentralization, rather it served as an enabling mechanism. The federal highway program provided the geographical infrastructure upon which other governmental programs fostered surburbanization. In 1934 the Federal Housing Administration (F.H.A.) was created as a means of stimulating the housing industry and thus the economy stricken by economic depression. The new organization insured mortgages made by private lenders, reducing the size of required downpayments as well as interest rates thus making houses more affordable. By 1972 it had helped some 11 million families to own houses, increasing the percentage of Americans living in owner-occupied dwellings from 44 to 63 percent.[33] In 1944 the Veterans Administration (V.A.) created similar mortgage programs to aid veterans.

Building standards suggested by the F.H.A. and V.A. programs inadvertently dictated the physical structuring of new neighborhoods. Subdividers and builders tended to adhere to recommendations regarding minimum lot size, setback, separation of houses, and character of yard. Spread-out places were the result. Missing were the conveniences of pedestrian travel traditional to older neighborhoods. Stores once close by at the ends of short blocks where streetcars ran, were removed upwards to several long blocks or even several miles. Travel by car became a necessity. Whereas narrow lots had been used to pack multiple-story houses close together in the old city, now wide lots, usually with single-story houses, prevailed in the new. In this scheme there was no place for row, terrace, or other traditional house forms. Indeed, 97 percent of all new single-family houses built between 1946 and 1975 were detached on open lots.[34] The "rambling ranch" with attached garage symbolized postwar affluence.

Affluent white Americans began to flood into the new suburbs during the 1950s, the black middle class excluded until after civil rights legislation of the subsequent decade. In 1970 median household income in the central cities was but 80 percent that of the suburban and, in 1980, 74 percent.[35] Economist Richard Muth[36] estimated that median income in metropolitan areas in the 1970s increased at about 8 percent with each mile traveled outward from a city center, income doubling every ten miles. The white middle class sought new housing to escape deteriorating inner-city neighborhoods fraught with social change as black and other minority groups concentrated there. The new suburbanites also sought tax benefits. Mortgage interest payments were deductible at income tax time. For businessmen, the 1954 tax code introduced accelerated depreciation on new buildings. Suburbia became a kind of tax haven for those who could afford (and obtain) the initial capitalization to live and do business there. Here was security, a place of stability where equity in private property could be protected.

Federal subsidy of municipal sewer and water systems not only accelerated urban sprawl, but encouraged the proliferation of municipal governments. Through World War II most big cities had easily annexed peripheral areas through control of public utilities. Suburban governments had faced especially prohibitive startup costs in providing water services. But after World War II, with such difficulty eliminated, suburban governments of all kinds proliferated. Today there are over 22,000 governmental units, each with their own taxing power, in the nation's Standard Metropolitan Statistical Areas (S.M.S.A.), an average of 86 per S.M.S.A.[37] New York City has some 1,400 governments, and Chicago over 1,000. With governmental authority so divided, it was difficult to plan the new metropolis. Thus suburbia has sprawled outward, the locating of subdivisions, shopping centers, highways, and other facilities largely uncoordinated. Kenneth Jackson writes of Los Angeles:

> Its vast amorphous conglomeration of housing tracts, shopping centers, industrial parks, freeways, and independent towns blend into each other in a seamless fabric of concrete and asphalt, and nothing over the years has succeeded in gluing this automobile-oriented civilization into any kind of cohesion—save that of individual routine.[38]

Today, individual routine for most suburbanites is inefficient timewise and wasteful of energy. Without cheap gasoline suburbia would come unglued. Automobiles consume about one-quarter of the nation's oil needs, and over half of that is consumed in intra-city driving. In 1980, the typical American worker took 44 minutes commuting 18.4 miles to and from work at an annual personal expense of some $1,270.[39] Instead of being concentrated geographically, as in the traditional city, jobs are now decentralized. As early as 1963, industrial employment in the United States was more than half suburban based, and by 1981 about two-thirds. Should mass transit regain popularity, as, for example, with a renewed energy crisis like that of the 1970s, its effectiveness would be substantially hindered by today's excessive dispersal of activity.

*Inner cities*

Central areas in most American cities have suffered decline (if not outright abandonment) in the face of suburbanization. Again, the ascendancy of the automobile has enabled and, indeed, directed change. Again, various federal programs in combination with highway building influenced substantially what we see in the landscape today. The 1949 Housing Act created urban renewal, intended urban revitalization through the bulldozing of slums. By removing physical decay, it was assumed that social decay also would be eliminated. By paying upwards to two-thirds the costs of land clearance, the program served more as a subsidy to real estate and building interests than as a mechanism for solving slum problems. Indeed, the threat of urban renewal did much to destabilize neighborhoods creating the very physical conditions planners were seeking to solve. Landlords disinvested buildings, failing to repair and maintain properties. Accelerated obsolescence reduced property values so reducing taxes collected. With decreased revenue, municipal governments began to disinvest public streets, parks, and schools. Police, fire and other public services were curtailed. By 1967 some 1,400 urban renewal projects had been launched in 700 cities.[40] In most cities, displaced residents crowded into adjacent neighborhoods fostering a spiral of slum development there. Four out of five families displaced were black.

Freeway construction had similar impact (Fig. 15.4). Engineers, and the political and economic interests that supported them, worked a tyranny on

**Figure 15.4**
Central Boston, seen from Charlestown looking south. New highways, cut through the old fabric of the city, have unraveled old neighborhoods. The pedestrian- and streetcar-oriented city has been sacrificed to the freeway designed to rush suburbanites downtown. The old city clings to life only in isolated pockets, as seen in the foreground.

inner-city communities. Whole neighborhoods were sacrificed to generate capital gains for the influential.[41] Planners seemed unresponsive to the human needs of people displaced or unappreciative of the neighborhoods and communities destroyed. The accepted values were those of business, government, and the supporting governmental bureaucracy. As commercial and industrial properties provided employment and paid substantive taxes, so those properties should be enhanced in worth. Where vacant land or other open space (such as parks) was unavailable, residential properties were readily sacrificed to freeway development. Even where neighborhoods were partially spared, traffic congestion, noise, and dirt generated by the new roads depressed property values. Often, surviving neighborhoods found their parts hopelessly disconnected by freeways which served as barriers to local movement. On the other hand, freeways have undeniably alleviated mounting urban traffic congestion.

*Central business districts*

Although favored by the new freeways, most large and small city business districts have suffered decline. Retail and wholesale trade and even administrative functions have joined the rush to the suburbs. Whereas corporate skyscrapers still dominate skylines, downtown is increasingly awash in a sea of widened streets and parking lots (Fig. 15.5). Over two-thirds of the land in most downtown business districts is covered by concrete and asphalt. Disappearing is the traditional downtown fabric comprised of modest buildings integrated along pedestrian streets. The change is slow: a building hauled down for a parking lot, then another, and another. One by one skyscrapers come to turn impersonal walls of stone and glass to sidewalks little used. Commuters depart in the evening leaving downtowns deserted. Business districts may still symbolize the metropolis as center, but for most cities it is a hollow ritual. Streetlife is increasingly concentrated in suburban business centers; the pedestrian, for his part, an animal increasingly caged in enclosed shopping malls.

Retailing changed when the affluent moved to the suburbs. Stores long located downtown, especially those selling convenience and expensive shopping goods, moved to peripheral shopping centers. In 1960 there were some 4,000 planned shopping centers in the United States.[42] What survives downtown in most cities are discount and remainder stores catering to low income, minority populations. Most of their customers are still public transit dependent and represent only a shrinking residual market for downtown merchants. In some cities new downtown shopping malls and retail facilities opened in historic districts promise to reverse some of the decline.

*Commercial strips*

No landscape reflects more the automobile's impact than the commercial strip.[43] It is a built environment created for the automobile, or, more precisely, the motorist as customer (Fig. 15.6). Automobile convenience is the underlying organizing principle of space utilization. Low, sprawling

**Figure 15.5**
Downtown Houston. Viewed
from an expressway, the
edge of the central area
displays three ecological
dominants: skyscraper,
street, and parking lot.
Impressive as tall buildings
may be when composing a
distant skyline, close up and
at ground level they stand as
isolates surrounded by
asphalt and automobiles.
Pedestrians here are
completely marginal.

buildings, dominated by giant signs, beckon motorists into adjacent parking lots. Street margins glitter with the array: supermarkets, discount stores, fastfood restaurants, motels, gasoline stations. There is a sameness in commercial strips everywhere: the same basic forms decorated to advertise the same or similar corporate enterprises. Here and there a shopping center disrupts the pattern by its scale. The goods and services sold relate directly to building form and styling through "place-product-packaging": merchandise and services symbolized at the scale of landscape.

Strip development came to dominate well-traveled highways outward from literally every American city and town. It was, and is, an elaboration of the "old road," and not merely a conduit to other destinations. Most strips were unplanned. They just evolved, neither aided nor hindered by government or other central authority. An implement dealer moved to the edge of town to intercept farmers, giving himself more room to store equipment. A supermarket chain located adjacent to a new subdivision and attracted a drug store and dry cleaners shop in addition. The accumulation began early. By 1935 over 300 gasoline stations and 400 other commercial establishments lined the 47 miles of U.S. Highway 1 between Newark and Trenton in New Jersey.[44] In Connecticut between New Haven and the New York State line, gasoline stations averaged one every 895 feet on U.S. Highway 1, and restaurants one every 825 feet.[45]

So pervasive has strip development become that a sort of sameness, born of roadside clutter, has emerged across the nation. As the suburbs are characterized for their homogeneity, so the roadside also suffers blandness. Lewis Mumford wrote of suburbia as a new kind of community characterized by uniform, indistinguishable houses, lined up inflexibly, at uniform

**Figure 15.6**
Pennsylvania's U.S. Route 30 near Breezewood. Here, businesses clamor for the motorist's attention along the commercial strip. A new esthetic has been born, rooted, perhaps, in the World's Fair concept of the midway with its array of forms, colors, and signs. Along the commercial strip, the car has transformed the midway into a nonstop marketplace.

distances, on uniform roads.[46] To J. B. Priestley the roadside communicated a similar message.[47] There was rapidly coming into existence a new way of living—fast, crude, vivid—perhaps even a new civilization, but, more likely, another barbaric age. And it was symbolized in the commercial strip seen everywhere. Gasoline stations, restaurants, and motels were trivial enough in themselves, but they pointed to the most profound change. Here was a way of life, informal and potentially equalitarian, "breaking through the old like a crocus through the wintry crust of earth." The American strip has permeated the urban mass as kudzu spreads through Southern groves. In an automobile world, it is unimpeachably convenient.

The automobile's hegemony over American landscapes is rooted in values which run deep. They are most certainly values inherited from a frontier experience whereby an essentially European culture brought a continent to heel, exploiting its resources and developing new possibilities socially and politically. At base was belief in individual freedom of action as well as respect for change as progress. Basic also was the pursuit of privatism, utilitarianism, and egalitarianism, values honed by pioneer circumstances.

Thus Americans were predisposed to embrace automobile technology. Indeed, no other invention of such far reaching geographical importance has ever diffused so rapidly across a society.

Almost universal access to the automobile promised freedom of a basic geographical kind. Geographical mobility, as it broadened opportunities through ease of access to new places, promised social mobility and enhanced status. Here was an important American core value supported by automobiles and highways. As an individual's fortunes waned, the opportunity of a fresh start could be had elsewhere—if not on a western, then on a suburban frontier. In city terms utopia lay in moving to a better neighborhood in the suburbs, as it had once meant moving west. Freedom carried, as before, an escapist theme. Americans were promised an equal right to compete for resources, not a guaranteed equal share of them. Change through mobility always has seemed requisite to this competition. The ability to reach new horizons has been a necessary ingredient for success.

A distorted kind of equality prevails when people and communities suffer the impact of dislocation dictated, for example, by city freeway construction condoned for the majority good—the majority interpreting the common benefit in terms of the rewards accorded those who succeed. Those unwilling or unable to conform to prevailing ideals of success tend to remain isolated in what remains of the pre-automobile city. Once public opinion is formed on such issues as freeway construction, conformity is expected and even demanded. There emerges what Alexis de Tocqueville identified in the 19th century as a "tyranny of the majority." "I know of no country," he wrote, "in which there is so little independence of mind and real freedom of discussion as in America."[48]

Although rooted in long standing values, America's reliance on the automobile did not evolve naturally following set preconditions. Automotive hegemony was created by men and women working hard to encourage favorable public opinion and establish private and public institutional mechanisms capable of realizing the profound environmental and social changes that, in fact, accrued. Deliberate decision making and not impersonal social forces continue to promote automobiles and highways as a basis for American life. The American citizenry has willingly assented. Promoters of the automobile fall into at least three categories: the vested interests of corporate capitalism, the politicians (supported by business entrepreneurs) who wield the public purse, and the bureaucrats in public service who translate political will into action.

Entrepreneurs such as Henry Ford championed the automobile as consumer product. The development of the automobile as a machine was rooted in corporate profit taking as vested interest. The lobbying for highways was intended to enhance that profitability. By convincing the American public of the automobile's desirability, major industries were created which ultimately came to dominate the American economy. Politicians, including American presidents such as Dwight Eisenhower, supported vigorously the highway lobby sensing strong widespread public support. Finally, men like Robert Moses created the highway programs through which the American environment was substantially remade, building bureaucratic empires in the process.

The niches filled by such men as Henry Ford and Dwight Eisenhower in American transportation history are hardly surprising in retrospect. What seems astonishing, however, is that such men as Robert Moses could exert such considerable power in remolding the American landscape. The highway engineers as planners and implementers of the new highway-oriented America brought an arrogance to environmental change even exceeding that of the railroad barons of the preceding era. With dedicated single-mindedness they built their highways, liquidating established places to create new places. Imposed was what Edward Relph labels "benevolent environmental authoritarianism." Persons and communities in the path of progress obtained little leverage in ordering their lives.[49]

The automobile became dominant in American life with amazing speed. Change has driven the fast lane. In only 80 years the automobile has evolved from an amusement for the very few to become a necessary adjunct of life for the vast majority. Values, resources, and technologies have been aligned toward a massive restructuring of the United States with profound economic benefit resulting. It remains to be seen whether the forces marshaled to produce automobile culture can be "fine-tuned" to resolve internal contradiction and wasteful inconsistency. The American nation stands challenged to place the automobile in humane perspective. It stands challenged to the making of new landscapes maximally enhancing the lives of all Americans.

# Chapter sixteen
# The imprint of central authority

## WILBUR ZELINSKY

IT WOULD BE shortsighted indeed to try to explain the humanized landscapes of our late 20th-century world without reckoning with the large, ever-expanding rôle of central authority: the workings of our more-or-less sovereign nation states and their varied agents and deputies. Nowhere is this more apt than in the United States. Perhaps nowhere else is there stronger visible evidence of the power and universality of the governmental presence. Yet, surprisingly, to date only two scholars[1] have seriously considered this focus on the visible scene anywhere on this Earth.

Such a peculiarly vivid inscription of the federal factor—and, to a lesser but still notable degree, of local authority—upon the form and content of domesticated America is the outcome of special historical circumstances. Indeed, the visible encoding within our public environment of the political powers that be is highly time-specific and reflects the evolving character of the nation, or rather state, and, even more broadly, the imperatives of a modernized mass society.

To begin at the beginning, the transplantation of European (cum African) individuals and communities into eastern North America in the 17th and 18th centuries was a relatively leisurely process by latterday standards, and essentially a replication of Old World models. As such, despite some abortive experiments in such places as earliest Pennsylvania or Georgia, there was little real control, no effective organizing center staffed by monarchs, proprietors, or local administrators to shape the geometry or appearance of the new settlements outside a very few urban places. Consequently, local peculiarity was the rule in the landscapes of pre-Revolutionary European America, and remains so to a noticeable degree within such tracts to this day.

But the large-scale shifting of persons and cultures across the Atlantic did meet up with a new situation quite at variance with European experience, namely, the almost total obliteration of antecedent societies and their landscapes. Thus, colonial Americans were able to refashion essentially wild, depopulated spaces into places of their own devising with no reference to any local past. Such a license for environmental manipulation, for drawing new panoramas on a blank canvas, was unthinkable in Europe with its deeply layered, historically fused, diachronic landscapes. But the implications of such liberation from the detritus of previous generations did not become truly clear until the 19th and, especially, the 20th century. The exceptional circumstances of the American story—that is, the creation of a set of novel landscapes by a society, initially localistic and libertarian, that has expanded at an explosive rate into every measurable dimension, but eventually came under the domination of a centrally managed corporate structure of government and business—provide the wherewithal for a nearly ideal case study of how such authority inserts itself into the tangible substance of our collective existence.

## The early federal presence

For most of the first century of national independence, the federal establishment was remarkably small in size, severely limited in scope of activity, and generally a passive agent performing only those minimal functions needed to preserve economic and political sovereignty plus a few essential services—to handle only those affairs beyond the competence of the locality. Thus in 1816 the aggregate civilian workforce employed by the United States government totaled only 4,857 persons,[2] while paid state and local government workers cannot have been much more numerous. Federal employment did increase to 36,672 by 1891; but, subsequently, govern-mental personnel has soared to stratospheric levels. As of December 1984, some 16,318,000 persons were on various governmental payrolls (more than four times the total national population in 1790), 2,824,000 of them at the federal level, thus making the U.S. government by far the country's—and almost certainly the entire capitalist world's—largest employer.

During the antebellum era, ordinary citizens would have detected few if any signals in their workaday surroundings that any sort of national government was active. And, although there would have been greater awareness of state and local government policies and activities, their impact on the visible scene must have been too slight to be obtrusive. True enough a certain number of forts and other military installations did exist, manned by a tiny standing army, and the young U.S. navy was a tangible presence in a handful of places. Customhouses were mandatory and relatively conspicuous in the major seaports, while the central regime was obliged to build and maintain lighthouses at crucial points along the Atlantic coast, an obligation local jurisdictions were unwilling or unable to undertake.[3]

The most obvious ways in which early congresses and the executive branch molded the physical structure of the young Republic are more readily appreciated by scanning maps and aerial photography than by reconnaissance on the ground. First, there are the international boundaries for the coterminous United States created by treaty and negotiation from 1783 to 1853. For many years, however, their reality was more cartographic than terrestrial. Only belatedly did Washington's minions survey precise locations, build boundary markers, create border stations for managing customs and immigration, and erect barriers along sections of the border with Mexico. Incidentally, these international boundaries may very well be the first to observe geodetic formulae. Such straight Euclidean slashes across the map were later adopted in Africa, certain parts of Central America, and, in a manner of speaking, Antarctica.

In the process of creating 34 new states and annexing Texas during the period 1791 to 1912, Congress delineated the interstate boundaries which, in contrast to most intercolonial delimitations, invariably included extended straight lines. In fact, in the extreme cases of Colorado and Wyoming we encounter pure rectangular lumps of territory, while Utah's shape is only slightly less simplistic. This fundamental framework, i.e., the familiar profiles of the states, is thus mostly the enduring handiwork of central authority, and the direct and indirect landscape and other geographical implications of such a bald application of geometry are far from trivial. Such a mechanistic carving up of the land would seem to have been prefigured by the provision in the Constitution for an (originally) diamond-shaped District of Columbia contained within four straight 10-mile sides.

Much more consequential for the life-patterns of that half of the American population inhabiting those places which were formerly part of the Public Domain is the strategy pursued by federal agencies in disposing of huge tracts of real estate. Acquired by purchase or cession from foreign countries and the original colonies, the lands once held by the central regime amounted to something close to three-quarters of the expanse of the coterminous United States. The American government proved to be a reluctant landlord, at least initially, and began almost immediately, in the late 1780s, to sell or donate (chiefly to military veterans and railroad companies) as many of its holdings as it could as quickly and painlessly as possible. And that is precisely what happened beyond the original 13 states and Texas, except for those tracts granted under antecedent French and Spanish titles and the various Indian and military reservations, national parks and forests, and various other areas not deemed suitable for traditional types of settlement. Such a program dovetailed neatly with the prevailing economic ethos, one in which individual and corporate enterprise flourished freely with minimal intervention by governmental bureaucracies.

The mode of land survey enacted by Congress—the carving up of the Public Domain into 6-by-6-mile square townships aligned as strictly as possible with compass directions and subdivided into 36 square-mile sections—was the ultimate in geometric simplicity. Initiated in northeastern Ohio in 1785, the system pushed onward quickly, barely keeping pace with eager settlers and speculators. It immensely facilitated legal and commercial transactions involving the sale or transfer of land. And, more to our immediate purpose, the resulting grid has been stitched indelibly into the fabric of the greater part of the American land surface. As Hildegard Binder

313

Johnson has so admirably demonstrated, the social, economic, and other implications, both positive and negative, of this pervasive cadastre have been varied, complex, and substantial. In landscape terms it has produced a repetitive checkerboard lattice of roads following section and half-section lines, one that is paralleled by the boundaries of fields, pastures, and woodlots in the lands within. In countless instances, it has predetermined the placement of county boundaries and the configuration of political townships. Many a village and city, large or small, has adopted the layout of its streets from what began as a design for rural settlement.

Visually insistent though it may be, the rectangular survey system is a residual legacy that does not genuinely validate the ideological or managerial brawn of the state. Instead it reminds us that during the first half of its history the federal establishment played a basically passive part in contriving the material framework of American life, that it relegated to the private sector most decisions as to what the country was to become and how it would look. If much of the Public Domain still remains in federal hands today, it has only been in recent decades, or within the past hundred years at most, that that fact has become noticeable to the casual observer.

Despite being weakly manned and underfunded, and enervated by political dispute, the federal establishment did gradually gather symbolic and material weight in the years leading up to the Lincoln Administration. Perhaps the most persuasive sign of growing strength was the building of federal courthouses in various cities, sometimes as much as status symbols as to meet genuine administrative needs.

> Towns everywhere clamored for federally funded buildings as an indication of stature. And Congressmen obligingly served them up. For example, Memphis received a courthouse even though no federal courts were held there. . . . Indeed to people in towns such as Dubuque, Iowa and Astoria, Oregon, federal buildings represented the latest in architectural style and technology and, symbolically, membership in the Union.[4]

The crucial juncture, the watershed event, in the maturation of the American nation–state, ultimately in landscape terms as in virtually every other department of our collective existence, was without question the Civil War. In the most decisive and bloodiest of terms, it settled once and for all the dispute as to whether the central state and its allied system of mercantile and budding industrial capitalism, as opposed to sectional, local, or agrarian interests and values, were to dominate the polity. The landscape implications began to be discernible shortly thereafter.

## Federal landscape influence after the civil war

The account that follows fits into a much broader schema developed in detail elsewhere.[5] In brief, we can trace the gradual evolution of the American community from its pristine Revolutionary and immediate post-

Revolutionary character as a nation, or ethnie, of a strikingly novel ideological bent—a situation in which the superstructure of a state was barely tolerated as a necessary nuisance—into a full-fledged, veritable textbook example of the nation–state, a condition in which the state is supreme in material and emotional fact and has coopted and absorbed into itself whatever lingers on of the former people-based nationalism. The case is most lucidly documented by chronicling the shifts in symbols that mediate relationships between individuals and the larger social–psychological entities which they inhabit. But one can also read a parallel progression in many corners of the visible landscape.

The decisive landscape innovation was that the federal establishment assumed an increasingly active rôle from the 1870s onward. Even when purposive behavior has not implanted immediate stigmata upon our surroundings, the indirect by-products of governmental programs and decisions have subtly, often profoundly, modified the look of the land. If a single date is needed to mark the transition, then 1872 may qualify, for that is when Congress created Yellowstone Park (Fig. 16.1).[6] It was not only the

28478   OLD FAITHFUL INN AND GEYSER, YELLOWSTONE NATIONAL PARK                    HAYNES

**Figure 16.1**
The pseudo-rustic style of Yellowstone Park's Old Faithful Inn, shown in this postcard view, has become almost mandatory for buildings in other national parks and many state parks as well.

first of that impressive constellation of national parks and, later, national monuments and historic sites to be administered by the National Park Service (and to enjoy immense patronage), it was the first in the world, setting a precedent imitated by other countries. These precious asylums, officially wild and geologically, biologically, or historically memorable places, do vary greatly in size, shape, and appearance, but there are certain family resemblances, visual clues that set them apart from ordinary terrain. The reception or visitor centers, the mode of fencing, signage at strategic points, the occasional museum, the general style of landscaping, minor physical appointments, and other small details speak to us of a wise and caring government.

Since their relatively low-key origins during the colonial and early republican periods, the number and acreage of military sites has expanded enormously, and especially so during the past several decades, even though statistics on such land use are not readily available. A variety of facilities falls under this heading: camps for the armed services (often associated with extensive tracts for training maneuvers);[7] munition dumps; the aviation and port facilities of the various services; the concrete silos in which I.C.B.M.s are nested; firing ranges and other testing facilities; navy docks, repair yards, and related structures; military hospitals; and various fortifications (many now obsolete or turned into museums), among other items. To such a roster one might legitimately add the places for manufacturing and testing nuclear weapons in the states of Washington and Nevada, along with the complex at Oak Ridge, Tennessee, even though they happen to be managed by the Department of Energy. Similarly, we can include the often imposing arsenals of the National Guard (nominally under the control of the 50 individual states) or the recruiting offices for the various armed services to be found in so many cities large and small. However diverse their immediate functions, the observer seldom has trouble recognizing the military personality of such places, or distinguishing them from civilian landscapes. In particular, the traditional military barracks resemble no other form of human habitation unless it be the "temporary" dormitories that mushroomed on college campuses immediately after World War II (Fig. 16.2). Equally distinctive in appearance are those large, bland yellow-brick Veterans Administration hospitals that punctuate the skylines of many of our cities and suburbs.

There are other settings, however, in which civilian and military elements meet and merge after a fashion. First there are American Legion and Veterans of Foreign Wars halls in virtually every town of any size. Their architecture is completely unpredictable, but seldom striking; we recognize them by virtue of signs and flags and the military hardware parked on the lawn. In social terms, few elements are more meaningful in the landscapes of our smaller communities. Second, there are community cemeteries where flags and other insignia decorate the graves of veterans and those fallen in battle. But these are much less distinctive places than the national military cemeteries, which, among other things, are peculiarly effective devices for promoting the statist mystique.[8] Prior to the American Civil War, no national government had given much thought to the advantages of organized burial of battle casualties and veterans; but in 1863 the United States initiated the practice—subsequently adopted by many other countries—with the dedication of the Gettysburg Battlefield.[9] Since then, the number of American examples has multiplied greatly. Many, but far from all, lie at or near the scene of battle; most are located within the homeland, but some are in northern France, the Philippines, and other distant locales. Their landscaping and design, which includes uniform headstones regimented in the neatest of geometric arrays, have been standardized.[10] They have not been ignored by the public; in fact, some, most notably Gettysburg and Arlington, have become major tourist attractions—with some visually questionable consequences.[11]

Much less obvious than militarized sites are the telltale indications of federal stewardship over those huge stretches of countryside, predominantly in the West, controlled by the Forest Service (Department of Agriculture) and the Bureau of Land Management (Department of the Interior), in part through lease arrangement. None the less such forests and rangelands, which have developed over the past 100 years, can be distinguished from privately held properties by the sensitive viewer.

**Figure 16.2**
This complex of army barracks happens to be located in Denver, Colorado, but virtually identical siblings are to be seen throughout the United States. Note the geometrical alignment of structures, the absence of landscaping, and the extreme plainness of the (non-) architecture.

## The emergence of Washington, D.C. as epitome and model

Although it is hard to avoid some visible manifestation of the power or majesty of central authority wherever one may chance to wander within the United States, it is in the nation's capital that we encounter by far the most intense, spectacular, indeed overwhelming expression of statist principles. In fact, the City of Washington was designed with just that purpose in mind:

> In the realm of broad (and somewhat trite) generalities, the most fundamental fact about Washington is that it was created for a definite purpose and has been developed according to a definite plan. Therein lies its unique distinction among American cities and among all existing capitals in the western world.[12]

Here is still another instance in which Americans can claim priority, for Washington was the first totally synthetic capital city, creating a precedent for Ottawa, Canberra, Brasilia, Islamabad, New Delhi, Ankara, Belmopan (Belize), and other such latterday efforts.[13] The only possible earlier claimant is St. Petersburg, which was founded in 1701; but that was a multipurpose development, one that did not become the seat of the Russian Empire until 1714.

As is well known, the original physical plan for the District of Columbia embodies the thoughts of Washington, Jefferson, and other luminaries as well as those of L'Enfant (Fig. 16.3).[14] The remarkable street layout and placement of official buildings resulting from their deliberations were, at least for the early decades of national existence, curiously at odds with the temper of the times and an egalitarian populace:

> All the baroque design motifs of European planning developed over the years in the old world suddenly and splendidly found application in this virgin setting for the capital of the newest of the world's nations. It was a supreme irony that the plan forms originally conceived to magnify the glories of despotic kings and emperors came to be applied as a national symbol of a country whose philosophical basis was so firmly rooted in democratic equality.[15]

And indeed for at least the first half-century this capital city of magnificent intentions was more of an international embarrassment than anything else, quite simply a physical ordeal to domestic and foreign sojourners alike. Sitting as it did on an unpleasantly mucky site, cursed with intolerable weather for more than half the year, and containing too few buildings and those separated by wide gaps, the unsightly young capital was desperately short of charm or symbolic prowess. Indeed for many years, the unfinished Capitol was the only structure to invite serious attention by reason of bulk or architectural aspiration. But gradually the situation improved. The Civil

318

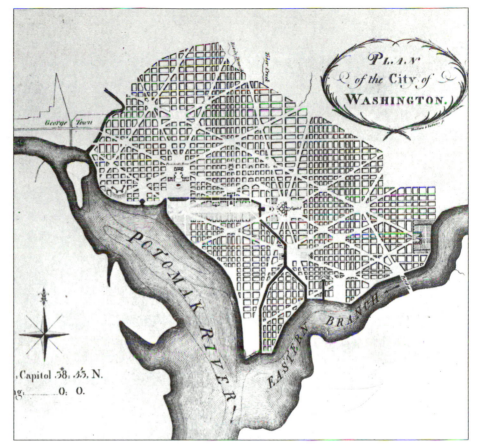

**Figure 16.3.**
The Plan of the City of
Washington, published in
1792. Basically the conception
and handiwork of Major
Pierre Charles L'Enfant, this
remarkable network of wide
diagonal avenues, named
after individual states, and
traffic circles superimposed
on a rectangular lattice of
streets remains very much
intact in the 1980s. Indeed,
the initial scheme has been
extended outward to the
District's boundary with
Maryland.

War began to energize what had been a sleepy quasi-southern town (a process pretty well consummated by the boom of World War II) with its surge of population, traffic, and official business. The implementation of the recommendations of the Macmillan Commission after the turn of the century, the cumulative efforts of one administration and congress after another, and the substantial accretion of population and wealth eventually yielded what we see today: the world's capital city *par excellence*, a metropolis of dazzling symbolic expressiveness, a nearly ideal pronouncement of the nation-state creed in material terms. L'Enfant's plan has been fleshed out—triumphantly. We behold a theatrical ensemble of majestic vistas, plazas, and fountains, overpowering phalanxes of embassies, government and national association offices, all of those grand shrines, museums, libraries, tombs, the most prestigious of burial places, all portentously designed, sophisticated landscaping that inspires more than a modicum of awe, and brilliant nighttime illumination of crucial structures and regiments of statuary (Fig. 16.4).

The impact of this uniquely potent assemblage of physical testimonials to the glory of the American nation–state extends far beyond the bounds of the Washington Metropolitan Area and its local aggregation of workers and

**Figure 16.4**

Looking northwest toward central Washington, D.C. from an airplane window during the summer of 1968, a view crowded with nationalistic objects. Clearly visible is the Mall, the principal axis of the L'Enfant plan and now a broad esplanade flanked by impressive government office buildings and museums. The National Capitol is situated at the Mall's eastern terminus and faces the Washington Monument and, beyond that, the Lincoln Memorial, while to the Capitol's rear we glimpse the two oldest structures in the Library of Congress complex.

residents. The capital is host each year to an enormous horde of tourists (who might realistically be labeled as pilgrims), along with many businessmen, officials, lobbyists, conventioneers, scholars, and others. The statistics on Washington's visitors are unsatisfactory, but it is safe to assume that they add up to an annual value of many millions. The fact that just one attraction, the Air and Space Museum, drew 10,014,892 persons in 1983 gives us a clue as to the total volume of the phenomenon.[16]

What draws most of these visitors to the shores of the Potomac are not the standard diversions of other tourist magnets but rather something out of the ordinary: the opportunity to gaze upon the sacred places and objects of Americanism, to join in a kind of nationalistic communion. To be sure, certain icons that symbolize the essence of America to the world and quicken the pulse of the patriot are to be found far beyond the District of Columbia—Niagara Falls, Brooklyn Bridge, Valley Forge, the Statue of Liberty, Grand Canyon, Independence Hall, and the Panama Canal among

320

them. Nevertheless, sightseers reveling in such tourist meccas as New York City, San Francisco, or New Orleans can, with a little luck, entirely escape any direct reminders of American nationhood or statehood. Such cultural amnesia is literally impossible in Washington. There is little question about the effectiveness of the Washington, D.C. strategy, even as early as the time of the Civil War: "The Union soldiers themselves were moved by their wartime experience in the city—visited previously only by their political representatives. Their actually seeing it was a fact of immeasurable psychological importance."[17]

Over and above the waves of standard tourists, there are all those who arrive for special occasions, for inaugurations, demonstrations, protests, and parades, by the tens, or even hundreds of thousands. If we regard a living landscape as embracing more than static objects, it is proper to include these milling crowds, along with the endless busloads and carloads of tourists, as integral elements of the Washington scene.

The outreach of this remarkable collection of nationalistic objects we call Washington, D.C. is not confined to those who experience it firsthand. For many years, reproductions of the major icons, e.g., the Capitol, White House, Washington Monument, Lincoln Memorial, Iwo Jima Memorial, and nearby Mount Vernon, have proliferated throughout the land in the form of newspaper and magazine illustrations, advertisements, posters, souvenirs, framed pictures, and other household decorations, and by the millions and hundreds of millions. Then, in recent years, these images show up daily and nightly on televised newscasts and other programs with the utmost regularity. It has become literally impossible to avoid some secondhand glimpse of the nation's capital in the course of an ordinary day.

There is still another channel through which the particular landscape ensemble of Washington, D.C. permeates the length and breadth of America: via the thousands of other cities and towns which act as administrative centers. The persuasiveness of the Washington example is apparent in many of the 50 state capitals, but even more widespread is a rather standardized formula for spelling out physically the sense of central authority in our more than 3,000 county seats, innumerable cities, and even some townships. The moral is most obvious in the realm of architecture. Clearly the single most influential model has been the National Capitol.[18] Although other federal buildings quite independently adopted a neoclassical form during the early 19th century, it was the Capitol (the name itself is significant) that most other official structures sought to emulate, especially after it finally assumed its present form during the Lincoln presidency. Indeed, the building has become far more than an architectural prototype, having risen to the level of transcendent national symbol.

The style of the National Capitol has been copied most slavishly in many of our state capitol buildings, but the process was gradual. "At the close of the eighteenth century there was no universally acceptable image of what an American state capitol should be."[19] It was during the 1820s and 1830s that

321  "statehouse design passed through a transition that led suddenly to the

adoption of a new architectural style, Greek Revival."[20] Then, after the National Capitol had become the symbolic anchor of the American Union in the 1850s, we find widespread mimicry of it in state capitols and other structures,[21] sometimes, as in the case of the buildings in Providence and Austin, virtual replicas.[22] During the late 19th and early 20th century, the architecture of official buildings, including state capitols, evolved through a series of interesting variations, but all still well within the general bounds of neoclassicism. Occasionally, as with Pennsylvania's capitol in Harrisburg, we encounter true magnificence.

The progression of styles for the much more numerous county courthouses has closely paralleled the history of state capitols.[23] After the initial generations of unprepossessing structures (but with lovely exceptions in central Virginia and a few other places), Greek Revival buildings dominated county seats during the second quarter of the 19th century, then persisted intermittently thereafter.[24] The designs of the post-Civil War era tended to move in tandem with the fashions in commercial and residential building. Scholars have just begun to survey the cityhalls of the United States,[25] but they are likely, when that task is completed, to document a similar procession of styles: the ascendancy of Greek Revival styles by mid-19th century, then a series of classically derivative designs up until the very recent past, all ultimately inspired by the examples in the District of Columbia.

Whatever the specific architectural styles and their hierarchical diffusion through space and time, the complex of governmental and symbolic items within state capitals represents a kind of delegated, relatively subdued grandeur radiated from Washington, although the sheer pomp of the Albany, New York achievement outshines the symbolic displays of more than half the national capitals of the world. Alongside the pretentious capitol building itself we are accustomed to seeing one or more large office structures to house a burgeoning bureaucracy, one or several monuments and pools, quite possibly a federal courthouse, and perhaps a museum or auditorium (or civic center). On a smaller scale, this is also what we usually find in county seats, but with the frequent addition of the county jail, Department of Agriculture, Social Security, and other federal branch offices (Fig. 16.5). It is interesting and significant to note that all these physical trappings of civil authority—these visually and locationally dominating landscape complexes—generally exclude the ecclesiastical, quite unlike the standard patterns of urban design in Latin America, Québec, or premodern Europe. The cathedrals of Washington, New York City, and other major metropolises, impressive though they may be in their own right, cannot claim pride of place—except, possibly, for Salt Lake City's remarkable temple. There is no question who occupies the driver's seat. Equally intriguing is the fact that the governmental-cum-ceremonial cluster is invariably offset from the commercial (also usually churchless) core of the city in all the state capitals as well as in Washington, even though they may be only a comfortable stroll apart. This description also holds for many, but far from all, county seats.[26]

There is more to be said about the direct and indirect impact of the federal government upon the look of the American land, but it is helpful to stand back a moment to try to grasp the sheer enormity of the present-day physical apparatus of the central government:

> By 1974 the federal government was a property holder with worldwide possessions worth $83 billion plus utility systems, roads, dams, bridges, and harbor and port facilities valued at $39.3 billion. It had gone from the construction of less than a dozen buildings annually in the early years of the Republic to a domestic inventory of over 400,000 buildings containing floor space equivalent to 1,250 Empire State Buildings. It leased properties in another 50,000 locations . . . on its 200th birthday in 1976 the Corps of Engineers could look back on a record of constructing 4,000 civil works, 25,000 miles of navigable waterways, and 400 man-made lakes.[27]

Undoubtedly the most ubiquitous manifestation of a federal presence has been that of the postal system. Although the system has existed for well over 200 years, our post office buildings have attained some degree of visual consistency only within the past several decades (Fig. 16.6). Operating out of special buildings, corners of shops, or even their own residences, postmasters served clustered settlements of all sizes and even some

**Figure 16.5**
The Edgar County Courthouse in Paris, Illinois, a characteristic late 19th-century structure sited within a central courthouse square, in this instance also the center of the business district. A Civil War monument is visible here, but not the law offices and various government bureaus that gravitate to county seats.

**Figure 16.6**
This post office, probably
built in the 1920s, resides in
anonymity in the author's
records, but it does not
matter. Close facsimiles of
this building, with its
inevitable flagpole, can be
found the length and breadth
of the country in small and
medium-sized cities. The
neoclassical style has
dominated post office
architecture from the turn of
the century until at least the
1950s.

completely rural neighborhoods. Quite apart from their service functions, these post offices are also often important sites for social interaction on a daily basis, especially in smaller towns. There were over 33,000 of these establishments around the turn of the century, when they were at their geographical apogee; since then, for various reasons, their number has dwindled by almost 50 percent. But even as attrition decimated their ranks, the buildings constructed by the General Services Administration, especially from the 1920s onward, began to be standardized. Their design has frequently been latterday classical, like many a contemporary bank, or some other nostalgic style, distinctive enough in appearance that strangers have little difficulty finding the post office somewhere near the town center. On a more intimate scale, we also find within all our cities countless mailboxes, formerly painted olive drab, but more recently a jaunty red, white, and blue. And if we include the mobile dimensions of our landscape, it is hard to ignore the fleet of thousands of postal trucks in the same colors dashing along our streets and highways.

## The New Deal and its legacy

Without any doubt the greatest leap forward in the history of the federal government's involvement with the American landscape occurred with the advent of the New Deal.[28] The qualitative change in the relationships between political center and hinterland that became so visually blatant then has continued and intensified in the course of World War II and a period of Cold War and relative prosperity that has persisted more than four decades.

Despite much campaign rhetoric about the wisdom of restoring power to the states and local communities, the absolute and relative strength of the nation–state continues to grow. The great transformations of the 1930s and afterwards were actually the flowering of processes that had been evident for some time. We have commented on the rôle of the postal system, and, as has already been suggested, the venerable Corps of Engineers has literally reshaped much of the surface of America. The most dramatic instances are of this century and include the taming (at least temporarily) of the Ohio River and the lower Mississippi (Fig. 16.7). The ecological and socio-economic as well as cosmetic effects of building an elaborate system of dams, levees, sluiceways, and other engineering works are complex and extend well beyond the banks of the streams throughout the regions drained by them. A definitive account of the geographical impact of all the Corps' many stream projects, canals, coast and harbor, and other enterprises—something no scholar has yet essayed—would fill a large monograph to overflowing.

As in certain other advanced nation–states, an even more momentous way by which the central regime has imprinted itself upon the land has been via a national highway system. Toward the beginning of the past century, when Albert Gallatin was a force to be reckoned with, an era of internal improvements almost came to pass. Although ambitious plans for a system of highways and canals were drafted, the only federally sponsored project to come close to completion was the National Road (later U.S. 40) running from Baltimore to central Illinois. But, then, for almost 100 years, Washington was only an indirect agent at best while hundreds of miles of canals and tens of thousands of miles of railroad track were generated by private enterprise, municipalities, and individual state governments (often

**Figure 16.7**
Dam and lock on the upper Ohio River a few miles below the Ohio–Pennsylvania line. The Corps of Engineers has managed to tame this formerly flood-prone stream, with important consequences for the location and operation of heavy industries. Virtually all the freight barged today in the United States uses waterways built or maintained by the federal government.

on land donated by the national regime). It was only in the wake of the automotive revolution of the early 20th century that the federal government finally bestirred itself and began to take charge. Still, it was not until 1925 that a federal agency mandated a national highway numbering system, began the installation of standardized road signs,[29] and made some gestures toward uniform engineering criteria and guidelines for roadside landscaping.[30] The watershed event, however, was the passage of the Federal-Aid Highway Act of 1956 and the initiation of an interstate highway system which, when nearly completed in 1983, included some 43,028 miles of limited-access roads.

When we consider either the immediate landscape implications or the socioeconomic by-products of what is certainly the world's greatest public works project, we must reach for superlatives. The existence of such long stretches of uniformly engineered pavement, the thousands of standardized bridges, overpasses, and lighting installations, broad swaths of rather monotonous roadside landscaping, the totally unsurprising service plazas, and all those signs of unvarying size, shape, color, and typography has become one of the central facts of American life, and a more than trivial portion of our collective sensory input. We are not prepared as yet to assess the impact of this grandiose web of concrete on our economy, society, ecology, and life-patterns—no geographer or other social scientist has been brave enough to try—but unquestionably it is staggering. The two sets of effects, the visual and socioeconomic, intersect and are most obvious in metropolitan areas, especially in the vicinity of beltways looping around such cities as Atlanta, Baltimore, Chicago, St. Louis, or Washington. Veritable mini-cities of innovative form and function have materialized at or near many of the interchanges, but the less obtrusive consequences of such high-speed roadways have filtered far out into suburbia and exurbia and, conversely, back into the inner cities.

The landscape legacy of the New Deal is rich and varied in kind and effect, ranging from total transformation of an area down to the most subtle of nuances. Unquestionably, the Tennessee Valley Authority (TVA) is a prime example of what a rich, determined central regime can achieve in terms of remaking the landscape of a region as well as its economy.[31] Other hydroelectric and reclamation projects of the same period, such as Hoover and Grand Coulee Dams and their associated new lakes, among many another in the West, have altered the visual scene greatly, and have also affected patterns of recreational facilities and land occupance near and far, but not to the same degree as in TVA country.

Some of the more idealistic New Deal ventures involved resettling distressed rural folk in such places as the Matanuska colony in Alaska[32] or the Cumberland Homesteads in West Virginia,[33] or the creation of such model communities as Greenbelt, Maryland with their distinctive patterns of street layout and landscaping. Much more widespread were the visible effects of the many programs initiated or executed by the U.S. Department of Agriculture under Henry A. Wallace, notably the Agricultural Adjustment

326

**Figure 16.8**
Only scattered patches of the
New Deal's Shelter Belt
project were ever actually
planted, and even fewer have
survived, as seen in this 1983
view of Red River Valley
farmland near Grand Forks,
North Dakota. But a majority
of farmsteads are sensibly
equipped with their own
private tree and brush
shelters along their northern
and western edges.

Administration, the Soil Conservation Service, and the Farm Security
Administration. Among the results were changes in absolute and relative
acreages of crops, wholesale implementation of contour plowing and
building of checkdams to retard soil erosion, the creation of thousands of
farm ponds, and the reforestation of marginal tracts. Although the Shelter
Belt, one of Franklin Roosevelt's pet programs—the planting of extensive
strips of trees and shrubs the length of the Great Plains to protect fields and
homesteads and, possibly, mitigate the impact of periodic droughts—was
never fully realized, enough was done to give a boskier look to much of the
region (Fig. 16.8).

A thick volume would be needed just to catalog all the projects with
landscape implications financed or directed by various emergency relief
agencies of the New Deal, notably the Public Works Administration, Civil
Works Administration, Civilian Conservation Corps, Works Progress
Administration, and National Youth Administration. Suffice it to say that
they are numerous, diverse in size and character, and located in all manner
of settings, urban and rural. Some have been durable, others ephemeral.
Many of the projects bear the unmistakable look of governmental
benevolence or supervision, but in many instances only an expert could
detect Uncle Sam's fine hand. Despite many *faux pas*, the aggregate social
and environmental results of all these efforts were definitely positive. Less
celebrated than some of the foregoing but ultimately more spatially
pervasive and certainly much vaster in social consequence has been the
work initiated by the Rural Electrification Administration in the 1930s. It is
difficult for us at this late date to visualize life and work when electrical
power was available to only a minute fraction of farms and not too many of

the small towns of the nation.[34] The addition of poles and wires to the scene is really minor compared to the truly revolutionary changes in economic and social behavior which, in turn, have spawned notable landscape results.

Within many major metropolises, the New Deal manufactured new cityscapes by funding inexpensive public housing for impoverished slum dwellers. The institutional look of such mass architecture is undeniable. The program survived the demise of the New Deal, in fact it intensified with the urgent demands for housing war industry workers from 1941 to 1945. Since then, public housing programs have persisted, but rather sporadically. They have usually involved some combination of federal and local planning, funding, and administration, and have also generated much acrimony when large areas of older housing have been razed (often for unconscionably long periods) and their residents shunted elsewhere.

Among the more colorful outcomes of New Deal relief programs were the thousands of works of art produced by mainly impoverished painters and sculptors under federal patronage.[35] Although most of the murals, easel paintings, and statues—many of considerable merit—are to be found inside post offices and other government buildings, we encounter a fair number outdoors.

There are still other ways in which the federal government has manifested itself in the American landscape, especially in recent times. Such communities as Oak Ridge, Tennessee and Los Alamos, New Mexico are purely and simply total federal artifacts, and certainly cannot be confused with ordinary cities. There is a strong case to be made for the claim that Huntsville, Alabama, Hanford, Washington, and the urban developments bordering Cape Canaveral are the offspring of federal largesse or that much of the same situation prevails in California's Silicon Valley, North Carolina's Research Triangle, and any number of other research and development districts on the outskirts of various metropolises and university towns. All such areas do share a distinctive appearance. Within the industrial realm, the Nuclear Regulatory Commission has veto power over both the design and siting of nuclear power plants, while the Environmental Protection Agency's regulations almost certainly have had a perceptible effect on where certain plants have located and what they look like, but the topic awaits investigation.

No one who has driven past such federal penitentiaries as those at Marion, Illinois, Lewisburg, Pennsylvania, or Leavenworth, Kansas, or has seen Alcatraz from afar is likely to forget them soon. More secluded and more ephemeral have been the euphemistically labeled "relocation camps" for Japanese-Americans during World War II or the detention facilities for Vietnamese and other refugees during the past few decades.

We have the federal and affected state governments to thank for the enactment and enforcement of strip-mining regulations that have gone so far to alleviate the scandal of thoroughly hideous, lifeless landscapes previously left behind by mining operations. Less esthetically pleasing perhaps than reclaimed surface mines but even more widely evident along the nation's highways is the rôle of Uncle Sam as advertiser. Billboards beyond counting tout bond sales, enlistment in the armed forces, and sundry government drives and programs. Although its basic function was that of advisor, coordinator, and general cheerleader, the American Revolution Bicentennial Administration did catalyze thousands of projects in and around the year 1976, a fair percentage of which yielded new or remodeled artifacts in public places.[36] There are some interesting regional differentials in the incidence of such projects with the North Central states scoring especially well.[37]

The impress of the American nation–state does not stop at our borders. As already noted, American military cemeteries are maintained in a number of overseas localities. American embassies and other buildings associated with them stand on conspicuous sites in more than a hundred foreign capitals, many of them designed to be visually assertive. No other country operates as many military installations on foreign soil as does the United States (or religious missions too for that matter), and the more important of them not only occupy great tracts of land but also have stimulated many private enterprises along their peripheries, as has happened around major bases within the United States. Frequent adjuncts to the American diplomatic and military presence are the "Little Americas," hermetic enclaves of residences, shops, schools, recreational and other facilities that inhibit serious dealings with the surrounding land and population.

It is an asymmetric situation, since, outside Washington and its embassies and some international headquarters, such as those for the World Bank and the United Nations complex in New York City, there is virtually no hint of the existence of foreign governments or international agencies to be sensed within the United States. But one might offer the same observation about the near-invisibility of supranational government in any of the advanced nation–states of the world, except Switzerland.

Visual symptoms of an international order are not the only potential authority-related items missing from the American scene. Because of the peculiarities of the political system and, ultimately perhaps, the basic nature of the collective cultural psyche, the country lacks anything approaching land use planning, zoning, or control at the national level, of the sort practiced in Scandinavia, the Netherlands, Great Britain, and many socialist countries. Also lacking is any centralized educational system (except for that run by the Bureau of Indian Affairs) and thus centrally determined school architecture such as prevails in any number of foreign lands. The United States does not own or operate a network of railroads, a national airline, or shipping company, unlike Canada, Mexico, or so many Old World countries. Consequently, their equipment and logos are missing from the scene.

329

## Indirect governmental influence on the landscape

We are far from finished with the federal factor even after considering the lengthy inventory of landscape features which demonstrate its direct operation. In their totality the ways in which federal legislation, policies, and regulations have acted obliquely to mold our environs may outweigh direct cause-and-effect phenomena. In fact, it is likely that no corner of this land has escaped being affected to some visible degree by the indirect workings of central authority. Perhaps the most obvious case is that of federal tax laws and V.A. and F.H.A. loan programs. There is a general consensus as to their crucial rôle in the explosive growth of suburbia since World War II and the character of its housing. Similarly, urban renewal, the boom in office buildings and condominiums, gentleman farming, and the historic preservation craze would have fared quite differently without certain tax advantages under federal law. Undoubtedly, it would be hard to identify a more potent force in the dynamics of the current landscape than the Internal Revenue Service, however indirect or devious the chain of causality. It is also easy to demonstrate the multifaceted effects of U.S.D.A. policy in the countryside via many channels, including its county agents and the work of the allied schools of agriculture at the land grant colleges: upon crop choices and acreages, modes of cultivation and storage, and much else. In related fashion, tariffs and import/export regulations have interesting landscape repercussions in both the manufacturing and agricultural sectors. Vivid confirmation of this assertion is apparent to anyone who scans the contrasting land use patterns along the Minnesota–Manitoba boundary.

There are many other ways, as yet unexplored by the scholar, in which a huge, manysided federal establishment has brought about important secondhand changes in our human geography during recent times. The availability of Social Security benefits and other federal welfare programs over the past 50 years has given many individuals, especially the elderly and unemployed, a latitude in choosing place of residence that was previously nonexistent, and the results have been quite substantial.

Plainly enough, the number and attributes of inhabitants is a prime factor in the making of landscapes. In so far as ethnicity is a visible phenomenon in this country—and few would argue to the contrary—the immigration laws and regulations that have been on the books for the past hundred years have contributed striking details to the landscapes of many sections of the United States. Taking a final example from among many other candidates, efforts at the national level to prohibit the production or consumption of alcohol and certain narcotics have certainly affected patterns of crop production, and also led to the existence of clandestine landscapes, notably those where marijuana fields or illicit stills are hidden.

Much of the foregoing discussion could be transferred to other advanced urban-industrial or post-industrial countries with only modest amounts of revision. But there is one respect in which the landscape expression of
central authority in the United States approaches uniqueness: the voluntary

**Figure 16.9**
The incidence of flag display
is especially noticeable
among commercial
establishments in the United
States. Was this Subaru
dealer aware of the irony in
his lavish exploitation of the
national emblem?

display by the citizenry and business community of the emblems of statehood (Fig. 16.9).[38] The leading items in question are the national flag and the American bald eagle, the latter being the national totem since its incorporation into the Great Seal in 1782. Less overt, but still quite meaningful, is the extensive use of the national colors, the red-white-and-blue combination, in virtually every possible context and the private and commercial display of the tricolor shield also derived from the Great Seal. All sovereign states have their flags, of course, and other obligatory national symbols, but nowhere else is the incidence of flag and totem display so prevalent in absolute or relative terms, and principally on residential, commercial, industrial, and other private properties in addition to their abundance in official buildings and grounds.

The explanation for such exceptionalism is not simple, but it has to do with a spontaneous "statefulness" on the part of an American population lacking a monarchy or the attachments to traditions rooted in ancient history and geography characteristic of other successful nation–states. And, like most of the other phenomena treated in this chapter, such veneration of flag and eagle is a time-dependent phenomenon and one in keeping with the evolutionary model for the American polity sketched earlier. Until the Civil War period, the flag was seldom seen outside official sites and military installations. Since then, the fragmentary evidence suggests steady proliferation in all manner of public and private space. Field work also indicates that the incidence of both flags and eagles is greatest in the northeastern quadrant of the country and lowest in the former Confederacy. The historical geography of the eagle is rather more complex than that of the flag. The latter has always been an essentially content-free emblem signifying no more than allegiance to a state. But the eagle has undergone a metamorphosis from its initial incarnation as a symbol of the early libertarian principles of American nationhood into a flaglike emblem expressing only identification with the nation–state.

## State and local government landscape elements

As we descend from the federal level to the state and other more localized jurisdictions, the landscape expression of the governmental factor is more limited, in territorial extent obviously, but also in terms of intensity and multiplicity of forms. Nevertheless, the visible impact of local government is much too important to be overlooked, and its salience for the landscape has been increasing over time. Two striking state-level examples ratify this point. Any traveler crossing into Nevada from an adjacent state by road or dropping from the sky into its airports would have to be blind (and also deaf) not to realize how great a difference gambling legislation can make in the ambience and economy of places. The visitor is assaulted by the blazing lights and blaring racket of the borderpoint casinos and satellite hotels and restaurants (Fig. 16.10). Much more soothing visually is one's entrance into Vermont with its sensitively maintained highways and roadsides, but especially its strict control of signs, which makes it a virtual paragon among the states in a landscape sense. Stateline liquor stores, fireworks stands, cut-rate cigarette emporia, and, once upon a time, shops selling colored margarine have been common sights, obviously battening on legal constraints just across the border.

**Figure 16.10**
It is not difficult to pinpoint the Nevada-California state line in this 1975 photo taken near Lake Tahoe. The contrast between the grandiose hotel–casinos in Nevada (background) and the smaller, relatively drab motels in California (foreground), where gambling is illegal is striking.

At a more restricted scale, we can find examples by the score or hundred of sharp visual breaks between a city and the communities which adjoin it. Thus, there is the City of Washington, with its limitations on building height (and other land use controls) nestled craterlike within the relatively unfettered Maryland and Virginia suburbs that loom above it. Equally jarring and abrupt is the passage from Chicago's West Side to the sylvan suburb of Oak Park, from Detroit to such outliers as Ferndale or elegant Grosse Pointe, or outward from the truly unique Carmel, California. In the author's hometown, one can traverse the line separating the Borough of State College (so intensely jealous of its appearance) and its satellite suburbs many thousands of times without ceasing to be startled by the sudden alteration of vistas. Even starker are the contrasts between city and environs when the former is the barony of a benevolent corporation, as has happened with Hershey, Pennsylvania or Dow Chemical's Midland, Michigan. The imprint of central authority is not limited to standard political jurisdictions. There are some notable instances where special districts, formed by interstate or intercity compact, have left their mark upon the land, but perhaps no example is more definitive than that of the New York Port Authority, which, under the napoleonic command of Robert Moses, imposed its dominating complex of bridges, tunnels, and other crucial constructions upon the New York and New Jersey scene.[39]

Thus we find that states, counties, incorporated municipalities, townships, and other local governmental entities do exercise certain powers that the federal government is generally unwilling or constitutionally unable to assert. Among these are the planning and zoning of land use, regulation of liquor sales and consumption, building codes, sign and tree ordinances, particular types of taxation, maintenance of educational, hospital, and welfare systems, licensing of utilities, refuse disposal, and the management of airports and harbors. In addition, of course, these lesser units parallel federal functions by operating highway systems, parks, forests, historical sites, and prisons. There may be a certain visual uniformity within their boundaries and discontinuities at borders. Thus, for example, each state highway system tends to have a visual personality of its own. The design of roadways and roadside, signage, rest areas, and picnic grounds all share a certain commonality. Quite unforgettable, for example, are the sculpture gardens that gladden the motorist's heart alongside the rest stops for Nebraska's interstates. The same observation applies to statewide systems of parks, forests, colleges, and historical sites. Is there a single state-supported college in Illinois that does not have its Altgeld Hall reeking of late Victorian fussiness? Even within our larger cities we can detect familial resemblances among primary and secondary school structures and in park buildings and playgrounds.

Almost endless is the roster of impacts subnational political jurisdictions have had upon the design of our lived-in American world, and by no means have all the ramifications, direct and indirect, of the hegemony of an overarching federal establishment been explored. But to bring this chapter to an end, perhaps two general observations can be made.

Even a casual survey of the history of the American landscape reveals a remarkable turnabout. There was a time less than two centuries ago when the handiwork of a puny, remote federal regime was almost never to be seen, and when the palpable imprint of local government was relatively feeble. Today, in total, stunning contrast, the impact of political authority, whether national or nearby, is inescapably intrusive. It is a revolutionary state of affairs reflecting the profound changes in the structure of our society and collective mentality, and is detectable in every department of socioeconomic interaction. We have only to look about us to collect the evidence.

Unfortunately, there has been extremely little in the way of systematic looking about. Most of the assertions presented above are undocumented, being based on personal observation and recollections of nonscholarly printed matter, for the simple reason that there are so few scholarly documents to cite. Thus this chapter is an introductory sketch and, in a sense, a programatic appeal; it should become hopelessly out of date before many more years have passed.

# Chapter seventeen
## Landscapes of private power and wealth

WILLIAM K. WYCKOFF

In order to gain and to hold the esteem of men it is not sufficient merely to possess wealth or power. The wealth or power must be put in evidence, for esteem is awarded only on evidence.

Thorstein Veblen

To dismiss Society as vanity or vanities or as a *chronique scandaleuse* is to throw away a rich segment of human experience, molded of wisdom and folly, graciousness and snobbery.

Dixon Wecter

ALTHOUGH ALEXIS DE TOCQUEVILLE was struck by "the general equality of condition among the people" of 19th-century America, the national landscape, from the graceful Georgian houses of its colonial era to the luxury condominiums of the present day, owes significant portions of its character and diversity to a numerically small but powerful upper class. These landscapes of private power and wealth represent the imprint of perhaps only one-half of 1 percent of the national population and yet their mark is pervasive, spanning every region of the country, and encompassing urban, suburban, and rural settings.[1]

The special rôle played by the nation's affluent class in shaping the American scene often has a complex expression on the modern landscape. Wealthy tastes have changed through time and the result is an accumulation of features that reflect the varied predilections for house styles, neighborhood settings, and resort playgrounds enjoyed by successive generations from 1700 to the present. Further complicating the picture is the fact that these landscapes are often partially obscured or profoundly transformed in their contemporary settings. Today, old mansions are converted and rural estates are subdivided to make way for suburban housing and shopping centers. In addition, there is a regional unevenness in the geography of such landscapes. Portions of the Virginia countryside, New York State's Hudson Valley, old Newport, or the smart suburbs of Hillsborough, San Francisco, Grosse Pointe, Detroit, or Dunwoody, Atlanta, literally reek of America's better sort, while in other settings, their signature is absent, forgotten, or substantially altered by subsequent changes to the landscape.

## Enduring themes

### English affinities

America's élite, from their colonial origins, have aped the English with enthusiasm and abandon. As one Virginian lamented in the 1760s, "Alas! Great Britain, their vices have been extended to America! . . . it must be stopped, or it will bear all before it with an impetuous sway."[2] Such warnings notwithstanding, America's prevailingly English roots are ubiquitously displayed, especially in the residential landscapes of the nation's upper class.[3] From 17th-century Virginia to 20th-century suburbia, the wealthy's fondness for English-style architecture has stamped the national scene in lasting ways. The epidemic of the balanced "colonial Georgian" house endures. English Gothic and Tudor revivals provide additional Anglo variants (Fig. 17.1). Gardens surrounding such homes almost inevitably echo English landscape tastes, whether they be the formal symmetrical displays of fountains, statuary, and arranged shrubbery inspired by Capability Brown or the presumably more natural assemblages of irregularly shaped lawns, wandering fieldstone paths, and rambling arbors and trellised vegetation of late Victorian era esthetics.[4] Even the swimming pool and private bathhouse, occasional residential additions by 1920, and increasingly common thereafter, were diffused through British traditions of garden and ornamental pool design.[5]

Beyond the home, the upper crust often identifies itself with distinctively British social institutions. The steady dignity of the Episcopalian church

**Figure 17.1** Stylized English countryhouse living in the affluent American suburb.

**Figure 17.2**
Lawrenceville School, Lawrenceville, New Jersey, showing original campus designed by Frederick Law Olmstead (upper center) and recent additions (bottom right).

perhaps is one of the more enduring symbols on the landscape which reflects the public expression of upper-class values and tastes.[6] It is often an integral part of the neighborhood élite scene, urban, suburban, or rural. In addition, the wealthy's hunger for private social clubs on the London model sparked the initiation of such metropolitan organizations after 1830,[7] and their wider appearance in the downtowns of most American cities is linked to the economic growth of the post-Civil War era.[8] Other Anglo traditions shape the proper education of élite youth.[9] Private day schools serve such needs within urban and suburban areas. In addition, élite boarding schools have been an educational option since prestigious Philips Academy began the tradition in Andover, Massachusetts in 1778. Regionally focused from New England south to Virginia, the private boarding school saw much renewed growth between 1880 and 1910.[10] Such institutions consciously copy the look and presumption of their English counterparts (Fig. 17.2). Traditionally rural or village-set campus landscapes are heavily Anglicized and such exclusive environments still pave the way for further education at élite private universities such as Harvard, Yale, and Princeton.[11]

America's élite also play the British way and many national landscapes of sport and leisure reflect these traditional connections. The aristocrat's penchant for fox hunting continues in northern Virginia, nearby areas of Maryland, the Kentucky Bluegrass country, and upstate New York.[12] The pleasures of the hunt are also replicated on the large woodland plantations of the South on acreage accumulated by monied Northerners who

337

purchased extensive tracts in portions of South Carolina, southern Georgia, and northern Florida after the Civil War.[13] Horse-racing became popular in late 17th-century England and the sport was readily transferred to Virginia, South Carolina, and Long Island.[14] The Kentucky Bluegrass affiliation with the horsey set began early: Louisville had its first racetrack in 1784 and Lexington in 1790, beginning a long regional élite tradition that persists today.[15] American pleasure-boating also has British roots.[16] The New York Yacht Club was organized in 1844 and their first cruise was to the nearby stylish resort of Newport, Rhode Island. In the present century, the older yachting communities of New England and Long Island and the newer Sun Belt marina landscapes of conspicuous consumption, replete with pleasure craft, dockside condominiums, and expensive restaurants, still display distinctive brands of American affluence.[17]

Modern golf, via England and Scotland, was introduced in the United States after 1880, precisely when the élite were busily suburbanizing on the edge of many larger American cities.[18] The result was the peculiarly American institution of the suburban country club. Golf typically has served as the sporting focal point in such settings since the Country Club was first established near Brookline, Massachusetts in 1882. By the 1920s over 5,000 golf courses, both private and public, dotted the American landscape as the sport diffused widely to the ranks of the middle class. Tennis followed a similar pattern.[19] Introduced via Bermuda to New York in 1875, the sport found ready acceptance in such élite haunts as Newport, Nahant, and suburban Germantown. By the 1920s the avocation spread to lesser social circles, although many of America's better sort still distinguish themselves by building their own backyard courts or, particularly in the Sun Belt, by improving their game and tan at any one of several hundred exclusive tennis resorts.[20] Polo, never widely adopted by the middle class, also arrived in America from Britain (who acquired it in 19th-century India). It quickly gained favor with the horse- and game-loving upper class once it was introduced in 1876 by J. G. Bennett.[21] Extensive suburban and often country club settings are best for the sport since regulation polo grounds require eight times the cleared level land necessary for a football field. Such sites continue as useful landscape signatures in identifying the rich today and modern concentrations focus on the suburban Northeast, the metropolitan clusters of Chicago, Los Angeles, and San Francisco, as well as traditional resort settings such as Saratoga and West Palm Beach (Fig. 17.3).

### Social and spatial exclusivity

According to social historian Mary Cable, "In America the rich always herd in colonies."[22] Indeed, the rich are an enclave-creating class and their desire for privacy and security often encourages them to congregate in private clubs, schools, resorts, and communities. Because the upper crust often do live near one another, they frequently concentrate their impact on the landscape in well-defined neighborhoods and exclusive districts. Within urban areas, persisting affluent neighborhoods were apparent in colonial

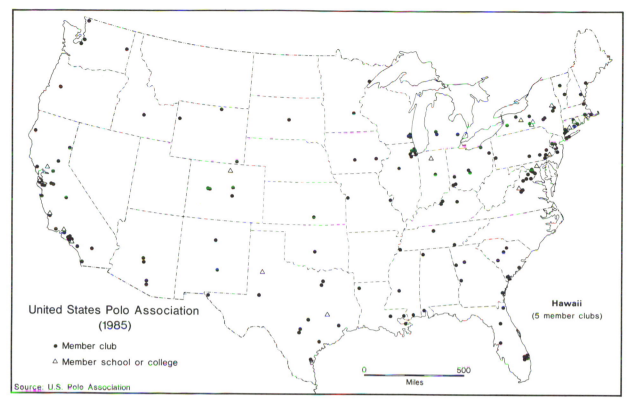

**Figure 17.3**

The geography of polo. This acquired taste is fairly well distributed across the United States, though adherents cluster somewhat in the urbanized Eastern seaboard, the Chicago area, and California.

---

and antebellum America. In the 1840s, over half of Philadelphia's wealthy lived on only three streets, and Boston's élite during the same period were quite concentrated just east and north of the Common.[23]

The desire for social homogeneity and spatial exclusivity is even more dramatically displayed in the consciously designed garden suburb of the late 19th and 20th centuries. These planned upper class communities originated in the 1860s with Llewellyn Park near West Orange, New Jersey, and in later decades the garden suburb became a well-developed and almost standard-ized landscape feature on the periphery of most sizable American cities.[24] These "capitalist communes" persist as bastions of the upper class and their landscapes reflect wealthy tastes and preferences for proper living.[25] They feature low-density housing on large lots, a lack of commercial land uses, often gently curving and landscaped streets, and a stylized architecture that blends well with a predominantly pastoral surrounding.

The managed landscapes of the garden suburb, both in the late 19th century and today, frequently are maintained through legal as well as social codes of conduct.[26] Restrictive covenants in deeds declare minimum lot sizes and acceptable standards of architecture and landscaping. Zoning ordin-ances are passed to exclude undesirable land uses. Well-known examples

339

include Tuxedo Park (near New York City, begun in the 1890s), Shaker Heights (outside Cleveland, constructed in two phases: 1910 and 1920), and River Oaks (an unusual planned enclave in an otherwise unplanned Houston, established in the 1920s). Undoubtedly one of the more dramatic recent displays is Fisher Island, Florida, just off the coast from Miami. The island, once the playground of the Vanderbilts, has been converted to an exclusive community of condominiums, villas, tennis courts, and swimming pools, all designed around a Mediterranean motif and accessible to the mainland only by boat or private helicopter (Fig. 17.4).

*Key social transformations*
Although social and spatial exclusivity are dominant themes in the landscapes of America's élite, there is a continuing tension between such tendencies and the desire on the part of the wealthy to display their success for all to see. But here an important distinction needs to be made between old and new affluence. Often the established aristocracy feels much less

340

**Figure 17.4**
(adjacent and opposite)
Social and spatial exclusivity.
Fisher Island, Florida,
according to promoters, "is
now being transformed into a
unique, exclusive enclave for
the élite . . . comfortably
insulated from the rest of the
world while being only
minutes away."

obliged to parade its inherited assets to the larger world, while the first generation wealthy are far more liable to be ostentatious.[27] In the residential landscapes of the former, houses are often smaller and older, well set back from the road, and sensitive to the integrity of original architectural design, while the latter, with a similar income, might have homes that are larger, newer, well in view of public thoroughfares, and that more freely display current fads and fashions (Fig. 17.5).[28] Indeed, the stress of not belonging to the established upper class may compel the newly-rich to display so lavishly the fruits of their recent accumulations. The free-wheeling years of the late 19th century perhaps produced the most opulent examples of new wealth on the American scene, but the process continues today as first generation recruits to the upper crust confirm their newly acquired status by prominently displaying it on the landscape.

Another related social process with even greater consequences for the larger American scene is the unrelenting desire of middle- and lower-class Americans to know about and emulate the life-styles of the rich and famous.[29] The methods of diffusing the fashions of high living include magazines, builder's guides, novels, the cinema, television, and, of course, the élite landscape itself. Large segments of the national scene have been shaped in the process. Specific architectural styles, from Georgian Colonial and Greek Revival to late Victorian have diffused down the socioeconomic

341

**Figure 17.5**
Old and new wealth on the
American landscape. A
secluded Georgian-style
country estate near
Charlottesville, Virginia (top)
and a recent neo-Georgian
suburban house in Athens,
Georgia (bottom).

hierarchy to mold the mass residential landscapes of middle- and lower-class American neighborhoods (Fig. 17.6).[30] The entire process of suburbanization, an élite phenomenon of the 19th century, spread to the middle class, along with the automobile and the decentralizing metropolis in the present century. Leisure-time activities follow similar paths of social diffusion.[31] The institution of the summer vacation is a miniature version of the élite's enduring penchant for seasonal travel to resorts, and the modern middle-class obsessions with golf, tennis, and boating trace their roots to originally élite inclination. It is an old and familiar story: as a colonial Virginian remarked, "Extravagance, love of gaieties, the taste for modish pleasures, are in a chain of imitation carried down to the lowest people, who would seem to have a notion of what high life is."[32]

**Figure 17.6**
The social and spatial diffusion of the Greek Revival. An affluent upstate New York farmstead in Wyoming County (top left), an antebellum version in Madison, Georgia (top right), a middle-class southern pyramid-style house with Greek styling, also in Madison, Georgia (bottom left), and a Grecian-style southern farmhouse in Morgan County, Georgia (bottom right).

## The lineage of landscape change

*Changing élite geography: town houses, country seats, and resorts*

Traditionally, rural and urban environments have been shaped by distinctive elements of America's upper crust (Fig. 17.7). But the record of
landscape change is complex because of the high mobility of élite
populations. Even in the colonial era, America's wealthier sort revealed an
avid predilection for maintaining multiple residences. Northern merchants
who kept townhouses as permanent homes often designed nearby country
retreats for seasonal living. The proper Philadelphia gentleman was obliged
to have a rural estate along the Delaware or Schuylkill Rivers, and even the
less ostentatious Bostonian might have a nearby, perhaps less showy retreat
in Milton, Medford, or Roxbury.[33] In the South, townhouses were relatively
uncommon for many of the colonial Virginia gentry, but Charleston, South
Carolina developed a distinctive and early urban aristocracy that included
many absentee landowners who spent summers removed from their rice
and indigo plantations.[34] Longer trips to colonial-era spas and resorts were
increasingly in vogue after 1760 and included excursions to take the waters
at Bristol and Yellow Springs near Philadelphia and to Warm Springs in

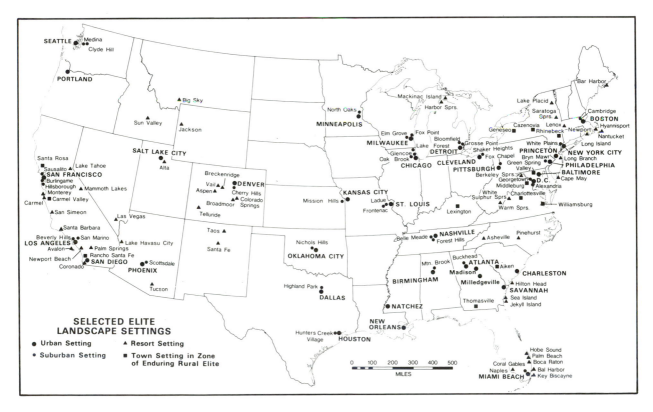

**Figure 17.7**
A typology of American landscape settings of the wealthy and powerful.

Berkeley County, Virginia.[35] Seaside resorts such as Newport, Rhode Island offered dancing, racing, and boating to an increasingly cosmopolitan colonial upper class.[36]

During the antebellum period, the southern élite's penchant for both rural and urban life expanded along with the cotton frontier. As a result, some of today's finest architectural displays of high living in the South are not in the countryside, where plantation houses often were quite modest in scale, but in towns such as Macon, Madison, and Milledgeville, Georgia and Natchez, Mississippi.[37] In the North, life in well-defined élite neighborhoods became ever more opulent in Philadelphia, New York, and Boston.[38] Increasingly, the wealthy also took advantage of improved steamboat and rail connections and maintained second homes, typically in rural or village settings within a few hours to a day's travel from their urban base. In fact, by the 1850s, improvements in urban-focused railroads in the Northeast were so great that a new option in life-styles was available. The creation of élite exurbs along the rail lines meant that it was possible to live in a low-density, pastoral, residential setting and yet have ready daily access to urban amenities and employment.[39]

Transport improvements also lessened travel times to more distant seasonal resorts. Although the older spa tradition remained popular in some areas (the interior South, Saratoga Springs, New York) most of the tremendous growth seen in the summer resort industry was focused in facilities providing a wide variety of diversions including swimming, boating, horse-racing, gambling, and dancing.[40] By 1860, regional variants of these resorts included mountain settings (the Catskills, White Mountains) as well as seaside locales (Nahant, Newport, Long Branch, and Cape May). Typically, these settings offered large several-story hotels in which one could associate with one's equals and enjoy life's luxuries. Within large cities, the antebellum period also witnessed the growth of the "palace hotel" tradition which made distant travel to urban areas more endurable.[41] Boston's elaborate Tremont House (1829) and the widely read architect's guide that followed sparked the construction of a multitude of huge and sumptuous downtown hotels (New York's St. Nicholaus, 1850s; Chicago's Palmer House, 1870s; San Francisco's Palace Hotel, 1870s), a tradition surviving today in the new luxury hotel chains of Hilton and Marriott that still offer the penthouse suite to those who can afford the view.

After the Civil War, the expanding national affluence, especially in the Northeast and Middle West, prompted a new cycle of concurrent changes. Within the city, townhouses quickly established new standards of size and luxury.[42] It was, after all, the age of J. P. Morgan's dictum, "Do something big." These voluminous urban residences were near increasingly plush theaters, social clubs, luxury hotels, and shopping districts. Spatially, they often extended linearly along key boulevards in grand avenues of display. New York's illustrious Fifth Avenue had its parallels in Boston's Commonwealth Avenue, Chicago's Prairie Avenue, and Cleveland's Euclid Avenue (Fig. 17.8, overleaf).

**Figure 17.8**
The changing élite landscape in New York City. This neo-Italian Renaissance structure, built in 1902 as the Morton Plant mansion, stood for 15 years as one of the many wealthy residences on Fifth Avenue. Since 1917, however, it has served as American headquarters of Cartier Jewelers.

Beyond these urban promenades of the new plutocracy, the late 19th-century railroad and the early 20th-century automobile accelerated the suburbanization process in which many of the upper class were drawn to convenient countryside living.[43] Frequently, the outreaching suburbs incorporated older élite enclaves, seasonal country retreats, or resorts. Such was the case for New York City's expanding élite suburban periphery as it worked its way northward up the Hudson Valley and eastward along the north shore of Long Island. Such processes produced complex expressions on the landscape. For example, even in the 1860s, Charles Sweetser describes how Salem's older élite, a class created from successful early 19th-century trade, was overwhelmed by the town's newer rôle as an outer Boston suburb. Of Salem, he notes, "by day it is almost depopulated, many of its most noteworthy citizens going to Boston for business purposes, and returning to dinner and domestic joys."[44]

New seasonal resorts and a new magnitude of luxury in resort living also characterized the late 19th century.[45] More isolated northeastern settings such as the Adirondacks and the Maine coast were opened as railroads, and then automobiles brought these areas closer to rapidly growing cities. The biggest shift, however, was towards both winter and summer élite resorts in the South and West. Georgia's sea islands and Florida's peninsula became popular winter enclaves, often with the help of land promoters, railroad investors, and hotel builders. Further west, a trickle of upper-crust visitors explored the curative powers of southern California's Mediterranean-like environment in the 1860s and 1870s. Quickly the trickle broadened to a torrent and, by the 1890s, communities such as San Diego, Pasadena, Santa Barbara, and Monterey sported large numbers of seasonal and even permanent residents, as well as the usual collection of resort hotels (Hotel Del Monte, near Monterey, 1880; Hotel Del Coronado, near San Diego, 1888). Colorado was an early élite destination in the Intermontane West.[46] Railroad promoter William Palmer designed Colorado Springs as an élite health resort in the 1870s and the image was successfully reinforced with the 1918 completion of the Mediterranean-style Broadmoor Hotel, replete with polo grounds, golf courses, and private landing strip (Fig. 17.9).

The regional spread of élite landscape influences continued in the present century. In the West, a sensitivity to the health-related and esthetic benefits of desert living prompted the creation of new resorts and permanent

**Figure 17.9**
The Broadmoor Hotel, near Colorado Springs, Colorado, a classic resort hotel boasting 350 rooms, built in 1918.

wealthy retreats. Elite haunts still include Sante Fe (after 1910), Palm Springs (after 1920), Phoenix (after 1925), and Las Vegas (after 1945). During the same period, the growth of skiing encouraged landscape changes in traditional eastern mountain resorts (Adirondacks, White Mountains) as well as large new investments in heretofore isolated western settings such as Sun Valley, Idaho, Alta, Utah, and Vail and Aspen, Colorado (Fig. 17.10).[47] This modern diffusion of élite landscapes has meant that today's wealthy have incredible financial and social freedom to live wherever they please, whether it is a Park Avenue apartment, a suburban estatelet, a Bluegrass horse farm, or an alpine chalet. In fact, many wealthy Americans are more prone than ever to own several homes and the more flamboyant members of the "jet set" demonstrate their hypermobility with almost unceasing movements between residences, resorts, and retreats, frequently in their own privately operated aircraft.

### Changing élite architectural tastes

Before the American Revolution, colonial excellence in Georgian-style architecture was nowhere better expressed than in Virginia, where plantation houses echoed the rigid elaborate symmetry, axial entrances, and

**Figure 17.10**
Élite landscape modification in the Intermontane West. High living in Vail, Colorado. Stacks of contemporary-styled condominiums crowd the valley below manicured ski slopes.

geometrical proportions made popular by Englishmen such as Christopher Wren and James Gibbs.[48] In northern urban areas, Georgian townhouses often were architecturally simpler, set on smaller grounds, but structurally as large as their Virginia counterparts. Although most of the northern urban élite recreated the same two-story, four-over-four room, rectangular Georgian style, differences between cities were apparent. In Philadelphia, the Quaker élite, perhaps because of the decline of their social pre-eminence, became increasingly sensitive to the need for grander visual displays of wealth, while more socially sure-footed and secure Boston bluebloods felt less compelled to reveal publicly their aristocratic status in the solid but hardly showy homes of North Square or the West End.[49] Elsewhere, the stubborn individuality of Charleston's upper crust already showed itself in a unique blend of British and West Indies architectural styles encouraging detached houses set perpendicular to the street.[50]

After the War of Independence, while acknowledging the continuing English pedigree, America's grand architecture reflects an increasing number of other influences. The Federal period ushered in a turn to lighter, more varied, ornamented, and delicate shapes and styles in élite houses, gardens, interior design, and furniture.[51] The shift drew upon the unique contribution of the Adam brothers in Scotland and was embellished further from our clearly closer affiliations with France and from the special genius of an increasing number of professionally trained domestic architects such as Boston's Charles Bullfinch.[52] In governments and in buildings, Thomas Jefferson, for one, felt emboldened to depart from the unending predictabilities of the Georgian style. He blended his francophilia with elements of classic Roman design.[53] Jefferson anticipated the major trend of the pre-Civil War era. Elite styles in houses, businesses, and public buildings evolved to draw strongly upon historical associations. "Grecian architecture" became the rage after 1825 (Fig. 17.6).[54] Drawing on the classic columns and pediments of the Parthenon, the style became the norm in Boston townhouses, upstate New York farms, and eventually across the South in the standardized antebellum plantation house. After 1835, in many areas outside the South, the spires, turrets, and steep gables of the Gothic Revival and the characteristic flat roof and often frescoed interior walls of the Italianate style signaled a turn toward an increasingly eclectic élite architecture and displayed an antebellum upper class that, according to Alan Gowans, was "growing ever richer, but not yet vulgarly aware of it."[55]

Between 1865 and 1925, America's upper-class esthetics leaned largely towards bigness and any decoration, European or otherwise, that displayed, if not one's good taste, then surely one's economic success and undoubtedly one's inviolate individualism.[56] It was a grand and gawdy era of ostentatious townhouses, mammoth resort "cottages," and plush metropolitan theaters. Architects such as R. M. Hunt, H. H. Richardson, and McKim, Mead, and White gave the wealthy whatever they wanted, whether it was a French Second Empire mansard roof, a Moorish minaret, a Victorian tennis court, or an Egyptian dining room. Regional divergences were evident, however.[57]

*349*

New York City bested all in its displays of riches. Other cities such as Chicago, Denver, and San Francisco did their best to emulate the trend, while older, more aristocratic, and more slowly growing Boston and Philadelphia shunned some of the more exotic and extreme styles of the Manhattan millionaires.

By the early 20th century, however, a powerful modernist–internationalist style was selectively adopted, combining various continental European (Raymond Schindler and Richard Neutra), American (Frank Lloyd Wright), and even vaguely oriental influences.[58] In addition, regionally, the innumerable versions, authentic and otherwise, of the Spanish Colonial Revival, became well developed in parts of California, Florida, and the American Southwest.[59] In mountain resort settings, the wealthy similarly borrowed from German, Swiss, and Austrian traditions, combined them with modernist shapes and styles, and produced the homogenized alpine landscape so favored by the ski set (Fig. 17.10).[60] In general, the present century has produced an American upper class with overwhelmingly eclectic tastes that are increasingly diffuse, often more informal, less attuned to any single arbiter of style, and broadly less dependent upon overt visual differences than the rest of American society.[61] The result is a modern élite esthetic in architecture as difficult to characterize as the upper class themselves, but one which repeatedly reveals the almost limitless range of choices available to those who can afford to pay.

## Reading the American élite landscape

### Evolutionary processes

Understanding the cumulative impact of powerful and wealthy Americans on the national scene is made more difficult by the fact that such imprints, once made, continue to evolve, becoming part of a long accumulation of dynamic landscape features often dating from the colonial era to the present. One expression of the process is the American readiness to append new architectural fashions on to their homes and other buildings.[62] In 1836, financier Nicolas Biddle, enamored with the Greek Revival, engaged an architect to add a Doric colonnade to the front of his Georgian-style mansion. As Gothic became the rage, scores of Georgian and Federal homes sprouted towers, turrets, and scrollwork. Mansard roofs and Victorian embellishments provided further modifications for late 19th century plutocrats. The accumulated results of these upper-crust tinkerings often produce exquisitely mongrelized landscape features (Fig. 17.11).

Significant functional changes in the use of upper class landscapes also complicate the pattern. In urban settings, most of the finer townhouses surviving demolition no longer serve as single-family residences.[63] Many are banks, museums, stores, educational centers, or professional offices (Fig. 17.11). Some remain as multifamily residential units. In central city

**Figure 17.11**
Evolutionary processes in the
élite landscape. At top a
Southern home, originally
built before the Civil War,
with popular mansard roof,
extensive front porch, and
entire rear half appended in
the late 19th and early 20th
centuries and, below, an
antebellum mansion recently
converted to a modern bank.

settings, increasing numbers of 19th-century mansions pass through long
cycles of decline, even abandonment, only to be renovated as new upper
class residences or businesses. In rural settings, especially on the suburban
fringe, originally large country estates of 50 acres or more frequently are
subdivided for smaller-scale and less exclusive upper-class housing on 1–5
acre lots.[64] Other estates become golf courses, shopping centers, and
donated public park lands, with original mansions serving as clubhouses,
meeting facilities, or even condominiums.[65]

351

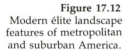

*The modern pattern*

The palimpsest of landscape signatures expressing the dynamic impact of upper-class tastes and values on the American scene is now a centuries-long accumulation of changing architectural styles and settlement patterns. At the scale of the modern metropolitan area, a checklist of inner-city élite landscape elements includes persisting high-status housing districts (more likely in larger cities), rundown or renovated élite housing, élite housing in other land uses (public or private), metropolitan social clubs, refurbished grand hotels, new luxury hotels, high-rise luxury condominiums, long established Episcopalian churches, and high-rent shopping and restaurant districts (also in larger cities) (Fig. 17.12). On the suburban fringe, landscapes of private power and wealth are best seen in exclusive high-status, low-density suburbs, larger intact élite estates (increasingly rare), country clubs, private day and boarding schools, and fashionable upper-class shopping areas (Fig. 17.12).

In the larger regional context, major cities such as Boston, New York, Philadelphia, and Chicago still display sizable zones of smart urban affluence. Inevitably, every good-sized northeastern or midwestern center

**Figure 17.12**
Modern élite landscape features of metropolitan and suburban America.

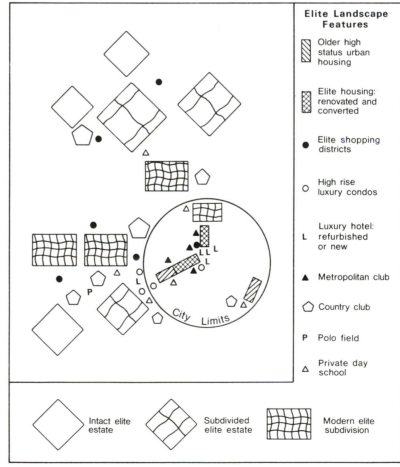

352

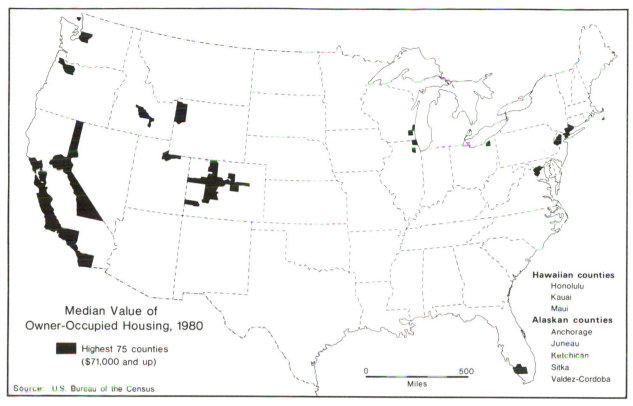

Median Value of
Owner-Occupied Housing, 1980

Highest 75 counties
($71,000 and up)

Source: U.S. Bureau of the Census

Hawaiian counties
Honolulu
Kauai
Maui
Alaskan counties
Anchorage
Juneau
Ketchican
Sitka
Valdez-Cordoba

0          500
Miles

**Figure 17.13**

The geography of high-cost housing. Key settings are in suburban counties near large eastern and midwestern cities and in wealthy suburban and high amenity environments of the American West.

also has its share of wealthy suburbs. In addition, older rural strongholds such as the Hudson Valley reflect the landed gentry's enduring impact. Traditional resort settings on the New England coast and in high amenity mountain and hill locales (White Mountains, Berkshires, and Catskills) are also fruitful areas of exploration.

The American South offers old coastal colonial-era centers (Charleston and Savannah), former plantation zones (eastern and middle Virginia, western and central Kentucky, the Cotton Belt), traditional places of leisure (woodland plantations, Georgia's sea islands, Florida's West Palm Beach), and the more recent affluence of the Sun Belt era, well represented in 20th-century suburbs (Atlanta's Buckhead district, Houston's Hunter Creek Valley) and in newly built resorts. High amenity zones in the American West are important and relatively recent regional additions to the geography of élite landscapes. Skyrocketing home prices reveal especially attractive areas (Fig. 17.13). Large urban centers such as Los Angeles, San Francisco, and Denver abound in affluent landscapes, shaped mostly by new money acquired and displayed in the post World War II era. Selective upper-class migrations to more isolated environments in California's Sierra Nevada, Wyoming's Tetons, Idaho's Sun Valley, and numerous alpine retreats in

353

Colorado put astounding pressure on housing markets and local resources.

De Tocqueville's observations notwithstanding, the result is a national landscape in which the impact of the wealthy and powerful, from Bar Harbor, Maine, to Palm Springs, California, is pervasive and enduring. It is surely the most opulent and self-consciously displayed theme in the making of the American scene. It is a visual record of changing landscape tastes, shifting regional patterns of wealthy accumulation, transforming social processes that diffuse upper-class values to the broader American mainstream, and dynamic historical forces which continue to alter the form and function of élite landscapes once they are created. It is, above all, a single yet complex expression of both greed and magnificence, an expression of the continually evolving American Dream that embodies the best of its optimism and native exuberance along with its naïve excesses and its uncritical acceptance of the good life.

# Chapter eighteen
# The house in the vernacular landscape

## JOHN BRINCKERHOFF JACKSON

O<small>F ALL THE STATES</small> in America, New Mexico contains perhaps the most extraordinary variety of house types—that is, types of dwellings. There are Pueblo-Indian, Spanish-American, and Navajo houses. Some house types, like those of the prehistoric ruins, are 800 or 900 years old and still their patterns of use are not entirely understood. Chaco Canyon, the largest archeological site in the United States, is a mystery from that point of view. But there are also house types like the trailer or mobile home that are new and still evolving, and the counterculture has also made its contribution. Over 50 years residence in the region has provided the author ample opportunity for observation and understanding.[1]

What is unusual about New Mexico is that many of these different types can be found side by side in the small community. Not only that, in many cases they are being lived in by the families who built them in the first place. This means that one can find out how they were built and how they are being used. There are many traditional house types in the East and in the South, of course, and they have been studied and often preserved. But they are usually old and have had so many owners and have gone through so many remodelings that the link between the original builders and the house as it now stands is hard to establish. The architectural historian or preservationist has to confine his or her work to investigating the construction of the house: the house as artifact—the materials, the tools, and the methods of building. Thanks to sophisticated archeological techniques we have learned a great deal about old construction processes, and about the ethnic or geographical origins of the builders, and we can restore the whole structure to something like its original condition. On the other hand, we can only speculate about how the house was used in daily life, how it was related to its landscape. So New Mexico has something to offer by way of insight into the nature of house types.

Most dwellings in New Mexico are small, and as works of art or architecture hardly worth a second glance. But they are what gives the landscape its character. They are of simple construction, not meant to last for long. That is because they are the homes of families with little money—small farmers, wage earners, day laborers, and men and women working in service jobs—people who often think of moving to where there are better work opportunities. If they can rent or sell the house they are lucky; they usually abandon it. New Mexico is very poor and it always will be. It is true that there are a number of handsome architect-designed houses in Albuquerque and Santa Fe, but traveling over the last half century through the less prosperous sections of the state, one could find village after village, and even small towns, where there was no such thing as a mansion, a so-called Great House, an expensive house, one clearly designed for a different life-style. Instead, almost everywhere were small, unpretentious one-story houses, sometimes clustered together, sometimes strung out along both sides of the road, sometimes sitting alone in the open country (Fig. 18.1): in most cases a sort of basic, all-purpose house type for a family with an income below the national average and an above national average number of children and of used cars.

**Figure 18.1**

Modest houses and outbuildings comprise the village of Truchas, New Mexico, set among winter fields against the backdrop of the majestic Sangre de Cristo Mountains. In the right foreground is a traditional Spanish-American adobe dwelling, complete with projecting flat roof beam.

# Vernacular dwellings in 1930s New Mexico

Newcomers to New Mexico are often attracted by the Spanish-American villages scattered throughout the ranch country. They seem very foreign. Back in the 1930s, most families supported themselves by farming and raising cattle or sheep. It was a hard life; many men had to work as sheepherders or cowhands on ranches in Wyoming or Colorado and were away from home for months at a time.

The villages were half hidden in the immense open rangeland and stood beside a stream that watered the small fields of corn and chili and beans. The surrounding landscape was organized in an almost medieval manner. Easterners are not always aware that communal control of the land and its use, with a large common for the livestock, existed in the Spanish Southwest before New England had been heard of. In places the system still survives. Each household had the right to graze its cows or sheep on the very extensive community range, to use water from the community irrigation ditch, and to take wood from the community forest. Furthermore the church belonged to the villagers and so did the few roads and trails. Whoever used those facilities had to help keep them up, and this enforced sharing of work and space and responsibility helps to explain the strong sense of local solidarity among the villagers. Everyone knew the names of local plants and game, and of the fields and mountains around the village. They could tell which village a stranger came from by his accent or his use of some word. Neighboring villages often had deep-seated mutual hostility and described each other by some abusive epithet. This kind of community, harking back to the late 16th century and brought in from Spain by way of Mexico, had already begun to fall apart in New Mexico by the Depression. Sizable private holdings had come into existence, and community obligations were more and more neglected. Younger men and women left to find work in town. But certain customs persisted. The community cattle roundup and rodeo were popular events, and so was the old-fashioned public celebration of Christmas and Easter. Everyone still went to the village church and on Sunday afternoons the young men, dressed in their finery, galloped up and down the one street.

Architecturally, the houses were far from remarkable: one-story structures with two or three rooms, usually of adobe. Often they had a pitched roof of corrugated tin that shone in the sun, and many had a long front porch (Fig. 18.2). They were all very much alike, for there is a limit to the variety that can be introduced into the plan of a house with two or three rooms. None had running water or electricity, and almost all had dirt floors. They were of different colors, however—bright green, or pink, or brown, with white window and door trim, and entirely without ornamentation. The manner in which they were sometimes connected in rows to form three sides of a common courtyard or plaza gave the village an almost urban aspect. Throughout the day the houses were quiet. They were scantily furnished, but gave the impression less of poverty than of an austere

**Figure 18.2**
Traditional, but more
modern, Spanish-American
adobe homes covered with
tin roofs in Las Vegas, New
Mexico. Typically, rooms
have been added over the
years as need dictated, each
with its own door to the
outside.

formality. In going to such a house one went not to the front door (painted
white and locked), but to the kitchen door and, as was the custom among
neighbors, one entered without knocking. It was usual to be met with the
sight of a taciturn mother-in-law minding the smallest children. Normally
the men would be out gathering the fuel, even job hunting. The wife might
have gone to the store.

This was almost always the case: at every house everybody was out
(Fig. 18.3); being "out" meant taking part in the life of the village. Early each
morning the man of the house would ride out to work in one of his fields or
to check on his livestock grazing in the common. He kept an eye on what
there was that he could use: a dead cedar tree to make a fence post, a stray
hen, a rare medicinal herb. Perhaps a passerby might tell him of a rancher
who needed extra hands for putting up hay, or building a fence. He would
stop at the store to get a sense of how his credit stood. In such poor
neighborhoods every item was of possible worth. Although always aware of
their own struggle for survival, it seemed that the men in the village were
also always aware that they were involved in sharing the land—the water,
the grass, the sand and the gravel, the game in the forest. They were also
always on the lookout for some abuse, some reason for holding a noisy
public meeting and clamoring for justice. And this incessant clamor
suggested not that justice was hard to get but that it could be had on
demand. Those who live in town think of the countryside as a place where
people farm or enjoy the beauties of nature. Actually it can be a stimulating
place, and politically speaking even the most somnolent village has much to
offer. That is where one sees custom in action, regulating movement and
ways of work and relationships between neighbors. It is where one
eventually grasps that the established order is not easily changed.

Remaining at home would not only be lonely, it would mean being deprived of the excitement of community existence and all its opportunities. In the pastoral New Mexico of half a century ago the distinction between the quiet domestic realm and the community was very clear cut; and the community mattered more than the house. Certainly the house was important; it stood for shelter and privacy, it was where family ritual was enacted, year after year. It was the place of origin and the place where you died. But it was remote. Its economic rôle was limited. It was not the place of work in the sense of being the place of gainful employment. It was not the place for conviviality, and it was not a personal work of art to be proud of. Indeed, the reason all houses resembled one another was that every man was capable of building one. Finally, the house was rarely associated with memorable family events: it contained neither mementoes of the family past

**Figure 18.3**

Vernacular interior: the living room of a small house in Rio Lucio, New Mexico. Furnishings are minimal, almost austere, functional. The aura of emptiness serves as a reminder that social life in the village takes place mostly elsewhere, in public places—outside.

nor provisions for the family future. Marriages and funerals and anniversaries and reunions were held in the church, or the school, or sometimes in the local dance hall. To be sure, even the simplest dwelling deserves respect for its rich symbolism and the memories it holds, but it has another more prosaic aspect: the house as a space or a composition of spaces and walls and doors that makes certain relationships possible and impedes others. The village houses seemed to serve as supplements to the larger, shared spaces of the community, being incomplete in themselves, fragments of a much more complex unit. The typical house did not pretend to be anything more than a container. What it contained in the way of family relationships was of infinite value, but these could and often did survive in another container, another house. Its rôle was to make visible how the inside world related to the outside, how the individual related to the village, and how the hours of working with others were distinct from the private routine of the home. Defining a vernacular dwelling in those days would easily have summoned to mind those Spanish American village houses, and furthermore the notion that it was a house which depended on its immediate environment for the satisfaction of its daily needs.

## Vernacular dwellings in New Mexico today

Fifty years, however, have brought many changes in the New Mexico landscape; the most striking is what has happened to some of the villages. They have degenerated into rural slums of the most abject kind. Fields have reverted to second growth, houses are in decay, roads and irrigation ditches are choked with rubbish and abandoned cars. It is not easy to account for this tragic decline, except to say that New Mexico is always subject to entropy. Farming no longer provides a living, most villages are too isolated, too lacking in resources, and too far from the highway to try another way of life. So now, 20 miles from Santa Fe with its opera, its 90 art galleries, its polo fields, one can find a squalor more hopeless than anywhere else in the United States.

Still, some of the villages *have* survived into the 1980s (Fig. 18.4). The men now work for wages in the service sector or do odd jobs in town. Thanks to the automobile the environment they depend on has expanded well beyond the village and ranch, and they think nothing of commuting 30 or 40 miles to work. The roads are paved and buses take the children to a consolidated school. When they come home in the afternoon and run down the street, their bright clothes and loud voices bring life to the village, and a way of marking the time of day. Every household seems to have at least three cars, one of them always a pickup. Cars in varying stages of roadworthiness are parked outside the bar, the convenience store, in front yards, in deserted corrals, and in vacant lots. With hoods raised, they seem about to devour the young men adjusting their carburetors. Spanish music comes from their radios. Although the villages are probably just as poor, comparatively

**Figure 18.4**

The small village of San Ysidro del Norte, New Mexico, tucked away in a small valley, showing signs of modest recent growth. Brick or concrete block have become building materials of choice. Increased commuting has meant less connection between the residents and their immediate surroundings.

speaking, as they were in the past, some now have more movement and perhaps more vitality.

What is particularly notable is the number of new dwellings and the decay and abandonment of the old. Adobe is no longer the most popular building material; cement block and frame houses are common as well as houses trucked in from elsewhere. The new ones are more comfortable than the old ones were: they have electricity and gas and running water. They indicate that a number of men in the village have been "in construction" and have learned about new materials, new ways of building, and how to use power tools.

A great deal of this new housing throughout New Mexico—and for that matter, throughout the whole country—consists of trailers. They are everywhere: tucked in between houses, attached to houses, even on top of houses; in alleys and gardens and out in the fields. In fact there are New Mexico villages where trailers outnumber conventional dwellings and where the newly arrived tourist cries out in delight at the glimpse of an adobe house. The old, close relationship between the houses, suggesting as it did a relationship between members of the same extended family, has been replaced by a more scattered arrangement, like that among friendly but self-sufficient neighbors. The newer, free-standing houses seem to prefer the margins of the road leading out of the village to the traditional compact patterns of plazas.

## The new trailer landscape

The prominence of those trailers in the landscape challenges the accepted definition of the vernacular (Fig. 18.5). Many Americans first became aware of the trailer in the years during and immediately after World War II. That was when they were widely used as a form of emergency housing. They clustered by the hundreds around army posts and construction sites, and after the war they invaded college campuses to accommodate married students. They were unsightly, but, at the time, no one cared. They were temporary, and in fact most of the wartime trailer communities have long since vanished.

Now, a generation later, America has more trailers than ever before. They are called mobile homes in the trade, and they are larger, more comfortable, and much more expensive. Some 13 million Americans, most of them young blue-collar families, live in trailers and (for the time being, at least) call them home.

But there is strong prejudice against them. Architectural historians who have learned to accept the bungalow, the split-level ranch house, and the A-frame still cannot bring themselves to recognize the trailer as a dwelling. Few property owners want a trailer as a residence. Few homeowners want trailers in their neighborhood, and style-conscious communities do what they can to relegate them to less visible parts of town. Trailer parks are often researched by sociologists who report on the deadly conformity among the tenants or on the tyrannical behavior of the trailer park managers.

Yet it is one thing to glimpse in passing the regimentation of a trailer park (Fig. 18.6), quite another to see the solitary trailer permanently part of the fabric of a neighborhood. Far from being hidden or disguised, it is often conspicuous.

Over the years the educated public, helped by architects and urban planners and environmentalists, has drawn up the indictment of the trailer.

**Figure 18.5**
A modern box-shaped trailer home in Vista del Valle, a fringe subdivision of Santa Fe, New Mexico, not known for its architect-designed houses. The trailer forms the kernel of a dwelling enlarged and financed mostly through the owner's personal "sweat equity."

**Figure 18.6**

A trailer park in Stockton, California, developed initially in the 1950s, as seen from an adjoining freeway embankment. Like water alleys in a marina, straight concrete strips separate tight rows of trailer lots—berths for their immobile home "craft." At some point, the concrete apron was widened to accommodate more cars and pickups that ferry residents to the outside world.

It is part esthetic judgement, part structural, with a touch of compassion for the people who are unfortunate enough to live in one. To begin with, the trailer is an industrial product, massproduced, low-cost, and disposable. It comes out of some Midwestern factory and is shipped by truck, quickly unloaded, and soon ready for occupancy. This means it has by-passed the craftsman and the architect and the landscape architect, and that the owner (or consumer) has no opportunity for self expression, or even a say in the ordering of the interior or in the outside decorations. Some trailers come completely furnished—the ultimate indignity.

Second, coming as it does off an assembly line, the trailer ignores all local architectural traditions and all local environmental constraints. Its uncompromising shape and boxlike appearance make any real composition of a group of trailers impossible. No matter how we site them in relation to one another, we can never achieve anything like a traditional village.

For all its conspicuous ugliness, the trailer is quite small and cramped, and long and narrow as it is, fails to provide a half-way satisfactory arrangement of rooms for a family. Although the trailer is often successful as a store or an office or a schoolroom, its awkward inflexibility means that it can never be a self-sufficient, autonomous dwelling. On the contrary, almost from its first day of occupancy it spills its contents—and its occupants—into its surroundings: parked cars, refrigerators, packing cases, children, and dogs and laundry invade the landscape. As time goes on the trailer becomes more and more dependent on the spaces provided by taxpayers: cars take up room, children need spaces for play. Yet, ironically enough, the trailer rejects assimilation: its potential mobility, its frequent changes in occupancy

363

and ownership, its ambiguous legal status all work against its acceptance. It is of light construction, easily destroyed by fire or toppled by a high wind. Literally as well as figuratively, the trailer has no real attachment to place.

Most of us would agree that these are valid criticisms, and we could probably add to them. But from the point of view of those who live in trailers they miss their mark. The villagers who have moved into trailers are in general satisfied. They wish their trailer were larger, and had better insulation. They object to the floor plan. Nevertheless, to them the advantages of the trailer far outweigh its faults. What they especially appreciate is how little the trailer costs, compared to even the smallest house, and how easy it is to finance. They regretted leaving the old adobe house with its associations, but it was a joy to move into a brand new home, clean and never used.

Newness is something we do not always appreciate, but perhaps at least a third of all Americans have never owned a new car and would very much like to. That is why there are spray cans which produce the smell—whatever it may be—of a new car interior. A new trailer has the same exciting appeal: stickers on the windows, books of instructions, and that indefinable smell of newness. It takes only a few days to realize how convenient and comfortable the trailer is, and how easy to maintain. The fact that it resembles all the other trailers in the vicinity is if anything a source of reassurance, for it means that the choice was a popular one, endorsed by other families. The most welcome feature of trailer living is that it brings with it no new responsibilities, no change or expansion in the traditional domestic routine. Nor does it alter the old relationship with the outside world: the man of the family can leave home as usual in the morning, only with the trailer there is no chopping of wood, no feeding of livestock. Life is simplified, and begins, as it always has, when we join others in work and conversation. Moreover, with fewer domestic chores the wife is at last free to move into the community. Trailers, as we all know, are rarely mobile in the literal sense of the word, but because of their impersonality, their part-exchange value, they are like automobiles: easy to trade and sell. When a better job becomes available somewhere else the family can at least consider the wisdom of selling, and of finding similar accommodation wherever they go.

The heart of the matter is that for a great many families the trailer is a sensible way of living. Indeed, it almost seems as if those shortcomings which critics never tire of mentioning—the lack of individuality, the functional incompleteness, the dependence on outside services and amenities—and even the lack of such traditional architectural qualities as firmness, commodity, and delight—all are what make the trailer useful and attractive to many of its owners.

In spite of the recommendations of their occupants, we need not be blind admirers of the trailer or mobile home. It is easy to see at first hand what is wrong with its plan and construction. But it remains the most practical low-cost dwelling we have, and is well adapted to a way of life that is becoming increasingly common in both urban and rural America.

## A broader meaning for vernacular housing

That way of life is identified with the blue-collar worker: the man or woman without capital, without any marketable skill, and with only a limited formal education. The man or woman of the family (in many cases both) has to work by the hour or the day at an unskilled or semi-skilled job away from home, with little assurance that it will last. These factors obviously have their effect on the kind of house they can afford, and how they use it.

There was a time when we would have used the term "proletarian" to describe this class of citizen. As long ago as the 16th century in England the word signified the worker who owned no land and who could produce nothing for the market. But Marxist theory has redefined "proletarian" to exclude the farmworker and craftsman and it now means the industrial worker alone; and of course the industrial worker is often highly skilled and well paid. So if we want a convenient term which would include all those who work in the less prestigious service jobs we should probably say unskilled wage earner, and, as described, the trailer and other forms of low-cost, massproduced housing seem to be part of that way of life.

This was the kind of dwelling so evident in the cities and towns of New Mexico, and in the industrial communities. It was missing in the prosperous suburbs and in the regions of condominiums and high-rise apartment houses, and so it was easy to associate it with urban working-class areas. It has been something of a surprise in more recent times to see those massproduced, prefabricated houses and trailers appearing with heightened frequency in some of the villages.

They certainly changed the appearance of the place: the old compactness, the old uniformity of forms and textures was shattered, and the new houses, most of them strung along the road, did catch the eye. Their very prevalence rendered them acceptable. Most of them, as far as size and location were concerned, fitted in with their neighbors well enough (Fig. 18.7). Even the newest showed signs of improvization and the use of

**Figure 18.7**
Trailer homes amid conventional houses in a low-income subdivision off Central Avenue in South Phoenix, Arizona. Trees and other plantings provide sufficient visual containment to blur the sharp distinctions between dwelling types on the street.

shortcuts to save time and money, and it seemed that it was only a matter of a few years before their rawness and sharpness of outline would be overcome. Most of them, in fact, were already surrounded by a drift of discarded objects and abandoned cars that is part of every New Mexico house. The panorama of every village was like a familiar and not very important public notice: a vanished letter or a garbled spelling made you look twice, but you soon saw that the meaning had not changed.

But what reconciled one to the presence of all those new houses, whatever their style or lack of style, was that to all appearances they were being used, being lived in, in much the same manner as were the older houses, and visits to a few of them confirm this. The resemblance between the life-style of the younger villagers and that of their families or grandfathers a half century earlier was striking. The houses were much more comfortable, much healthier than the old ones ever were, and they were better furnished. No wonder the families were proud of them and happy to show them off. But certain traditional relationships—between the house and the family, the house and the community, the house and the place of work—had changed little or not at all. They were much the same as they had been in the adobe houses, for generations. In short, these brand new houses or trailers were bona fide vernacular.

Many contemporary American students of the vernacular, and many architectural historians might disagree. The usual scholarly approach to the vernacular is to concentrate on the construction of the house, the materials and techniques used, and on the geographical or ethnic origin of its structural features. As a result of scientific or technological research we have a very impressive literature on what might be called architectural archeology, and we have a wider knowledge of house types, often of a very obscure kind. But the emphasis has inevitably been on the old, the pre-technological structure. From the architectural point of view that is probably more stimulating. However, the word "vernacular" now covers many lively aspects of popular culture, especially contemporary popular culture, and by concentrating almost exclusively on the anatomical aspects of old buildings, the field of vernacular architecture runs the risk of being essentially antiquarian.

The solution, it would seem, is to explore the history of the vernacular dwelling, not merely here in the United States, but as far back as we can go—at least in the history of the Western world. When we eventually undertake this, we will discover that the vernacular dwelling, the dwelling of the laborer or peasant as distinguished from the dwelling of the aristocrat, has been the subject of constant control and regulation and at the same time the recipient of definite rights and privileges. Far from being a small and primitive version of the house of the nobleman or merchant it has been and still is a distinct form with its own distinct way of life.

# The social uses of vernacular dwelling spaces

Americans are reluctant to discuss class distinctions in their culture, probably on grounds that this would be undemocratic and adversarial. Nevertheless, the difference in the houses lived in by the working class and those lived in by the rich do seem recognizable, and this difference is often less a matter of size and cost than it is of how space, interior as well as exterior, is organized and used. The average white-collar home is likely to contain a great variety of what anthropologists call monofunctional spaces: spaces of one kind or another set aside for a special use or a special person. This was always characteristic of the aristocratic household, even in the remote past, but its prevalence in the houses of the middle class is something relatively new. Many scholars have discussed the development of the elaborate floor plan in domestic architecture, Philippe Aries and Yi Fu Tuan among them. The 19th century seems to have been the time when the obsession with monofunctional spaces or rooms reached its climax. The contemporary middle-class dwelling manages to survive with fewer spaces, but in the guise of a free flow of space, new ones keep emerging: media entertainment centers, hobby rooms, exercise rooms, and super bathrooms. The modern hi-tech kitchen is becoming a cluster of monofunctional spaces.

There are several interesting things about this segmentation of domestic space. In the first place it is merely a small scale, architectural version of a widespread tendency to organize *all* spaces in the landscape in terms of some special function. It has reorganized the farm, the city, the industrial plant, and the university—it has reorganized the map of the world.

But equally significant is the fact that the working-class house has been largely immune to the appeal of the monofunctional space. The house may well contain many rooms, but most of those rooms serve several uses, uses which can change from hour to hour or from day to day. The garage serves

**Figure 18.8**
A "basic" house with two rooms, each with an outside door, in the Spanish-American Milltown district of Albuquerque, New Mexico. Its interior spaces are generic, adaptable to multiple uses, and family functions easily spill outside when necessary. Vernacular space thus has no inherent identity, but is defined by the momentary pattern of its use.

*367*

as a storage room, then becomes a workshop. The kitchen is where we watch television and cook and eat; the dining room—if there is one—is for homework. The out-of-work brother-in-law sleeps on the living room couch, and the men in the family tune up the second-hand car on the patch of lawn. These are strictly temporary expedients. All or almost all spaces in the house can be shared and used in a variety of ways (Fig. 18.8). This reflects what might be called a vernacular concept of space: a space has no inherent identity, it is simply defined by the way it is used. The middle-class or establishment concept is almost the direct opposite: each space is unique and can in fact affect the activity taking place within it, and so in the design of domestic spaces and their relationship the skill of the architect and planner is always called for.

Nowhere is the contrast between the planned, specialized organization of domestic space in the establishment household and the fluid, undifferentiated spaces in the working-class dwelling more striking than in the provisions each makes for hospitality. When we enumerate the spaces and symbols devoted to hospitality—or exclusion—in even the average middle-class dwelling we are likely to be surprised by their profusion: the formal front door with door bell or chime, the formal lobby or entrance hall with clothes closet and so-called powder room, the drawing room (or library), the guest bedroom and bath, and formal dining room—each of them containing discrete symbols of the family status; to say nothing of a parking lot. All of them together constitute a sizable fraction of the area of the house, and along with this lavish use of space for hospitality often goes a very demanding domestic schedule of hospitality, fixed many days in advance. All of this apparatus for hospitality has its justification; the guest is ceremoniously introduced and admitted to a private and exclusive domain, to a territory of which the host or hostess is sovereign. We can criticize the formality of what we now call 'entertaining,' but even its modest contemporary version represents a distinctly establishment definition of the house as an autonomous, self-sufficient territory, a focus of power and influence, a space where the stranger is formally admitted to be a member of a group.

The vernacular dwelling knows no such tradition. Its hospitality, though no less generous and welcoming, is informal and unpremeditated: no special rooms, no special days or hours, no special china or special cooking are called for. The guests who appear, often uninvited, are not there for negotiating alliances or soliciting favors: they come to be included in the daily routine of the family.

There is nothing mysterious about this. It seems entirely consistent with the vernacular concept of the dwelling as a refuge from the workaday world, a place for the rituals of privacy, not for the pursuit of influence and power. The wage-earner dwelling delegates as many functions as it can to the public realm, reserving for itself the rôle of providing shelter and the perpetuating of family awareness. Unlike the middle-class house, the vernacular house is not a jealously guarded territory, and the outsider undergoes no entrance examination. As a member of the extended family or of the neighborhood, he or she is automatically included in the domestic order.

Hospitality, in short, is less an initiation into the house as an autonomous territory than it is a celebration of the super family, and the best kind of celebration, the most generous kind of hospitality is that which is staged *outside* the home. The graduation party, the wedding reception, the grandparents' anniversary, the family reunion, each such occasion takes over the school gymnasium, the parish hall, the hall of the local protective fraternal order, and for the time being the super family shares it as if it belonged to them and no one else. From behind the closed doors come sounds of revelry: of flash photography, of laughter, and of long emotional toasts. Live music plays on through the night. Outside in the darkness a shiny car, decorated with crêpe paper flowers and streamers, waits for the bride and groom, bound for a honeymoon weekend in Las Vegas.

This is the kind of event and the kind of space the vernacular dwelling has to have in order to survive. Its dependence on its immediate environment is not servitude, it is something that can always be counted on, something morally dependable. For that is what distinguishes vernacular space from territorial space: it belongs to *us*. We have no legal title to it, but custom, unwritten law tells us we can use it in meeting our daily needs. Vernacular space is to be shared, not exploited or monopolized. It is never a source of wealth or power, it is in the literal sense of the term a common ground, a common place, a common denominator which makes each vernacular neighborhood a miniature commonwealth. So the way to begin the study of the vernacular landscape is with the house; not as an autonomous realm but as a structure which achieves completeness by relating to its environment.

# Afterword

## MICHAEL P. CONZEN

WE HAVE TRIED here to look at the American landscape from the perspective of the major historical forces that have shaped it. Sometimes this has meant considering those processes that stem from a broad but generally unified ethnic or cultural presence, such as that of the English or the French, or the new American social formation. Sometimes it has meant defining historical force in terms of Toynbeean challenge and response: the colonizing of forest, grassland, and desert, or the evolution of the plantation system in regions suited to crops best raised that way. And sometimes historical force has meant a grand transformation of the social condition through economic or technological change, such as the process of industrialization or radical improvements in transportation or governance.

The selection of the particular "large forces" is of course open to debate, and the emphasis given to each in different historical periods likewise begs alternative construction. While there is a rough chronological progression in the sequence of topics explored we do not mean to imply that Indian or Spanish influences in landscape making do not continue to this day. Indian presence continues as a force in many of today's landscapes, not just on the official reservations but also, for example, in land claims and water management affairs. Spanish influence continues in the enduring popularity of Spanish architectural styles, as well as in the growing vitality of hispanic culture in many regions and cities of the nation, even if the link to the colonial past is indirect. Alternatively, large industrial activity, new means of transportation, and the impress of government are not manifestations merely of the modern period. But questions of definition and chronology aside, we have aimed for what we hope is a judicious balance of critical importance in each major phase of landscape making in America.

The approach, then, has been largely thematic. While the forces explored in some chapters have by historical circumstance been salient in particular regions and not others, most are seen to reach into many corners of the nation, and a number to approach virtual ubiquity—as with the influence of the automobile. This perspective leads almost inevitably to a sense of the

American landscape as a giant amalgam of features reflecting the swirl and flow of great human and natural forces. Each systematic grouping of forces is represented by a vast litter of objects throughout the land, with variations in density, to be sure, but a scatter none the less. Reading this record thus becomes an exercise in mobile detective work, ranging over large territory to discover the complete set of features connected with any particular shaping force, wherever each is to be found. Where does this lead? What kind of synthesis of landscape understanding can be envisioned that draws together the spatially disparate findings of the thematic approach followed in this book?

The complementary perspective that recommends itself, of course, is to look at the American landscape as a vast congeries of regional landscapes, each with its own distinctive character and relative unity. Thus, each regional landscape, however small in orbit—and, indeed, however recognized in practice as a regional landscape—represents a distillation in place of all the historical forces that made a difference in that locality and together actually shaped it. This view sees landscapes not merely as abstract or incidental settings for individual objects (however symbolic of complex associations they may be in themselves) but as ensembles in their own right, in which the admixture and juxtaposition of landscape features creates a localized whole greater than the sum of the parts.

A regional view of American landscape—the recognition and study of regionally distinctive landscapes—invokes a form of consciousness that draws on American traditions of fiction, visual arts, and travel description, but that needs to transcend each of these to combine the elements of discourse within a disciplined but imaginative geographical and historical framework. Immediately, one is confronted with nagging questions. How many regional landscapes are there in the United States? How do we know where one ends and another begins? Are they territorially exclusive, or do certain types of landscape "nest" within larger ones? Are there "hierarchies" of regional landscapes? Are the number and boundaries of regional landscapes immutable over time, and if not how do we deal with the pace of change? The answers to these questions properly belong in a work devoted to the regional approach to American landscapes, and inklings about them are to be gleaned in the rich but often casual literature on localities to be found in any library or bookstore catering to the curious observer. There is as yet no equivalent in the United States to the series of book-length historical treatments of English regional landscapes inspired and organized by W. G. Hoskins. But, increasingly, professional and lay geographers, historians, and others in America are publishing attractive interpretations of the landscape history of small regions in various parts of the country.

As a link between the thematic perspective of this book and the complementary regional viewpoint acknowledged here, we can offer a very crude cartographic summary of the kinds of historical influences examined as they play out across the country and the implicit "landscape regions" that might be out there waiting to be recognized (Figs. A.1a & b). An attempt has been made in Figure A.1a to show how various cultural impulses have originated and spread across space. Several "hearth" areas have been recognized by geographers in which reformulations of cultural values and landscape habits occurred in critical periods as a result of colonization and immigration, some fashioned from one dominant group and others from the intermingling of many. Strong impulses then were carried over broad territory as settlers migrated from these core areas to newer lands, spreading landscape traits as they went, changing them also in the process as new conditions or competing impulses were encountered. As the 19th century wore on modernization took an increasing hold of the artifactual basis of landscape making (represented on the map symbolically by impulse lines radiating from Chicago) so that most western areas were touched by a multiplicity of weak original influences and a gathering force of modern impulses, though with plenty of scope for new, indigenous but generalized Western forms to emerge. This schematic interpretation is based on the results of a great deal of painstaking research by cultural geographers, folklorists, and others in various regions, and reflects those patterns over which there is a fair consensus. Some additional impulses mooted in the technical literature, such as the putative southwestern "hearth" in east-central Texas, are omitted because the evidence is as yet inconclusive. Clearly, continued scholarly research is bound to change the macroscopic picture in time.

If we accept that such a view provides at least a rudimentary synthesis of the large historical forces as they swept across the nation and placed the imprint of mixed cultures upon the land, what might the resulting mosaic of regional landscapes in the aggregate look like? Figure A.1b is an attempt to suggest just how intricate that mosaic may be. It consists of areal units formed by the varying incidence of regional boundaries defined by three separate criteria. Culture regions as delineated by several geographers provide a first principle of division: each area bounded by a culture region (or subregion) boundary is presumed to display some uniformity of culture traits across that area. Clearly, the more traits considered the more the uniformity of such a region will be compromised. To these divisions have been added, second, boundaries marking off areas within them of contrasting land resources, mainly the economic support of each locality, whether it be a type of farming, forest culture, rangeland, specialty produce, or something else. Where boundaries run close together according to official delineations, they have been generalized for the sake of clarity as a unified boundary in Figure A.1b, with the cultural divide given precedence. Third, physiographic regions and subregions have been added, because the difference between, say, absolutely flat plains and plains with low hills, or tablelands and intermontane basins, is sufficient to imply differences in the way the cultural imprint appears in each case. Again, many such physical boundaries coincide with cultural and economic ones, so these are given precedence where overlap occurs. The resulting map is simply a heuristic device, not intended to say that these are necessarily the zones in which distinct landscapes will be found, but rather to suggest the scale and

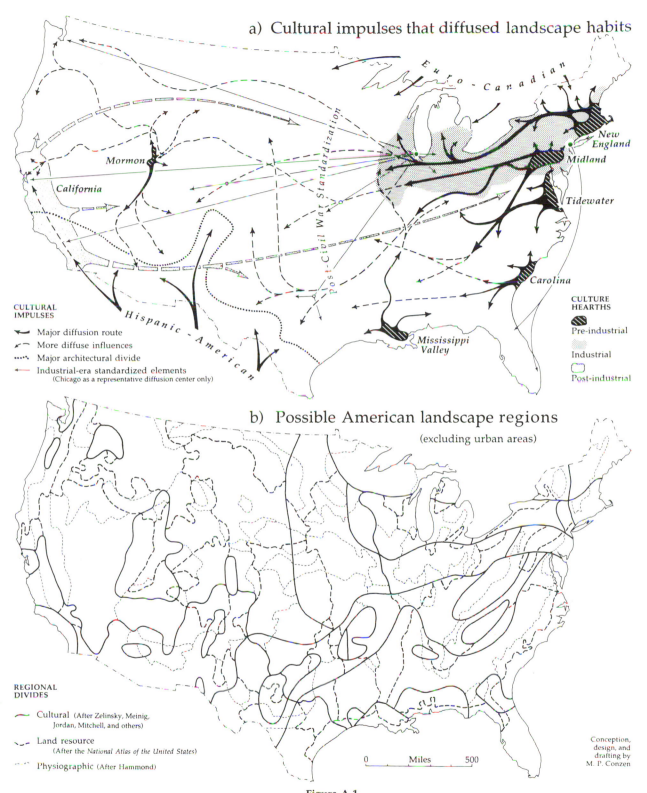

## a) Cultural impulses that diffused landscape habits

Euro-Canadian

New England

Midland

Tidewater

Carolina

Mormon

California

Mississippi Valley

Post-Civil War Standardization

Hispanic-American

CULTURAL
IMPULSES

➤ Major diffusion route
⌐ More diffuse influences
····· Major architectural divide
+— Industrial-era standardized elements
(Chicago as a representative diffusion center only)

CULTURE
HEARTHS

▨ Pre-industrial

Industrial

Post-industrial

## b) Possible American landscape regions
### (excluding urban areas)

REGIONAL
DIVIDES

Cultural (After Zelinsky, Meinig,
Jordan, Mitchell, and others)

Land resource
(After the *National Atlas of the United States*)

Physiographic (After Hammond)

0   Miles   500

Conception,
design, and
drafting by
M. P. Conzen

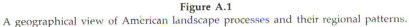

**Figure A.1**
A geographical view of American landscape processes and their regional patterns.

intricacy of landscape variation as attention shifts from place to place. Clearly, much exploration and study awaits those interested in producing an improved national map of actual, contiguous cultural landscapes!

These two maps merely summarize and raise further questions about the themes considered in this book. It is unneccesary to point out how much more could be done to clarify additional historical forces at work in the American landscape, to identify further objects and features associated with each major landscape forming process, to delineate the regional landscapes within which the associations are seen to best advantage, and to deepen understanding of the symbolic meaning of landscapes for each generation that has experienced them. Suffice it to say that concepts such as process, object, and ensemble—and their social meanings—represent valuable dimensions along which study of the American landscape can advance.

It is hoped that this collection of essays may have opened up some worthwhile avenues of thought about the making of the American landscape. It was put together in the belief that there is benefit in a broader awareness of the landscape as an active ingredient in the everyday culture of America. This thought stems not only from a painful awareness of the national consequences of comparative ignorance of Earth geography, but also of a common state of mind in which individuals appear to drift blithely through geographical space without landmarks or moorings, living a life of locational and visual indifference. Such a mode of living may well suffice, but environmental blindness ultimately is neither practical nor enriching.

There are individual satisfactions to be gained from an intellectual understanding of and an emotional resonance towards the ordinary and extraordinary landscapes around us. In this book we have striven not to overdraw the distinction between vernacular and élite landscapes, since the actual record contains the monuments of both in endlessly varied proportions from place to place. More significance lies in perceiving the ebb and flow of human energy and creativity in molding our habitat somewhat to our liking, and in grasping what underlies the patterns produced.

There are wider social implications of landscape understanding. Neither nature nor humankind is static or steady-state; landscapes change to reflect altered needs, and competing agendas ensure that change is typified and valued differently by different groups. There are shifting scales and spatial impacts of change, and changing rates of landscape change. If any generalization may be ventured, it is that change usually appears to any historical generation smaller-scale and slower in the past than in the present. In some respects the pace of economic modernization and gathering global interdependence over the last two centuries has accelerated quantitatively and spatially, so that many earnest observers foresee great dangers in failing to maintain a balance. Landscape characteristics are then often resorted to as the measure of the misfit between ideal and actual: how much do we interfere with change, and on what basis? Do certain areas warrant preservation, for reasons of salubrity or sanity? How resilient are landscapes in absorbing change, and what price landscape extinction (as if equated with biological impoverishment through the death of species)?

A scholarly purist would maintain that all facets and trends in landscape evolution are inherently interesting and as such neither overtly good nor bad. Those committed to progress are likely to harbor strong preferences and to seek guidelines for social policies that profoundly affect the character, and in their view the quality, of the landscape. Urban sprawl and the denaturing of agriculture through technology exemplify such issues. Whatever ideological positions are favored, only an extreme libertarian would quibble with the concept of custodianship and reasonable management of the cultural landscape as a social resource. Since Americans "manage" much of the landscape through the institution of private property, they have only by stages developed a concept of the landscape as a public good. From the days when the first national parks were set up for the benefit and enjoyment of all to the latterday programs of historic preservation of old and worthy buildings, there has been a secular increase in the breadth of definition of what constitutes valued landscape. As the United States approaches and surpasses the quincentenary of Columbus's landfall, perhaps the landscape transformations he set in motion will become even better understood and more widely appreciated.

# Contributors

KARL W. BUTZER is Dickson Centennial Professor of Liberal Arts in the Department of Geography at the University of Texas at Austin.

MICHAEL P. CONZEN is Professor of Geography at the University of Chicago.

RICHARD COLEBROOK HARRIS is Professor of Geography at the University of British Columbia.

SAM BOWERS HILLIARD is Alumni Professor of Geography at Lousiana State University.

DAVID HORNBECK is Professor of Geography at California State University at Northridge.

JOHN C. HUDSON is Professor of Geography at Northwestern University.

JOHN BRINCKERHOFF JACKSON, founder of *Landscape* magazine, lives and writes in Santa Fe, New Mexico.

JOHN A. JAKLE is Professor of Geography at the University of Illinois at Champaign-Urbana.

HILDEGARD BINDER JOHNSON lives in Minneapolis, and is Professor Emerita of Geography at Macalester College, St. Paul.

PEIRCE F. LEWIS is Professor of Geography at the Pennsylvania State University.

DONALD W. MEINIG is Maxwell Professor of Geography at Syracuse University.

DAVID R. MEYER is Assistant Professor of Sociology at Brown University.

EDWARD K. MULLER is Associate Professor of History at the University of Pittsburgh.

STANLEY W. TRIMBLE is Associate Professor of Geography at the University of California at Los Angeles.

JAMES E. VANCE, JR., is Professor of Geography at the University of California at Berkeley.

JAMES L. WESCOAT, JR., is Assistant Professor of Geography at the University of Colorado.

MICHAEL WILLIAMS is University Lecturer in Geography at the University of Oxford and a Fellow of Oriel College.

WILLIAM K. WYCKOFF is Associate Professor of Geography at Montana State University.

WILBUR ZELINSKY is Professor Emeritus of Geography at the Pennsylvania State University.

# Notes

## Introduction

1 Cosgrove 1984, pp. 1–5, 11.
2 Good examples of reading the landscape for orientation in an urban setting are Lynch (1960) and Clay (1973). The classic statement on the historical record of human adjustment to the Earth is contained in Thomas (1956). The affective dimension of landscape is treated in such works as Tuan (1976, 1979).
3 Mikesell 1968, p. 576; Jackson 1964.
4 Cosgrove 1984, p. 20.
5 Lowenthal 1962–3.
6 Mikesell 1968, p. 578.
7 Mattern 1965–6, p. 14.
8 Coones 1985.
9 As noted in Peirce Lewis' excellent primer on "reading" the American landscape. See Lewis, "Axioms for reading the landscape: Some guides to the American scene" in Meinig (1979, pp. 26–7).
10 Meinig 1979, pp. 33–48.
11 Books on this theme are legion, and the literature devoted to nature in particular localities is almost without count. Attractive examples of general treatments are Shimer (1959), Farb (1963), Thornbury (1965), Watts (1975), and Sullivan (1984).
12 Anderson 1976.
13 Cases in which environmental awareness is treated in direct relation to American landscapes can be found in Lowenthal & Riel (1972), Zube (1973), and Tuan (1974, esp. pp. 66–70).
14 Appleton 1975, pp. 41, 55; Taylor 1976; Watson 1970–1; Cosgrove 1984.
15 Marx 1964; Jakle 1977; Mulvey 1983.
16 Harris, N. 1966; Rees 1978; Salter 1978; Mallory & Simpson-Housley 1987.
17 Tunnard & Pushkarev 1963; Nairn 1965; Greenbie 1981. Some geographers, however, have contributed to the debate, notably Lewis *et al.* (1973) and Luten (1986).
18 For an overview, see Kennedy *et al.* (1988).
19 A hint of the reasons behind this may lie in David Lowenthal's argument that "For many Americans the past is still only a foreign body, alien and intrusive in the great national landscape of today and a positive impediment to realizing the greater creations of tomorrow" (See Lowenthal 1975, p. 111; 1985, pp. 105–24).
20 The best works on the geographical shaping of America, that is, offering a general societal framework within which to view landscape development, are Meinig

(1986) and Mitchell & Groves (1987).

21 The seminal study of the English landscape is Hoskins (1955). A brief and lucid introduction to the general subject is Knowles (1983), containing a succinct but excellent bibliography. Modern writing on American landscape history owes its impetus to J. B. Jackson, who in 1951 founded *Landscape*, the influential magazine devoted to the origins and character of landscapes everywhere. While some of Jackson's writings on the history of the American landscape appear in various anthologies (see Jackson 1980, 1984), and he produced a book-length interpretation of a crucial decade of change in the 19th century (Jackson 1972), many see his most comprehensive framework for dealing with the topic reflected in Stilgoe (1982). A searching assessment of Hoskins' and Jackson's approaches is offered in Meinig (1979, pp. 195–244). In recent years historians have taken an increasing interest in the creation of American landscapes through their exploration of environmental history. While not always making explicit use of the concept of landscape, several studies show a keen eye for the rôle of human action in shaping the visible environment: see, for example, Worster (1979), White (1980), Cronon (1983), and Schuyler (1986).

22 The book also mixes in exotic comparisons with Britain, Germany, and South Africa (Hart 1975).

23 These range from the resolutely scholarly compendia such as Upton & Vlach (1986), which is restricted to architecture, to popular overviews such as Smithsonian Exposition Books (1979), exhibiting a catholic set of commentaries, only some of which are historical.

24 Serious histories of particular urban landscapes—a more manageable scale—are somewhat more common. In the thin American genre of topographical histories the classic treatment of Boston in Whitehill (1968) stands out. Among more modern work, see Mayer & Wade (1969), and Lewis (1976). More often books on a city's historical evolution treat the cityscape as graphic accompaniment rather than central focus. Occasionally, technical treatises in architectural history and landscape architecture devote a chapter to the total landscape evolution of the district considered; for example, as in the study of northwest Cambridge, Mass., in Krim *et al.* (1977, pp. 2–55); and in some Vermont townscapes in Williams *et al.* (1987, pp. 35–43).

25 Lowenthal 1968, p. 81.

26 And even this required two volumes to encompass it (see Noble 1984).

27 Such a book series of regional landscape histories has appeared in Britain, thanks to the inspiration of Hoskins. For a listing, see Knowles (1983).

## 1 Nature's continent

1 Excellent introductions to the physical make-up of the United States can be found in Shimer (1959), Dury & Mathieson (1976), Redfern (1983), and White *et al.* (1985).

2 Hart 1972.

3 A good summary of current knowledge of the ecology of this period is contained in Wright (1983).

4 For a general introduction to regional American physiography, see Fenneman (1931 and 1938), Atwood (1940), Lobeck (1957), Hunt (1974), Chapman & Putnam (1984), and Pirkle & Yoho (1985). For a solid introduction to the distribution of soils, see Steila 1976, and for vegetation see Bowman (1914) and Küchler (1964).

5 Gilbert 1917.

6 Cooke & Reeves 1976.

7 On the Colorado River, for example, see Graf (1985).

8 Quoted in Parkman 1946.

9 Trimble 1985.

10 Hart 1975.

11 John Trotwood Moore, "The Basin of Tennessee," c. 1920.

12 Sauer 1927.

## 2 *The Indian legacy in the American landscape*

I am deeply indebted to William E. Doolittle (Austin), for sharing his library and experience with me. Fred Eggan (Chicago), B. L. Turner II (Worcester), as well as Stephen A. Hall, Robert A. Ricklis and Michael D. Blum (Austin) provided discussion, suggestions, or information. The maps were ably drawn by John V. Cotter (Austin).

1 See McManus *et al.* 1983.

2 Hopkins *et al.* 1982.

3 Reeves 1983.

4 Regarding the Alaskan site, see Hopkins *et al.* (1982) and West (1983); for the Pittsburgh site, see Adovasio *et al.* (1987).

5 West 1983.

6 Porter 1983; Bryant & Holloway 1985.

7 Martin & Klein 1984.

8 Thompson *et al.* 1986.

9 Concerning the High Plains, see Frison (1978), Johnson & Holliday (1986).

10 Ford 1985; Delcourt *et al.* 1986.

11 The sedimentation evidence is presented in Guthrie (1984).

12 Johnson & Holliday 1986; Meltzer & Collins 1987.

13 Hall 1977; Waters 1986.

14 Butzer 1977. Wiant *et al.* (1983) have provided a new set of bore profiles for the Koster Archaic site, Illinois Valley, and a few new dates, arrived at by radiocarbon dating, that confirm earlier observations (Butzer 1977). Rates of sedimentation of colluvial soil across the site can now be refined: 23.2 cm. (9.1 in.) per century ca. 10,000–8200 BP, 14.4 cm. (5.7 in.) per century 8200–4800 BP, and 3.7 cm. (1.5 in.) per century 4800–2100 BP, correcting for distortion of the time scale by radiocarbon calibration. Peak soil erosion upslope led to accumulation of 57.1 cm. (22.5 in.) of sediment per century about 8500 BP, 13.0 cm. (5.1 in.) per century about 5200 BP.

15 Ford 1985; Delcourt *et al.* 1986.

16 For the last 2500 years or so radiocarbon dating has been "corrected" according to the bristlecone pine calibration (Klein *et al.* 1982), in order to avoid a distorted time scale and bring such ages in line with tree-ring and archeomagnetic dates.

17 Frison 1978.

18 Schwarcz *et al.* 1985.

19 Brose & Greber 1979.

20 Butzer 1977.

21 Schwarcz *et al.* 1985.

22 Cohen & Armelagos 1984.

23 Smith 1974; Yerkes 1987.

24 Blum n.d.

25 Smith 1978.

26 Fowler 1978. The "Cahokia Climax" during the Stirling and Moorehead phases has conventional 14C dates of AD 1050–1250, which compares to AD 1135–1290

when calibrated.

27 Gregg 1975.
28 Cohen & Armelagos 1984.
29 Sauer 1971, 1980.
30 Ritchie 1980; Ricklis n.d.
31 Caldwell & Henning 1978.
32 Rohn 1978; Ford 1985.
33 For dating, see Eighmy & Doyel (1987).
34 Mortar appears to have been first introduced to Mexico and the Southwest by the Spanish.
35 Doolittle 1985; Crown 1987.
36 Nicholas & Neitzel 1984; flow data from Masse (1981).
37 However, precarious segments of Hohokam canals were sometimes strengthened by applying fire to a fresh adobe lining, to "bake" it, in lieu of cement (Haury 1976).
38 Midvale 1968; Masse 1981; Nicholas & Neitzel 1984.
39 Nicholas & Neitzel 1984.
40 Fish & Fish 1984; Crown 1987.
41 Wood & McAllister 1984.
42 The drought evidence is discussed in Dean & Robinson (1978).
43 Minnis 1985.
44 The Zuñi archeological evidence is presented in Fish & Fish (1984); on the Spanish estimates, see Sauer (1980).
45 Hornbeck 1982.
46 Fladmark 1986.
47 Herndon 1967.
48 Sauer 1971, 1980.
49 Sauer 1980.
50 Ubelaker 1976; Sturtevant 1978. The problem is illustrated by New Mexico and Arizona, for which Ubelaker (1976) gives a contact population of 113,800. The 1582 Gallegos report estimates at least 5,932 houses in 54 pueblos, specified as having several stories of up to eight rooms (family units), with no less than 130,000 people (see Sauer 1980, pp. 39–40); the Hopi, with a further 300–500 houses, were not included. The 1630 Benavides memorial estimates 56,500 Christian converts, a figure generally multiplied by 1.3 to include children, in 86 pueblos; this represents 73,450 agricultural people under partial Spanish control, with a further 1,750 in Santa Fe, and a plausible total of almost 80,000 (see Sauer 1980, pp. 61–2). These figures do not include other large groups, such as Apache and Navajo, or smaller ones such as the Pima, Papago, Maricopa, Yuma, Mohave, Hualipai, so that 250,000 would seem a conservative figure for New Mexico and Arizona in 1582, reduced to perhaps 150,000 in 1630, prior to the first recorded pandemics.
51 Denevan 1976.
52 Kay 1979; Albers & Kay 1987.
53 This growing economic interdependency and its environmental implications are examined by Ray & Freeman (1978) and a critical review of the growing literature is given by Peterson & Anfinson (1984).
54 Members of De Soto's group noted Chickasaw tending pigs during their own stay, and feral pigs were reported by the Spanish in Florida as early as 1539; the hogs reportedly kept by the Iroquois in 1687 may have been of such early, Spanish origin (see Sauer 1971, 1980).
55 Goodwin 1977; Newman 1979; Delcourt *et al.* 1986.
56 Hilliard 1972; Utley & Washburn 1977.

57 Hudson 1976.

58 Wishart 1979.

59 Zelinksy 1973.

60 Recent pollen studies have become so refined as to provide dramatic evidence regarding the scope of Indian agriculture, expressed in forest clearance, weed "explosions" and the pollen and macro-botanical remains of cultivated as well as collected or tended plants (Delcourt *et al.* 1986).

61 Jordan 1989.

62 Nash 1982; Axtell 1981.

63 Brown 1983; LeCompte 1978.

64 Mudbrick housing is limited to a very few, out-of-the-way locations in southeastern and east-central Spain, and flat roofs are only characteristic in parts of Granada, Murcia and the island of Ibiza. None of these areas contributed to the stream of emigrants to the New World (Butzer 1988).

## 3 *Spanish legacy in the Borderlands*

1 Bolton 1921; Bannon 1968.

2 Gold 1969.

3 Bolton 1917.

4 Some good general works on this topic are Caroso (1963), Bannon (1974), and McDermott (1974).

5 Nasatir 1976.

6 Wright 1971.

## 4 *French landscapes in North America*

1 A good introduction to the geographical dynamics underlying the development of French-influenced landscapes in North America can be found in Harris & Warkentin (1974). A major new source for interpreting the evolving geography of New France, along with many of its landscape features, is the recently published *Historical atlas of Canada*, vol. I: *Beginnings to 1800* (Harris 1987).

2 A useful overview of the early Maritime fisheries is Head (1976).

3 Clark 1968.

4 Harris, R. C. 1966.

5 Lewis 1976a.

6 Belting 1948; Gentilcore 1957.

7 Johnson 1958.

8 For an excellent geographical overview of the Acadian migrations that included Louisiana as a destination, see LeBlanc (1979); a recent detailed account of the Acadian settlement of Louisiana is found in Brasseaux (1987; see especially maps, pp. 93, 97); the Cajun building traditions developed in Louisiana are treated in Kniffen (1965), Heck (1978) and Rooney *et al.* (1982, p. 79). For discussion of 19th-century French Canadian migrations to the United States, see McQuillan (1979).

5 *The Northeast and the making of American geographical habits*

1 Throughout most of American history, Americans have been torn between the urge to tame the land and a conflicting almost mystical urge to conserve it—even to worship it. The motivations, of course, pit economics against esthetics and even theology—at best a complicated matter. Three intelligent treatments of this intricate subject are White (1967), R. Nash (1973) and Cronon (1983).
2 Cooper 1810.
3 Ravenstein 1885, 1889.
4 Kurath 1973.
5 Meinig 1966.
6 The first major treatment of this New England diaspora was Rosenberry (1909).
7 Kniffen 1965; Lewis 1975; Hudson 1986.
8 Holbrook 1950.
9 Glass 1986.
10 Lewis 1976b.
11 It is noteworthy that Pennsylvania, for all its wealth and population, has produced just one American president, the hapless James Buchanan (1857–61), mainly remembered for keeping the presidential chair warm while the nation prepared to tear itself apart in Civil War. See also the scathing commentary on the membership of Pennsylvania's congressional delegation in Barone *et al.* (1988, p. 1008).
12 This view is not mere subjective opinion, but is supported by meticulous comparative enumerations of leaders from the two regions; see Baltzell (1979).
13 Gowans 1976.
14 Zelinsky 1977.
15 Paint, however, was another matter. In colonial and early national times, paint was very expensive, and only wealthy people could afford to use it. As a result, the bulk of New England's wooden houses simply went unpainted and turned a weathered gray. The tendency to paint all New England houses white is a fashion of fairly recent date. Meantime, Pennsylvanians often painted their red bricks red—presumably to help preserve them from the weather.
16 Gowans 1976.
17 Classical place-naming was not confined to New York State, of course, but the region between Utica and Rochester contains perhaps the densest and most exuberant collection of classical names in North America. Almost all of them were bestowed in the first three decades of the 19th century (Zelinsky 1967).
18 This amazing episode has been chronicled by Cross (1950).
19 Classical styles were adopted by élite folk in the South as well, but they are by no means as common as viewers of *Gone with the wind* would have been led to believe. In vernacular housing built before the Civil War, aspects of southern classicism are much more restrained (see Trimble (1988)). In a meticulous count of dwellings in Georgia in the early 1950s, Zelinsky found Classical Revival houses to be concentrated mainly on the Piedmont, and mainly in towns. Classical mansions in the country, *à la* Tara, were very rare, and it seems doubtful if Sherman's army could have burned them all down (see Zelinksy (1954)). New England's western extension in the upper Great Lakes region still contains the densest concentration of vernacular classical buildings in the United States.
20 Hubka 1984.
21 Glass 1986, Ch. 2, n. 10.
22 Midwesterners commonly added a gambrel roof and red paint to the basic Pennsylvania model, to produce the "standard" American barn of popular image. Both features are also common in central Sweden, but they apparently diffused throughout the rest of the farm belt through the efforts of county extension

agents from a number of university colleges of agriculture.

23 Conzen 1980b.

24 Wood 1982.

25 This geopolitical terminology is peculiar to New England and New York State, which was largely organized by New Englanders. Elsewhere in the United States, the closest thing to a New England town is called a "township," which is usually merely a political subdivision of a larger county. Outside the New England region, townships often have very little significance, but in New England, true to its origins, towns possess a huge amount of political autonomy and power—often including zoning authority. Regional planning is hard enough in the United States, but in New England, with wildly fragmented authority over land-use decisions, planning is a nightmare.

26 For an excellent discussion of the New England village as a feature of the vernacular landscape, see Wood (1986).

27 Some of our most potent geography, of course, is not tangible, but is in the form of mental images. For penetrating discussions of the New England village as geographic image, see Meinig (1979) and Wood (1987).

28 Lewis 1983.

29 For a vivid and witty chronicle of what happened to one section of domestic vernacular landscape in the process, see Watts (1975).

## 6 *Plantations and the molding of the southern landscape*

1 Hilliard 1982b, p. 131.

2 Jones 1957, p. vii.

3 Prunty 1955, p. 460.

4 Hilliard 1982b, p. 133.

5 Robert 1949, Preface.

6 *Ibid.*, pp. 7–8

7 *Ibid.*

8 *Ibid.*, p. 18.

9 According to the first Federal Census; see Wiley (1970, p. 11).

10 Robert 1938, pp. 6–7.

11 The Piedmont expands from a region approximately 45 miles wide at the Potomac, to 165 miles wide at the Virginia–North Carolina border, to its widest point of 175–180 miles in North Carolina (Robert 1938, p. 16).

12 Compared with 8–10 acres of cotton, or 20 acres of corn or wheat (Robert 1938, p. 18).

13 Robert 1938, p. 19. This size is considerably smaller than the definition usually given for plantation sizes, i.e., over 500 acres, but these were the original plantations in the South and were limited by the vagaries of tobacco cultivation already mentioned. For a discussion of this see Parkins (1938, p. 189).

14 Hilliard 1982b, p. 131.

15 Parkins 1938, pp. 190ff.

16 Parkins 1938.

17 South Carolina's agriculture was established in the 17th century, but the Georgia colony was not founded until 1733.

18 Winberry 1979, pp. 91–102.

19 Hilliard 1978, p. 92.

20 Heyward 1937, p. 4.

21 Heyward 1937. Dr. Woodward also had the distinction of being the first English settler in the region (see Salley 1919).

22 Salley 1919.
23 Hilliard 1978, p. 94.
24 *Ibid.*, pp. 97–8; Heyward 1937, pp. 12–14.
25 Hilliard 1978, pp. 98–104.
26 *Ibid.*, pp. 111–12.
27 Civil government had been established by the United States in Florida only in 1822, so settlement here lagged somewhat behind (see Parkins 1938, pp. 111–12).
28 Newton 1974, pp. 143–54; Otto & Anderson 1982, 89–98.
29 In the upper Mississippi Valley the increase in towns with populations of 2,500 or more, in the years between 1820 and 1870, was from 1 to 235; in the lower Mississippi Valley (Kentucky, Tennessee, Alabama, Mississippi, Arkansas, Louisiana, and Texas) the increase was from 3 to 46 (see Still 1974, p. 103).
30 Pease & Pease 1985, p. 8.
31 Pease & Pease 1985.
32 *Ibid.*, p. 9.
33 Rubin 1967, pp. 14–15.
34 Although there were scattered mill villages and some manufacturing in larger cities, like Richmond, which reflected efforts of small groups of investors to encourage local industry (see Still 1974, p. 104).
35 Radford 1983.
36 Prunty 1955, p. 462.
37 Hilliard 1979, p. 255.
38 *Ibid.*, p. 258, see also Rehder 1978, pp. 135–50.
39 Hilliard 1980, p. 414.
40 Prunty 1955, pp. 467–68.
41 The exception to this development, which was most extreme on the cotton plantations, were the sugar plantations, which continued to rely on "gang" labor of the type slaves had provided prior to the Civil War (Prunty 1955). The reason given for this was the apparent difficulty in dividing effectively the sugar between laborers and the owners of the land and sugar mills (*ibid.*, p. 472.).
42 A caveat must be added to the discussion of sharecropping. The system existed throughout the South, but was most common in the cotton and tobacco regions. Because of the high level of technology employed in the sugar-making process, sharecropping was much less used on sugar plantations. Moreover, sharecropping is so much identified with blacks that we forget its impact on poor whites as well. In many parts of the South, white sharecroppers *outnumbered* black sharecroppers.
43 Aiken 1978, pp. 151–65.
44 Wall 1981, pp. 251–62.
45 On neo-plantations see Prunty (1955, pp. 459–91).
46 Aiken 1973, pp. 196–224.

## 7 Towards a national landscape

1 See Pattison 1957, pp. 38, 63–6.
2 Franz Joseph Marschner's original map, after one copy was made, was sent to the Director of the Lake State Experiment Station in St. Paul, Minnesota. The Washington copy was sent to the same place in April, 1963, redrawn and published in color on the original scale in 1974.
3 See Pattison (1957, Chs. 5, 6) for Seven Ranges with map.
4 Thrower 1966.
5 Stewart 1935, pp. 16–23, 46, 88–9 (picture of solar compass), 114, 174–5. Long out

of print, this history of surveying was reprinted in a limited edition in 1975, through the efforts of the surveyors' societies in Michigan, Wisconsin and Minnesota, by Meyers of Minneapolis.

6 Marx 1974.

7 Johnson 1957.

8 Horton 1902, p. 58.

9 The four scenes are reproduced in Thompson (1966, pp. 365–7), Havighurst (1960, pp. 188–9) and in Johnson (1978, pp. 19–20).

10 Sauer 1963, p. 38.

11 Conzen 1984a & b.

12 Thrower 1961, pp. 365–72.

13 Johnson 1978; Rohrbough 1968, p. 51; Gates 1978, pp. 107–8.

14 Johnson 1976, p. 140.

15 Hart 1972, p. 258.

16 For a list of townsites with dates of entry up to 1880, see Donaldson (1884, pp. 300–5).

17 Borchert 1967, p. 305.

18 Conzen 1980a.

19 Personal communication from L. M. Sebert, 1977.

20 Stewart 1935, p. 45 (Fig. 6 Reynolds County).

21 Langewiesche 1950, p. 188.

22 Johnson 1976, pp. 191–6 (for Coon Creek watershed, see *ibid.*, p. 194).

23 Nassauer 1986.

24 Quay 1966, p. 77.

25 Meinig 1979, p. 167; and Jackson 1979, p.158.

26 Laforc 1971.

27 *New Yorker* January 1, 1979, 21.

28 Cirlot 1962, p. 293.


## 8 *The clearing of the forests*

1 See Hall 1836.

2 Hindle 1975, 1981; Van Ravenswaay 1970.

3 Williams 1987.

4 Dobyns 1966; Jacobs 1974.

5 For reviews see Day (1953), Martin (1973) and Maxwell (1910).

6 Strachey 1620.

7 Belknap 1791, pp. 131–7; Cooper 1810, pp. 117–18; Dwight 1821, pp. 125–6, 325–6.

8 Danhof 1969; Bidwell & Falconer 1923; Russell 1976.

9 Chastellux 1789.

10 Turner 1849.

11 De Brahm 1856.

12 Nairne 1732.

13 Williams 1982.

14 Shurtleff 1939.

15 Dwight 1821, pp. 295–7; Crévecoeur 1770, pp. 114–15.

16 Glassie 1975; Gould 1965.

17 Flint 1828, vol. 2, pp. 75–6.

18 Cooper 1810, pp. 127–8; Oliver 1843, pp. 239–40.

19 Gray & Thompson 1933, vol. 2, p. 533; Russell 1976, pp. 104–7.

20 Hart 1968; Hendrickson 1933.

21 Frothingham 1919.

22 A cord is a cubic measure of wood, 8x4x4 feet or 128 cubic feet.

23 Crévecoeur 1770, p. 144; Gates 1972; Muntz 1959; Reynolds & Pierson 1942.

24 Bridenbaugh 1938.

25 Muntz 1959.

26 Eavenson 1942.

27 Hart 1968, 1980.

28 A board foot, or b.f., is a common measure for timber in the United States. It is 1 foot x 1 foot x 1 inch, and 12 b.f. equal 1 cubic foot. The metric equivalent of 1 cubic foot is 0.02832 cubic metres.

29 Steer 1948.

30 North 1961; Robbins 1982.

31 Dinsdale 1965.

32 Illick 1924; Latham 1957; Van Tassel & Bluestone 1940.

33 Fox 1902; Wood 1935.

34 Hough 1878, vol. 1, p. 446.

35 Fries 1951, pp. 60–83, 141–60; Rector 1953.

36 Fries 1951, pp. 204–21; Rohe 1972, 1986.

37 Erickson 1965.

38 Fries 1951; Benson 1976; Smith 1973.

39 Hartt 1900.

40 Holbrook 1943; Pyne 1982.

41 Hartman & Black 1931.

42 Carstenson 1958; Clark 1956; Helgeson 1953, 1962; Kane 1954.

43 Williams 1982.

44 Hickman 1952, 1962.

45 Bryant 1913; Hickman 1962.

46 Allen 1961; Creel 1915; Stokes 1957.

47 For an excellent account of life in such a town, Fullerton, LA, see Richardson (1983).

48 Forbes 1923.

49 Stokes 1957.

50 U.S. Congress, Senate 1909 and 1920.

51 Cox 1974.

52 Erickson 1965; Van Tassel & Bluestone 1940.

53 Thomas 1864.

54 Temin 1964.

55 Schallenberg 1975.

56 Lesley 1859; Warren 1973.

57 Ransom 1966.

58 Beatley 1953; Williams 1982.

59 Fishlow 1965.

60 Schob 1977; Williams 1980.

61 Sargent 1884.

62 Cole 1970.

## 9 Settlement of the American grassland

1 See Alwin 1981.

2 Hart 1972, p. 268.

3 Sauer 1944, p. 552.

4 Webb *et al.* 1983, p. 163.

5 Borchert 1950.

Notes

6 Hewes & Jung 1981; Hewes 1981.
7 Sauer 1971, pp. 142–7.
8 Hudson 1978.
9 Hudson 1975.
10 Johnson 1957.
11 Hudson 1986b.
12 Hart 1972.
13 Hewes 1951.
14 Hart 1986.
15 Hudson 1986a.
16 Malin 1947.
17 Webb 1931.
18 Hargreaves 1957.
19 Kollmorgen 1969; Mather 1972.
20 Jordan 1977.
21 Atherton 1961.
22 Reps 1979.
23 Hudson 1985.

## 10 Challenging the desert

1 See Smythe 1905; Lee 1980.
2 U.S. Congress 1874; White 1960; Powell 1962; Abbey 1975.
3 Limerick 1985.
4 Shepard 1981.
5 White 1960; Kelso et al. 1973; Wolman & Wolman 1986.
6 Upham 1984.
7 McPhee 1971.
8 Templer 1978; Wescoat 1984.
9 Hundley 1966, 1975.
10 Dobyns & Byrkit 1981.
11 Haury 1976; DiPeso 1979; Plog 1980.
12 Ezell 1983.
13 Ibid.
14 Castetter & Bell 1942; Bohrer 1971.
15 Hackenberg 1983.
16 Smith 1972.
17 Doyel 1980.
18 cf. Doyel (1980) and Plog (1980).
19 For example, see Nabhan (1984).
20 Simmons 1972.
21 Vivian 1974.
22 Cordell 1979.
23 Clark 1960.
24 Simmons 1982.
25 Meyer 1984.
26 Ibid.
27 Meinig 1971.
28 Templer 1978.
29 Meinig 1965.
30 Harris 1940.
31 Haglund & Notarianni 1980.

32 cf. Locke's natural theory of property.
33 Hudson 1962.
34 See Francaviglia (1978) on esthetic debates during recent decades.
35 Arrington 1975.
36 Maass & Anderson 1978.
37 Graf 1985; Quin 1968; National Research Council 1968.
38 U.S. Congress 1947.
39 Meyers 1966.
40 U.S. Congress 1950.
41 Venturi *et al.* 1977.
42 Lawton *et al.* 1976.
43 McPhee 1971.

## 11 Democratic utopia and the American landscape

1 Vance 1977.
2 Bridenbaugh 1938.
3 Powell 1963.
4 Francaviglia 1978.
5 Porter & Lukermann 1976.
6 For a recent discussion of the values underlying this philosophical commitment, see Vogeler (1981).
7 Bridenbaugh 1938.
8 Vance 1977.
9 Jackson 1985.

## 12 Ethnicity on the land

1 The working definition of ethnicity employed here regards members of an ethnic group as sharing traits that are a product of their common heredity and cultural traditions. In the American context Amerindians and African-Americans form the basis for ethnic groups, as do, for example, Chinese, Japanese and a host of traditionally distinguishable European groups. Not included in this definition are groups bound together merely on the basis of a particular religion or ideology. Baptists, for example, do not constitute an ethnic group. The Mormons are a possible exception in so far as their early history involved considerable geographical isolation and inbreeding, conditions suitable for the rapid development of a set of strong social traits that created a distinct settlement landscape in an initially localized area (see Francaviglia 1978).
2 An authoritative guide to the historical provenance and general characteristics of the many groups is contained in Thernstrom (1980). Their geographical distribution in the 20th century is presented cartographically at the county and large-city level in Allen & Turner (1988). For an able discussion of other mapping of ethnic groups, at a variety of scales, see Raitz (1978).
3 The terminology of memory versus experience is drawn from Upton (1986, p. 10).
4 This is the argument for "simplification" of old world cultural traits versus the potency of "cultural baggage." For a recent assertion of the former view, see Harris (1977).
5 For literature on sod houses, see Noble (1981); regarding adobe construction in American dwellings, see Spears (1986).

*Notes*

6 Jordan & Kaups 1989.

7 Kouwenhoven 1972, pp. 48–9, 64; Zink 1987; Cummings 1979.

8 Meixner 1956; Glassie cited in Upton (1986, pp. 74–9).

9 For a good modern discussion of the historical geography of colonial settlement see Mitchell & Groves (1987, Ch. 5).

10 For a useful survey of these topics, see Jordan (1985).

11 The Germanic basis is well argued in Jordan (1985); Swedish ancestry is noted in Meixner (1956).

12 Jordan & Kaups 1989, pp. 7–14, 35–7.

13 For discussion of the English colonial building traditions in New England and the Chesapeake Bay, see Noble (1984); also Carson cited in Upton (1986, pp. 54–61).

14 Weaver 1986. Another well researched example of a localized early German landscape in the East is the Massanutten settlement in Virginia's Shenandoah Valley (see Chappell 1980). The classic Pennsylvania German farmscape is laid out in Long (1972).

15 Ludwig 1945.

16 Nor is there anywhere a comprehensive guide to this subject. But for a succinct review of the chief visual characteristics of building traditions attributable to several ethnic groups in America, see Upton (1986).

17 Space permits only cursory treatment of a few of the many possible traits mentioned. Emphasis here is on the larger, continuously visible elements, such as building architecture, land and village patterns and religious signatures. However, the other aspects mentioned are no less intrinsic to the overall cultural imprint on the landscape. For an illustration of one ethnic group's contribution to naming places in America, that of the Swedes, see Landelius (1985).

18 Vernacular forms are those of ordinary people performing everyday functions. While often in some way inspired by high-style, professionally designed forms, vernacular forms remain largely domestic or craft-based in origin and use.

19 See Ch. 17 above.

20 Noble 1984, vol. I, pp. 32, 41–2.

21 Henning & Palmqvist in Upton 1986, pp. 149–59; Selkurt 1985, p. 252; on stone construction, see Jaderborg (1981) and Breisch & Moore (1986, pp. 64–71).

22 Noble 1984, vol. 1, p. 119; Van Ravenswaay 1977, p. 151; and Tishler 1986. For Texas, see Jordan (1964) and Wilhelm (1971).

23 Half hip/half gable.

24 Laatsch 1988; Calkins & Laatsch in Upton 1986.

25 Kaups 1983.

26 Peterson 1976; Koop & Ludwig 1984; Peterson 1984.

27 Tishler & Witmer 1986; Marshall 1986.

28 Alanen & Tishler 1980.

29 Long 1972, pp. 122–33.

30 *Ibid.*, pp. 134–55; Calkins & Laatsch 1979; Conzen & Conzen 1988.

31 Mather & Kaups 1963.

32 Johnson 1955.

33 Jordan 1964; Milner 1975; Van Ravenswaay 1977, p. 151.

34 Chs. 3, 4 & 7 above.

35 McHenry 1986.

36 Wilson 1972.

37 Ingalls 1986.

38 Trewartha 1943.

39 Gerlach 1976.

40 Davis 1936.

41 Isaksson & Hallgren 1969.

42 P. R. Johnson 1984.

43 Vogeler 1976.
44 Calkins & Laatsch in Upton (1986, p. 101).
45 Vlach 1986.
46 Godfrey 1988.
47 Arreola 1981, 1984.
48 Kory 1978.
49 Geraniotis 1986.
50 Rice 1973.
51 Palmqvist 1983, pp. 101–2.
52 A good illustration of this gradual process of adjustment is given in Chappell (1980).
53 This "island" terminology is used explicitly in Noble (1985).
54 Dockendorff 1986; Vogeler 1976.
55 Conzen & Conzen 1988.
56 Zelinsky 1973, pp. 13–14.
57 Meinig 1965; Francaviglia 1978; Peterson & Bennion 1987.


## 13  *The new industrial order*

1 See Trinder 1982.
2 Walton & Sheperd 1979.
3 Goldenberg 1976.
4 U.S. Bureau of the Census 1975, Series Z1–Z19.
5 Bining 1933, Apendix F.
6 Paskoff 1983.
7 Meyer 1983.
8 Temin 1964.
9 Taylor 1951, pp. 132–5.
10 Segal 1961, p. 172.
11 U.S. Bureau of the Census 1975, Series Q321–328.
12 Davis *et al.* 1972, p. 494.
13 Pred 1980.
14 Armstrong 1969.
15 Kulik *et al.* 1982.
16 Hunter 1979, vol. 1, pp. 221–7.
17 Stilgoe 1983.
18 Taylor & Neu 1956; U.S. Bureau of the Census 1975, Series Q284–328.
19 Fishlow 1965, p. 585.
20 Chandler 1977.
21 Davis *et al.* 1972, pp. 433, 447.
22 James 1983.
23 Temin 1964.
24 Warren 1973.
25 Clark 1929, vol. 2, p. 514.
26 Perloff *et al.* 1960.
27 Cox 1974.
28 Clark 1929, vol. 3, pp. 245–52.
29 Greever 1963.
30 Peterson 1977.
31 Williamson & Daum 1959; Williamson *et al.* 1963.
32 Stilgoe 1983, pp. 77–103.
33 Chandler 1977, pp. 240–83.

34 Devine 1983.

35 Dunn 1983; Jones 1938.

36 Dunn 1983.

37 Warren 1973.

38 Clark 1929, vol. 3, pp. 157–64; Dunn 1983, vol. 2, pp. 151–2.

39 U.S. Bureau of the Census 1975, Series Q148–162.

40 Hall & Markusen 1985.

## 14 *The Americanization of the city*

1 For a popular description of the modern American city, see Lockwood & Leinberger (1988, pp. 31–56).

2 Bellah 1986, Ch. 2; Lemon 1972, Preface and pp. 1–13; Warner 1968, pp. ix–xii.

3 Teaford 1975.

4 Vance 1971, pp. 101–20

5 Vance 1977, pp. 245–69.

6 Reps 1979.

7 Muller 1980, pp. 747–55.

8 Barth 1980, pp. 110–47.

9 Goldberger 1981.

10 Stilgoe 1983, pp. 30–45.

11 Mollenkopf 1983.

12 Muller 1981, Ch. 4.

13 Hoover & Vernon 1962, pp. 21–73.

14 Burstein 1981, pp. 174–203.

15 Ward 1971; and Zunz 1982.

16 Bodnar *et al.* 1982.

17 Gottlieb 1987.

18 Spear 1967; Kusmer 1976.

19 Hirsch 1983.

20 Wright 1981, Ch. 2.

21 Jackson 1985, pp. 45–137; Doucet & Weaver 1985, pp. 560–87; Warner 1962.

22 Jackson 1985, pp. 157–282; Muller 1981, Chs. 2 & 3.

23 Rothman 1971.

24 Teaford 1984; Lubove 1969; Scott 1969; Tunnard & Reed 1956, pp. 136–53.

25 Gelfand 1975.

26 Bauman 1987.

27 Wilson 1987; Lukas 1985.

28 Daly 1987.

29 Wissink 1962; Lichtenberger 1970, pp. 45–62.

## 15 *Landscapes redesigned for the automobile*

1 See Dodds 1961, p. 146.

2 *Ibid.*

3 Wik 1972, p. 233.

4 Jackson 1985, p. 161.

5 Rae 1981, p. 57.

6 Jackson 1985, p. 162.

7 Dodds 1961, p. 147.

8 Jackson 1985, p. 163.
9 Flink 1975, p. 55.
10 Hugill 1982.
11 Mason 1957.
12 Anon. 1935.
13 Rose 1950, p. 742.
14 Miller 1950.
15 Fuessle 1915, p. 26.
16 Jackson 1985, p. 170.
17 Horvath 1974.
18 Davies 1975, p. 42.
19 Warner 1972, p. 41.
20 *Ibid.*, p. 39.
21 Goodman 1971, p. 73.
22 Mumford 1964, p. 234.
23 Goodman 1971, p. 73.
24 Davies 1975, p. 28.
25 Leavitt 1970, p. 13.
26 Davies 1975, p. 36.
27 Guiness & Bradshaw 1985, p. 217.
28 Snow 1967.
29 Muller 1981, p. 4.
30 *Ibid.*, p. 51.
31 Jackson 1985, p. 7.
32 Lewis 1979, p. 186.
33 Jackson 1985, p. 205.
34 *Ibid.*, p. 239.
35 *Ibid.*, p. 8.
36 Muth 1968, p. 285.
37 Jackson 1985, p. 277.
38 *Ibid.*, p. 250.
39 *Ibid.*, p. 10.
40 Higbee 1976, p. 150.
41 Mumphery & Seley 1972.
42 Muller 1981, p. 122; Johnston 1982, p. 220.
43 Liebs 1985.
44 Tunnard & Pushkarev 1963, p. 162.
45 Robinson 1971, p. 52.
46 Mumford 1961, p. 486.
47 Priestly 1937, p. 88.
48 De Tocqueville 1956, pp. 114, 117.
49 Relph 1981, p. 94.

## 16 *The imprint of central authority*

1 See Knight 1971; Whittlesey 1935.
2 Craig 1978, p. 163.
3 Stilgoe 1982, pp. 109–11.
4 Craig 1978, p. 163.
5 Zelinksy 1988.
6 Nash 1970.
7 Rhyne 1979.

8 *Ibid.*
9 Mosse 1979, pp. 7–8; Patterson 1982.
10 Mollenhoff 1983; Steere 1953–4a, 1953–4b, 1953–4c.
11 Patterson 1974.
12 Federal Writers' Project 1937, pp. 3–4.
13 Fifer 1981; Henrikson 1983, p. 124.
14 Bush 1977, pp. 39–41; Cosgrove 1984, pp. 181–3; Green 1962–3; Fifer 1981; Gutheim & Washburn 1976; Reps 1967.
15 Reps 1967, p. 21.
16 National Capital Planning Commission 1984.
17 Henrikson 1983, p. 134.
18 Fairman 1927; Feeley 1957; Gowans 1981, pp. 123–4; Hitchcock & Seale 1976, pp. 121–46; Krythe 1968, pp. 140–67; Miller 1966, pp. 40–78; Scully 1984.
19 Hitchcock & Seale 1976, p. 48.
20 *Ibid.*, p. 9.
21 Craig 1978, p. 141.
22 Hitchcock & Seale 1976, p. 187.
23 Harper 1971; Ohman 1985, pp. 67–70; Pare 1978.
24 Hitchcock & Seale 1976, pp. 172–84.
25 Goodsell 1984; Lebovich 1984.
26 Price 1968.
27 Craig 1978, p. 440.
28 Cutler 1985.
29 Stewart 1953, pp. 13–14.
30 Roberts 1987.
31 Cutler 1985, pp. 133–44.
32 Stone 1950.
33 Cutler 1985, pp. 116–32.
34 For an eloquent account of the situation in Lyndon Johnson's Texas Hill Country, see Caro (1983, pp. 502–15).
35 Alexander 1980; Contreras 1983; Larson 1983; Marling 1982; McKinzie 1973.
36 Lowenthal 1977.
37 Stump 1985.
38 Zelinsky 1984.
39 Caro 1974.

## 17 *Landscapes of private power and wealth*

1 See Domhoff 1967, pp. 7–8; Pessen 1973, pp. 302–3.
2 Shi 1985, p. 55.
3 Wecter 1937; Persons 1973, pp. 31–3; Lewis 1975, pp. 3–4.
4 Lowell 1902; Wright 1928, vol. 2, pp. 421–42; Clifford 1966; Highstone 1982, pp. 1–10.
5 Humphreys 1914, pp. 74–97.
6 Wecter 1937, 475–80; Baltzell 1962, pp. 252–93.
7 Philadelphia Club founded in 1834; Union Club, New York, founded in 1836.
8 Chicago Club founded in 1869; Bohemian Club, San Francisco, founded in 1872; Wecter 1937, pp. 255–67; Baltzell 1962, pp. 373–403; Pessen 1973, pp. 223–7; Thompson 1981, pp. 191–5; Bushnell 1982.
9 McLachlan 1970; Baird 1977; Waller 1985.
10 Boarding schools were established at Lawrenceville, 1883, at Groton in 1884, and at Deerfield in 1903.

11 Baltzell 1962, pp. 363–71.

12 Wecter 1937, pp. 444–7; Slater 1967; Spears & Swanson 1978, pp. 69–70.

13 Prunty 1963; Breukheimer 1982.

14 Betts 1974; Spears & Swanson 1978.

15 Betts 1974, p. 10; Raitz 1980, pp. 18–23.

16 Wecter 1937, pp. 448–57; Betts 1974; Spears & Swanson 1978.

17 Robinson 1981.

18 Wecter 1937, pp. 270–6; Betts 1974; Spears & Swanson 1978; Bremer 1981.

19 Betts 1974; Spears & Swanson 1978.

20 Humphreys 1914, pp. 240–51; Tarshis & Waller 1984; Michael 1985.

21 Bent 1929; Wecter 1937, pp. 447–8; Betts 1974.

22 Cable 1984, p. 150.

23 Pessen 1973.

24 Wecter 1937, pp. 272–4; Gowans 1976, pp. 313–4; Roth 1979, pp. 105–7; Cable 1984, p. 31.

25 Louw 1983, pp. 79–80.

26 Sobin 1968, pp. 99–110; Banham 1971, p. 147; Duncan 1973, p. 337; Burns 1980; Cook & Kaplan 1983; Louw 1983.

27 Wecter 1937, pp. 5–9; Domhoff 1967, p. 30; Sobin 1968, pp. 152–6; Jaher 1980, pp. 197–201.

28 Duncan 1973; Hugill 1980; Cable 1984, pp. 148–50.

29 Lynes 1955, pp. 8–11, 229–37; Sobin 1968, p. 34; Gowans 1976, pp. 313–4.

30 Lynes 1955, pp. 240–1; Streatfield 1977, p. 234; Roth 1979, p. 98.

31 Dulles 1965, pp. 202, 359–60; Betts 1974, pp. 156–60; Starr 1984, p. 28.

32 Shi 1985, p. 51.

33 Baltzell 1962, pp. 206–8; Andrews 1978, pp. 36–8.

34 Lewis 1975, pp. 10–12; Andrews 1978, pp. 22–8.

35 Bridenbaugh 1946; Lawrence 1983.

36 Dulles 1965, p. 64.

37 Lewis 1975; Bonner 1977; Andrews 1978, p. 137.

38 Pessen 1973.

39 Sweetser 1868, pp. 146–7; Baltzell 1962, pp. 223–5; Vance 1972; Andrews 1978, pp. 107–9; O'Brien 1981, pp. 141–5.

40 Sweetser 1868; Dulles 1965; Lawrence 1983.

41 Lynes 1955, pp. 81–9.

42 Wecter 1937, pp. 108–56; Dulles 1965, pp. 232–8; Sobin 1968, pp. 10–11; Jaher 1973; Hammack 1982; Cable 1984.

43 Sobin 1968, pp. 28–32; Burns 1980; O'Brien 1981, pp. 202–6.

44 Sweetser 1868, p. 48.

45 Bachelder 1875; Baedecker 1904; Amory 1952; Kramer 1978.

46 Sprague 1980.

47 Dulles 1965, pp. 360–1; Dunleavy 1981; Allen 1983.

48 Gowans 1976, pp. 715–63; Andrews 1978, pp. 1–31; Roth 1979, pp. 1–52.

49 Whitehill 1968, pp. 22–46; Andrews 1978, pp. 34–54; Baltzell 1979; Shi 1985, pp. 33–4.

50 Andrews 1978, pp. 22–31.

51 Gowans 1976, pp. 164–72.

52 Wecter 1937, pp. 73–4; Whitehill 1968, pp. 47–72; Andrews 1978, pp. 86–96; Roth 1979, pp. 59–68.

53 Gowans 1976, pp. 243–65; Andrews 1978, pp. 56–62.

54 Gowans 1976, pp. 267–84; Roth 1979, pp. 53–100.

55 Gowans 1976, pp. 291–328; Bonner 1977; Andrews 1978, pp. 97–143; Roth 1979, pp. 100–25.

56 Jaher 1973; Gowans 1976, pp. 329–86; Andrews 1978, pp. 144–97; Roth 1979,

pp. 126–227; Hammack 1982.

57 Wecter 1937, pp. 142–3; Jaher 1973, pp. 258–9; Cable 1984, p. 28.
58 Lynes 1955, pp. 220–2; Andrews 1978, pp. 222–45; Roth 1979, pp. 192–359; Howett 1982.
59 McWilliams 1946, pp. 77–83, Streatfield 1977, pp. 231–2; Ferrell 1984.
60 Louw 1983, p. 161.
61 Allen 1952, pp. 219–22; Lerner 1957, pp. 481–6.
62 Gowans 1976, pp. 304–5; Roth 1979, p. 92; Hugill 1980, p. 10.
63 Whitehill 1968, pp. 236–7; Goldstone 1974; Lewis 1976, pp. 86–90; Findsen 1984.
64 Sobin 1968; Burns 1980; O'Brien 1981, pp. 202–59.
65 Ruhling 1986.

## 18 The house in the vernacular landscape

1 Three books I have found very helpful in writing this chapter are Sack (1986), Kent (1984), and Hillyer & Hanson (1984).

# Bibliography

Abbey, E. 1975. *Desert solitaire: a season in the wilderness*. New York: Ballantine.

Adovasio, J. M., A. T. Boldurian & R. C. Carlisle 1987. "Who are those guys? Early human populations in eastern North America." Paper presented to the Mammoths, mastodons and human interaction Symposium, Baylor University, Waco, Texas, October.

Agg, T. R. 1920. *American rural highways*. New York: McGraw-Hill.

Aiken, C. S. 1973. "The evolution of cotton ginning in the southeastern United States." *Geographical Review* **63**, April, 196–224.

Aiken, C. S. 1978. "The decline of sharecropping in the lower Mississippi Valley," in "Man and environment in the lower Mississippi Valley." *Geoscience and Man* **19**, 151–65.

Alanen, A. R. & W. H. Tishler 1980. "Finnish farmstead organization in Old and New World settings." *Journal of Cultural Geography* **1**, Fall/Winter, 66–81.

Albers, P. & J. Kay 1987. "Sharing the land: a study in American Indian territoriality." In *A cultural geography of North American Indians*, T. E. Ross & T. G. Moore (eds.), 47–91. Boulder: Westview Press.

Alexander, C. C. 1980. *Here the country lies: nationalism and the arts in twentieth-century America*. Bloomington: Indiana University Press.

Allen, E. J. B. 1983. "Winter culture: the origins of skiing in the United States." *Journal of American Culture* **6**, 65–8.

Allen, F. L. 1952. *The big change: America transforms itself 1900–1950*. New York: Harper.

Allen, J. P. & E. J. Turner 1988. *We the people: an atlas of America's ethnic diversity*. New York: Macmillan.

Allen, R. A. 1961. *East Texas lumber workers: an economic and social picture*. Austin: University of Texas Press.

Alwin, J. A. 1981. "Jordan Country, a Golden Anniversary look." *Annals of the Association of American Geographers* **71**, 479–98.

Amory, C. 1952. *The last resorts*. New York: Harper.

Anderson, W. 1976. *A place of power: the American episode in human evolution*. Santa Monica, CA: Goodyear.

Andrews, B. T. & M. Sansone 1983. *Who runs the rivers? Dams and decisions in the New West*. Stanford: Stanford Environmental Society.

Andrews, W. 1978. *Architecture, ambition, and Americans: a social history of American architecture*. New York: Free Press.

Anon. 1935. *The Lincoln Highway: the story of a crusade*. New York: Dodd, Mead.

Appleton, J. 1975. *The experience of landscape*. London: J. Wiley.

Armstrong, J. B. 1969. *Factory under the elms: a history of Harrisville, New Hampshire, 1774–1969*. Cambridge, Mass.: MIT Press.

Arreola, D. P. 1981. "Fences as landscape taste: Tucson's barrios." *Journal of Cultural Geography* **2**, 96–105.

Arreola, D. P. 1984. "Mexican American exterior murals." *Geographical Review* **74**, October, 409–24.

Arrington, L. J. 1975. "'A different mode of life': irrigation and society in nineteenth century Utah." *Agricultural History* **49**, 3–20.

Atherton, L. E. 1961. *The cattle kings*. Lincoln: University of Nebraska Press.

Atwood, W. W. 1940. *The physiographic provinces of North America*. Boston: Ginn.

Axtell, J. 1981. *The European and the Indian: essays in the ethnohistory of colonial North America*. New York: Oxford University Press.

Bachelder, J. B. 1875. *Popular resorts and how to reach them*. Boston: J. B. Bachelder.

Baedecker, K. 1904. *The United States*. Leipzig.

Baerwald, T. J. 1978. "The emergence of a new 'Downtown'." *Geographical Review* **68**, 308–18.

Baird, L. L. 1977. *The élite schools*. Lexington, Mass.: Lexington Books.

Baltzell, E. D. 1962. *An American business aristocracy*. New York: Free Press.

Baltzell, E. D. 1979. *Puritan Boston and Quaker Philadelphia: two protestant ethics and the spirit of class authority and leadership*. New York: Free Press.

Banham, R. 1971. *Los Angeles: the architecture of four ecologies*. Harmondsworth: Penguin.

Bannon, J. F. (ed.) 1968. *Bolton and the Spanish Borderlands*. Norman, OK: University of Oklahoma Press.

Bannon, J. F. 1974. *The Spanish Borderlands frontier, 1513–1821*. Albuquerque: University of New Mexico Press.

Barone, M., G. Ujifusa & D. Matthews 1988. *The Almanac of American politics, 1988*. Washington, D.C.: The National Journal.

Barth, G. 1980. *City people: the rise of modern city culture in nineteenth-century America*. New York: Oxford University Press.

Bauman, J. F. 1987. *Public housing, race, and renewal: urban planning in Philadelphia, 1920–1974*. Philadelphia: Temple University Press.

Beatley, J. C. 1953. "The Primary Forests of Vinton and Jackson Counties, Ohio." Ph.D. Dissertation, Ohio State University.

Belknap, J. 1791. *The history of New Hampshire*. Boston: printed for the author.

Bellah, R. N., R. Madsen, A. Swindler, S. M. Tipton & W. M. Sullivan 1986. *Habits of the heart: individualism and commitment in American Life*. New York: Harper & Row.

Belting, N. M. 1948. *Kaskaskia under the French Regime*. Urbana, IL: University of Illinois Press.

Bender, G. L. (ed.) 1982. *Reference handbook on the deserts of North America*. Westport, Conn.: Greenwood Press.

Benson, B. E. 1976. "Logs and lumber: the development of the lumber industry in Michigan's lower peninsula 1837–1870." Ph.D. Dissertation, Indiana University.

Bent, N. 1929. *American polo*. New York: Macmillan.

Berger, M. L. 1979. *The devil wagon in God's country: the automobile and social change in rural America, 1893–1929*. Hamden, Conn.: Archon Books.

Betts, J. R. 1974. *America's sporting heritage: 1850–1950*. Reading, Mass.: Addison-Wesley.

Bidwell, P. W. & J. I. Falconer 1923. *History of agriculture in the northern United States, 1620–1860*. Washington, D.C.: Carnegie Institute.

Bining, A. C. 1933. *British regulation of the colonial iron industry*. Philadelphia: University of Pennsylvania Press.

Blum, M. D. "A geoarcheological approach to habitat-specific modeling of Mississippian settlement patterns." In preparation.

Bodnar, J., R. Simon & M. Weber 1982. *Lives of their own: blacks, Italians, and Poles in Pittsburgh, 1900–1960*. Urbana: University of Illinois Press.

Bogue, A. G. 1963. *From prairie to Corn Belt: farming on the Illinois and Iowa Prairies in the nineteenth century*. Chicago: University of Chicago Press.

Bohrer, V. L. 1971. "Paleoecology of Snaketown." *Kiva* **36**, 11–19.

Bolton, H. E. 1917. "The mission as a frontier institution in the Spanish-American colonies." *American Historical Review* **23**, 42–61.

Bolton, H. E. 1921. *The Spanish Borderlands: A chronicle of Old Florida and the Southwest*. New Haven, Conn.: Yale University Press.

Bonner, J. C. 1977. "House and landscape design in the antebellum South." *Landscape* **21**, 2–8.

Borchert, J. R. 1950. "The climate of the central North American grassland." *Annals of the Association of American Geographers* **40**, 1–39.

Borchert, J. R. 1967. "American metropolitan evolution." *Geographical Review* **57**, 301–22.

Bowman, I. 1914. *Forest physiography*. 2nd edn. New York: Wiley.

Brasseaux, C. A. 1987. *The founding of New Acadia: the beginnings of Acadian life in Louisiana, 1765–1803*. Baton Rouge: Louisiana State University Press.

Breisch, K. A. & D. Moore 1986. "The Norwegian rock houses of Bosque County, Texas: some observations on a nineteenth-century vernacular building type." In *Perspectives in vernacular architecture, II*, C. Wells (ed.), 64–71. Columbia, MO: University of Missouri Press, for the Vernacular Architecture Forum.

Bremer, W. W. 1981. "Into the grain: golf's ascent in American culture." *Journal of American Culture* **4**, 120–32.

Bridenbaugh, C. 1938. *Cities in the wilderness: the first century of urban life in America, 1625–1742*. New York: The Rowland Press.

Bridenbaugh, C. 1946. "Baths and watering places of colonial America." *William and Mary Quarterly* **3**, 151–81.

Brose, D. S. & N. Greber 1979. *Hopewell archaeology*. Kent, OH: Kent State U.P.

Brown, J. S. H. 1983. "Women as center and symbol in the emerence of Métis communities." *Canadian Journal of Native Studies* **3**, 39–46.

Brown, R. 1948. *Historical geography of the United States*. New York: Harcourt Brace & World, 1948.

Bruekheimer, W. R. 1982. *Proceedings: Tall Timbers Ecology and Management Conference* **16**. Tallahassee, FL: Tall Timbers Research Station.

Bryan, K. 1929. "Flood-water farming." *Geographical Review* **19**, 444–56.

Bryant, R. C. 1913. *Logging: the principles and general methods of operation in the United States*. New York: Wiley.

Bryant, V. M. & R. G. Holloway (eds.) 1985. *Pollen records of Late Quaternary North American sediments*. Dallas: American Association of Stratigraphic Palynologists Foundation.

Burns, E. K. 1980. "The enduring affluent suburb." *Landscape* **24**, 33–41.

Burstein, A. N. 1981. "Immigrants and residential mobility: the Irish and Germans in Philadelphia, 1850–1880." In *Philadelphia: work, space, family, and group experience in the 19th century*, T. Hershberg (ed.), 174–203. New York: Oxford University Press.

Bush, C. 1977. *The dream of reason: American consciousness and cultural achievement from independence to the Civil War*. New York: St. Martin's Press.

Bushnell, G. D. 1982. "Chicago's leading men's clubs." *Chicago History* **11**, 79–88.

Butzer, K. W. 1977. "Geomorphology of the lower Illinois Valley as a spatial-temporal context for the Koster Archaic site." *Illinois State Museum Reports of Investigations* **34**, 1–60.

Butzer, K. W. 1988. "Cattle and sheep from Old to New Spain: historical antecedents." *Annals of the Association of American Geographers* **78**, 29–56.

Cable, M. 1984. *Top drawer*. New York: Atheneum.

Caldwell, W. W. & D. R. Henning 1978. "North American plains." In *Chronologies in New World archaeology*, R. E. Taylor & C. W. Meighan (eds.), 113–46. New York: Academic Press.

Calkins, C. F. & W. G. Laatsch 1979. "The Belgian outdoor ovens of Northeastern Wisconsin." *Pioneer America Society Transactions* **2**, 1–12.

Caro, R. A. 1974. *The power broker: Robert Moses and the fall of New York*. New York: Vintage.

Caro, R. A. 1983. *The years of Lyndon Johnson: The path to power*. New York: Vintage.

Caroso, J. A. 1963. *The southern frontier*. New York: Bobbs-Merrill.

Carstenson, V. 1958. *Farms or forests: evolution of a state land policy for northern Wisconsin, 1850–1932*. Madison: University of Wisconsin, College of Agriculture.

Castetter, E. F. & W. H. Bell 1942. *Pima and Papago agriculture*. Albuquerque: University of New Mexico Press.

Chandler, A. D., Jr. 1977. *The visible hand: the managerial revolution in American business*. Cambridge, Mass.: Belknap Press of Harvard University.

Chapman, L. J. & D. F. Putnam 1984. *The physiography of southern Ontario*, 3rd edn. Ontario: Ministry of Natural Resources.

Chappell, E. A. 1980. "Acculturation in the Shenandoah Valley: Rhenish houses of the Massanutten settlement." *Proceedings of the American Philosophical Society* **124**, 55–89. Reprinted 1986 in *Common places: readings in vernacular architecture*, D. Upton & J. M. Vlach (eds.), 25–57. Athens: University of Georgia Press.

Chastellux, F. J. Marquis de 1789. *Travels in North America in the years, 1780, 1781, and 1782*, 2 vols. New York: White, Gallaher & White.

Cirlot, J. E. 1962. *Dictionary of symbols*. Translated by Jack Sage. New York: Philosophical Library.

Clark, A. H. 1968. *Acadia: the geography of Early Nova Scotia to 1760*. Madison: University of Wisconsin Press.

Clark, J. I. 1956. *Farming the cutover: the settlement of northern Wisconsin*. Madison: State Historical Society.

Clark, R. E. 1960. "The pueblo rights doctrine in New Mexico." *New Mexico Historical Review* **35**, 265–83.

Clark, V. S. 1929. *History of manufactures in the United States*, 3 vols. New York: McGraw-Hill.

Clay, G. 1973. *Close-up: how to read the American city*. New York: Praeger.

Clifford, D. 1966. *A history of garden design*. New York: Praeger.

Cohen, M. N. & G. J. Armelagos (eds.) 1984. *Paleopathology and the origins of agriculture*. Orlando, FL: Academic Press.

Cole, A. H. 1970. "The mystery of fuel wood marketing in the United States." *Business History Review* **44**, 339–59.

Coleman, K. (ed.) 1968. "How to run a Middle Georgia cotton plantation in 1885: a document." *Agricultural History* **42**, 55–60.

Contreras, B. R. 1983. *Tradition and innovation in New Deal art*. Lewisburg, PA: Bucknell University Press.

Conzen, M. P. 1980a. "The morphology of nineteenth-century cities in the United States." In *Urbanization in the Americas: the background in comparative perspective*, W. Borah, J. Hardoy, & G. Stelter (eds.), 119–41. Ottawa: National Museum of Man.

Conzen, M. P. 1980b. "What makes the American landscape." *Geographical Magazine* **53**, 36–41.

Conzen, M. P. 1984a. "Maps for the masses: Alfred T. Andreas and the midwestern county atlas trade." In *Chicago mapmakers: essays on the rise of the city's map trade*, 47–63. Chicago: Chicago Historical Society, for the Chicago Map Society.

Conzen, M. P. 1984b. "The county landownership map in America: its commercial development and social transformation, 1814–1939." *Imago Mundi* **36**, 9–31.

Conzen, M. P. & K. N. Conzen 1988. "Luxembourg building traditions in the New World." Paper presented to the Luxembourg Heritage Conference, Old World Wisconsin, Eagle, WI, October.

Cook, C. O. & B. J. Kaplan 1983. "Civic élites and urban planning: Houston's River Oaks." In *Houston: a twentieth century urban frontier*, F. A. Rosales & B. T. Kaplan (eds.), 22–33. Port Washington, N.Y.: Associated Faculty Press.

Cooke, R. U. & R. W. Reeves 1976. *Arroyos and environmental change in the American South-West*. Oxford: Oxford University Press.

Coones, P. 1985. "One landscape or many? A geographical perspective." *Landscape History* **7**, 5–12.

Cooper, W. 1810. *A guide in the wilderness, or the history of the first settlements in the western counties of New York, with useful instructions to future settlers in a series of letters addressed by Judge Cooper of Cooperstown to William Sampson, Barrister, of New York*. Dublin: Gilbert & Hodges.

Cordell, L. S. 1979. "Cultural resources overview of the middle Rio Grande Valley." Washington D.C.: U.S. Government Printing Office.

Cosgrove, D. E. 1984. *Social formation and symbolic landscape*. London: Croom Helm.

Cox, T. R. 1974. *Mills and markets: a history of the Pacific coast lumber industry to 1900*. Seattle: University of Washington Press.

Craig, L. A. & Federal Architecture Project Staff 1984. *The federal presence: architecture, politics, and symbols in United States buildings*. Cambridge, Mass.: MIT Press.

Creel, G. 1915. "The feudal towns of Texas." *Harper's Weekly*, January 23, 76–8.

Crévecoeur, J. H. St. J. de 1970. *Sketches of eighteenth century America*, H. Boudin (ed.). New Haven, Conn.: Yale University Press.

Cronon, W. 1983. *Changes in the land: indians, colonists, and the ecology of New England*. New York: Hill & Wang.

Cross, W. 1950. *The burned-over district: the social and intellectual history of enthusiastic religion in western New York, 1800–1850*. Ithaca: Cornell University Press.

Crown, P. L. 1984. "Adaptation through diversity: an examination of population pressure and agricultural technology in the Salt-Gila Basin." In *Prehistoric agricultural strategies in the Southwest*, S. K. Fish & P. R. Fish (eds.), 5–25. Tempe: Arizona State University, Anthropological Research Paper no. 33.

Crown, P. L. 1987. "Classic Hohokam settlement and land use in the Casa Grande ruins area, Arizona." *Journal of Field Archaeology* **14**, 147–62.

Cummings, A. L. 1979. *The framed houses of Massachusetts Bay, 1625–1725*. Cambridge, Mass.: Harvard University Press.

Cutler, P. 1985. *The public landscape of the New Deal*. New Haven, Conn.: Yale University Press.

Daly, J. R. 1987. "The changing image of the city: planning downtown Omaha, 1945–1973." Ph.D. Dissertation, University of Pittsburgh.

Danhof, C. H. 1969. *Change in agriculture: the northern United States, 1820–1870*. Cambridge, Mass.: Harvard University Press.

Davies, R. O. 1975. *The age of asphalt: The automobile, the freeway, and the condition of metropolitan America*. Philadelphia: J. B. Lippincott.

Davis, D. H. 1936. "Amana: a study of occupance." *Economic Geography* **12**, July, 217–30.

Davis, L. E., R. A. Easterlin & W. N. Parker 1972. *American economic growth*. New York: Harper & Row.

Day, G. M. 1953. "The Indian as an ecological factor in the northeastern forest." *Ecology* **34**, 329–46.

De Brahm, J. G. W. 1856. "Philosophico-historico-hydrogeography of South Carolina, Georgia and east Florida." In *Documents connected with the history of South Carolina*, P. C. J. Weston (ed.), 155–227. London: Private edn.

de Tocqueville, A. 1956. *Democracy in America*. New York: Mentor.

Dean, J. S. & W. J. Robinson 1978. *Expanded tree-ring chronologies for the southwestern United States*. Tucson: University of Arizona, Laboratory of Tree Ring Research.

Delcourt, P. A., H. R. Delcourt, P. A. Cridlebaugh & J. Chapman 1986. "Holocene ethnobotanical and paleoecological record of human impact on vegetation in the Little Tennessee River Valley, Tennessee." *Quaternary Research* **25**, 330–49.

Denevan, W. M. (ed.) 1976. *Native populations of the Americas in 1492*. Madison: University of Wisconsin Press.

Devine, W. D., Jr. 1983. "From shafts to wires: historical perspective on electrification." *Journal of Economic History* **43**, 347–72.

Dinsdale, E. M. 1965. "Spatial patterns of technological change: the lumber industry in northern New York." *Economic Geography* **41**, 252–74.

DiPeso, C. C. 1979. "Prehistory: O'otam." *Handbook of the North American Indians*, vol. 9, W. C. Sturtevant (ed.), 91–9. Washington, D.C.: Smithsonian Institute Press.

Dobyns, H. F. 1966. "Estimating aboriginal America population: an appraisal of techniques with a new hemispheric estimate." *Current Anthropology* **7**, 395–416.

Dobyns, H. F. & J. W. Byrkit 1981. *From fire to flood: historic human destruction of Sonoran Desert riverine oases*. Socorro, N.M.: Bellena Press.

Dockendorff, T. P. 1986. "Cultural geography of eastern Stearns County: God, granite, and Germans." In *AAG '86 twin cities field trip guide*, T. J. Baerwald & K. L. Harrington (eds.), 184–93. Washington, D.C.: Association of American Geographers.

Dodds, J. W. 1961. *American memoir*. New York: Rinehart & Winston.

Domhoff, G. W. 1967. *Who rules America?* Englewood Cliffs, N.J.: Prentice-Hall.

Donaldson, T. 1884. *The Public Domain and its history*. Washington D.C.: Government Printing Office.

Doolittle, W. E. 1985. "The use of check dams for protecting downstream agricultural lands in the prehistoric Southwest." *Journal of Anthropological Research* **41**, 279–305.

Doucet, M. J. & J. C. Weaver 1985. "Material culture and the North American house: the era of the common man, 1870–1920." *Journal of American History* **72**, 560–87.

Doyel, D. 1980. "Hohokam social organization in the Sedentary to Classic transition." In *Current issues in Hohokam prehistory*, D. Doyel & F. Plog (eds.), 23–40. Tempe: Arizona State University.

Drache, H. 1964. *The day of the bonanza*. Fargo: North Dakota Institute of Regional Studies.

Driver, H. E. 1961. *Indians of North America*. Chicago: University of Chicago Press.

Dulles, F. R. 1965. *A history of recreation: America learns to play*. New York: Appleton-Century-Crofts.

Duncan, J. S., Jr. 1973. "Landscape taste as a symbol of group identity: a Westchester County village." *Geographical Review* **63**, 334–55.

Dunleavy, J. E. 1981. "Skiing: the worship of Ullr in America." *Journal of American Culture* **4**, 75–85.

Dunn, E. S., Jr. 1983. *The development of the U.S. urban system*, 2 vols, 2nd edn. Baltimore: Johns Hopkins University Press.

Dury, G. H. & R. S. Mathieson 1976. *The United States and Canada*, 3rd edn. London: Heinemann.

Dwight, T. 1821. *Travels in New England and New York in 1821*. 4 vols. New Haven, Conn.: T. Dwight.

Eavenson, H. N. 1942. *The first century and a quarter of the American coal industry*. Pittsburgh: privately printed.

Eighmy, J. L. & D. E. Doyel 1987. "A reanalysis of first reported archeomagnetic dates from the Hohokam area, southern Arizona." *Journal of Field Archaeology* **14**, 331–42.

Elazar, D. J. 1966. *American federalism: a view from the states.* New York: Thomas Y. Crowell.

Erickson, K. 1965. "The morphology of lumber settlements in western Oregon and Washington." Ph.D. Dissertation, University of California, Berkeley.

Ezell, P. H. 1983. "History of the Pima." *Handbook of North American Indians,* vol. 10, W. Sturtevant (ed.), 149–60. Washington, D.C.: Smithsonian Institution Press.

Fairman, C. E. 1927. *Art and artists of the Capitol.* Washington, D.C.: Government Printing Office.

Farb, P. 1963. *Face of North America: the natural history of a continent.* New York: Harper & Row.

Federal Writers' Project 1937. *Washington: city and capital.* Washington, D.C.: Government Printing Office.

Fenneman, N. M. 1931. *Physiography of western United States.* New York: McGraw-Hill.

Fenneman, N. M. 1938. *Physiography of eastern United States.* New York: McGraw-Hill.

Ferrell, S. 1984. "Addison Mizner's Florida fantasy." *Historic Preservation* **3**, June, 25–30.

Fifer, J. V. 1981. "Washington, D.C.: the political geography of a federal capital." *Journal of American Studies* **15**, 5–26.

Findsen, O. 1984. "A lucky find in Cincinnati." *Historic Preservation* **36**, December, 8–12.

Finlayson, W. D. & R. H. Pihl 1980. "Some implications for the attribute analysis of rim sherds from the Draper site, Pickering, Ontario." In *Proceedings of the 1979 Iroquois Pottery Conference,* C. F. Hayes (ed.) 113–31. Rochester: Rochester Museum and Science Center, Research Division.

Fish, S. K. & P. R. Fish (eds.) 1984. *Prehistoric agricultural strategies in the southwest.* Anthropological Research Papers 33. Tempe: Arizona State University.

Fishlow, A. 1965. *American railroads and the transformation of the ante-bellum economy.* Harvard Economic Studies 127. Cambridge, Mass.: Harvard University Press.

Fladmark, K. R. 1986. *British Columbia prehistory.* Ottawa: National Museums of Canada.

Flink, J. J. 1975. *The car culture.* Cambridge, Mass.: MIT Press.

Flint, T. 1828. *A condensed geography and history of the western states or the Mississippi Valley,* 2 vols. Cincinnati: W. M. Farnsworth.

Forbes, R. D. 1923. "The passing of the piney woods." *American Forestry* **29**, 121–36, 185.

Ford, R. I. (ed.) 1985. *Prehistoric food production in North America.* Anthropological Paper 75. University of Michigan: Museum of Anthropology.

Fowler, M. L. 1978. "Cahokia and the American Bottom: settlement archaeology." In *Mississippian settlement patterns,* B. D. Smith (ed.), 455–78. New York: Academic Press.

Fox, W. F. 1902. *History of the lumber industry in the state of New York.* United States Department of Agriculture, Bureau of Forestry, Bulletin no. 34, Washington, D.C.: Government Printing Office.

Francaviglia, R. V. 1978. *The mormon landscape: existence, creation, and perception of a unique image in the American West.* New York: AMS.

Fries, R. F. 1951. *Empire in pine: the story of lumbering in Wisconsin, 1830–1900.* Madison: State Historical Society of Wisconsin.

Frison, G. C. 1978. *Prehistoric hunters of the High Plains.* New York: Academic Press.

Frothingham, E. H. 1919. *The status and value of farm wood-lots in the eastern United States.* United States Department of Agriculture, Bureau of Forestry, Bulletin no. 481. Washington, D.C.: Government Printing Office.

Fuessle, N. A. 1915. "The Lincoln Highway—a National Road." *Travel* **24**, 26–9.

Gaines, F. P. 1925. *The southern plantation: a study in the development and the accuracy of a tradition.* New York: Columbia University Press.

Garner, W. W. 1946. *The production of tobacco.* Philadelphia: Blakiston.

Gates, P. W. 1972. "Problems of agricultural history, 1790–1840." *Agricultural History* **46**, 33–51.

Gates. P. W. 1978. "The nationalizing influence of the public lands: Indiana." In *This land of ours: the acquisition and disposition of the Public Domain,* 103–26. Indianapolis: Indiana Historical Society, Indiana American Revolution Bicentennial Symposium.

Gelfand, M. I. 1975. *A nation of cities: the federal government and urban America, 1933–1965.* New York: Oxford University Press.

Gentilcore, R. L. 1957. "Vincennes and French settlement in the old Northwest." *Annals of the Association of American Geographers* **47**, 285–97.

Geraniotis, R. M. 1986. "German architectural theory and practice in Chicago, 1850–1900." *Winterthur Portfolio* **21**, Winter, 293–306.

Gerlach, R. L. 1976. *Immigrants in the Ozarks: a study in ethnic geography.* Columbia, MO: University of Missouri Press.

Gilbert, G. K. 1917. "Hydraulic mining debris in the Sierra Nevada." *United States Geological Survey Professional Paper* **105**.

Gilchrist, D. T. (ed.) 1967. *The growth of seaport cities, 1790–1825.* Charlottesville: University Press of Virginia.

Glass, J. W. 1986. *The Pennsylvania culture region: a view from the barn.* Ann Arbor: UMI Research Press.

Glassie, H. H. 1975. *Folk housing in middle Virginia.* Knoxville: University of Tennessee Press.

Glymph, T. (ed.) 1985. *Essays on the postbellum southern economy.* College Station: Texas A & M University Press.

Godfrey, B. J. 1988. *Neighborhoods in transition: the making of San Francisco's ethnic and non-conformist communities.* Berkeley: University of California Press.

Gold, R. L. 1969. *Borderlands empires in transition: the triple-nation transfer of Florida.* Carbondale: Southern Illinois University Press.

Goldberger, P. 1981. *The skyscraper.* New York: Knopf.

Goldenberg, J. A. 1976. *Shipbuilding in Colonial America.* Charlottesville: University Press of Virginia.

Goldstone, H. H. & M. Dalyrymple 1974. *History preserved: a guide to New York City landmarks and historic districts.* New York: Simon & Schuster.

Goodman, R. 1971. *After the planners.* New York: Simon & Schuster.

Goodsell, C. T. 1984. "The city council chamber: from distance to intimacy." *Public Interest* **74**, 116–31.

Goodwin, G. C. 1977. *Cherokees in transition: a study of changing culture and environment prior to 1775.* University of Chicago, Department of Geography, Research Paper 181.

Gottlieb, P. 1987. *Making their own way: Southern blacks' migration to Pittsburgh, 1916–30.* Urbana: University of Illinois Press.

Gould, M. E. 1965. *The early American house.* Rutland, VT: Tuttle.

Gowans, A. 1976. *Images of American living: four centuries of architecture and furniture as cultural expression.* New York: Harper & Row.

Gowans, A. 1981. *Learning to see: historical perspectives on modern popular/commercial arts.* Bowling Green: Bowling Green University Popular Press.

Graf, W. L. 1985. *The Colorado River: instability and basin management.* Washington, D.C.: Association of American Geographers, Resource Publications in Geography.

Gray, L. C. & E. K. Thompson 1933. *History of agriculture in the southern United States to 1860,* 2 vols. Publication no. 430. Washington, D.C.: Carnegie Institute of Washington.

Green, C. M. 1962–3. *Washington: village and capital, 1800–1878,* 2 vols. Princeton,

N.J.: Princeton University Press.

Greenbie, B. B. 1981. *Spaces: dimensions of the human landscape*. New Haven, Conn.: Yale University Press.

Greever, W. S. 1963. *The Bonanza West: the story of the Western mining rushes, 1848–1900*. Norman: University of Oklahoma Press.

Gregg, M. L. 1975. "A population estimate for Cahokia." In *Perspectives in Cahokia archaeology*, 126–36. Urbana: University of Illinois, Illinois Archeological Survey Bulletin 10.

Guinness, P. G. & M. Bradshaw 1985. *North America: a human geography*. Totowa, N.J.: Barnes & Noble.

Gutheim, F. A. & W. E. Washburn 1976. *The federal city: plans and realities*. Washington, D.C.: Smithsonian Institution Press.

Guthrie, R. D. 1984. "Mosaics, allelochemics and nutrients: an ecological theory of Late Pleistocene megafaunal extinctions." In *Quaternary extinctions*, P. S. Martin & R. G. Klein (eds.), 259–98. Tucson: University of Arizona Press.


Hackenberg, R. A. 1983. "Pima and Papago ecological adaptations." *Handbook of the North American Indians*, vol. 10, W. Sturtevant (ed.), 161–77. Washington, D.C.: Smithsonian Institution Press.

Haefner, H. 1970. *Höhenstufen, öffentliche Ländereien und private Landnützung auf der Ostseite der Sierra Nevada (U.S.A.)*. Zürich: Juris.

Haglund, K. T. & P. F. Notarianni 1980. *The avenues of Salt Lake City*. Salt Lake City: Utah State Historical Society.

Hall, J. 1836. *Statistics of the West*. Cincinnati: J. A. James.

Hall, P. & A. Markusen (eds.) 1985. *Silicon landscapes*. Boston: Allen & Unwin.

Hall, S. A. 1977. "Late Quaternary sedimentation and paleoecologic history of Chaco Canyon, New Mexico." *Geological Society of America Bulletin* **88**, 1593–618.

Hammack, D. C. 1982. *Power and society: greater New York at the turn of the century*. New York: Russell Sage Foundation.

Hargreaves, M. W. 1957. *Dry farming in the northern Great Plains, 1900–1925*. Cambridge, Mass.: Harvard University Press.

Harper, H. L. 1971. "The antebellum courthouses of Tennessee." *Tennessee Historical Quarterly* **30**, 3–25.

Harris, C. D. 1940. *Salt Lake City, a regional capital*. Chicago: University of Chicago Library.

Harris, N. 1966. *The artist in America: the formative years, 1790–1860*. Chicago: University of Chicago Press.

Harris, R. C. 1966. *The seigneurial system in early Canada: a geographical study*. Madison: University of Wisconsin Press.

Harris, R. C. 1977. "The simplification of Europe overseas." *Annals of the Association of American Geographers* **67**, December, 469–83.

Harris, R. C. (ed.) 1987. *Historical atlas of Canada*, vol. 1: *From the beginning to 1800*. Toronto: University of Toronto Press.

Harris, R. C. & J. Warkeutin 1974. *Canada before Confederation: a study in historical geography*. New York: Oxford University Press.

Hart, J. F. 1968. "Loss and abandonment of cleared farm land in the eastern United States." *Annals of the Association of American Geographers* **58**, 417–40.

Hart, J. F. 1972. "The Middle West." *Annals of the Association of American Geographers* **62**, 258–82.

Hart, J. F. 1972. *The look of the land*. Englewood Cliffs, N.J.: Prentice-Hall.

Hart, J. F. 1980. "Land use change in a Piedmont county." *Annals of the Association of American Geographers* **70**, 492–527.

Hart, J. F. 1986. "Change in the Corn Belt." *Geographical Review* **76**, 51–72.

Hartman, W. A. & J. D. Black 1931. *Economic aspects of land settlement in the cutover region of the Great Lakes states.* United States Department of Agriculture, Circular 160. Washington, D.C.: Government Printing Office.

Hartt, R. L. 1900. "Notes on a Michigan lumber town." *Atlantic Monthly*, January, 101–9.

Haury, E. W. 1976. *The Hohokam: desert farmers and craftsmen.* Tucson: University of Arizona Press.

Havighurst, W. 1960. *Land of the long horizons.* New York: Coward-McCann.

Head, C. G. 1976. *Eighteenth century Newfoundland: a geographer's perspective.* Toronto: McClelland & Stewart.

Healy, R. G. 1985. *Competition for land in the American South: agriculture, human settlement, and the environment.* Washington, D.C.: The Conservation Foundation.

Heck, R. W. 1978. "Building traditions in the Acadian parishes." In *The Cajuns: essays on their history and culture*, G. R. Conrad (ed.), 161–72. Lafayette: University of Southwestern Louisiana, Center for Louisiana Studies.

Helgeson, A. C. 1953. "Nineteenth century land colonization in northern Wisconsin." *Wisconsin Magazine of History* 36, 115–21.

Helgeson, A. C. 1962. *Farms in the cutover: agricultural settlement in northern Wisconsin.* Madison: State Historical Society.

Hendrickson, C. I. 1933. "The agricultural land available for forestry." In *A national plan for American forestry* by U.S. Forest Service (Copeland Report), vol. 1, 151–69. Washington, D.C.: Government Printing Office.

Henrikson, A. K. 1983. "A small, cozy town, global in scope: Washington, D.C." *Ekistics* **50**, 123–45.

Herndon, G. M. 1967. "Indian agriculture in the southern colonies." *North Carolina Historical Review* **44**, 283–97.

Hewes, L. 1951. "The northern wet prairie of the United States: nature, sources of information, and extent." *Annals of the Association of American Geographers* **41**, 307–23.

Hewes, L. 1981. "Early fencing on the western margin of the Prairie." *Annals of the Association of American Geographers* **71**, 499–526.

Hewes, L. & C. L. Jung 1981. "Early fencing on the Middle Western prairie." *Annals of the Association of American Geographers* **71**, 177–201.

Heyward, D. C. 1937. *Seed from Madagascar.* Chapel Hill: University of North Carolina Press.

Hickman, N. W. 1952. "Logging and rafting timber in south Mississippi, 1840–1910." *Journal of Mississippi History* **19**, 154–72.

Hickman, N. W. 1962. *Mississippi harvest; lumbering in the long-leaf Pine Belt, 1840–1915.* University: University of Mississippi.

Higbee, E. C. 1976. "Centre cities in Canada and the United States." In *The American environment: perceptions and policies*, W. Watson & T. O'Riordan (eds.), 145–60. London: Wiley.

Highstone, J. 1982. *Victorian gardens.* San Francisco: Harper & Row.

Hilliard, S. B. 1972. "Indian land cessions." *Annals of the Association of American Geographers* **62**, Map Supplement 16.

Hilliard, S. B. 1978. "Antebellum tidewater rice culture in South Carolina and Georgia." In *European settlement and development in North America: essays in honour and memory of Andrew Hill Clark*, J. R. Gibson (ed.), 91–115. Toronto: University of Toronto Press.

Hilliard, S. B. 1979. "Site characteristics and spatial stability of the Louisiana sugercane industry." *Agricultural History* **53**, 254–69.

Hilliard, S. B. 1980. "Plantations created the South." *Geographical Magazine* **52**, 409–16.

Hilliard, S. B. 1982a. "Headright grants and surveying in northeastern Georgia." *Geographical Review* **72**, 416–429.

Hilliard, S. B. 1982b. "The plantation in antebellum southern agriculture," *Proceedings, Tall Timbers Ecology and Management Conference*, February 22–24, 1979, 127–39. Tallahassee, FL: Tall Timbers Research Station.

Hillyer, W. & J. Hanson 1984. *The social logic of space*. New York: Cambridge University Press.

Hindle, B. (ed.) 1975. *America's Wooden Age: aspects of its early technology*. Tarrytown, N.Y.: Sleepy Hollow Press.

Hindle, B. 1981. *Material culture of the Wooden Age*. Tarrytown, N.Y.: Sleepy Hollow Press.

Hirsch, A. R. 1983. *Making the second ghetto: race and housing in Chicago, 1940–1960*. London: Cambridge University Press.

Hitchcock, H. R. & W. Seale 1976. *Temples of democracy; the state capitols of the U.S.A.* New York: Harcourt, Brace Jovanovich.

Holbrook, S. H. 1943. *Burning an empire: the story of American forest fires*. New York: Macmillan.

Holbrook, S. H. 1950. *The Yankee exodus: an account of migration from New England*. Seattle: University of Washington Press.

Hoover, E. M. & R. Vernon 1962. *Anatomy of a metropolis*. New York: Doubleday.

Hopkins, D. M., J. V. Matthews, C. E. Schweger & S. B. Young 1982. *Paleoecology of Beringia*. New York: Academic Press.

Horgan, P. 1984. *Great river: the Rio Grande in North American history*, revised edn. Austin: Texas Monthly Press.

Hornbeck, D. 1982. "The California Indian before European contact." *Journal of Cultural Geography* **2**, 23–39.

Horton, W. F. 1902. *Land buyer's, settler's and explorer's guide*. Minneapolis: Press of Byron & Willard.

Horvath, R. J. 1974. "Machine space." *Geographical Review* **64**, 167–88.

Hoskins, W. G. 1955. *The making of the English landscape*. London: Hodder & Stoughton.

Hoskins, W. G. 1988. *The making of the English landscape*. With an Introduction and Commentary by Christopher Taylor. London: Hodder & Stoughton.

Hough, F. B. 1878. *Report upon forestry*, vol. 1. Submitted to Congress by the Commissioner of Agriculture. Washington, D.C.: Government Printing Office.

Howett, C. M. 1982. "Frank Lloyd Wright and American residential landscaping." *Landscape* **26**, 33–40.

Hubka, T. C. 1984. *Big house, little house, back house, barn: the connected farm buildings of New England*. Hanover, N.H.: University Press of New England.

Hudson, C. M. 1976. *The southeastern Indians*. Knoxville: University of Tennessee Press.

Hudson, J. 1962. *Irrigation water use in the Utah Valley, Utah*. Research Paper no. 79. University of Chicago, Department of Geography.

Hudson, J. C. 1975. "Frontier housing in North Dakota." *North Dakota History* **42**, 4–15.

Hudson, J. C. 1978. "North Dakota's frontier fuels." *Bulletin of the Association of North Dakota Geographers* **28**, 1–15.

Hudson, J. C. 1985. *Plains country towns*. Minneapolis: University of Minnesota Press.

Hudson, J. C. 1986a. "Who was 'Forest Man'? Sources of migration to the plains." *Great Plains Quarterly* **6**, 69–83.

Hudson, J. C. 1986b. "Yankeeland in the Middle West." *Journal of Geography* **85**, September/October, 195–200.

Hugill, P. J. 1980. "Houses in Cazenovia: the effects of time and class." *Landscape* **24**, 10–15.

Hugill, P. J. 1982. "Good roads and the automobile in the United States, 1880–1929." *Geographical Review* **72**, 327–49.

Humphreys, P. W. 1914. *The practical book of garden architecture*. Philadelphia, Penn.: J. B. Lippincott.

Hundley, N. 1966. *Dividing the waters: a century of controversy between the United States and Mexico*. Berkeley: University of California Press.

Hundley, N. 1975. *Water and the West: the Colorado River Compact and the politics of water in the American West*. Berkeley: University of California Press.

Hunt, C. B. 1974. *Natural regions of the United States and Canada*. San Francisco: Freeman.

Hunter, L. C. 1979. *A history of industrial power in the United States, 1780–1930*, 2 vols. Charlottesville: University Press of Virginia.

Illick, J. S. 1924. "The story of the American lumbering industry." In *A popular history of American invention*, W. Kaempffert (ed.), 150–98.

Ingalls, M. R. 1986. *Historical perspective of the Welsh settlement in Big Rock township, Kane County, Illinois* (mimeo). Geneva, IL: Kane County (Illinois) Rural Structures Survey.

Isaksson, O. & S. Hallgren 1969. *Bishop Hill, Illinois: a utopia on the prairie*. Stockholm: Solna, Seelig.

Jackson, J. B. 1964. "The meanings of landscape." *Kulturgeografi* **16**, 47–50.

Jackson, J. B. 1970. *Landscapes: selected writings of J. B. Jackson*. E. H. Zube (ed.). Amherst, Mass. University of Massachusetts Press.

Jackson, J. B. 1972. *American space: the centennial years, 1865–1876*. New York: W. W. Norton.

Jackson, J. B. 1979. "The order of a landscape: reason and religion in Newtonian America." In *The interpretation of ordinary landscapes*, D. W. Meinig (ed.), 153–63.

Jackson, J. B. 1980. *The necessity for ruins and other topics*. Amherst, Mass.: University of Massachusetts Press.

Jackson, J. B. 1984. *Discovering the vernacular landscape*. New Haven, Conn.: Yale University Press.

Jackson, K. T. 1985. *Crabgrass frontier: the suburbanization of the United States*. New York: Oxford University Press.

Jacobs, W. R. 1974. "The tip of the iceberg: pre-Columbian Indian demography and some implications for revisionism." *William and Mary College Quarterly* **31**, 123–33.

Jaderborg, E. 1981. "Swedish architectural influence in the Kansas Smoky Valley community." *Swedish Pioneer Historical Quarterly* **32**, January, 65–79.

Jaher, F. C. (ed.) 1973. "Style and status: high society in late nineteenth century New York." In *The rich, the well born, and the powerful: elites and upper classes in history*, 258–84. Urbana: University of Illinois Press.

Jaher, F. C. 1980. "The gilded elite: American multimillionaires, 1865 to the present." In *Wealth and the wealthy in the modern world*, W. D. Rubenstein (ed.), 187–276. New York: St. Martin's Press.

Jakle, J. A. 1977. *Images of the Ohio Valley: an historical geography of travel, 1740–1860*. New York: Oxford University Press.

Jakle, J. A. 1985. *The tourist: travel in twentieth century North America*. Lincoln: University of Nebraska Press.

James, J. A. 1983. "Structural change in American manufacturing, 1850–1890." *Journal of Economic History* **43**, 433–59.

Jennings, J. D. (ed.) 1978. *Ancient Native Americans*. San Francisco: Freeman.

Jillick, J. S. 1924. "The story of the American lumbering industry." In *A popular history of American invention*, W. Kaempffert (ed.), 150–98. New York: Scribners.

Johnson, A. 1955. "Sweden gave America the rail fence." *American Swedish Monthly* **49**, June, 6–7, 29.

Johnson, E. & V. T. Holliday 1986. "The archaic record at Lubbock Lake." *Plains*

*Anthropologist Memoir* **21**, 7–54.

Johnson, H. B. 1957. "Rational and ecological aspects of the Quarter Section: an example from Minnesota." *Geographical Review* **47**, 330–48.

Johnson, H. B. 1958. "French Canada and the Ohio country." *Canadian Geographer* **15**, 1–10.

Johnson, H. B. 1976. *Order upon the land: The U.S. rectangular land survey and the upper Mississippi country*. New York: Oxford University Press.

Johnson, H. B. 1978. "Perceptions and illustrations of the American landscape in the Ohio Valley and the Midwest." In *This land of ours: the acquisition and disposition of the Public Domain*, pp. 1–38. Indianapolis: Indiana Historical Society, Indiana American Revolution Bicentennial Symposium.

Johnson, P. R. 1984. "Communal imprints on the Wisconsin landscape: St. Nazianz, 1854-1873." *Bulletin of the Wisconsin Council for Geographic Education*, Spring, 34–43.

Johnston, R. J. 1982. *The American urban system; a geographical perspective*. New York: St. Martin's Press.

Jones, C. F. 1938. "Areal distribution of manufacturing in the United States." *Economic Geography* **14**, 217–22.

Jones, K. M. 1957. *The plantation South*. New York: Bobbs-Merrill.

Jordan, T. G. 1964. "German houses in Texas." *Landscape* **14**, Autumn, 24–26.

Jordan, T. G. 1977. "Early northeast Texas and the evolution of western ranching." *Annals of the Association of American Geographers* **67**, 66–87.

Jordan, T. G. 1985. *American log buildings: an old world heritage*. Chapel Hill: University of North Carolina Press.

Jordan, T. G. "The Anglo-American Mestizos: genetic and cultural legacy of the American Indian." *Geographical Review*, in press.

Jordan, T. G. & M. Kaups 1989. *The American backwoods frontier: an ethnic and ecological interpretation*. Baltimore: Johns Hopkins University Press.

Kane, L. 1954. "Selling the cutover lands in Wisconsin." *Business History Review* **28**, 236–47.

Kaups, M. 1983. "Finnish log houses in the upper Middle West, 1890–1920." *Journal of Cultural Geography* **3**, Spring/Summer, 2–26.

Kay, J. 1979. "Wisconsin Indian hunting patterns, 1634–1836." *Annals of the Association of American Geographers* **69**, 402–18.

Kehoe, A. B. 1981. *North American Indians: a comprehensive account*. Englewood Cliffs, N.J.: Prentice-Hall.

Kelso, M., W. E. Martin & L. E. Mack 1973. *Water supplies and economic growth in an arid environment: an Arizona case study*. Tucson: University of Arizona Press.

Kennedy, C. B., J. L. Sell & E. H. Zube 1988. "Landscape aesthetics and geography." *Environmental Review* **12**, 31–55.

Kent, S. 1984. *Analyzing activity areas*. Albuquerque, N.M.: University of New Mexico Press.

Klein, J., J. C. Lerman, P. E. Damon & E. K. Ralph 1982. "Calibration of radiocarbon dates." *Radiocarbon* **24**, 103–50.

Kniffen, F. 1965. "Folk housing, key to diffusion." *Annals of the Association of American Geographers* **55**, 549–77.

Knight, D. B. 1971. "Impress of authority and ideology on the landscape: a review of some unanswered questions." *Tijdschrift voor Economische en Sociale Geographie* **62**, 383–87.

Knowles, C. H. 1983. *Landscape history*. London: Historical Association.

Kollmorgen, W. M. 1969. "The woodsman's assault on the domain of the cattlemen." *Annals of the Association of American Geographers* **59**, 215–39.

Koop, M. & S. Ludwig 1984. *German-Russian folk architecture in southeastern South Dakota*. Vermillion, S.D.: State Historical Preservation Center.

Kory, W. B. 1978. "Ethnic churches and ethnicity." *Pennsylvania Geographer* **16**, September, 21–30.

Kouwenhoven, J. A. 1972. *The Columbia historical portrait of New York: an essay in graphic history*. New York: Harper & Row.

Kramer, J. J. 1978. *The last of the grand hotels*. New York: Van Nostrand Reinhold.

Krim, A. J. & Staff of Cambridge Historical Commission 1977. *Northwest Cambridge*. Report Five, Survey of Architectural History in Cambridge. Cambridge, Mass.: MIT Press, for the Cambridge Historical Commission.

Krutch, J. W. 1955. *The voice of the desert: a naturalist's interpretation*. New York: William Morrow.

Krythe, M. R. 1968. *What so proudly we hail*. New York: Harper & Row.

Küchler, A. 1964. *Potential natural vegetation of the coterminous United States*. Special Publication no. 36. New York: American Geographical Society.

Kulik, G., R. Parks & T. Z. Penn 1982. *The New England mill village, 1790–1860*. Cambridge, Mass.: MIT Press.

Kurath, H. 1973. *Handbook of the linguistic geography of New England*. New York: A.M.S. Press.

Kusmer, K. L. 1976. *A ghetto takes shape: black Cleveland, 1870–1930*. Urbana: University of Illinois Press.

Laatsch, W. G. 1988. "Wisconsin's Belgians." *World & I*, October, 498–509.

Laforc, L. 1971. "In the sticks." *Harper's Magazine*, October, 108–55.

Landelius, O. R. 1985. *Swedish place-names in North America*. Carbondale: Southern Illinois University Press, for the Swedish-American Historical Society.

Langewiesche, W. 1950. "The U.S.A. from the air." *Harper's Magazine*, October, 179–98.

Larson, G. O. 1983. *The reluctant patron: the United States government and the arts, 1943–1965*. Philadelphia: University of Pennsylvania Press.

Latham, B. 1957. *Timber: its development and distribution. A historical survey*. London: Harrap.

Lawrence, H. W. 1983. "Southern spas: source of the American resort tradition." *Landscape* **27**, 1–12.

Lawton, H. W., P. J. Wilke, M. DeDecker & W. M. Mason 1976. "Agriculture among the Paiute of Owens Valley." *Journal of California Anthropology* **3**, 13–50.

Leavitt, H. 1970. *Superhighway—Superhoax*. New York: Ballantine.

LeBlanc, R. A. 1979. "Les migrations Acadiennes." *Cahiers de Géographie du Québec* **23**, 99–124.

Lebovich, W. L. 1984. *America's city halls*. Washington, D.C.: Preservation Press.

LeCompte, J. 1978. *Pueblo, hardscrabble, greenhorn: the upper Arkansas, 1832–1856*. Norman: University of Oklahoma Press.

Lee, L. B. 1980. *Reclaiming the American West: an historiography and guide*. Santa Barbara, Calif.: ABC–Clio.

Lemon, J. T. 1972. *The best poor man's country*. Baltimore: Johns Hopkins University Press.

Lerner, M. 1957. *America as a civilization: life and thought in the United States today*. New York: Simon & Schuster.

Lesley, J. P. 1859. *The iron manufacturers' guide to the furnaces, forges and rolling mills of the United States*. New York: John Eiley.

Lewis P. F. 1975. "Common houses, cultural spoor." *Landscape* **19**, 1–22.

Lewis, P. F. 1976a. *New Orleans: the making of an urban landscape*. Cambridge, Mass.: Ballinger.

Lewis, P. F. 1976b. "The Land of Penn's woods: the early settlers." In *Pennsylvania 1776*. R. Secor & J. M. Pickering (eds.), 17–31. University Park: Pennsylvania State University Press.

Lewis, P. F. 1979. "The unprecedented city." *Smithsonian* **10**, 184–92.

Lewis, P. F. 1983. "The galactic metropolis." In *Beyond the urban fringe: land use issues of non-metropolitan America*, R. H. Platt & G. Macinko (eds.), 23–49. Minneapolis: University of Minnesota Press.

Lewis, P. F., D. Lowenthal & Y. Tuan 1973. *Visual blight in America*. Washington, D.C.: Association of American Geographers, Commission on College Geography, Resource Paper no. 23.

Lichtenberger, E. 1970. "The nature of European urbanism." *Geoforum* **4**, 45–62.

Liebs, C. H. 1985. *Main street to miracle mile: American roadside architecture*. Boston: Little, Brown.

Limerick, P. N. 1985. *Desert passages: encounters with the American deserts*. Albuquerque: University of New Mexico Press.

Lobeck, A. K. 1957. *Physiographic diagram of the United States*. Maplewood, N.J.: Hammond.

Lockwood, C. & C. B. Leinberger 1988. "Los Angeles comes of age." *Atlantic Monthly*, January, 31–56.

Long, A. Jr. 1972. *The Pennsylvania German family farm: a regional architectural and folk cultural study of an American agricultural community*. Breinigsville: Publications of the Pennsylvania German Society, vol. 6.

Louw, R. 1983. *America II*. Los Angeles: Jeremy P. Tarcher.

Lowell, G. (ed.) 1902. *American gardens*. Boston: Bates & Guild.

Lowenthal, D. 1962–3. "'Not every prospect pleases'." *Landscape* **12**, 19–23.

Lowenthal, D. 1968. "The American scene." *Geographical Review* **58**, 61–88.

Lowenthal, D. 1976. "The place of the past in the American landscape." In *Geographies of the mind: Essays in historical geography in honor of John Kirtland Wright*, D. Lowenthal & M. J. Bowden (eds.), 89–117. New York: Oxford University Press.

Lowenthal, D. 1977. "The bicentennial landscape: a mirror held up to the past." *Geographical Review* **67**, 253–67.

Lowenthal, D. 1985. *The past is a foreign country*. New York: Cambridge University Press.

Lowenthal, D. & M. Riel 1972. *Publications in environmental perception, numbers 1–8*. New York: American Geographical Society.

Lubove, R. 1969. *Twentieth century Pittsburgh: government, business, and environmental change*. New York: Wiley.

Luckingham, B. 1982. *The urban southwest: a profile history of Albuquerque, El Paso, Phoenix, and Tucson*. El Paso: Texas Western Press.

Ludwig, G. M. 1945. "The influence of the Pennsylvania Dutch in the Middle West." *Publications of the Pennsylvania German Folklore Society* **10**, 1–108.

Lukas, J. A. 1985. *Common ground: a turbulent decade in the lives of three American families*. New York: Knopf.

Luten, D. B. 1986. *Progress against growth: Daniel B. Luten on the American landscape*. T. R. Vale (ed.). New York: Guilford Press.

Lynch, K. 1960. *The image of the city*. Cambridge, Mass.: MIT Press.

Lynd, R. S. & H. M. Lynd 1929. *Middletown: a study in American culture*. New York: Harcourt, Brace.

Lynes, R. 1955. *The tastemakers*. New York: Harper.


Maass, A. & R. L. Anderson 1978. *And the desert shall rejoice: conflict, growth, and justice in arid environments*. Cambridge, Mass.: MIT Press.

McDermott, J. F. (ed.) 1974. *The Spanish in the Mississippi Valley, 1762–1804*. Urbana: University of Illinois Press.

McGuire, R. H. & M. B. Schiffer (eds.) 1982. *Hohokam and Patayan: prehistory of southwestern Arizona*. New York: Academic Press.

McHenry, S. G. 1986. "Eighteenth century field patterns as vernacular art." In

*Common places: readings in American vernacular architecture*, D. Upton & J. M. Vlach (eds.), 107–23. Universtiy of Georgia Press.

McKinzie, R. D. 1973. *The New Deal for artists*. Princeton, N.J.: Princeton University Press.

McLachlan, J. 1970. *American boarding schools: a historical study*. New York: Scribners.

McManus, D. A., J. S. Creager, R. J. Echols & M. L. Holmes 1983. "The Holocene Transgression on the Arctic Flank of Beringia." In *Quaternary coastlines and marine archaeology: towards the pre-history of land bridges and continental shelves*, P. M. Masters & N. C. Flemming (eds.), New York: Academic Press.

McPhee, J. 1971. *Encounters with the Archdruid*. New York: Farrar, Straus & Giroux.

McQuillan, D. A. 1979. "French-Canadian communities in the American upper midwest during the nineteenth century." *Cahiers de Géographie du Québec* **23**, 53–72.

McWilliams, C. 1946. *Southern California country: an island on the land*. New York: Duell, Sloan & Pearce.

Malin, J. C. 1947. *The grassland of North America: prolegomena to its history*. Lawrence, KS: published by the author.

Mallory, W. E. & P. Simpson-Housley (eds.) 1987. *Geography and literature: a meeting of the disciplines*. Syracuse, N.Y.: Syracuse University Press.

Mandle, J. R. 1974. "The plantation states as a sub region of the post bellum South." *Journal of Economic History* **34**, 732–38.

Marling, K. A. 1982. *Wall-to-wall America: a cultural history of post-office murals in the great depression*. Minneapolis: University of Minnesota Press.

Marshall, H. W. 1986. "The Pelster housebarn: endurance of Germanic architecture on the midwestern frontier." *Material Culture* **18**, 65–104.

Martin, C. 1973. "Fire and forest structures in the aboriginal eastern forest." *Indian Historian* **6**, 38–42.

Martin, P. S. & R. G. Klein (eds.) 1984. *Quaternary extinctions: a prehistoric revolution*. Tucson: University of Arizona Press.

Marx, L. 1964. *The machine in the garden: technology and the pastoral ideal in America*. New York: Oxford University Press.

Marx, L. 1974. *The American Revolution and the American landscape*. Washington, D.C.: Bicentennial Lecture, American Enterprise Institute for Public Policy Research.

Mason, P. P 1957. "The League of American Wheelmen and the Good-Roads Movement." Ph.D. Dissertation, University of Michigan.

Masse, W. B. 1981. "Prehistoric irrigation systems in the Salt River Valley, Arizona." *Science* **214**, 408–15.

Mather, E. C. 1972. "The American Great Plains." *Annals of the Association of American Geographers* **62**, 237–57.

Mather, E. C. & M. Kaups 1963. "The sauna: a cultural index to settlement." *Annals of the Association of American Geographers* **53**, December, 494–504.

Mattern, H. 1965–6. "The growth of landscape consciousness." *Landscape* **15**, 14–20.

Maxwell, H. 1910. "The use and abuse of the forests by the Virginia Indians." *William and Mary College Quarterly* **19**, 73–104.

Mayer, H. M. & R. C. Wade 1969. *Chicago: growth of a metropolis*. Chicago: University of Chicago Press.

Meinig, D. W. 1965. "The Mormon culture region: strategies and patterns in the geography of the American West, 1847–1964." *Annals of the Association of American Geographers* **55**, 191–220.

Meinig, D. 1966. "Geography of expansion." In *The geography of New York State*, J. H. Thompson (ed.), 140–71. Syracuse: Syracuse University Press.

Meinig, D. 1971. *Southwest: three peoples in geographical change, 1600–1970*. New York: Oxford University Press.

Meinig, D. 1976. "The beholding eye: ten versions of the same scene." *Landscape Architecture* **66**, 47–54.

Meinig, D. 1979. *The interpretation of ordinary landscapes*. New York: Oxford University Press.

Meinig, D. 1986. *The shaping of America*, vol. 1: *Atlantic America, 1492–1800*. New Haven, Conn.: Yale University Press.

Meixner, E. C. 1956. "Swedish landmarks in the Delaware Valley." *Swedish Pioneer Historical Quarterly* **7**, 21–34.

Meltzer, D. J. & M. B. Collins 1987. "Prehistoric water wells in the southern High Plains: clues to altithermal climate." *Journal of Field Archaeology* **14**, 9–28.

Meyer, D. R. 1983. "Emergence of the American manufacturing belt: an interpretation." *Journal of Historical Geography* **9**, 145–74.

Meyer, M. C. 1984. *Water in the hispanic Southwest: a social and legal history*. Tucson: University of Arizona Press.

Meyers, C. J. 1966. "The Colorado River." *Stanford Law Review* **19**, 1–75.

Michael, J. W. 1985. "The sun spas." *Town and Country*, May, 136.

Midvale, F. 1968. "Prehistoric irrigation in the Salt River Valley, Arizona." *Kiva* **34**, 28–32.

Mikesell, M. W. 1968. "Landscape." In *International encyclopedia of the social sciences*, D. L. Sills (ed.), 575–80. New York: Macmillan/Free Press.

Miller, L. B. 1966. *Patrons and patriotism: the encouragement of the fine arts in the United States, 1790–1860*. Chicago: University of Chicago Press.

Miller, S., Jr. 1950. "History of the modern highway in the United States." In *Highways in our national life*, J. Labatut & W. J. Lane (eds.), 88–119. Princeton, N.J.: Princeton University Press.

Milner, J. D. 1975. "Germanic architecture in the New World." *Journal of the Society of Architectural Historians* **34**, December, 299.

Minnis, P. E. 1985. *Social adaptation to food stress: a prehistoric southwestern example*. Chicago: University of Chicago Press.

Mitchell, R. D. & P. A. Groves (eds.) 1987. *North America: the historical geography of a changing continent*. Totowa, N.J.: Rowman & Littlefield.

Mollenhoff, G. 1983. "VA national cemeteries: America's military dead and military culture." Paper presented at the Biennial Meeting of American Studies Association, Philadelphia, Penn.

Mollenkopf, J. H. 1983. *The contested city*. Princeton, N.J.: Princeton University Press.

Morgan, W. N. 1980. *Prehistoric architecture in the eastern United States*. Cambridge, Mass.: MIT Press.

Mosse, G. L. 1979. "National cemeteries and national revival: the cult of fallen soldiers in Germany." *Journal of Contemporary History* **1**, 1–20.

Muller, E. K. 1980. "Distinctive downtown." *Geographical Magazine* **53**, 747–55.

Muller, P. O. 1981. *Contemporary suburban America*. Englewood Cliffs, N.J.: Prentice-Hall.

Mulvey, C. 1983. *Anglo-American landscapes: a study of nineteenth-century Anglo-American travel literature*. Cambridge: Cambridge University Press.

Mumford, L. 1961. *The city in history: its origins, its transformations, and its prospects*. New York: Harcourt, Brace & World.

Mumford, L. 1964. *The highway and the city*. New York: Mentor Books.

Mumphrey, A. J. & J. E. Seley 1972. *Metropolitan neighborhoods: participation and conflict over change*. Resource Paper no. 16. Washington, D.C.: Association of American Geographers.

Muntz, A. P. 1959. "The changing geography of the New Jersey woodlands, 1600–1900." Ph.D. Dissertation, University of Wisconsin, Madison.

Muth, R. F. 1968. "Urban residential land and housing markets." In *Issues in urban economics*, H. S. Perloff & L. Wingo (eds.), 285–333. Baltimore: Johns Hopkins University Press.

412   Nabhan, G. P. 1984. "Replenishing desert agriculture with native plants and their

symbionts." In *Meeting the expectations of the land*, W. Jackson, W. Berry & B. Colman (eds.), 172–82. San Francisco: North Point Press.

Nairn, I. 1965. *The American landscape: a critical view*. New York: Random House.

Nairne, T. 1732. *A letter from South Carolina: giving an account of the soil, air, product, trade, government, laws, religion, people, military strength, etc. of that province*. London: A. Baldwin.

Nasatir, A. P. 1976. *Borderlands in retreat: from Spanish Louisiana to the far Southwest*. Albuquerque: University of New Mexico Press.

Nash, G. B. 1982. *Red, white, and black: the peoples of early America*, 2nd edn. Englewood Cliffs, N.J.: Prentice-Hall.

Nash, G. 1973. *The American West in the twentieth century: a short history of an urban oasis*. Englewood Cliffs N.J.: Prentice-Hall.

Nash, R. 1970. "The American invention of national parks." *American Quarterly* **22**, 726–35.

Nash, R. 1973. *Wilderness and the American mind*, revised edn. New Haven, Conn.: Yale University Press.

Nassauer, J. I. 1986. "Illinois farmers view the landscape: a functional aesthetic." Lecture to the Department of Landscape Architecture, University of Minnesota, January 10.

National Capital Planning Commission 1984. *Comprehensive plan for the national capital. Visitors to the national capital*. Washington, D.C.: National Capital Planning Commission.

National Research Council 1968. *Water and choice in the Colorado River Basin: an example of alternatives in water management*. Washington, D.C.: National Academy of Sciences.

Newman, R. D. 1979. "The acceptance of European domestic animals by the eighteenth century Cherokee." *Tennessee Anthropologist* **4**, 101–07.

Newton, M. 1974. "Cultural preadaptation and the upland South." In "Man and cultural heritage." *Geoscience and Man* **5**, 143–54.

*New Yorker* 1979. "Notes and comment." January 1.

Nicholas, L. & J. Neitzel 1984. "Canal irrigation and sociopolitical organization in the lower Salt River Valley: a diachronic analysis." In *Prehistoric agricultural strategies in the Southwest*, S. K. Fish & P. R. Fish (eds.), 161–78. Tempe: Arizona State University, Anthropological Research Papers 33.

Noble, A. G. 1981. "Sod houses and similar structures: a brief evaluation of the literature." *Pioneer America* **13**, 61–66.

Noble, A. G. 1984. *Wood, brick, and stone: the North American settlement landscape*, Vol. 1: *Houses*. Vol. 2: *Barns and Farm Structures*. Amherst: University of Massachusetts Press.

Noble, A. G. 1985. "Rural ethnic islands." In *Ethnicity in contemporary America: a geographical appraisal*, J. O. McKee (ed.), 241–57. Dubuque, IA: Kendall-Hunt.

North, D. C. 1961. *The economic growth of the United States, 1790–1860*. Englewood Cliffs, N.J.: Prentice-Hall.

O'Brien, R. J. 1981. *American sublime: landscape and scenery of the lower Hudson Valley*. New York: Columbia University Press.

Ohman, M. M. 1985. *A history of Missouri's counties, county seats, and courthouse squares*. Columbia: University of Missouri.

Oliver, W. 1843. *Eight months in Illinois with information to immigrants*. Newcastle upon Tyne: published by the author.

Otto, J. S. & N. E. Anderson 1982. "The diffusion of upland South folk culture, 1790–1840." *Southeastern Geographer* **22**, November, 89–98.

Owsley, F. L. 1949. *Plain folk of the Old South*. Baton Rouge: Louisiana State University Press.

Palmqvist, L. A. 1983. *Building traditions among Swedish settlers in rural Minnesota: material culture—reflecting persistence or decline of traditions.* Stockholm: Emigrant Institute, Nordiska Museet.

Pare, R. (ed.) 1978. *Court house: a photographic document.* New York: Horizon.

Parkins, A. E. 1938. *The South: its economic-geographic development.* Westport, Conn.: Greenwood Press.

Parkman, F. 1946. *The Oregon trail.* New York: Doubleday.

Paskoff, P. F. 1983. *Industrial evolution: organization, structure, and growth of the Pennsylvania iron industry, 1750–1860.* Baltimore: Johns Hopkins University Press.

Patterson, J. S. 1974. "Zapped at the map: the battlefields at Gettysburg." *Journal of Popular Culture* **7**, 825–37.

Patterson, J. S. 1982. "A patriotic landscape: Gettysburg, 1863–1913." In *Prospects: the Annual of American Cultural Studies*, J. Salzman (ed.), 315–33. New York: Burt Franklin.

Pattison, W. D. 1956. "Use of the U.S. public land survey plats and notes as descriptive sources." *Professional Geographer* **8**, 10–15.

Pattison, W. D. 1957. *Origins of the American rectangular land survey system, 1784–1800.* University of Chicago, Department of Geography Research Paper No. 50.

Pease, W. H. & J. H. Pease 1985. *The web of progress: private values and public styles in Boston and Charleston, 1828–1843.* New York: Oxford University Press.

Perloff, H. S., E. S. Dunn, Jr., E. E. Lampard & R. F. Muth 1960. *Regions, resources, and economic growth.* Baltimore: Johns Hopkins University Press.

Persons, S. 1973. *The decline of American gentility.* New York: Columbia University Press.

Pessen, E. 1973. *Riches, class, and power before the civil war.* Lexington, Mass.: D.C. Heath.

Petersen, A. J. 1976. "The German-Russian house in Kansas: a study in persistence of form." *Pioneer America* **8**, 19–27.

Peterson, F. W. 1984. "Norwegian farm homes in Steele and Traill Counties, North Dakota: The American dream and the retention of roots, 1890–1914." *North Dakota History* **51**, Winter, 4–13.

Peterson, G. B. & L. C. Bennion 1987. *Sanpete scenes: a guide to Utah's heart.* Eureka, UT: Basin Plateau Press.

Peterson, J. & J. Anfinson 1984. "The Indian and the fur trade." In *Scholars and the Indian experience*, W. R. Swagerty (ed.), 223–57. Bloomington: Indiana University Press.

Peterson, R. H. 1977. *The Bonanza kings: the social origins and business behavior of western mining entrepreneurs, 1870–1900.* Lincoln: University of Nebraska Press.

Pirkle, E. C. & W. H. Yoho 1985. *Natural Landscapes of the United States*, 4th edn. Dubuque, Iowa: Kendall.

Plog, F. 1980. "Explaining culture change in the Hohokam Preclassic." In *Current issues in Hohokam prehistory*, D. Doyel & F. Plog (eds.), 4–22. Anthropological Research Paper, no. 23. Tempe: Arizona State University Press.

Porter, P. W. & F. E. Lukermann 1976. "The geography of utopia." In *Geographies of the mind: essays in historical geography in honor of John Kirtland Wright*, D. Lowenthal & M. J. Bowden (eds.), 197–223. New York: Oxford University Press.

Porter, S. C. (ed.) 1983. *Late-Quaternary environments of the United States.* Minneapolis: University of Minnesota Press.

Powell, J. W. 1962. *Report on the arid region of the United States*, W. Stegner (ed.). Cambridge, Mass: Harvard University Press.

Powell, S. C. 1963. *Puritan village: the formation of a New England town.* Middletown, CT: Wesleyan University Press.

Pred, A. 1980. *Urban growth and city-systems in the United States, 1840–1860.* Cambridge, Mass.: Harvard University Press.

Price, E. T. 1968. "The central courthouse square in the American county seat." *Geographical Review* **58**, 29–60.

Priestley, J. B. 1937. *Midnight on the desert.* New York: Harper.

Primack, M. L. 1962. "Land clearing under nineteenth century techniques: some preliminary calculations." *Journal of Economic History* **22**, 485-86.

Prunty, M. C., 1955. "The Renaissance of the southern plantation." *Geographical Review* **45**, 459–91.

Prunty, M. C. 1963. "The woodland plantation as a contemporary occupance type in the South." *Geographical Review* **53**, 1–21.

Prunty, M. C. 1970. "Some contemporary myths and challenges in southeastern rural land utilization." *Southeastern Geographer* **10**, 1–12.

Pyne, S. J. 1982. *Fire in America: a cultural history of wild land and rural fire.* Princeton, N.J.: Princeton University Press

Quay, J. R. 1966. "Use of soil surveys in subdivision design." In *Soil surveys and land use planning*, L. J. Bartelli (ed.), 76–86. Madison: American Society of Agronomy.

Quinn, F. 1968. "Water transfers: must the American West be won again?" *Geographical Review* **58**, 108–32.

Radford, J. P. 1983. "Regional ideologies and urban growth on the Victorian periphery: southern Ontario and the U.S. South." In "North American cities in the Victorian age." *Historical Geography Research Series* **12**, 32–57.

Rae, J. B. 1981. *The road and the car in American life.* Cambridge, Mass.: MIT Press.

Raitz, K. B. 1978. "Ethnic maps of North America." *Geographical Review* **68**, July, 335–50.

Riatz, K. B. 1980. *The Kentucky Bluegrass: a regional profile and guide.* Chapel Hill: University of North Carolina, Department of Geography.

Ransom, J. M. 1966. *The vanishing ironworks of the Ramapos: story of the forges, furnaces and mines of the New Jersey–New York border areas.* New Brunswick, N.J.: Rutgers University Press.

Ravenstein, E. G. 1885/9. "The laws of migration." *Journal of the Royal Statistical Society* **48**, 167–235 and **52**, 241–305.

Ray, A. J. & D. Freeman 1978. *Give us good measure: an economic analysis of relations between the Indians and the Hudson's Bay Company before 1763.* Toronto: University of Toronto Press.

Rector, W. G. 1953. *Log transportation in the Lake States lumber industry, 1840–1918: the movement of logs and its relationship to land settlement, waterway development, railroad construction, lumber production and prices.* Glendale, Calif.: Arthur H. Clark.

Redfern, R. 1983. *The making of a continent.* New York: Times Books.

Rees, R. 1978. "Landscape in art." In *Dimensions of human geography: essays on some familiar and neglected themes*, K. W. Butzer (ed.), 48–68. Chicago: University of Chicago Department of Geography, Research Paper No. 186.

Reeves, B. O. K. 1983. "Bergs, barriers and Beringia: reflections on the peopling of the New World." In *Quaternary coastlines and marine archaeology: towards the pre-history of land bridges and continental shelves*, P. M. Masters & N. C. Flemming (eds.), 389–411. New York: Academic Press.

Rehder, J. B. 1978. "Diagnostic landscape traits of sugar plantations in southern Louisiana," in "Man and environment in the lower Mississippi Valley." *Geoscience and Man* **19**, 135–50.

Relph, E. 1981. *Rational landscapes and humanistic geography.* London: Croom Helm.

Reps, J. W. 1967. *Monumental Washington: the planning and development of the capitol center.* Princeton: Princeton University Press.

Reps, J. W. 1979. *Cities of the American West: a history of frontier urban planning.* Princeton, N.J.: Princeton University Press.

Reynolds, R. V. & A. H. Pierson 1942. *Fuel wood used in the United States, 1630–1930.*

United States Department of Agriculture, Circular no. 641. Washington, D.C.: Government Printing Office.

Rhyne, D. W. 1979. "The army post in American culture: a historical geography of army posts in the United States." M.S. thesis, Pennsylvania State University.

Rice, J. G. 1973. *Patterns of Ethnicity in a Minnesota County*. Umeå, Sweden: University of Umeå, Geography Reports no. 4.

Richardson, O. D. 1983. "Fullerton, Louisiana, an American monument." *Journal of Forest History* **27**, 192–201.

Ricklis, R. A. "Iroquois Cultural Development on the Colonial Frontier." In press.

Ritchie, W. A. 1980. *The archaeology of New York State*. Harrison, N.Y.: Harbor Hill Books.

Robbins, W. G. 1982. *Lumberjacks and legislators: political economy of the U.S. lumber industry, 1890–1941*. College Station: Texas A & M University Press.

Robert, J. C. 1938. *The tobacco kingdom: production, market, and factory in Virginia and North Carolina, 1800–1860*. Durham, N.C.: Duke University Press.

Robert, J. C. 1949. *The story of tobacco in America*. New York: Knopf.

Roberts, C. E. 1987. "From parkway to freeway: the evolution of the public roadside." M.A. thesis, Pennsylvania State University.

Robinson, B. 1981. *Cruising: the boats and the places*. New York: W. W. Norton.

Robinson, J. 1971. *Highways and our environment*. New York: McGraw-Hill.

Rohe, R. E. 1972. "The landscape and the era of lumbering in northeastern Wisconsin." *Geographical Bulletin* **4**, 1–27.

Rohe, R. E. 1986. "The evolution of the Great Lakes logging camp, 1830–1930." *Journal of Forest History* **30**, 17–28.

Rohn, A. H. 1978. "American Southwest." In *Chronologies in New World archaeology*, R. E. Taylor & C. W. Meighan (eds.), 201–22. New York: Academic Press.

Rohrbough, M. J. 1968. *The land office business in Indiana: the settlement and administration of American public lands, 1789–1837*. New York: Oxford University Press.

Rooney, J. F., W. Zelinsky & D. R. Louder (eds.) 1982. *This remarkable continent: an atlas of United States and Canadian society and cultures*. College Station: Texas A & M University Press, for the Society for the North American Cultural Survey.

Rose, A. C. 1950. "The Highway from the railroad to the automobile." In *Highways in our national life*, J. Labatut & W. J. Lane (eds.), 77–87. Princeton N.J.: Princeton University Press.

Rosenberry, L. M. 1909. *The expansion of New England: the spread of New England settlement and institutions to the Mississippi River, 1620–1865*. Boston: Houghton-Mifflin.

Roth, L. M. 1979. *A concise history of American architecture*. New York: Harper & Row.

Rothman, D. J. 1971. *The discovery of the asylum: social order and disorder in the New Republic*. Boston: Little, Brown.

Rubin, J. 1967. "Urban growth and development." In *The growth of seaport cities: 1790–1825*, D. T. Gilchrist (ed.), 3–21. Charlottsville: University of Virginia Press.

Ruhling, N. A. 1984. "Manors for the masses." *Historic Preservation* **38**, 51–55.

Russell, H. S. 1976. *The long deep furrow: three centuries of farming in New England*. Hanover, N.H.: University Press of New England.

Sack, R. D. 1986. *Human Territoriality: its theory and history*. New York: Cambridge University Press.

Salley, A. S., Jr. 1919. "The introduction of rice culture into South Carolina," *Bulletin of the Historical Commission of South Carolina* **6**.

Salter, C. L. 1978. "Signatures and settings: one approach to landscape in literature." In *Dimensions of human geography: essays on some familiar and neglected themes*, K. W. Butzer. Chicago: University of Chicago Department of Geography, Research Paper no. 186.

Bibliography

Sargent, C. S. 1984. *Report on the forests of North America (exclusive of Mexico)*. Tenth Census of the United States, vol. 9. Washington, D.C.: Government Printing Office.

Sauer, C. O. 1927. *Geography of the Pennyroyal*. Frankfort, KY: Kentucky Geological Survey.

Sauer, C. O. 1944. "A geographic sketch of early man in America." *Geographical Review* **34**, 529–73.

Sauer, C. O. 1963. "Homestead and community on the middle Border." In *Land and life: a selection from the writings of Carl Ortwin Sauer*, J. Leighly (ed.), 32–41. Berkeley: University of California Press.

Sauer, C. O. 1971. *Sixteenth century North America: the land and the people as seen by the first Europeans*. Berkeley: University of California Press.

Sauer, C. O. 1980. *Seventeenth century North America*. Berkeley, Calif.: Turtle Island Press.

Schallenberg, R. H. 1975. "Evolution, adaption and survival: the very slow death of the American charcoal iron industry." *Annals of Science* **32**, 341–58.

Schob, D. E. 1977. "Woodhawks and cordwood: steam boat fuel on the Ohio and Mississippi Rivers, 1820–1860." *Journal of Forest History* **21**, 124–32.

Schuyler, D. 1986. *The new urban landscape: the redefinition of the city form in nineteenth-century America*. Baltimore: Johns Hopkins University Press.

Schwarcz, H. P., J. Melbye, M. A. Katzenberg & M. Knyf 1985. "Stable isotopes in human skeletons of southern Ontario: reconstructing paleodiet." *Journal of Archaeological Science* **12**, 187–206.

Scott, M. 1969. *American city planning since 1890*. Berkeley: University of California Press.

Scully, M. A. 1984. "The triumph of the capitol." *Public Interest* **74**, 99–115.

Segal, H. H. 1961. "Cycles of canal construction." In *Canals and American economic development*, C. Goodrich (ed.), 169–215. New York: Columbia University Press.

Selkurt, C. 1985. "The domestic architecture and cabinetry of Luther Valley." *Norwegian-American Studies* **30**, 247–72.

Shepard, S. 1981. *True West*. New York: Bantam.

Shi, D. E. 1985. *The simple life: plain living and high thinking in American culture*. New York: Oxford University Press.

Shimer, J. A. 1959. *This sculptured Earth: the landscape of America*. New York: Columbia University Press.

Shurtleff, H. R. 1939. *The log cabin myth: a study of the early dwellings of the English colonies in North America*. Cambridge, Mass.: Harvard University Press.

Simmons, M. 1972. "Spanish irrigation practices in New Mexico." *New Mexico Historical Review* **47**, 135–50.

Simmons, M. 1982. *Albuquerque: a narrative history*. Albuquerque: University of New Mexico Press.

Slater, K. 1967. *The hunt country of America*. New York: A. S. Barnes.

Smith, B. D. 1974. "Middle Mississippian exploitation of animal populations: a predictive model." *American Antiquity* **39**, 274–91.

Smith, B. D. (ed.) 1978. *Mississippian settlement patterns*. New York: Academic Press.

Smith, C. L. 1972. *The Salt River Project: a case study in cultural adaptation to an urbanizing community*. Tucson: University of Arizona Press.

Smith, J. B. 1973. "Lumbertowns in the cutover: a comparative study of the stage hypothesis of urban growth." Ph.D. dissertation, University of Wisconsin, Madison.

Smith, W. (ed.) 1964. *Cities of our past and present*. New York: Wiley.

Smithsonian Exposition Books 1979. *The American land*. New York: W. W. Norton.

Smythe, W. E. 1970. *The conquest of arid America*. London: 1900; reprint edn., Seattle: University of Washington Press.

*417*

Snow, J. T. 1967. "The new road in the United States." *Landscape* **17**, 13–16.

Sobin, D. P. 1968. *Dynamics of community change: the case of Long Island's declining Gold Coast*. Port Washington, N.Y.: Ira J. Freidman.

Spear, A. H. 1967. *Black Chicago: the making of a negro ghetto, 1890–1920*. Chicago: University of Chicago Press.

Spears, B. 1986. *American adobes: rural houses of northern New Mexico*. Albuquerque: University of New Mexico Press.

Spears, B. & R. Swanson 1978. *History of sport and physical activity in the United States*. Dubuque, Iowa: William C. Brown.

Sprague, M. 1980. *Newport in the Rockies*. Chicago: Sage.

Starr, K. 1984. "The sporting life." *California History* **63**, 26–31.

Steer, H. B. 1984. *Lumber production in the United States, 1799–1946*. United States Department of Agriculture, Miscellaneous Publication no. 669. Washington, D.C.: Government Printing Office.

Steere, E. 1953–4a. "Expansion of the national cemetery system, 1880–1900." *Quartermaster Review* **33**, 20–21, 131–37.

Steere, E. 1953–4b. "National cemeteries and memorials in global conflict." *Quartermaster Review* **33**, 18–19, 130–36.

Steere, E. 1953–4c. "National cemeteries and public policy." *Quartermaster Review* **33**, 18–19, 142–54.

Steila, D. D. 1976. *The geography of soils*. Englewood Cliffs, N.J.: Prentice-Hall.

Stewart, G. R. 1953. *U.S. 40: cross section of the United States of America*. Boston: Houghton Mifflin.

Stewart, L. O. 1935. *Public land surveys: history, instructions, methods*. Ames, IA: Collegiate Press.

Stilgoe, J. R. 1982. *Common landscape of America, 1580 to 1845*. New Haven, Conn.: Yale University Press.

Stilgoe, J. R. 1983. *Metropolitan corridor: railroads and the American scene*. New Haven, Conn.: Yale University Press.

Still, B. 1974. *Urban America: a history with documents*. Boston: Little, Brown.

Stokes, G. A. 1957. "Lumbering and western Louisiana cultural landscapes." *Annals of the Association of American Geographers* **47**, 250–66.

Stoltman, J. B. & D. A. Baerreis 1983. "The evolution of human ecosystems in the eastern United States." In *Late-Quaternary environments of the United States*. vol. 2: *The Holocene*, H. E. Wright (ed.), 252–68. Minneapolis: University of Minnesota Press.

Stone, K. H. 1950. *Alaska group settlement: the Matanuska Valley colony*. Washington, D.C.: Bureau of Land Management.

Stracey, J. 1849. *The historie of travails into Virginia Britannia*. London: 1620, reprinted edn. London: Hakylut Society.

Streatfield, D. C. 1977. "The evolution of the California landscape: the great promotions." *Landscape Architecture* **67**, 229–39.

Stump, R. W. 1985. "Toward a geography of American civil religion." *Journal of Cultural Geography* **5**, 87–95.

Sturtevant, W. C. (ed.) 1978. *Handbook of North American Indians*, 15 vols. Washington, D.C.: Smithsonian Institution Press.

Sullivan, W. 1984. *Landprints: on the magnificent American landscape*. New York: Times Books.

Sweetser, C. H. 1868. *Book of summer resorts*. New York: Evening Mail Office.

Tarshis, B. & K. Waller 1984. "John Gardiner's courtly resort." *Town and Country* **138**, 110ff.

Taylor, G. R. 1951. *The transportation revolution, 1815–1860*. New York: Holt, Rinehart & Winston.

Taylor, G. R. & I. D. Neu 1956. *The American railroad network, 1861–1890*. Cambridge, Mass.: Harvard University Press.

Taylor, J. C. 1976. *America as art*. New York: Harper & Row.

Teaford, J. C. 1975. *The municipal revolution in America: origins of modern urban government, 1650–1825*. Chicago: University of Chicago Press.

Teaford, J. C. 1984. *The unheralded triumph: city government in America, 1870–1900*. Baltimore: Johns Hopkins University Press.

Temin, P. 1964. *Iron and steel in nineteenth century America: an economic enquiry*. Cambridge, Mass.: MIT Press.

Templer, O. W. 1978. "The legacy of the past and its impact on water resources management." *Journal of Historical Geography* 8, 11–20.

Thernstrom, S. (ed.) 1980. *Harvard encyclopedia of American ethnic groups*. Cambridge, Mass.: Harvard University Press.

Thomas, J. J. 1864. "Culture and management of forest trees." In *United States Department of Agriculture Annual Report 1864*, 43–7. Washington, D.C.: Government Printing Office.

Thomas, W. L. (ed.) 1956. *Man's role in changing the face of the Earth*. Chicago: University of Chicago Press.

Thompson, J. 1981. *The very rich book*. New York: William Morrow.

Thompson, J. H. (ed.) 1966. *Geography of New York State*. Syracuse, N.Y.: Syracuse University Press.

Thompson, R. S., L. Benson & E. M. Hattori 1986. "Revised chronology for the last Pleistocene lake cycle in the Central Lahontan Basin." *Quaternary Research* 25, 1–9.

Thornbury, W. D. 1965. *Regional geomorphology of the United States*. New York: Wiley.

Thrower, N. J. W. 1957. "Cadastral surveys and roads in Ohio." *Annals of the Association of American Geographers* 47, 181–2.

Thrower, N. J. W. 1961. "The county atlas of the United States." *Surveying and Mapping* 21, 365–73.

Thrower, N. J. W. 1966. *Original survey and land subdivision: a comparative study of the form and effect of contrasting cadastral surveys*. Chicago: Rand McNally.

Tishler, W. H. 1986. "Fachwerk construction in the German settlements of Wisconsin." *Winterthur Portfolio* 33, Winter, 275–92.

Tishler, W. H. & C. S. Witmer 1986. "The housebarns of east-central Wisconsin." In *Perspectives in vernacular architecture*, vol. 2, C. Wells (ed.), 102–110. Columbia, MO: University of Missouri Press.

Trewartha, G. T. 1943. "The unincorporated hamlet: one element in the American settlement fabric." *Annals of the Association of American Geographers* 33, March, 32–81.

Trimble, S. W. 1985. "Perspectives on the history of soil erosion control in the eastern United States." *Agricultural History* 59, 162–180.

Trimble, S. W. 1988. "Ante-bellum domestic architecture in middle Tennessee: forms, facades, styles, materials, geographic distribution, and regional significance." In "The American South." *Geoscience and Man* 25, 97–117.

Trinder, B. S. 1982. *The making of the industrial landscape*. London: Dent.

Tuan, Y.-F. 1974. *Topophilia: a study of environmental perception, attitudes, and values*. Englewood Cliifs, N.J.: Prentice-Hall.

Tuan, Y.-F. 1976a. "Geopiety: a theme in man's attachment to nature and to place." In *Geographies of the mind: essays in historical geosophy in honor of John Kirtland Wright*, D. Lowenthal & M. Bowden (eds.), 11–39. New York: Oxford University Press.

Tuan, Y.-F. 1976b. *Landscapes of fear*. New York: Pantheon Books.

Tunnard, C. & B. Pushkarev 1963. *Man-made America: chaos or control?* New Haven, Conn.: Yale University Press.

Tunnard, C. & H. H. Reed 1956. *American skyline*. New York: New American Library.

Turner, O. 1849. *Pioneer history of the Holland Purchase of western New York*. Buffalo, N.Y.: Jewett Thomas.

Ubelaker, D. H. 1976. "Prehistoric New World population size: historical review and current appraisal of North American estimates." *American Journal of Physical Anthropology* **45**, 661–66.

United States Bureau of the Census 1975. *Historical Statistics of the United States, Colonial times to 1970*. Bicentiennal edn., 2 parts. Washington, D.C.: Government Printing Office.

U.S. Congress. House 1874. *Irrigation: its evils, the remedies, and the compensation*, by George Perkins Marsh. S. Misc. Doc. 55, 43rd Cong., 1st sess. Washington, D.C.: Government Printing Office.

U.S. Congress. House 1947. *The Colorado River: a natural menace becomes a national resource*. U.S. Department of the Interior. H. Doc. 419, 80th Cong., 1st sess.

U.S. Congress. Senate 1909. *Report of the National Conservation Commission*, 3 vols. H. Gannett (ed.) S. Doc. 676, 60th Cong., 2nd sess. Washington, D.C.: Government Printing Office.

U.S. Congress. Senate 1920. *Timber depletion, lumber prices, lumber exports and concentration of timber ownership* [Capper Report]. U.S. Forest Service. S. Rept. on S. Res. 311, 66th Cong., 2nd sess.

U.S. Congress. Senate 1950. *Boulder City, Nevada: a federal municipality*, by Henry Reining, Jr. 81st Cong., 2nd sess. Washington, D.C.: Government Printing Office.

U.S. Congress. Senate 1982. *An analysis of the timber situation in the United States, 1952–2030*. Forest Research Report no. 23. Washington, D.C.: Government Printing Office.

Upham, S. 1984. "Adaptive diversity and southwestern abandonment." *Journal of Anthropological Research* **40**, 235–56.

Upton, D. (ed.) 1986. *America's architectural roots: ethnic groups that built America*. Washington, D.C.: Preservation Press.

Upton, D. & J. M. Vlach (eds.) 1986. *Common places: readings in American vernacular architecture*. Athens: University of Georgia Press.

Utley, R. M. & W. E. Washburn 1977. *The Indian wars*. New York: American Heritage.

Van Ravenswaay, C. 1970. "America's age of wood." *Proceedings of the American Antiquarian Society* **809**, 49–66.

Van Ravenswaay, C. 1977. *Art and architecture of German settlements in Missouri: a survey of a vanishing culture*. Columbia, MO: University of Missouri Press.

Van Tassel, A. J. & D. W. Bluestone 1940. *Mechanization in the lumber industry: a study of technology in relation to resources and employment opportunity*. Philadelphia, Penn.: Work Projects Administration.

Vance, J. E. 1971. "Land assignment in the precapitalist, capitalist, and postcapitalist city." *Economic Geography* **47**, 101–20.

Vance, J. E. 1972. "California and the search for the ideal." *Annals of the Association of American Geographers* **62**, 185–210.

Vance, J. E. 1977. *This scene of man: the role and structure of the city in the geography of western civilization*. New York: Harper & Row.

Vance, R. B. & N. J. Demerath (eds.) 1954. *The urban South*. Chapel Hill: University of North Carolina Press.

Venturi, R., D. Scott-Brown & S. Izenour 1977. *Learning from Las Vegas: the forgotten symbolism of architectural form*, revised edn. Cambridge, Mass.: MIT Press.

Vivian, R. G. 1974. "Conservation and diversion: water control systems in the Anasazi Southwest." In *Irrigation's impact on society*, T. E. Downing & M. Gibson (eds.), 95–112. Anthropological Papers of the University of Arizona, no. 25.

Vlach, J. M. 1986. "The shotgun house: an African architectural legacy." In *Common places: readings in American vernacular architecture*, D. Upton & J. M. Vlach (eds.), 58–78. Athens: University of Georgia Press.

Bibliography

Vogeler, I. 1976. "The Roman Catholic culture region of central Minnesota." *Pioneer America* **8**, July, 71–83.

Vogeler, I. 1981. *The Myth of the family farm: agribusiness dominance of U.S. agriculture.* Boulder, CO: Westview Press.

Wall, R. T. 1981. "The vanishing tenant houses of rural Georgia." *Georgia Historical Quarterly* **65**, Fall, 251–62.

Waller, K. 1985. "Groton at 100: the charmed circle." *Town and Country* **139**, 150ff.

Walton, G. M. & J. F. Shepherd 1979. *The economic rise of early America.* Cambridge: Cambridge University Press.

Ward, D. 1971. *Cities and immigrants: a geography of change in nineteenth century America.* New York: Oxford University Press.

Warner, S. B., Jr. 1962. *Streetcar suburbs: the process of growth in Boston, 1870–1900.* Cambridge, Mass.: Harvard University Press.

Warner, S. B. 1968. *The Private City: Philadelphia in Three Periods of Its Growth.* Philadelphia: University of Pennsylvania Press.

Warner, S. B. 1972. *The urban wilderness: a history of the American city.* New York: Harper & Row.

Warren, K. 1973. *The American steel industry, 1850–1970: a geographical interpretation.* Oxford: Clarendon Press.

Waters, M. R. 1986. *The geoarchaeology of Whitewater Draw, Arizona.* Tucson: Anthropological Papers of the University of Arizona, no. 45.

Watson, J. W. 1970. "Image geography: the myth of America in the American scene." *Advancement of Science* **27**, 71–79.

Watts, M. T. 1975. *Reading the landscape of America.* New York: Collier.

Weaver, W. W. 1986. "The Pennsylvania German house: European antecedents and New World forms." *Winterthur Portfolio* **21**, Winter, 243–64.

Webb, T., E. J. Cushing & H. E. Wright 1983. "Holocene changes in the vegetation of the Midwest, 1983." In *Late Quaternary environments of the United States*, vol. 2: *The Holocene*, H. E. Wright (ed.), 142–65. Minneapolis: University of Minnesota Press.

Webb, W. P. 1931. *The Great Plains.* New York: Ginn.

Wechter, D. 1937. *The saga of American society: a record of social aspiration, 1607–1937.* New York: Scribners.

Wescoat, J. L. 1984. *Integrated water development: water use and conservation practice in western Colorado.* University of Chicago, Department of Geography, Research Paper no. 210.

West, F. H. 1983. "The antiquity of man in America." In *Late Quaternary Environments of the United States*, vol. 1: *The Late Pleistocene*, S. C. Porter (ed.), 354–84. Minneapolis: University of Minnesota Press.

White, C. L., E. J. Foscue & T. L. McKnight 1985. *Regional geography of Anglo America*, 6th edn. Englewood Cliffs, N.J.: Prentice-Hall.

White, G. F. 1960. "The changing role of water in arid lands." *University of Arizona Bulletin* **32**.

White, L. 1967. "The historical roots of our ecologic crisis." *Science* **155**, 1203–7.

White, R. 1980. *Land use, environment, and social change: the shaping of Island County, Washington.* Seattle: University of Washington Press.

Whitehill, W. M. 1968. *Boston: a topographical history.* Cambridge, Mass.: Harvard University Press.

Whittlesey, D. 1935. "The impress of effective central authority upon landscape." *Annals of the Association of American Geographers* **25**, 85–97.

Wiant, M. D., E. R. Hajic & T. R. Styles 1983. "Napoleon Hollow and Koster Site stratigraphy." In *Archaic hunters and gatherers in the American Midwest*, J. L. Phillips & J. A. Brown (eds.), 147–64. New York: Academic Press.

421

Wik, R. M. 1972. *Henry Ford and grassroots America*. Ann Arbor: University of Michigan Press.

Wiley, B. I. 1970. "Slavery in the United States." *American History Illustrated* **5**, 10–17.

Wilhelm, H. G. H. 1971. "German settlement and folk building practices in the hill country of Texas." *Pioneer America* **3**, July, 15–24.

Williams, M. 1980. "Products of the forest: mapping the Census of 1840." *Journal of Forest History* 24, 4–23.

Williams, M. 1982. "Clearing the United States forests: the pivotal years, 1810–1860." *Journal of Historical Geography* **8**, 12–28.

Williams, M. 1989. *Americans and their forests: an historical geography*. New York: Cambridge University Press.

Williams, N., E. H. Kellogg & P. M. Lavigne 1987. *Vermont townscape*. New Brunswick, N.J.: Center for Urban Policy Research.

Williamson, H. F. & A. R. Daum 1959. *The American petroleum industry: the age of illumination, 1859–1899*. Evanston, IL: Northwestern University Press.

Williamson, H. F., R. L. Andreano, A. R. Daum & G. C. Klose 1963. *The American petroleum industry: the age of energy, 1899–1959*. Evanston, IL: Northwestern University Press.

Wilson, C. W. 1972. "The Salzburger long-lots of colonial Georgia." *Papers of the Twenty-Seventh Annual Meeting, Southeast Division, Association of American Geographers, 1972*, Vol. 2, *Methodological, Cultural, and Physical*, 134–38. Miami, FL: The Division.

Wilson, W. H. 1983. "Moles and skylarks." In *Introduction to planning history in the United States*, D. A. Krueckeberg, (ed.) 88–121. New Brunswick, N.J.: Rutgers University, Center for Urban Policy Research.

Wilson, W. J. 1987. *The truly disadvantaged: the inner city, the underclass, and public policy*. Chicago: University of Chicago Press.

Winberry, J. J. 1979. "Indigo in South Carolina: a historical geography." *Southeastern Geographer* **19**, November, 91–102.

Wishart, D. 1979. *The fur trade of the American West 1807–1840: a geographical synthesis*. Lincoln: University of Nebraska Press.

Wissink, G. A. 1962. *American cities in perspective*. Assen, Netherlands: Royal Van Gorcum.

Wolman, M. G. & A. Wolman 1986. "Water supply: persistent myths and recurring issues." In *Geography, resources, and environment II*, R. W. Kates & I. Burton (eds.), 1–27. Chicago: University of Chicago Press.

Wood, J. S. 1982. "Village and community in early colonial New England." *Journal of Historical Geography* **8**, 333–46.

Wood, J. S. 1986. "The New England village as an American vernacular form." In *Perspectives in vernacular American architecture II*, C. Wells (ed.), 54–63. Columbia: University of Missouri Press.

Wood, J. S. 1987. "The three faces of the New England village." *North American Culture* **3**, 3–14.

Wood, J. S. & M. E. McAllister 1984. "Second foundation: settlement patterns and agriculture in the northeastern Hohokam periphery, central Arizona." In *Prehistoric agricultural strategies in the Southwest*, S. K. Fish & P. R. Fish (eds.), 271–80. Tempe: Arizona State University, Anthropological Research Papers no. 33.

Wood, R. G. 1935. *A history of lumbering in Maine, 1820–1861*. Orono: University of Maine Press.

Worster, D. E. 1979. *Dust Bowl: the southern Plains in the 1930s*. New York: Oxford University Press.

Wright, G. 1981. *Building the dream: a social history of housing in America*. Cambridge, Mass.: MIT Press.

Wright, H. E. (ed.) 1983. *Late Quaternary environments of the United States*, 2 vols. Minneapolis: University of Minnesota Press.

*Bibliography*

Wright, J. L. 1971. *Anglo-Spanish rivalry in North America*. Athens: University of Georgia Press.

Wright, W. P. 1928. *A history of garden art*, 2 vols. London: Dent.

Yerkes, R. W. 1987. *Prehistoric life on the Mississippi floodplain*. Chicago: University of Chicago Press.

Zelinsky, W. 1954. "The Greek Revival house in Georgia." *Journal of the Society of Architectural Historians* **13**, 9–12.

Zelinsky, W. 1967. "Classical town names in the United States: the historical geography of an American idea." *Geographical Review* **57**, 463–95.

Zelinsky, W. 1973. *The Cultural geography of the United States*. Englewood Cliffs, N.J.: Prentice-Hall.

Zelinsky, W. 1977. "The Pennsylvania town: an overdue geographical account." *Geographical Review* **67**, 127–47.

Zelinsky, W. 1984. "O say, can you see? Nationalistic emblems in the landscape." *Winterthur Portfolio* **19**, 77–86.

Zelinsky, W. 1988. *Nation into state: the shifting symbolic foundations of American nationalism*. Chapel Hill: University of North Carolina Press.

Zink, C. W. 1987. "Dutch framed houses in New York and New Jersey." *Winterthur Portfolio* **22**, Winter, 265–94.

Zube, E. H. (ed.) 1970. *Landscapes: selected writings of J. B. Jackson*. Amherst: University of Massachusetts Press.

Zube, E. H. 1973. "Rating every day rural landscapes of the northeastern United States." *Landscape Architecture* **63**, 92–7.

Zunz, O. 1982. *The changing face of inequality: urbanization, industrial development and immigrants in Detroit, 1880–1920*. Chicago: University of Chicago Press.

# Index

431